Teaching, Training and Learning

A Practical Guide

Sixth Edition Revised

Ian Reece and Stephen Walker

Business Education Publishers Limited

© Ian Reece and Stephen Walker 2007

ISBN 1 901888 56 8
ISBN 978 1 901888 56 0

First published in 1992
  Reprinted 1993
Second Edition 1994
  Reprinted 1995, 1996
Third Edition 1997
  Reprinted 1998, 1999, 2000
Fourth Edition 2000
  Reprinted 2000, 2001, 2001, 2001, 2002, 2002, 2002, 2003
Fifth Edition (Edited by Caroline Walker-Gleaves) 2003
  Reprinted 2003, 2004, 2004, 2005

Sixth Edition 2006
  Reprinted 2007
Sixth Edition Revised 2007

Cover Design, Tim Murphy, Bradley O'Mahoney Creative Ltd.

Published in Great Britain by
Business Education Publishers Limited,
evolve Business Centre,
Cygnet Way,
Rainton Bridge Business Park,
Tyne and Wear, DH4 5QY

Telephone: 0191 3055165
Fax: 0191 3055506

British Library Cataloguing-in-Publications Data
A catalogue record for this book is available from the British Library

The publisher has made every effort to obtain permission to reproduce material in this book from the appropriate source. If there are any errors or omissions please contact the publisher who will make suitable acknowledgement in the reprint.

Printed in Great Britain by CPD Wales

Acknowledgements

We would like to thank members of the Further Education Teacher Training team at New College Durham for their contribution to debates and discussions over many years and, in particular Phyll Bryning and Alan Lilley. We would also like to pay tribute to our teacher students from whom we have learned a great deal, especially during practical teaching visits. Of these, special thanks must go to Carl Gill, Janice Flint, Janet Ford, Andrew Lindley and Carolyn Piggford, whose original ideas have greatly enhanced this book.

The authors would particularly like to express their thanks to Sid Knight of the FETT team at New College Durham for his continued support and suggestions for changes in the second edition.

We are particularly grateful for the comments and suggestions for the third edition made by two of our colleagues Carole Rosethorn and John Hunt.

Gwyn Rose, Gail Thompson, Richard Harvey and Denise Heslop have been particularly helpful with ideas for the fourth edition.

We are grateful for the hard work and perseverance of Caroline Walker-Gleaves the editor of the fifth edition.

For this sixth edition, we would like to thank David Clues and Maureen Charlton for their expertise in ILT and their supportive critique of the impact of the New Professional Standards.

Our thanks go to all at Business Education Publishers, particularly Sonya Miller and Moira Page whose help was invaluable in producing this publication, and Paul Callaghan, whose positive attitude and professionalism have been a constant source of motivation in writing this book. Our particular thanks go to Andrea Murphy who has managed the production of the fourth, fifth and sixth editions so well.

Finally thanks to Margery, Susan, Timothy, Martin and Ruth for their tolerance and understanding as this book has gone through its various stages.

Durham
August 2006
IHR
SW

Preface

The first edition of this book was published in 1992 which was a period of great change in post-compulsory education. In the early 1990s post-16 education and training involved the design of new vocational qualifications using a competence-based approach, the introduction of self-management of educational organisations (i.e. the incorporation of FE and sixth-form colleges) and a new funding system for the sector with the introduction of the Further Education Funding Council (FEFC).

The first edition was primarily intended as a support for the City and Guilds 730 programmes: the more traditional 7307 and the then new, competence-based, 7306 and the first year of the Certificate in Education/PGCE. Its concentration was upon the skills required for effective 'classroom' performance with chapters relating to lesson planning, designing visual aids, assessment of student learning and so on.

The rate of change of post-16 education and training continued to accelerate in the two years after the first edition. Some of these changes, together with some of the many valuable and constructive criticisms made by readers, led to the second edition being published in 1994 with modifications being made to most chapters. Such modifications particularly related to the section dealing with National Vocational Qualifications and the sections dealing with assessment of student learning and self evaluation of teaching were enhanced.

The third edition, published in 1997, reiterated the fundamental principles which had been the underpinning of its two predecessors. To these it added aspects of change which had continued. There were three main changes to this edition: (i) the inclusion of further examples to provide clarity for the application of assessment of student learning; (ii) additions to the student learning chapter in an attempt to be more comprehensive; and (iii) further clarification to the section dealing with the writing of objectives. Again, such changes were as a result of suggestions made by readers and colleagues.

Since 1997 a debate in the training of teachers of post-16 education and training has taken place. The competence movement and the incorporation of colleges has allowed much more control to be placed upon the curriculum itself. Such control is evidenced by the inspection process which was controlled by the funding councils. In 1999 the training of teachers in post-16 education and training was influenced by two National Training Organisations: for the university sector The Higher Education Training Organisation (THETO) outlined a set of national standards for the training of HE lecturers; and in further education Further Education set up its own Lead Body, the Further Education National Training Organisation (FENTO) and has produced a set of national standards for FE lecturers.

The fourth edition, published in 2000, attempted to encompass this movement and the debate in the post-16 sector of education. Each of the chapters, which are the basis of an initial teaching qualification for post-16 education and training, outlined FENTO standards.

It is now eleven years since the initial publication and, by 2003, it was realised that it was time for a major revision to take place. The previous alterations had been 'bolt-on' changes and integrations and, on occasions, this interfered with the flow of the materials. The fifth edition was more concise than its predecessor and the sequence has been altered to help with the flow. It contains additional material covering learning technologies, learning styles and strategies, and using electronic multimedia.

There were aspects of the text that needed updating like some of the references and the names of examining and validating bodies which have changed. Additionally, the layout has been modified. There are wider margins and more visible headings, giving the text a greater visual appeal. The tables and diagrams have also been redesigned to provide better organisation and a cleaner visual appeal.

The sixth edition reflects the ever-changing world of education in general and teacher training in particular. The importance of teacher training in the post-compulsory sector is recognised in the LLUK (Lifelong Learning UK) standards. The essential content of Teaching Training and Learning remains the same, but we have linked the theory and practice we have discussed herein to the new LLUK Professional Standards*. At the end of each chapter we have indicated the relevant standards and have suggested how you may achieve them. All of the ideas are grounded in the fact that the best way to show your competence is to base your evidence on your own teaching situation. This edition also places more emphasis on the use of ILT and includes examples of good practice.

We hope this sixth edition is as well received by you, the reader, as its predecessors. We have used many sources to write this new edition and have made every effort to cite original materials. If we have failed to give due credit, we sincerely apologise and will rectify this at the soonest available opportunity. Please contact us if you have any ideas or suggestions for the next edition. We will be pleased to hear from you. We wish you well.

Ian Reece
Stephen Walker

* You can download the current standards from www.lifelonglearning.uk.org.

Contents

Chapter 4
Resources for Teaching and Learning

Chapter 5
Curricula, Courses and Lessons: Planning and Design

Chapter 6
Communication, Teaching and Learning

Chapter 7
Assessment of Learning and Achievement

Chapter 8
Evaluating and Improving Professional Practice

Appendix I

Glossary of Educational Terms

Bibliography

Index

LLUK Professional Standards

To achieve the LLUK Standards, teachers in the lifelong learning sector need to have the following knowledge and understanding	Chapter 1 Teachers and Teaching: Principles and Practices	Chapter 2 Learners and Learning: Principles and Practices	Chapter 3 Teaching Strategies and Learning Styles	Chapter 4 Resources for Teaching and Learning	Chapter 5 Curricula, Courses and Lessons: Planning and Design	Chapter 6 Communication, Teaching and Learning	Chapter 7 Assessment of Learning and Achievement	Chapter 8 Evaluating and Improving Professional Practice
Domain A: Professional values and practice								
Teachers in the lifelong learning sector know and understand:								
AK1.1 What motivates learners to learn and the importance of learners' experience and aspirations.		✓					✓	
AK2.1 Ways in which learning has the potential to change lives.		✓						
AK2.2 Ways in which learning promotes the emotional, intellectual, social and economic well-being of individuals and the population as a whole.	✓	✓					✓	
AK3.1 Issues of equality, diversity and inclusion.						✓		
AK4.1 Principles, frameworks and theories which underpin good practice in learning and teaching.	✓	✓						
AK4.2 The impact of own practice on individuals and their learning.							✓	✓
AK4.3 Ways to reflect, evaluate and use research to develop own practice, and to share good practice with others.	✓							✓
AK5.1 Ways to communicate and collaborate with colleagues and/or others to enhance learners' experience.						✓		
AK5.2 The need for confidentiality, respect and trust in communicating with others about learners.	✓						✓	
AK6.1 Relevant statutory requirements and codes of practice.					✓			
AK6.2 Ways to apply relevant statutory requirements and the underpinning principles.			✓	✓	✓			
AK7.1 Organisational systems and processes for recording learner information.	✓						✓	
AK7.2 Own role in the quality cycle.								✓
AK7.3 Ways to implement improvements based on feedback received.								✓
Domain B: Learning and teaching								
Teachers in the lifelong learning sector know and understand:								
BK1.1 Ways to maintain a learning environment in which learners feel safe and supported.			✓	✓	✓			
BK1.2 Ways to develop and manage behaviours which promote respect for and between others and create as equitable and inclusive learning environment.			✓	✓	✓			
BK1.3 Ways of creating a motivating learning environment.		✓					✓	
BK2.1 Principles of learning and ways to provide learning activities to meet curriculum requirements and the needs of all learners.		✓	✓	✓		✓		
BK2.2 Ways to engage, motivate and encourage active participation of learners and learner independence.			✓	✓	✓	✓		
BK2.3 The relevance of learning approaches, preferences and skills to learner progress.		✓	✓					
BK2.4 Flexible delivery of learning, including open and distance learning and on-line learning.		✓	✓					
BK2.5 Ways of using learners' own experiences as a foundation for learning.		✓	✓					
BK2.6 Ways to evaluate own practice in terms of efficiency and effectiveness.								✓
BK2.7 Ways in which mentoring and/or coaching can support the development of professional skills and knowledge.			✓					

To achieve the LLUK Standards, teachers in the lifelong learning sector need to have the following knowledge and understanding	Chapter 1 Teachers and Teaching: Principles and Practices	Chapter 2 Learners and Learning Principles and Practices	Chapter 3 Teaching Strategies and Learning Styles	Chapter 4 Resources for Teaching and Learning	Chapter 5 Curricula, Courses and Lessons: Planning and Design	Chapter 6 Communication, Teaching and Learning	Chapter 7 Assessment of Learning and Achievement	Chapter 8 Evaluating and Improving Professional Practice
Domain B: Learning and teaching								
Teachers in the lifelong learning sector know and understand:								
BK3.1 Effective and appropriate use of different forms of communication informed by relevant theories and principles.						✓		
BK3.2 A range of listening and questioning techniques to support learning.	✓		✓					
BK3.3 Ways to structure and present information and ideas clearly and effectively to learners.	✓		✓	✓	✓	✓		
BK3.4 Barriers and aids to effective communication.						✓		
BK3.5 Systems for communication within own organisation.								
BK4.1 Good practice in meeting the needs of learners in collaboration with colleagues.								
BK5.1 The impact of resources on effective learning.	✓			✓	✓			
BK5.2 Ways to ensure that resources used are Inclusive, promote equality and support diversity.				✓	✓			
Domain C: Specialist learning and teaching								
Teachers in the lifelong learning sector know and understand:								
CK1.1 Own specialist area including current development.								
CK1.2 Ways in which own specialism relates to the wider social, economic and environmental context.								
CK2.1 Ways to convey enthusiasm for own specialist area to learners.		✓					✓	
CK3.1 Teaching and learning theories and strategies relevant to own specialist area.			✓	✓	✓			
CK3.2 Ways to identify individual learning needs and potential barriers to learning in own specialist area.							✓	
CK3.3 The different ways in which language, literacy and numeracy skills are Integral to learners' achievement in own specialist area.						✓		
CK3.4 The language, literacy and numeracy skills required to support own specialist teaching.						✓		
CK3.5 Ways to support learners in the use of new and emerging technologies in own specialist area.	✓	✓	✓	✓	✓	✓	✓	
CK4.1 Ways to keep up-to-date with developments in teaching in own specialist area.								
CK4.2 Potential transferable skills and employment opportunities relating to own specialist area.								
Domain D: Planning for learning								
Teachers in the lifelong learning sector know and understand:								
DK1.1 How to plan appropriate, effective, coherent and inclusive learning programmes that promote equality and engage with diversity.	✓				✓			
DK1.2 How to plan a teaching session.	✓					✓		
DK1.3 Strategies for flexibility in planning and delivery.	✓				✓			
DK2.1 The importance of including learners in the planning process.	✓		✓	✓	✓	✓	✓	✓
DK2.2 Ways to negotiate appropriate individual goals with learners.					✓		✓	
DK3.1 Ways to evaluate own role and performance in planning learning.	✓		✓	✓	✓	✓	✓	✓
DK3.2 Ways to evaluate own role and performance as a member of a team in planning learning.								

To achieve the LLUK Standards, teachers in the lifelong learning sector need to have the following knowledge and understanding	Chapter 1 Teachers and Teaching: Principles and Practices	Chapter 2 Learners and Learning: Principles and Practices	Chapter 3 Teaching Strategies and Learning Styles	Chapter 4 Resources for Teaching and Learning	Chapter 5 Curricula, Courses and Lessons: Planning and Design	Chapter 6 Communication, Teaching and Learning	Chapter 7 Assessment of Learning and Achievement	Chapter 8 Evaluating and Improving Professional Practice
Domain E: Assessment for learning								
Teachers in the lifelong learning sector know and understand:								
EK1.1 Theories and principles of assessment and the application of different forms of assessment, including initial, formative and summative assessment in teaching and learning.	✓						✓	
EK1.2 Ways to devise, select, use and appraise assessment tools including, where appropriate, those which exploit new and emerging technologies.	✓						✓	
EK1.3 Ways to develop, establish and promote peer – and self-assessment.	✓						✓	
EK2.1 Issues of equality and diversity in assessment.	✓						✓	
EK2.2 Concepts of validity, reliability and sufficiency in assessment.							✓	
EK2.3 The principles of assessment design in relation to own specialist area.	✓						✓	
EK2.4 How to work as part of a team to establish equitable assessment processes.								
EK3.1 Ways to establish learner involvement in and personal responsibility for assessment of their learning.	✓						✓	
EK3.2 Ways to ensure access to assessment within a learning programme.	✓				✓		✓	
EK4.1 The role of feedback and questioning in assessment for learning.	✓						✓	
EK4.2 The role of feedback in effective evaluation and improvement of own assessment skills.							✓	✓
EK5.1 The role of assessment and associated organisational procedures in relation to the quality cycle.								✓
EK5.2 The assessment requirements of individual learning programmes and procedures for recording internal and/or external assessments.							✓	✓
EK5.3 The necessary/appropriate assessment information to communicate to others who have a legitimate interest in learner achievement.								
Domain F: Access and progression								
Teachers in the lifelong learning sector know and understand:								
FK1.1 Sources of information, advice, guidance and support to which learners might be referred.	✓		✓	✓				
FK1.2 Internal services which learners might access.								
FK2.1 Boundaries of own role in supporting learners.			✓					
FK3.1 Progression and career opportunities within own specialist area.								
FK4.1 Professional specialist services available to learners and how to access them.	✓							
FK4.2 Processes for liaison with colleagues and other professionals to provide effective guidance and support for learners.								

Chapter 1

Teachers and Teaching: Principles and Practices

1. The Role of the Teacher

- Being Positive about Learning
- Learning and the Individual
- Groups and Learning

2. Planning Learning

- Identify Learning Outcomes
- Classifying ways of Learning
- Planning Lessons
- Planning Learning Programmes

4. Assessing Learning

- Types of Assessment
- Other Assessment Techniques
- Uses of Assessment
- Evaluating the Impact of Good Teaching

3. Managing Learning

- Delivery Methods
- Resources
- The Wider Learning Environment

This chapter provides an introductory level to the main aspects of teaching. It covers your role as a teacher including planning, teaching and assessing.

LLUK Professional Standards

The Knowledge and Understanding within the LLUK Professional Standards incorporated in this chapter are:

Domain A: Professional values and practice

AK2.2   Ways in which learning promotes the emotional, intellectual, social and economic well-being of individuals and the population as a whole.

AK4.1   Principles, frameworks and theories which underpin practice in learning and teaching.

AK4.3   Ways to reflect, evaluate and use research to develop own practice, and to share good practice with others.

AK5.2   The need for confidentiality, respect and trust in communicating with others about learners.

AK7.1   Organisational systems and processes for recording learner information.

Domain B: Learning and Ttaching

BK3.2   A range of listening and questioning techniques to support learning.

BK3.3   Ways to structure and present information and ideas clearly and effectively to learners.

BK5.1   The impact of resources on effective learning.

Domain C: Specialist learning and teaching

CK3.5   Ways to support learners in the use of new and emerging technologies in own specialist area.

Domain D: Planning for learning

DK1.1   How to plan appropriate, effective, coherent and inclusive learning programmes that promote equality and engage with diversity.

DK1.2   How to plan a teaching session.

DK1.3   Strategies for flexibility in planning and delivery.

DK2.1   The importance of including learners in the planning process.

DK3.1   Ways to evaluate own role and performance in planning learning.

Domain E: Assessment for learning

EK1.1   Theories and principles of assessment and the application of different forms of assessment, including initial, formative and summative assessment in teaching and learning.

EK1.2   Ways to devise, select, use and appraise assessment tools, including, where appropriate, those which exploit new and emerging technologies.

EK1.3   Ways to develop, establish and promote peer and self-assessment.

EK2.1   Issues of equality and diversity in assessment.

EK2.3   The principles of assessment design in relation to own specialist area.

EK3.1   Ways to establish learner involvement in and personal responsibility for assessment of their learning.

EK3.2   Ways to ensure access to assessment within a learning programme.

EK4.1   The role of feedback and questioning in assessment for learning.

Domain F: Access and progression

FK1.1   Sources of information, advice, guidance and support to which learners might be referred.

FK4.1   Professional specialist services available to learners and how to access them.

1. The Role of the Teacher

1.1 Being positive about learning

Traditionally, the role of the teacher has been as a purveyor of information; the teacher has been the fount of all knowledge. This suggests a picture of students sitting in rows in front of the teacher who is talking and transmitting information to students, while the students listen passively.

This, of course, is not true any more. A teacher is now a facilitator: a person who assists students to learn for themselves. Instead of only having students sitting in rows, they are likely to be in groups, all doing something different; some doing practical tasks, some writing, some not even in the room but in another part of the building using specialist equipment or looking up something in the library. All of the students might well be at different stages in their learning and consequently, the learning is personalised to suit individual requirements and abilities.

This change from the traditional model is the result of a number of factors. First, it is recognised that adults have a wealth of experience and are often able to plan their learning quite efficiently. Second, not all individuals learn in the same manner, so that if a teacher talks to students some might benefit, but others might not. Third, everyone learns at their own pace and not, of necessity, at the pace set by the teacher. Hence, the individualising of learning has definite advantages.

Research into the ways that people learn has not, however, provided teachers with any specific answers. If it had, all teachers would be using the same techniques and all teaching would be effective and successful. Researchers have identified that learning is more effective if it is based on experiences – either direct experiences or experiences that have been read about. Of the two types of experiences, the former is likely to be more effective than the latter. Thus concepts that are able to be practised or seen are more likely to be learned. To apply this in a practical situation in post-16 education and training, learning is more likely to be effective when it is related to, and conducted in, the knowledge of a student's experience.

We need, at this stage, to consider how we as teachers might best provide the experiences so as to make the learning as easy and quick as possible. We might consider two possible approaches to the design of a programme of learning and teaching.

(i)   A programme where the content is carefully derived from an analysis of the student's personal, social and/or vocational needs, and which is implemented by you in such a controlled and organised manner that the student is almost certain to learn, and is aware when the learning has taken place. By this method motivation is generated by immediate success and the avoidance of failure.

Unfortunately this rarely takes place because it has a fundamental drawback. Apart from the requirement for the students to place themselves in the hands of the teacher and so develop a relationship of dependency, it confirms to them that learning is a process which is organised by someone who knows better. It does not help students to learn on their own.

(ii)   The other approach starts from the experience of the student: experience that has taken place as part of life or which has been organised as part of the programme. It then depends upon the student identifying and accepting a need to learn. Such an approach has been described as 'problem solving', 'student-centred learning', 'participative learning', and so on.

The problem with this approach is to ensure that important areas of learning are not omitted and that the 'right' balance is struck between these, and that each area is learned as effectively as possible.

Teaching methods which allow this second approach to be implemented include:

Project work derived from students' current experiences.

Discussions which allow students to recognise and consolidate what the experience has taught them, and also lead them to identify what else they need to learn and practise.

The learning of specific problem-solving techniques which can be applied to a range of situations.

Activities designed to provide opportunities for specific learning outcomes.

An *Experience, Reflection, Learning Model,* embodies the principles that:

(i)   The process should be focused on the student's current experience.

(ii)   It recognises the adult nature of the learner by according responsibility for what is learned.

(iii)   The learning can take place in a variety of contexts.

This suggests that the learning process should be considered in three phases; first, the student's *experience* needs to be followed by, secondly, some organised *reflection*. This reflection ensures that the student learns from the experience and also helps, thirdly, to identify any need for some *specific learning* before further experience is acquired. This model is expressed diagrammatically in Figure 1.1.

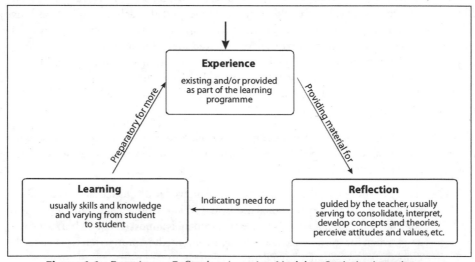

Figure 1.1   *Experience, Reflection, Learning Model to Optimise Learning*

The diagram shows that (i) the model is cyclic in nature and (ii) it has a definite starting point. Such a cyclic nature probably reflects an individual's learning process which takes place naturally. What is not so natural, but very important, is that reflection takes place to ensure that learning from the experience has taken place. Many teachers recognise the importance of the provision of experiences in their classrooms and workshops, but then forget to provide an activity which is designed not only to consolidate the learning, but also to ensure that all of the learning opportunities take place.

Although the three activities are shown as separate entities in the diagram, they should not be seen as separate lessons; they may well be part of the same lesson. Indeed, if they are separated by too long a time span, some of the aspects may be forgotten. The *experience* may be any student-centred activity such as simulation, role play, workshop task, or watching a TV programme. However, as suggested above, the experience may not be part of the programme but may be something that has previously taken place at work and away from the learning environment, they may be past experiences.

When the experience is part of the learning process, the *reflection* can very effectively be undertaken in groups. The teacher's role is very much an enabling one. When this is the case it will be the intention to elicit ideas, perceptions and views from the students and also to enable them to learn from each other. For this to take place effectively, the basic teacher requirement is that of good listening. Some stimulus materials might facilitate this process, such as a well designed questionnaire, or a problem solving strategy.

The *specific learning* part of the cycle will often take the form of specific skills to be practised or learned and particular information to be acquired. It is likely that individual students will vary greatly in what they need to learn and how they might best learn it. For example a text might be available for students to read through when they need help in the learning of specific information. This might be associated with a particular piece of written work which will allow the practise of the application of the information.

The use of the *Experience, Reflection, Learning Model* allows us to devise a teaching and learning scheme or it can be used to analyse an existing scheme. The format could well be used for the design of a lesson where each of the three components form part of the lesson itself.

Our task as teachers is to make this process work in some way and the Basic Teaching Model gives us some help with this. The Model suggests that we start with what we want our students to learn (the objective or 'terminal behaviour' of the students), go through 'entry behaviour' (what the students already know about the topic), 'teaching techniques' (this involves experiences and reflections) until finally assessing what has been learned. Thus, the model involves the aspects in Figure 1.2.

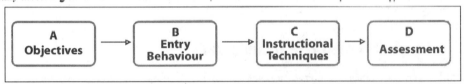

Figure 1.2   *Aspects of the Basic Teaching Model*

The model sub-divides the teaching process into four components and, in so doing, provides us with an uncomplicated yet fairly adequate concept of the teaching process, allowing us to plan and implement an effective learning sequence.

Objectives involve the determination of what our students should be able to do when they have completed a segment of instruction. Objectives vary in scope and character and we will discuss them in some detail in Chapter 5. They can consist of very general statements of aims or much more specific objective statements or competences. Determining our objectives is first in the sequence because knowing where we are taking the students, means there is more likelihood of us getting them there.

Entry behaviour describes the student's level of understanding of the topic before instruction begins. It refers to what the students have previously learned about the objective, their intellectual abilities and development, their motivational state and their learning abilities.

Instructional or Teaching techniques describes the teaching processes, which results in those changes in student behaviour that we call 'learning'.

Finally *assessment* consists of tests and observations that we use to determine how well the student has achieved the objectives. If this assessment tells us that all of the students, or even some of them, have fallen short of their objectives, then one or more of the previous components of the model may need adjustment. The feedback loops shown in Figure 1.3 provide the complete diagram and will be discussed further in section 4.4.3 of this chapter.

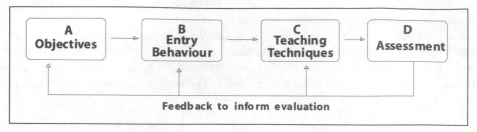

Figure 1.3   *Complete Basic Teaching Model*

Both the *Experience, Reflection, Learning Model* and the *Basic Teaching Model* give you the basis on which you can establish a positive attitude towards learning. In order to be motivated to learn, students have to be interested in their work. One of the best ways to motivate your students is to provide a variety of student activity; variety coming from the direct experiences and the subsequent reflection. The Basic Teaching Model tells you that you need to know where you are going (the objectives), to focus the learning on the needs of the students, to ensure that the level is neither too low or too high (entry behaviour) and, finally, after you have provided a variety of learning activity, to assess how much has been learned.

Your role as a teacher is to provide a positive learning environment and it will help you to do this if you take all of these aspects into consideration. Without a positive environment, your students will not reach their full potential. They will find their learning boring, will not devote the required time to it and, even during periods of learning, will find their minds wandering.

1.2   Learning and the individual

All students are individuals and no two students learn in the same way. One student may prefer to read information and to learn individually. Another student may have problems with reading and only learn through direct experiences by actually doing things. A third may learn through a mixture of experience and thinking about that experience and learn best as a member of a group where competition is an important element in the learning process. Thus, although you may have a number of students in a class, they are all individuals and need to be treated as individuals.

The question for you is, 'How do you treat a class of students as individuals?' Adult students (and, in this context, post-16 year olds are classed as adults) all have their own individual expectations and it is important that you meet these. Your students have all, successfully or unsuccessfully to a greater or lesser extent, completed at least eleven years of primary and secondary education and some will have also completed a number of years of tertiary education. During this time they have built up a series of expectations which have been based on their previous experiences. Your task is to discover their preferences, to concentrate upon those that have been successful and transform those that have been unsuccessful. There are four main general expectations that are common in adult learners and we describe each of these below.

First, adults *expect to be taught and expect to learn*. Adults become involved in post-16 education and training for a variety of reasons but in the main they come of their own volition. This, often for the first time in their life, is education because they choose it. Previously at school, their attendance had been mandatory. Because the students choose to give up their own (or their employer's) time, they have expectations that they *will* learn as a result of their attendance and their hard work. Thus, most adults expect there to be a relationship between your teaching and their learning – not an unreasonable assumption.

This, of course, does not mean that you have to talk or lecture to them the whole time. Kolb, (1984), shows us the importance of variety in teaching techniques. It does, however, mean that you need to find out the techniques that are most appropriate to individuals and to teach each individual according to their needs and preferences.

Second, adult students *expect to have to work hard*. Many adults have already come to the realisation that education does not come easily and that success only comes from hard work on an individual basis. They know that not only will they have to concentrate in the learning environment, but that they will also have to devote some time to private study. Your task is to make sure that they do work hard both in the learning environment and outside it at home.

The third main adult expectation is that the *work is related to the vocation*. All too often, especially in secondary education, students are not too sure why they have to learn the subjects they are asked to study and may be too immature to recognise that learning for its own sake is a useful exercise, and will be useful in later life. In post-16 education, it is important to make these links clear and to make sure that all of our students know why they are being encouraged to work hard. This means that you must set exercises that can be adapted to individual requirements, making sure that some of the exercises are work based.

The fourth and final adult expectation is that your *learners expect to be treated as adults*. Treating people with respect, dignity, seriousness and care is what we should expect as basic rights in a teaching situation. But further, adults tend to be much more intense about their learning and this is what makes teaching adults so satisfying.

Each of these four expectations, although stated in general terms, need to be interpreted as an individual need. Your students may vary in age from sixteen to over sixty. They are of different genders, of different marital states, have different backgrounds, cultures and religions and all have been through different experiences. If you are to treat them as individuals, the more you can find out about them (both in class and outside of it) the greater the likelihood of you being able to treat them as individuals, relate their learning to their needs and, in consequence, improve their learning potential.

The following assumptions, values and beliefs relate to how adults learn and the conditions under which they learn. The statements emerge largely from the growing literature on *Andragogy* but they have been extended by tutors experienced in working with adults. The following is based on work by Farrington (1996). In general, it is assumed that adults learn best when they:

> *Are involved in negotiation:* Negotiation and evaluation should be continuous, beginning before the course begins. There should be a mechanism for mutual planning. Overall, the adult accepts a share of the responsibility for planning, implementing and evaluating the course.

> *Derive their own goals:* Adults need to derive their own goals from their own practice, experience and future needs.

> *Diagnose their own needs for learning:* Adults should be helped to diagnose their own learning needs, beginning with the decision to attend the course in the first place (pre-course counselling) and ending with plans for further study when the course is completed.

> *Accept that learning is an internal process:* That is, learning is something that occurs 'inside' the adult and not something that the teacher 'does' to them.

> *Become autonomous:* The adult learner is enabled to move from a state of dependency (on the teacher as 'appointed leader') to one of inter-dependency and autonomy. This involves learning how to learn from one's own experience and from that of others.

Have responsibility for learning: Adults should have (and be prepared to take) equal responsibility for their own learning and that of others.

Share ideas and feelings: Adults in a group should be encouraged to share their ideas and feelings with others in the group from a very early stage. This will be harder for some than for others and it will be a major initial responsibility for the tutor to help build the sense of trust and membership that will enable sharing to take place fully and fairly.

Experience openness, trust, respect, commitment etc.: There should be an emphasis on the development of equality, mutual trust and respect, mutual helpfulness, openness, care, commitment, freedom of expression and acceptance of differences.

Are in a climate conductive to learning: The establishment of a suitable 'climate' should follow upon the successful building of a group feeling and the attainment of earlier values.

Are willing to alter their way of thinking: This might be another way of saying 'willing to learn'. For some adults their presence on a course indicates that they are passing through a major transition in their life requiring a new way of thinking (redundancy, training for a new job, a change of marital status, enforced leisure, etc.). Others will resist changing long established habits, assumptions and beliefs.

Are able to accept uncertainty: This follows immediately upon the point above and carries equal risk. For many adults, their earlier education (and their own need for security) makes it difficult for them to accept that some questions don't have answers!

Learn and think with others: Teaching adults is a process which involves learning and thinking with others who are also learning and thinking. It is a reciprocal process with a need to be both learner and teacher. Only in this way is it possible to facilitate the learning of others.

Make use of their experience: That is, a course and a tutor should try to take account of each adult's reservoir of experience. The adult may well have a highly structured understanding of the world which has been created over a lifetime and this can enhance or inhibit learning.

Fully utilise their willingness to learn: Adults will tend to have a readiness to learn which will come from their need to undertake developmental tasks associated with existing or proposed social roles, e.g. as workers, professionals, parents, members of sports groups, etc.

Are present-centred: The interests of the adult tend to be more present-centred. They look for more immediate gratification of needs and are less willing to postpone that gratification.

Learn from problems rather than subjects: There should be an emphasis on the tackling of problems and issues which are grounded in the present practice of course members rather than on the teaching and learning of 'subjects'.

Are activity-based: Adults should be helped to move from passivity to activity in their approach to their own learning. They learn best when they are actively involved in the learning process.

Focus on principles: there may well be a need to move from an initial focus on particulars (specific details and concrete examples) to the development of principles (general rules, concepts and, ultimately, theory) for each individual.

Reflect upon experience: Adults should be encouraged to reflect upon their own experience and praxis and use this as a source of learning. This may require an initial 'unfreezing' and learning how to learn from experience.

Acknowledge the importance of process: A group of adults should acknowledge the importance of the process of learning. They should be willing to reflect upon and help change their own and other people's learning processes.

Have a sense of progression: Adults need to have a sense of progression towards the goals which they agree are worth achieving.

Value Transitions: Adults should welcome the contribution that life's transitions make towards their learning. In this sense, even 'failure' can be interpreted as an opportunity to learn and change.

Are integrated in their thinking: There is value in integrated thinking and learning. Fragmentation and the separation of ideas and practice should be avoided.

Can create knowledge: Adults should come to understand that knowledge is something that can be created as well as used. Not all knowledge comes from 'authoritative sources'.

Can change: Adults have the potential to undergo further qualitative changes in their thinking throughout their entire life-span. In so doing they move towards increasing control over their own thinking.

Think critically: Education for adults is about critical thinking, questioning, problem-posing, synthesis and discovery in a cycle so that from each end emerges a new beginning. This can be unsettling and personally distressing for some adults, as they begin to question attitudes, behaviours and abilities that seemed set in stone. But ultimately, good and purposeful teaching can facilitate learning which creates and supports changes which can be truly transforming in people's lives and careers.

1.3   Groups and learning

Much of the art of the management of groups of students lies in preparation. You must always be prepared and be ready for any eventuality. This means that you must be ready to change your prepared teaching plan and strategy both for the group and for individuals.

All sessions, whether they are classroom, laboratory or workshop based, should have an introduction, a development and a conclusion and as such, all of these lesson phases present you with opportunities for both group and individual activities.

Follow the basic teaching model that we discussed earlier and relate this to the three phases of a lesson. In the introduction (which includes an assessment of the immediate needs of individuals – their entry behaviour) the group activities can include question and answer or a discussion of the objectives of the session to find out what your students already know about the topic. The development phase may involve you in some formal input of the material to be covered but, following the Experience, Reflection, Learning Model, students should then reflect and conceptualise the material. This can be achieved by completing some sort of group exercises (discussion groups, role play, group problem solving, gaming) to assist the learning process. The final conclusion phase is to find out how much the students know and this might be achieved through, for example a group assignment. The activities related to each of the lesson phases are summarised in Figure 1.4.

Lesson Plan	Basic Teaching Model Aspect	Group Activity	Individual Activity
Introduction	Objectives	Question and answer or discussion	Notes on session objectives
	Entry Behaviour		Entry behaviour test
Development	Instructional Techniques	Group work to apply learning	Notes on lecture
			Completing examples to apply learning
Conclusion	Assessment	Group assignment	Test

Figure 1.4   *Activities Related to Lesson Phases*

With this type of group activity, the question is asked, 'How do we manage the groups?' In effect, the role of the teacher in group work is very different to that when students are working individually or when you are controlling the learning through lecture or other forms of formal teaching methods. With group work the students control both the pace and the direction of the learning; they need to pool their knowledge and learning styles so that they learn from each other. Your role is to provide information *only* when it is asked, to point your students in the right direction (for example, where they might find the information that they require) but *not* to supply the answers. If groups are straying from the point or from the right direction, you can ask questions to bring their minds back but do not tell them the direction. Your role is that of guide and counsellor and not as the purveyor of information. This is summarised in Figure 1.5 giving the possible teacher and student roles for the different learning situations.

Learning Situation	Teacher Role	Student Role
Lecture-type situation	Control of time and pace of learning. Giving information and help.	Listening and taking notes.
Individual work	Assisting learners to know and apply their learning.	Asking questions. Working at own pace.
Group work	Guiding groups of students but not telling them.	Learning from each other by pooling knowledge. Learning and displaying group skills (leading and following). Working at pace of the group.

Figure 1.5   *Teacher and Student Roles in Learning Situations*

2. Planning Learning

2.1 Identifying learning outcomes

It is important for you to know where you want your students to finish and what you want them to learn. In this way you know when they have got there. In educational language, this involves you identifying the learning outcomes. These *learning outcomes* can be stated as aims and objectives. They are dealt with in greater detail in Chapter 5 but, at this stage, it is only necessary to state that they are what the students will be able to do by the end of their learning.

Aims are *goals* that are set, either by you as a teacher or by the curriculum designers in the curriculum documents (syllabus), to state what the learner will achieve. They are 'ultimate' goals to indicate what the students will be able to do at the end of the course, or subject; they give direction for both the teaching and the learning. Aims can be written at different levels. Course aims are fairly general and are designed to describe the overall purpose of the course. At a subject level they are more specific and are even more specific at lesson level. Examples at the different levels are:

Course Aim: To provide an introduction to the vocation of catering.

Subject Aim: To develop the skills required in kitchen work.

Lesson Aim: To give a working knowledge of the standard methods of cooking by roasting.

These statements are of most use when they are stated in terms of student behaviour; what the learners will be able to do at the end of the course, subject or lesson. Learning outcomes at lesson level are often stated in terms of objectives as opposed to aims. However, at this stage, it is sufficient to identify these as student terminal behaviour. Chapter 5 gives details of writing objectives and competences.

2.2 Classifying ways of learning

The way in which we learn depends to a certain extent on the type of learning that is involved. One theory of learning classifies three main types, or *domains*, and they are:

Psychomotor: Relates to the measurement of the student's manual skill performances and, therefore, the performance required will involve the manipulation of objects, tools, supplies or equipment.

Cognitive: Includes those learning behaviours which require 'thought processes' for specific information such as 'define the terms', 'select a suitable material' and 'summarise the topic'. All of these involve thought processes.

Affective: The behaviour required in this domain involves the demonstration of feelings, emotions or attitudes towards other people, ideas or things.

2.2.1 Teaching students to learn to DO something (psychomotor domain)

Learning to do something (learning a psychomotor skill) usually involves three distinct aspects:

(i)   *Purpose:* In order to learn a skill the student needs some understanding of what it is that is to be achieved – that is the aim or objective.

(ii)   *Procedures:* Skills need some procedures or rules that are necessary in order to complete them efficiently.

(iii)   *Practice:* All skills need practice so that they are completed correctly, quickly and, like riding a bicycle, automatically. This part is very important so that the movements are *right* from the start, unlearning of wrong movements can be difficult to rectify.

Thus, as the word 'psychomotor' suggests, learning in this domain involves a 'psycho' aspect – a cognitive aspect which must be remembered or understood, and a 'motor' aspect – the movement and co-ordination between brain and limbs. Usually, but not always, the hands.

Psychomotor skills are usually learned either from a demonstration or from written instructions or, preferably, from a mixture of the two.

When demonstrating a skill to students you should:

(i)   Give emphasis to the required body movements; which hand and foot is being used, when sight, sound, smell and touch are required.

(ii)   Encourage students to *ask questions* until they understand what is being done.

(iii)   Emphasise the key points so that the sequence is learned and any difficult aspects can be concentrated upon. These points could be highlighted on a chalkboard or in a handout or noted by the students themselves.

(iv)   Ensure that all safety aspects are covered.

Demonstrations should be short because, in the main, students will be inactive, watching what is being done. Anything that you do that can give students an activity will help them to concentrate upon the important points, for instance getting them to complete a handout, noting the key points, sketching some aspects, or even assisting. If the demonstration is too long, consider dividing it into two parts.

Demonstrations are designed to assist with the cognitive aspects of learning. Give the students some practice as soon as possible; too long a gap between the demonstration and the subsequent practice will mean that they may have forgotten many of the points.

2.2.2 Teaching students to memorise (cognitive domain)

Some students have good memories while others are not so good, (and the same might be said of teachers!). Memory relates to the factual information which is the basis of all subjects. It is not concerned with understanding but only with the *recall* of the factual information.

You can help your students to memorise information by:

(i)   Verbal or visual association, that is grouping things together verbally (like knife, fork and spoon) or keeping the location of things always the same (like the layout of the kitchen and the drawers so that equipment can always be visualised in the same place and, hence, remembered).

(ii) Repetition, for instance, we remember our telephone number by dialling it time and time again. We can do the same with facts. By writing them out a number of times, repeating them aloud as in poetry, listening to a tape several times or reading a number of times.

(iii) Testing, this is a form of repetition which asks learners to recall and repeat the information either verbally or in writing.

(iv) Special aids like rhyme rules (30 days has September, etc.) or mnemonics (ROYGBIV) which can either be designed by you for your learners or by the learners themselves.

A number of conditions help good recall. These include: (a) trying to avoid errors; (b) testing frequently to increase learning; (c) the more the students concentrate, the more they will be able to recall; (d) the greater the importance of the learning, the more effective it will be, and (e) the more students can relate the material to other things that have been learned previously, the greater the likelihood of recall.

2.2.3 Teaching students to understand (cognitive domain)

Learning to *understand* something involves giving answers to the questions of 'Why?' and 'How?'. Students need to give explanations or summaries to show that they understand something.

To summarise these points, learning to *do* something involves learning a procedure and then practising it; avoiding errors if possible.

Memorising involves using various methods to enable students to recall facts; practice, in the form of repetition or testing is helpful and, as with learning to do something, errors must be prevented if possible. Learning to *understand* something is different in a number of crucial aspects. Repetition is *not* helpful whereas errors can be. Another difference lies in the fact that memorising and doing, once accomplished, are always practised or repeated in the same way. By contrast, understanding is an active mental process involving thoughts which link or group ideas together in a *new* way in our minds.

An aid to understanding two similar concepts is to *compare and contrast* them. So we can list the features they have in common i.e. compare, and then list features which are distinct to each, i.e. contrast.

For example, Guidance and Counselling are often used interchangeably or together but they are different. Figure 1.6 shows how you can start to compare and contrast the two activities.

Same	Different	
	Guidance	**Counselling**
Helping students to make informed choices	• May be in small groups	• Usually one-to-one
Helping students with problems	• Usually not confidential	• May be confidential
May need to seek information for a student	• Usually concerned with future	• Usually concerned with now
May need to refer to another for help	• Planned event in student life	• Often response to unexpected event
Appointment basis	Etc.	

Figure 1.6 *'Compare' and 'Contrast' as an Aid to Understanding Similar Concepts*

Helping students to understand involves making sure that they ask questions so that the topic makes sense to them. They must be made to work at making comparisons and trying to solve problems. Thus, there are three techniques that you might use to help students understand; questioning, making comparisons and solving problems.

Getting students to ask questions can be achieved by them asking you as teacher or by them asking other students. Thus, a discussion on the topic can assist understanding. Questions such as 'Why' usually identify the reasons for what goes on and are likely to be helpful. 'Who?', 'What?', 'Where?' and 'When?' only gain information and are not helpful for understanding.

After finding out by questioning as much as they can about the new facts or ideas, you can ask students 'How is the information the same or different from ideas that you have already?' Questioning is being used here for the specific purpose of comparing what is known with what has been recently learned.

Working out a problem expands students' understanding by making them adapt and transfer the body of knowledge that they have to a variety of different circumstances. Figure 1.7 summarises helpful and unhelpful activities for doing, memory and understanding types of learning.

Type of Learning	Helpful Activities	Unhelpful Activities
Doing	Identifying key points from a demonstration followed by practice.	Errors must be prevented.
Memorising	Practice in the form of repetition and testing.	Errors must be prevented.
Understanding	Errors can be helpful. Learners should ask questions, make comparisons and solve problems.	Repetition is unhelpful.

Figure 1.7 *Helpful and Unhelpful Activities for Different Learning*

2.2.4   Teaching students to learn attitudes (affective domain)

The learning of attitudes is equally, if not more, important than the learning of cognitive and psychomotor elements. It could be argued that, unless your students have the 'correct' attitude, then other learning is superfluous.

Attitudes like 'showing concern for safety', 'working effectively as a group member' and 'checking work after completion' are all important aspects for your students. But, how do you teach them? You can tell students again and again about an incorrect attitude but, unless they really see the necessity for it and internalise it as part of their character, then they are not likely to display it.

The most effective technique for the teaching of attitudes is to set up a discussion (that is a discussion itself, or case study, role play and so on, all of which involve students discussing with each other) where students can learn from each other. Examining attitude through being critical is an excellent way to understand why students think the way they do, and can help to change deep seated feelings and motivations.

2.3   Planning lessons

It is evident from the previous section that:

(a)   The type of plan for a learning session depends upon the learning that is required for that session. The requirements are different for a psychomotor skill session compared with a knowledge session.

(b)   It is important to classify the requirements of a session into the domain that it predominantly falls and, if it involves cognitive learning, the level in that domain.

We have already said from the Basic Teaching Model (Section 1.1) that the formulation of objectives (or aims) for a session provides the starting point. Within these objectives (or aims) lie the clues to the required domain through the verbs that are used. These are summarised in Figure 1.8.

Domain	Possible Verbs (student behaviours)
Psychomotor	Assemble, build, cook, mend, sing.
Cognitive (Knowledge)	Know, define, list, name, state.
Cognitive (Understanding)	Understand, interpret, translate, explain, summarise.
Affective	Appreciate, choose, answer, comply, study.

Figure 1.8   *Student Behaviours Related to Domains of Learning*

Thus, the wording of the required student behaviour can indicate the domain into which the learning predominantly falls. Of course, as we have already said, the requirement of a psychomotor skill also relies upon cognitive knowledge and attitudes and vice-versa. What we have discussed in the previous section now has to be put into practice with the design and production of a plan for a learning session, a lesson plan.

2.3.1   Lesson planning

A lesson plan has two functions:

1.   A strategy or plan for 'teaching'.

2.   A series of cues to be used during the lesson.

It is not to be confused with *lesson notes* which are details of the actual subject matter content of the session. The lesson plan is intended to help you to proceed logically without being bound to your notes, but, even with detailed planning, every eventuality cannot be catered for, so the lesson plan is essentially tentative and flexible. A lesson plan should not limit you in your approach and it should contain sufficient flexibility to cater for circumstances as they arise in the session.

You can usefully divide your lesson plans into two:

(a)   Initial information.

(b)   Body of the plan.

The initial information should contain:

1.   The title of the lesson.

2.   Details of the class (name, size, etc.).

3.   The time of the lesson.

4. The expected entry behaviour of the class (expressed in terms of what the students should know or be able to do).

5. The aims/objectives of the lesson (expressed in the same sort of terms as the entry behaviour).

An example of initial information is shown in Figure 1.9.

Title:	Calculating Area
Class:	First Year Business Studies – 18 Students
Time:	9.00 – 10.00
Entry Behaviour:	Multiplication of numbers, shapes of plane figures
Objectives:	1. Explain how to calculate the area of plane shapes 2. Solve problems relating to area

Figure 1.9 *Initial Information in a Lesson Plan*

Once the essential preliminaries have been completed you need to plan the strategy. Planning should relate to the principles stated at the start of this chapter (that is following the Experience-Reflection-Learning and Basic Teaching Models). You will need to plan an introduction, a development and a conclusion within the time available, give students an experience, make them reflect on the experience and provide variety for them so that they are motivated throughout the session.

2.3.2 Planning a cognitive lesson

The expansion of the three phases of a lesson (introduction, development and conclusion) depends upon the type of learning and the subject matter.

Planning a cognitive lesson depends on whether the aim or objective relates to knowledge (memorising) or understanding. For a lesson based on knowledge there needs to be an emphasis on verbal or visual association, repetition and testing, whereas, for a lesson based on understanding, questioning, comparing with what is already known, and problem solving is appropriate.

You may find the following steps helpful when you are planning a lesson where *information* is to be remembered:

1. Tell the student *what* is expected to be learned and *why* it is important that it is learned.

2. Provide a meaningful context to the information to be learned. Logically organise the information.

3. Relate new information with previous experience or learning.

4. Provide for adequate practice and reinforcement of correct responses.

5. Assess students' performances.

If, on the other hand, the objectives of the lesson require that the students *understand* the subject matter and are required to solve problems to show their understanding, you will find the following steps useful.

1. Tell the students the lesson objectives.

2. Assess the students' entry behaviour for the concepts and principles they will need in order to solve the problem.

3. Have students recall the necessary concepts and principles.

4. Provide verbal direction to the students' thinking (an algorithm or paradigm) short of giving them the solution to the problem.

5. Verify students' learning by requiring them to give a full demonstration of the problem solution.

The headings that can usefully be employed for the expansion of the three phases are:

1. *Time*   It is helpful to give an indication of the time that is likely to be needed for each of the phases and each of the sub-topics within a phase.

2. *Content*   This should be restricted to brief cues or key words and they should be made to stand out clearly.

3. *Teacher Activity*   This should specify the strategies which are intended to be used during the lesson. If a question or questioning technique is to be used then key questions should be stated.

4. *Student Activity*   The parts played by students should be clearly stated so that variety can be planned. Students should have a change of activity at least every 15 minutes.

5. *Resources*   All audio-visual materials should be specified.

An example of the body of the plan using the introductory information from Figure 1.9, might be as shown in Figure 1.10.

Time	Content	Teacher Activity	Student Activity	Resources
9.00	**Introduction** Assess entry behaviour.	Questions about multiplication.	Answering.	
9.05	Objectives.	Tell students objectives and the importance of them.	Listening.	OHP.
9.10	**Development** Area of Square.	Exposition.	Listening.	Handout A1.
		Individual Tutorials.	Examples.	
9.20	Area of triangle.	Individual Tutorials followed by chalkboard.	Groups to predict the formula.	Handout A2.
		Individual Tutorials.	Examples.	
9.35	Area of parallelogram.	Individual Tutorials.	Individuals to predict formula.	Handout A3.
9.45	**Conclusion** Review of formulae.	Questions with C/B overview.	Answers.	
	Test.		Individual work.	
10.00	**End**			

Figure 1.10 *Body of a Plan for a Cognitive Lesson*

2.3.3 Planning a psychomotor skills lesson

We have all learned psychomotor skills. These include walking, tying our shoe laces and riding a bicycle. These, however, were learned automatically. They might have taken quite a long time to learn and might have been learned by trial and error. You are required to teach psychomotor skills so that they are learned in the most effective way and this generally means them being learned quickly and with a minimum of error.

Five steps can be identified in the teaching and learning of a skill. These are:

1. Analyse the skill.
2. Assess the entry behaviour of the student.
3. Arrange for training in the component parts.
4. Describe and demonstrate the skill.
5. Arrange for the three basic learning conditions of contiguity, practice and feedback.

Each of these steps will be examined in detail.

1.   Analyse the skill

The first step involves a detailed analysis of the skill so that it is broken down into its constituent parts, the sequence of operation is identified, and the key abilities are noted. For example, if you assume that you are teaching 'sharpening a Pencil with a Knife' the skills analysis will involve for a right handed person:

To cut wood:

1. Hold pencil in left hand about 2.5 cm from the end.
2. Hold knife in right hand and rest blade with blunt edge uppermost at an angle of about 30 degrees to the centre line of the pencil.
3. Cut off wood with slow, sure cuts removing pressure at the end of the stroke.
4. Rotate pencil in left hand to take equal cuts around the pencil.
5. Cut until about 5 mm of lead is exposed from the wood, equally around the circumference.

To put point on lead:

6. Position knife so that it makes an angle of approximately 90 degrees with the centre line of the pencil.
7. Sharpen lead with swift sure strokes rotating pencil in left hand.

From this analysis the key abilities can be identified as:

(a) Ability to keep the angle of the knife around the pencil constant.
(b) Ability to judge angle of knife for correct depth of wood.
(c) Ability to remove pressure towards the end of the stroke of the knife.
(d) Ability to sharpen exposed lead to a point without breaking the lead.

2.   Assess the entry behaviour

The skills analysis results in a chain of activities in the form of a sequence of component skills. You must make sure that the students have learned all of the pre-requisite skills. For example, in the sharpening of a pencil you must make sure that the student can cut with a knife, hold the knife at 30 and 90 degrees and so on.

3.   Arrange for training of component skills

This provides opportunity for the student to:

(a)   Learn any missing links in the chain and to develop the required abilities.

(b)   Learn the skill components (or some of them) so well that they can focus attention on new aspects of the more complex task that is being learned.

4.   Describe and demonstrate the skill to the student

Describing and demonstrating is a very important and skilled part of your job. It is necessary to show students the chain involved in the skill and the links in the chain. This part of the learning of the skill is, for the students, the cognitive part; they must learn to verbalise the skill so that they *know* what is required and, secondly, the demonstration provides a clear visual picture of what is required in completing the skill, what the task will look like after each stage. The demonstration method is described in Chapter 3 and will not be discussed here. Sufficient to say that it is an important part of your job.

5.   Arrange for the three basic learning conditions

The first condition for efficient and effective learning is *contiguity*, that is the almost simultaneous occurrence of the links in the chain so that each part of the chain is linked. Once the links are contiguously formed, they occur almost simultaneously. Thus, you must teach students the correct sequence, co-ordination and timing. To achieve this you can teach students (a) the whole method involving all of the links being learned at one time, or (b) the part method involving sub-dividing the skill into sections and learning a section at a time. For a complex skill, the part method has the advantage that the simple skills can be mastered before the more complex ones. It does, however, have the disadvantage that the sections have then to be joined.

The other conditions are *practice* and *feedback*. Practice should be given directly after the demonstration so that students do not have the chance to forget what is required. Feedback is the information to the students about their performance. Feedback can be intrinsic (which comes from within the student by, for example, noting the finish produced or by the kinaesthetic or sensory feel of doing the job right) or extrinsic (which is provided by someone else like you as the teacher). The best type of feedback is intrinsic because you will not always be available to provide information to the student. In consequence, any form of extrinsic information should always lead to the provision of intrinsic feedback. For this reason feedback should be immediate or given as soon as possible after the event.

Using the pencil example, intrinsic feedback could be given through telling students the criteria of acceptable performance and them ensuring that the lead does not break during the sharpening process. Extrinsic feedback could be given by you commenting upon the angles of the knife during the practice periods and through assessment of both process and product.

2.3.4 The skills lesson plan

As with a the cognitive lesson, the main components of a skills lesson involve introduction, development (demonstration, explanation, practice and assessment) and conclusion.

Introduction

It is vital to arouse interest in the first few minutes of a skill lesson. For a new topic, a short clear statement of what the students are going to be doing (the aim/objective) and why it is important for them to be doing this. The importance can often be the link with what they are doing at work. In a continuation lesson testing the work already completed will focus attention on the subject and provide the necessary link with the previous lesson.

Development

A demonstration of the skill to be learned can follow the introduction. This should be followed by an explanation of the key points which can usefully be reinforced with questions and answers. As soon as possible each student should be given the opportunity to practice the skill so that the sub-tasks are integrated. The necessary extrinsic feedback can be given on a one-to-one basis during the practice period to complement the intrinsic feedback that should be encouraged.

When students have practised the skill sufficiently to become competent, they can be assessed. This assessment may need to be followed by a further period of practice if sufficient competence has not been achieved.

Conclusion

You should plan the ending of the lesson with just as much care as the introduction and development. Sufficient time must be allowed for the cleaning of the practical area, returning tools and equipment and washing (if this is required). You should plan a short period in which you summarise what has been learned and prepare students for the next session. A useful summary is to place all of the student work on the bench and to formally, but anonymously, assess each piece of work. In this way the students see what their peers have achieved as well as having the main points emphasised.

The example plan given in Figure 1.11 shows the design of a lesson to teach the sharpening of a pencil with a knife.

Title:	Pencil Sharpening
Class:	First Year – 18 Students
Time:	2.00 – 3.00
Entry Behaviour:	Use of knives – Know 30 and 90 degrees
Objectives:	1. Show skill in sharpening a wood pencil with a knife so that 5 mm of lead is exposed concentrically

Time	Content	Teacher Activity	Student Activity	Resources
2.00	**Introduction** Assess entry behaviour	How do you use a knife?	Answering	
2.05	Objectives	Tell students objectives and importance of sharp point in drawing	Listening	OHP
2.15	**Development** Removal of wood	Demonstration	Watching	
		Tutorials	Practise	Pencils & Knives
2.30	Sharpen to a point	Demonstration	Watching	
		Tutorials	Practise	
		Assessment	2nd Practise	Template
2.45	**Conclusion**	Display on front desk of all pencils for critique. Identification of criteria	Listening. Identification and notes	
2.55			Clearing away and returning equipment	
3.00	**End**			

Figure 1.11 *Psychomotor Skills Lesson Plan*

2.3.5 Introductions and conclusions

When we are planning our lessons we have a tendency to concentrate upon the main body of the lesson and often neglect the start and the end. However, the start of a lesson and the end, are very important and should be part of our normal planning process.

Introduction

The *introductory* phase is intended to motivate the students to want to know more; it should motivate the students by providing links with what has gone on before, by informing them of what is to take place in the lesson and suggest why the topic is important and how the information might subsequently be used. Figure 1.12 shows some of the possible purposes (the inner circle) and processes (outer circle) that might be used in this introductory phase of the lesson.

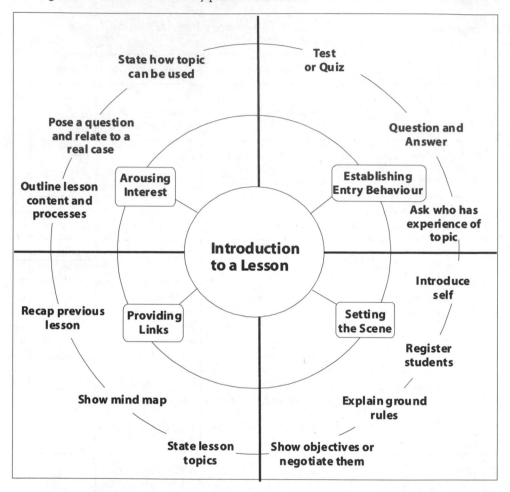

Figure 1.12   *Possible Purposes and Processes of Introductions*

This indicates that there are four possible purposes, and for each purpose, there are a number of possible processes that can be used. It is not, however, suggested that only one of these are used or that all of them are used for each introduction. The intention is to indicate the options that are available so that you can choose those options that are most appropriate for your students and for a particular topic.

So, how do we choose what is appropriate for a particular lesson? The over-riding criterion is to motivate the students. If the lesson is in the middle of a sequence of topics you might establish the entry behaviour of the students through question and answer of the previous lesson's content, set the scene by informing the students of the objectives of the session, and arouse interest by stating how the topic might be used in the future.

Conclusion

The conclusion to a lesson should be planned with as much precision as the introduction. All too often a teacher who does not monitor the time carefully will suddenly realise that the allotted time has been completed and, in consequence, there is either no conclusion or a very short one. The conclusion should be planned to take about 10% of the total time of the lesson.

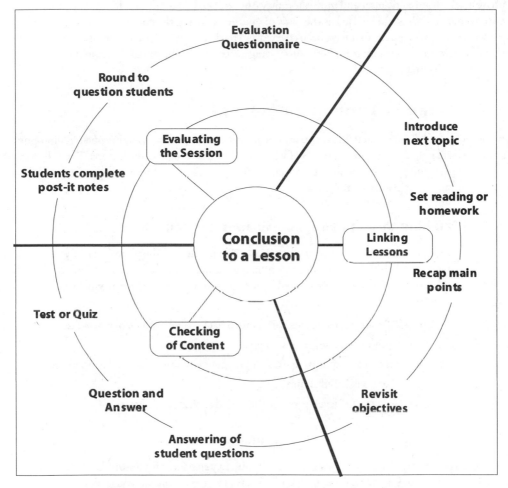

Figure 1.13 *Possible Purposes and Processes of Conclusions*

In any lesson much information passes between you, the teacher and your students. The intention of a conclusion is to remind students of the main aspects covered during the lesson and to start the transfer of the information from the short-term to the long-term memory. If this is repeated in the introduction to the next session this will further assist the process.

Figure 1.13 provides an overview of the possible purposes (the inner circle) and processes (the outer circle) that may be used. The three purposes that are suggested include (i) checking the student understanding of the content, (ii) linking the content and structure to other learning and (iii) evaluating the session. Each of these purposes have their own suggested processes associated with them. Thus, the checking of the understanding of the content might include a test or quiz of the main points that have been covered, it may involve question and answer based on the objectives of the session or it may involve you answering any questions that students may have for you. Some of these are teacher-centred and some student-centred. The former can check the understanding of all the students whilst the latter can only check some of the students. The decision of which might be more appropriate, will probably rest on how much time you have available as any student-centred activity is likely to take longer than teacher-centred ones.

A useful ploy in any session is to have your objectives displayed for students on either an OHP transparency or on the whiteboard or flipchart. In this way they can be displayed in the introduction phase as an advance organiser and motivator; they can be ticked off in the development phase as they are covered; and they can be used as the basis of questions during the conclusion phase to remind students of the main points that have been covered and to check on their understanding of them. Any visual aid that can be used on three occasions during a session must be worth the time and effort that you put into its preparation!

2.4   Planning learning programmes

It is important to decide what it is that you want to teach from the point of view of course 'philosophy', since this will help to guide you in terms of what to include in your specific lessons. The following aspects of planning will help you formulate exactly what you want to achieve in any programme that you teach, from first principles, to first sessions.

1.   Thinking through your course aims and objectives

The first important aspect to think about when involved in planning is the philosophy of your course and its main aims and objectives. The decisions that you come to about the courses philosophy will have a direct bearing on all of your planning decisions that follow. The following will help you with this. Is your course:

(a)   A 'basic skills' course for students with limited background knowledge or skills?

(b)   A general education course for all students?

(c)   A higher level course requiring the development of cognitive and practical activities?

(d)   A vocational or skills-based course?

(e)   A course requiring the development of ideas and critical faculties?

2.   Thinking about the actual course content

For this step you'll need to ask yourself whether the content you choose for lessons is 'core', 'principle-based', or 'skills-based', and in answering such questions, to what extent can you achieve these in class and how much can you expect students to develop *outside* your sessions. So, in essence:

> Does your course model 'behaviours' for a specific job/career and how will you show this in your teaching?
>
> Does your course only involve ideas and principles?
>
> Does your course need to develop key skills amongst the course goals?

3.   Thinking through how you will Structure your Course Content and Lesson Structure

It may be surprising to realise that the way the content is structured in your course and lessons, can have a major influence on the way that students learn not only the subject in question, but how that subject is applied, and its relevance in their everyday life. Consequently, you should arrange your course content bearing in mind that:

Structure of the material should reflect the way that the subject is organised in reality, e.g. through time and relationships, etc.

Concepts need to be arranged to demonstrate the fullest variation that subjects may demonstrate, e.g. science through logic, education through discussion and dialogue etc.

The importance that you attach to certain areas gives strong messages about how you see that subject, e.g. teaching 'simple' concepts first gives the impression that a subject should be dealt with hierarchically, or that some concepts are complex.

If a subject is vocational, working with employers is important.

Students need to learn continually how to apply and re-evaluate their learning if they are to become truly autonomous. Only ever demonstrating one method of approaching problems does not lead to creative thinking.

Dealing with values and affective domain aspects of a topic is often relegated to the ends of a course: if you want to engage your students with different ways of looking at the world, you must meet those issues early on in your course.

4.   Thinking about the Relationships between Teaching and Learning

So far, we have dealt with aspects of planning which are more to do with your teaching and preparation of your material. But thinking about the students who will be studying under you makes that necessary leap from *your* planning to *their* understanding, so you also need to consider *why* your students are taking this course and how you can best approach their diverse motivations:

Are the students here to get a qualification for a job?

Are the students here because they just want to learn and enjoy their subjects?

Are students here because the course forms an entry requirement for higher level study?

Are the students here because they have to be, in order to receive benefits, etc?

Are the students here because the course is a 'core' or an option'?

5.   Thinking about Teaching and Learning

No matter what subject or variety of students who you will be teaching, you need to use a variety of teaching and learning strategies. Rather than simply being common sense, this is also, importantly, a question of respect for diversity and difference and in fact will enhance the learning experience of *all* your students. So you should use both 'passive' and 'active' strategies of teaching, and include:

Discussion

Case study

Instruction

Lecture

Tutorial

Labs

Fieldwork/visits

Role play

Debate

Presentations

Project work

3.   Managing Learning

3.1   Delivery methods

A teaching strategy maybe defined as 'a purposeful combination of student activities supported by the use of appropriate resources to provide a particular learning experience (process) and/or to bring about the desired learning (product)'. Notice, in the definition, the emphasis is placed firmly on the needs of the student and not on the teacher. A teaching strategy is what you do for the benefit of student learning. There is a vast range of teaching strategies, some of which are detailed in Chapter 3. Here it is sufficient that you familiarise yourself with that range and know what each of them entails. Some of the more popular strategies are outlined below:

Lecture:	One way communication by the teacher with no feedback from students. May last from 5 minutes to more than two hours.
Question and Answer:	Teacher-centred interaction with the students.
Group Discussion:	A network of interaction between students with the teacher setting the discussion but subsequently playing only a minor role.
Practicals:	Real or simulated situations with students learning from experience.
Tutorial:	Interaction between the teacher and one or a small group of students providing opportunity for guidance and support.
Individual Learning:	Situations where students work alone with books, equipment and other resources.
Demonstration:	Teacher shows the basic steps and sequence of a skill, or the main attributes of a concept with students watching.
Seminar:	Students either individually or in small groups are set a task to research and from which they report their findings to the whole group and lead a subsequent discussion.
Case Study:	The examination of a real or simulated situation so that learning can take place through the discussion of each of its facets.
Role Play:	Students are invited to enact, in the training situation, the role they will be called upon to play in their job of work.
Project:	The particular task is laid down by the teacher but the lines to be followed to achieve the objectives are left for the student to decide. Projects have an end product and tend to be integrated activities.
Assignment:	Similar to a project but usually of shorter duration and not as open-ended.
Problem Solving:	Teacher sets a problem which students solve either individually or in groups.

It has already been suggested that the use of one strategy may be more appropriate in a given situation than another. Research into the advantages and limitations of the various methods, however, is not always clear cut. It is possible to make some crude choices, based on the way that you analyse your objectives. Figure 1.14 makes suggestions for the general choices of matching strategies to objectives.

When your objective is to teach a motor skill	When your objective is to impart knowledge and understanding	When your objective is to change attitudes
Assignment Demonstration Individual Practice Tutorial Project	Case Study Project Seminar Individual Learning Problem Solving Lecture Question and Answer Assignment	Case Study Discussion Role Play

Figure 1.14 *Matching Strategies to Objectives*

Making the choice, of course, does not mean that a lecture (for instance) cannot change attitudes, or that role play will not impart knowledge.

3.2 Resources

You will remember from the previous section that the definition of a teaching strategy was given as a combination of student activities supported by appropriate resources. The main resources with which you should have familiarity and be able to use fairly effectively are:

Chalk and whiteboard or flipchart: — Can be used as a planned visual aid but also to give a résumé of student work like responses to questions.

Handout: — Information given to students on paper which can either be given complete to supplement a lecture or incomplete to provide a student activity. Worksheets fall into this latter category.

OHP transparency: — Pictures or words projected onto a screen which are used to provide students with the information needed to reach the lesson objectives. Used like a chalkboard but with the advantage that the transparencies can be prepared prior to the lesson to save time in writing.

Chapter 4 goes into some detail about the design and use of resources. You must remember that resources are an extremely useful aspect of your teaching repertoire. They can:

(a) Provide concrete experience (Experience-Reflection-Learning Model).

(b) Motivate and arouse learner interest.

(c) Increase retention (we remember more of what we see than we do of what we hear).

(d) Provide variety in learning.

(e) Provide experience not otherwise easily obtained.

(f) Make better use of class contact time.

(g) Improve your communicative skills.

With all of these advantages, you must ensure that you are skilful in the design and use of resources.

3.2.1 Boardwork

Figure 1.15 suggests some guidelines that you can use for your boardwork including chalk, white or flipchart.

Boardwork

Preparation: Keypoints and diagrams should be planned on lesson plan.

Lettering: Minimum size should be 5cm upper case and 3cm lower case.
Lower case is easier to read than upper case.
Emphasis can be given by:
      * UPPER CASE
      *colour
      *<u>underlining</u>
      *s p a c i n g
Avoid symbols, abbreviations, vertical or angled words.

Diagrams: Avoid clutter.
Use colour but not too much to be confusing.
Label directly, avoid a key.
Use templates for accuracy and recurring need.

Location: Ensure it is visible to all learners and is suitably lit.

Testing: Check visibility from rear of room.
Avoid obscuring students' vision.

Figure 1.15   *Guidelines for Boardwork*

3.2.2 Handouts

Handouts are useful in the presentation of information and as worksheets. They may be loosely categorised as:

Information handouts

These aim to provide learners with the information needed to achieve the lesson objectives. They may be further divided into:

(a)   Notes that relate directly to the content of the lesson, for example an overview of the main points of a lecture, a summary or outline of an experiment, a full transcript of a seminar.

(b)   Supporting handouts which may be used to introduce a session, give formal statements such as definitions or formulae, present data to support arguments, e.g. graphs or maps.

Worksheets (incomplete handouts)

The student is expected to write on the handout either during the lesson or afterwards. Workcards are similar to worksheets but the crucial difference is that they are reusable because the students do the associated work on a separate page.

You should consider various things when using handouts. The following questions need answering before you decide to design and duplicate the handout.

(a)   Why use a handout? Is it to save time and make the learning easier for the students?

(b)   At what stage in the lesson do you intend using the handout? Remember that, if they are *Information Handouts,* it is better to give them at the start of your lecture/ exposition as the students can read them at the same time as listening to you.

(c)   Are the students clear as to how they can use the handout? Do they use it as background to be read later? Do they make their own notes on it? There is nothing worse than spending time, effort and money on their design and duplication and finding that they are subsequently left on the desks or, even worse, in the wastebasket at the end of the lesson!

(d)   What type of handout do you intend to use? In general, an incomplete handout is preferable to the information type. The former can be personalised and you can ensure that they are read and used.

(e)   Do you intend to assess the students' use of the handout? This is a useful way to ensure that the material that they contain is learned. One way which this can be achieved is to plan the questions that you are to ask in order to draw out the information from the class, which students then write in the appropriate spaces provided.

Preparing handouts

Choose the best format to clearly and simply illustrate the idea you are seeking to teach. Remember your aim is to provide motivation and to ensure achievement. The handout should be clear, logical, straightforward, concise, error free and legible.

You must write at a vocabulary level which will be understood by the student. Simple, short sentences rather than complex, compound ones are more likely to be understood. Illustrations are invaluable; a picture can be worth much more than words and a table is more likely to be looked at than a paragraph.

You should avoid large blocks of type. 'White space' makes a handout easier to read. If possible colour should be used where it is necessary to differentiate between different aspects. For differentiation purposes, different phases, topics or subjects can be duplicated on different coloured paper.

3.2.3 OHP transparencies

The Overhead Projector has several advantages including: (a) it can be used in daylight conditions; (b) you face the class and can therefore more easily control the group; (c) it can be used in conjunction with other aids; (d) material can be prepared before a lesson or can be developed as the lesson proceeds; (e) material can be stored and used again.

You should site the OHP 'off centre', and then turned so that the projected image is directed diagonally towards the screen which should be placed in the darkest corner at the front of the room.

You may find it necessary to adjust the screen to avoid a 'keystoning' effect where the image at the bottom of the screen is wider than at the top with the result that it is distorted. To prevent this, tilt the top edge of the screen towards the projector.

Operating the OHP

You should adhere to the following principles when using the OHP: (a) face the students at all times; (b) stand or sit to one side of the projector and not behind it. All writing on the transparencies should be done while standing at the side; (c) place the prepared transparencies on the projector with the light off. Switch off between each transparency; (d) if it is necessary to *point* at the transparency this should be done by pointing at the projector; (e) do not move the projector while it is hot as this may reduce the bulb life.

Preparing transparencies

(i) Materials

The transparency material is made from acetate sheet and different thicknesses are available. The thicker material is easier to use and handle than the very thin.

Two types of ink pen are available: spirit based and water based. If a permanent transparency is to be produced, then use a spirit based ink pen. If you have to erase the ink from a spirit-based pen, special erasing spirits are available.

Adhesive lettering such as *'Letraset'* can be applied directly to the acetate film. Care should be taken when using photocopies from books, magazines or other published material. Apart from the laws relating to copyright, the printing can be too small for classroom purposes. If you do resort to this, ensure that you enlarge the print prior to copying onto acetate film.

(ii) Considerations of use

Many teachers prepare their own transparencies. If you do this, careful thought must be given to how you will use the aid and how you will integrate it with other learning activities. For instance: (a) what do you expect the students to do while the transparency is being projected?; (b) are they to make notes or copy in full the displayed material and should an associated handout be prepared?; (c) what questions are to be asked to draw out information from the students?

(iii) Key Design Principles

Often, transparencies have far too much material on them. The overall principle relates to simplicity. So you should: (a) keep the transparency simple. Preferably, a transparency should deal with only one main point; (b) use large lettering (a minimum of 6 mm in height) and, as with boardwork, lower case is easier to read than upper case; (c) do not overuse colour; (d) water based pens can easily be erased so use spirit based permanent ones when you intend to store the transparency for future use.

3.2.4 Using Information and Learning Technology (ILT)

ILT has a very important role to play in teaching and learning. It can be used as a resource, in assessment, in evaluating a lesson and in Key Skills. Often, the role of ILT has been seen as a replacement for existing methods. For example:

> the whiteboard is replaced by an interactive whiteboard;
>
> the OHP is replaced by the data projector and Personal computer;
>
> multiple-choice questions are replaced by software that create such questions;
>
> an evaluation of a session is replaced by an electronic voting device.

However, it is interesting to see *how* learning takes place through the use of ILT. The use of ILT allows study to take place where and when the student chooses. The use of email allows you to keep in touch with your students, mark assignments and give them advice. The creation of electronic portfolios enables students to gather a range of evidence in image, sound and video as well as in the traditional written format.

In section 1:2 we considered how to plan lessons for cognitive and psychomotor skills. In this section we are going to look at developing a lesson using ILT. Figure 1.16 shows a lesson plan for colleagues who are undertaking staff development.

The objectives of the session are that colleagues will:

>   identify ILT resources that their students have used and the problems using these resources;
>
>   discuss ways of overcoming the problems;
>
>   identify a range of resources in their own area of teaching;
>
>   discuss how the resources could be used to assist with differentiation, cater for different learning styles, develop assessment, and accessibility issues.

The lesson is located in a room which has access to computers, data projector and an interactive whiteboard. The intention is to make use of the experience of the group and the problems that they have encountered when using IT with their students.

Time	Title	Teacher Activity	Colleague Activity	Resources
10.00	Introduction.	Identify Outcomes Show video and lead responses.	Watch short video clip and comment.	'Be Inspired' video clip from Ferl Practitioners Programme.
10.10	Problems with ILT.	Lead small groups discussion methods used with students and problems with using ILT with own students. * Make notes on interactive whiteboard and summarise. Print summary for colleagues. * Lead discussion on how we can make ILT happen and the resources available.	Group Working. Write key points in PowerPoint. Present and feedback to whole group. Discussion.	PowerPoint to present group findings. Interactive whiteboard print out of notes.
10.30	Demonstrate ready made ILT resources.	Demonstration to include: * Word. * PowerPoint. * Video. * Assessment.	Working in groups colleagues identify how the materials can enable differentiation. * Cater for different learning styles. * Can be used in assessment. * Key skills. * Accessibility.	Word activities Acweb.doc * Isacbity.doc. * NLN resources: safety, Numeracy. * Hot Potatoes crossword multi-choice. * Excel Numberwork
10.50	Discussion.	Lead discussion with each of the groups. Place points raised directly into PowerPoint.	* Groups feedback.	PowerPoint.
11.10	PowerPoint.	Play back key points.	Question and Answer.	
11.15	End of Session.			

Figure 1.16 *Interactive Lesson Plan*

The lesson plan is designed to be displayed on the interactive whiteboard during the session. All of the links to Word and PowerPoint documents, video, etc., are shown as hypertext (underlined) links in the right-hand resource column of the lesson plan. Simply clicking on a title takes you to the required resource.

The lesson plan appears no different to any other. The lesson is planned in sections of not longer than 20 minutes. It starts with the class watching a short video clip to assist them in the identification of ILT teaching and learning methods that might be used and the problems that could be encountered. The identification of methods and problems is completed in small groups with key points noted in PowerPoint by each group. This is followed by a teacher-led demonstration of the use of different ILT hardware and software resources and groups are required to identify which **areas** these assist with learning. The following could be a typical response:

Enabling differentiation:

Word	- use of 'pop-up' comments to explain difficult terms;
	- using 'drop-down' boxes to limit wrong choices;
	- using 'drag and drop' to reinforce procedures.
PowerPoint	- use of visual cues to help with written answers;
	- non-linear pathway so students can choose the direction.
Hot Potatoes	- allowing a range of assessment methods to be used.

Allowing for different learning styles:

Word	- written word;
PowerPoint	- visual format which can incorporate images and music;
Excel	- simulation involving numbers and graphs;
Video	- visual format incorporating images, voice and music;
Hot Potatoes	- allowing hands-on experiences.

Providing self-assessment:

Hot Potatoes	- production of a range of different assessment materials such as crossword and multiple-choice;
Video	- built in assessment materials;
PowerPoint	- built-in assessment materials.

Accessibility Issues:

Word	- test reader can scan documents easily, making it suitable for students with sight problems;
PowerPoint and Video	- visual images make PowerPoint suitable for students with dyslexia but disadvantages partial sighted or blind students;
Quizzes	- printed in a range of text sizes on coloured backgrounds assists with reading problems.

Assisting with Key Skills:

Excel	- uses numeracy;
NLN materials	- National Learning Network (NLN) resources contain images and sound clips and can be used in assisting with communication and numeracy skills.

3.3   The wider learning environment

A very important task for you is to make learning as easy and as enjoyable as possible for your students. We have already laid down some principles like: all students learn differently, at their own pace and in their own way; students' experiences should be interspersed with periods of reflection; different strategies are applicable for different domains of objectives; a variety of teaching strategies are most likely to be useful to a class of students to maintain motivation; well designed and correctly used visual aids assist the learning process.

All of these, and more, are means which you can use to assist your students in their learning. You must think about the environment of your classrooms and workshops and make them as amenable to the learning process as possible.

3.3.1   Room layout

The traditional image of post-16 teaching is fast disappearing. This old image is one which involves a lecturer, chalk and talk, teacher centred methods that are syllabus bound and examination oriented, dictated notes, pitching the teaching at the average ability level, rows of desks and strong teacher control.

You should see yourself as a facilitator with much of your work being done out of the classroom in preparation for individualised learning: you should value resource-based learning where student participation and activity is high, curriculum negotiation is common and the teaching of transferable skills takes place at all stages.

In order to accommodate these changes, your classroom has to become more of a resource centre and less of a lecture room. You need to have books, magazines and articles readily available for your students. The walls could be covered with charts, drawings, photocopied articles and the like, about the subject. They also require constant changing so that they keep up with the changes in the curriculum area being followed. The desk layout needs to be flexible so that they can easily be moved from the more formal situations, to groups of them being put together for discussions and then apart for individual work.

3.3.2   Study skills

Why should you try to introduce new approaches?

> The exam results might be better.
>
> You should not rely on always teaching traditional courses and should be developing some of the skills that the newer FE courses require.
>
> Even if it does not improve the end product (exam results), development of more interactive teaching may improve the quality of experience of the course and the process of learning.
>
> You should value some degree of student independence in learning for its own sake which should make students more adaptable and able to learn for themselves. Students will develop more critical ways of looking at topics, which can be enhanced by multiple modes of teaching and learning.

If students are to be asked to learn for themselves then you should assist them in this process and teach them the study skills that are necessary for this to take place. In its many forms, teaching study skills basically means teaching people to learn effectively from whatever 'delivery mode' is being used either presently, or in a more general sense, as a life skill. The common study skills are described in detail in Chapter 6 but, in general terms those often required by adults are:

Planning a project or an assignment.

Reading (SQ3R – Survey, Question, Read, Recall, Review).

Taking notes.

(a) from a lecture

(b) from a book.

Essay writing.

Planning study time.

You need to consider including the teaching of these skills, particularly in the beginning part of your courses, in order to assist your students in their learning. They are going to have enough difficulty with the subject matter without having the added problem of not knowing how to study effectively.

4. Assessing Learning

You must make many decisions in your teaching job. Some of these are:

> Which students are successful.
>
> What teaching strategies to use.
>
> Where to start teaching depending on the ability of the students.
>
> What additional teaching is to be given to less successful students.
>
> When students have achieved the objectives.

The basis upon which you make these decisions is generally related to information that you collect. This information is often based on 'tests' that you give to your students. A test is:

> a way of measuring a sample of a student's behaviour or achievement in order to evaluate that learning.

A distinction is drawn between assessment and evaluation. Assessment is the measure of student learning (generally through testing) whereas evaluation involves much more than this and can include the quality of the learning experience, pass rates, attendance levels etc.

So, assessment is the process of *obtaining information* about how much the student knows and evaluation involves using that information to form *judgments* which, in turn, are to be used in *decision making*.

The three concepts that are outlined are:

Information: Facts about students, materials, resources, processes, and so on that you need to collect.

Judgments: Interpreting the facts or information to help determine present conditions or predict future performance.

Decisions: Deciding upon a course of action from among several possibilities.

The Basic Teaching Model indicates that assessment is required at two major stages of the process. You will need to assess the entry behaviour of your students and you will need to make an assessment to see how well they have achieved the objectives after the learning has taken place. Thus, assessment of the student is necessary for the following types of instructional decisions. The list is not exhaustive and you could think of many more decisions that follow assessment tests. It does, however, illustrate the various points:

> Identifying where to start instruction.
>
> Planning remedial action for students.
>
> Identifying student learning difficulties.
>
> Finding student readiness for learning new topics.
>
> Improving teaching methods or resources.
>
> Planning activity-wide groupings of students.
>
> Grading students.

4.1   Types of assessment

Achievement testing usually involves the use of certain instruments. These include:

> A written test.
>
> An oral test.
>
> A practical test.

There are, however, many objectives in education for which tests are not appropriate. For these objectives, non-test methods need to be employed. Some of the techniques used for this purpose are:

> Self-report techniques.
>
> Observational techniques.
>
> Profiles.

As all courses require a variety of objectives for their successful completion, it is necessary that you use a variety of test and non-test instruments to decide if all your objectives are being met by your students.

It is not our intention in this chapter to make you an expert in the design of the various types of test, only to make you familiar with the different types together with where they might be most appropriately used. In this way you can include them in your lesson plans in order to take the decisions described above. Greater detail will be found in Chapter 7.

A written test is made up of a variety of questions. One way of classifying these is from the point of view of how the students are expected to respond. They can either:

> Select the right response from a set of given responses (called selection-type questions)
>
> or
>
> Supply the answer to a given question (called supply-type questions).

4.1.1   Selection type questions

Items of the selection type include alternative choice, multiple-choice and matching block types. The time needed to answer this type of question is only a matter of seconds.

Alternative-choice type

Items of this type, also known as true-false items, contain statements for which there are only two possible responses. The type of responses can be: true or false; yes or no; agree or disagree.

Multiple-choice type

Multiple-choice questions consist of two parts: a stem and a number of options. The stem consists of the question or statement which must be answered by choosing one of the options. The *options* are plausible answers or concluding statements from which one option must be selected.

Matching block type

The matching block type consists of a series of premises in one column, and the response options are listed in another column. The student is asked to select the response options that match each of the stems.

Example:

Here are two columns. Match the decimals in the left-hand list with the appropriate prefix in the right-hand list by completing the table.

Decimal		Prefix	
(i)	0.000 001	a.	centi
(ii)	0.000 000 001	b.	milli
(iii)	0.001	c.	pico
(iv)	0.01	d.	micro
		e.	nano
		f.	deca

Table

Decimal	0.000 001	0.000 000 0001	0.001	0.01
Letter of Appropriate Prefix				

4.1.2 Supply type questions

Questions of this type include short answer, structured response essay, extended response essay and practical questions. The time needed to answer this type of question is much longer than for the selection type.

Short answer questions

There are two types of short answer questions:

(a) Where a question is posed and the student supplies the answer by using a word or phrase.

e.g. In what year did the first person land on the moon?

(b) Where an incomplete sentence is given and students must complete it by inserting the appropriate word or phrase.

e.g. In the year .... the first person landed on the moon.

Structured essay questions

This is an essay-type question taking 15-25 minutes to answer, but the response is structured for the student. This type can include calculation questions.

Example:

Using the following headings, state briefly how to grow a lettuce crop in the open:

(a) Soil preparation.

(b) Sowing.

(c) Thinning.

(d) Harvesting.

Essay type

In this type no restrictions or limits are placed on the student responses. Again, they are usually allocated 15-25 minutes to answer.

Example:

Give a brief account of growing an outdoor lettuce crop.

4.1.3 Practical test

The term practical 'test' refers to a test in which students perform a practical exercise according to instructions prepared in advance and assessed according to a marking scheme.

The practical test involves the completion of psychomotor skills. This type of test might also be called an assignment or project when it involves the completion of written work to accompany the psychomotor skills.

Example:

The following example shows how such a test can be operated and consists of specific instructions for the students and a marking scheme which will also be given to them.

Task

Apply undercoat and gloss paint to wall surfaces by brush.

Preparation

You will require a wall area (plaster, plaster board or building board) of between 7 and 8 sq. metres with a height of at least 1.5 metres and a cutting edge of at least 4 metres. The surface should be prepared, made good and ready to receive undercoat.

The test is to be organised over two days to allow sufficient drying time. Colours must be selected with care to ensure that no opacity weaknesses reduce your chance of meeting the standards.

Instructions
1. Protect the surrounding area.
2. De-nib surfaces.
3. Apply one coat of undercoat by brush.
4. Wet or dry flatten to a smooth even surface.
5. Apply one coat of alkali type gloss finish by brush.
6. Check and clean tools and equipment and return to store after each process.
7. Clean surroundings after each process.
8. Check assessment schedule for standards to be achieved.

Assessment:

Standard of Finish	Tolerances	Yes	No	Comments
Are bits and nibs visible but not excessive?				
Are brush marks laid off correctly and not pronounced?				
Is work free from grinning?				
Does work have full even gloss?				
Free from runs and tears?	1 run 5mm max			
Free from curtains?	1 allowed 50mm max.			
Free from misses?	Invisible from 1m			
Etc.				

4.2   Other assessment techniques

The objectives that are applicable to these methods include:

> Communicating effectively with a range of people and in a variety of situations.
>
> Showing a capacity for organisation and leadership.
>
> Working safely with a range of equipment and materials to an agreed standard.
>
> Identifying own strengths and weaknesses.
>
> Recognising the need for a personal career plan.

These objectives are all affective domain objectives which deal with attitudes and personal competences.

4.2.1 Self-assessment techniques

You can argue, especially in the case of adults, that the only true assessment of the type of objective or competence identified above, is self-assessment. No one else really can know how well a person is able to 'communicate with a range of people' or 'recognise the need for a personal career plan'. The only true assessment is that made by the individual. Hence, self-assessment is becoming widely recognised as an important assessment technique especially when used with adults.

When you adopt this technique, you will need to identify the objectives or, even better, competences that are to be achieved together with explicit criteria for assessment for each of the competences, so that students have a clear idea upon which to base their self-assessment.

4.2.2 Profiles

A profile is a way of reporting student achievements; it is not an assessment technique in itself. Profiles can be used during the course of study to provide a basis for action by both students and teachers and, at the end of the course, to provide a basis for action by employers and teachers. They also provide a system of reporting progress on areas (that is the affective domain areas) that are difficult to assess when using the traditional techniques of assessment. Thus, profiles attempt to pass on information to students, employers and other teachers about student progress and achievements in all areas of study.

You will see that several types of profile are discussed in Chapter 7. One type, the 'Free Response' type is given as an example in Figure 1.17. Others have much greater structure than this and are more firmly linked to lists of objectives or competences.

The intention is that this will be completed by you as the teacher but that you will discuss it with your students and, more importantly, get the student to sign it. This is of particular importance where goals are to be set for the student in the space for areas where improvements need to be made. It has already been stated that profiling is a process; it takes place in an on-going (formative) framework. There are four basic principles that you should follow when profiling.

1.   It requires one-to-one teacher-student reviews on a regular basis.

2.   It involves negotiation with individual student.

3.   It is a strategy which allows students to, reflect on their success and failure and take responsibility for their own learning, development and assessment.

4.   It should record positive statements of achievement with respect to: abilities and skills demonstrated, personal qualities exhibited, and tasks and activities experienced.

Please comment on the following:
Communication Skills:
Practical and Numerical Skills:
Attitude to Training:
Planning and Problem Solving:
Manual Dexterity:
Computer Literacy:
Aptitude and Areas for Improvement: (Give here areas in which the student shows a particular aptitude and areas in which improvements need to be made).

Signed:	Teacher:	Student:	Date:

Figure 1.17 *Free Response-Type Profile Sheet*

4.2.3 Observation techniques

It has come to be realised over the past few years that the traditional techniques of assessment (like examinations involving paper and pencil tests) are very unreliable and are not really achieving the intended result. They only assess the end product and, generally, completely neglect the process that is involved in achieving that product. In consequence, the instruments that have been used for some time in the assessment of practical work have become more widely accepted for other tasks and are based on *direct observation*.

This observation is necessary to increase the validity and reliability of the assessment procedures. The observation may take place over a relatively long period of time or may be related to the assessment of a specific task. It is evident that this technique can assess the process elements of a task as well as the finished product.

There are four common methods of direct observation but the first of these, global impressions, although included here for the sake of completeness, is unreliable and not really suggested for common use. The four methods are:

(i) *Global impression:* which is essentially a 'look and see' technique. The method is very unreliable but is a useful first step when starting to develop an assessment procedure.

(ii) *Semi-structured:* consists of a number of open questions which have been determined in advance and are relevant to the different aspects of the task. The observer writes answers and/or comments during and after the observation.

(iii) *Rating schedules:* are where the rater gives a score on a scale of the impression of each component of the task on a scale from poor to good.

(iv) *Checklists:* are where the rater marks, usually with a tick or a cross, whether the student did or did not carry out the specific features of a task.

Examples of each of these methods are detailed in Chapter 7.

4.3 Uses of assessment

Each of the type of assessment techniques can be used in a variety of situations. One of your roles is to decide which type to use in a particular situation. Some suggestions for this are made in Figure 1.18.

Assessment Type	Possible Uses
Multiple Choice	Measurement of a variety of learning outcomes such as vocabulary, facts, explanations and applications. Providing diagnostic assessment of entry behaviour or to assess objectives quickly at the end of a session.
Alternate-Choice	These are not particularly helpful as they are very susceptible to guessing.
Matching Block	Testing of lower level knowledge (matching dates with events and symbols with units). When associations between things are to be identified.
Short Answer/Completion	When the learning outcome is to recall rather than to recognise information. Simple computational problems. When a selection type is too obvious.
Structured and Extended Essay	When the objectives specify writing or recall rather than recognition of information. When the sorting and presentation of an argument is required.
Practical	When the assessment of psychomotor skills is necessary.
Self Assessment	Especially useful for adults where affective and high level cognitive assessment required.
Profile	For recording on-going assessment during a course to give and negotiate specific feedback to students.
Observation	Particularly for psychomotor and affective domain objectives.

Figure 1.18   *Situations where Different Assessment Techniques may be Used*

4.4   Evaluating the impact of good teaching

4.4.1   Evaluating teaching

There is no single good way to teach. Good teachers have different attributes and behaviours. Much research has been undertaken (and continues to be undertaken) regarding effective teaching. Current research into good teaching (e.g. Entwistle (2000), Shulman (2002), Warren Little (2003), Kreber (2002), etc.) illustrates the diversity of what can be described as good teaching; but broadly defined, suggests that good teachers:

> Plan and manage learning effectively.

> Evaluate students' learning experiences continually, and place students' support needs centrally.

> Plan and manage learning experiences which promote critical and inquiring thought and engage learners intellectually, ethically and sensually.

> Place equality of opportunity and promotion of equal rights centrally in all learning and teaching.

> Are able to articulate a 'theory of teaching and learning'.

> Promote and actively engage in professional and personal development continually.

Engage in and disseminate findings publicly, of a scholarship of teaching, and in so doing promote a wider community of inquiry amongst colleagues.

When we have a new group of students working towards the City and Guilds 740, Cert Ed or PGCE, we often use the following activity:

Think of the best teacher you ever had, at school, at university or during your own training – think of a real person – and then list the qualities that made them so good.

After this we ask individuals to contribute their thoughts and we write these on the board as a basis for discussion. The following are the thoughts of one group of students. From the results, you can see a close correlation to that of the current research into good teaching.

The ideal teacher is described as having the following characteristics:

Is expert in own subject.

Is expert in the teaching role, well organised, well prepared.

Is confident, open to suggestions, other viewpoints, is flexible and approachable.

Is interested in individual students, and spends time with them.

Is consistent in the treatment of everyone.

Is consistent in behaviour – always fair, always even tempered.

Is friendly, with a sense of humour.

Shares, with students, the teaching aims and objectives.

Knows the students as individuals – their strengths and their weaknesses.

Communicates well in a variety of modes, including non-verbal.

Leads well, with appropriate pace.

Is flexible and willing to change the approach.

Gives feedback within an appropriate timescale.

In addition to this paragon, the ideal learning process is described as one where students like:

To be stimulated and motivated.

To be involved.

To have clear goals.

To feel a sense of openness and trust.

To enjoy the lesson and feel part of it.

To have a role model.

To see the overall picture and the underlying model.

The topic to be relevant or be made relevant.

All of the above research can be used to gauge the qualities that are required by a 'good' teacher. They indicate:

(i)   The qualities that are necessary (e.g. enthusiastic, warm, approachable).

(ii) The teaching attributes that are required (e.g. have clear aims and objectives, be a subject expert, and be open to other views).

When it comes to evaluating teaching, evaluation needs to be systematic if you are to get a realistic picture of what you are good at and what aspects need more thought and practise. Self-evaluation is a core aspect of the whole process of being insightful and continually reflective in teaching. As such, it should form part of a system of 'triangulation' of feedback from students, peers, external examiners, inspectors, and through the process of assessment. Only then will you be truly able to develop your teaching to a higher level.

Concerning self-evaluation though, probably one of the most helpful methods is to keep a diary of what has gone on in our learning sessions. The type of headings that you might consider in such a diary are given in Figure 1.19 with associated questions. These questions can be used as a checklist, or alternatively you can rate yourself on, say, a four point scale (one for poor and four for excellent) for each of the aspects, or you might make comments alongside each of the aspects.

Aspect	Question
Preparation	Have you: • Analysed the topic/subject area? • Indicated expected student learning? • Identified the needs of your students? • Selected appropriate teaching strategies? • Written systematic lesson plans? • Selected and prepared learning resources?
Presentation	• Implemented selected teaching strategies? • Responded flexibly to classroom situations? • Used learning resources effectively? • Conformed to safety requirements?
Classroom Relationships	• Secured student participation in your lesson? • Provided leadership to your students? • Promoted a classroom climate which facilitated learning?
Communications	• Used appropriate language registers? • Developed students' communication skills? • Effectively employed skills of non-verbal communication?
Assessment	• Used an assessment method to consider if the objectives have been achieved?
Subject Matter	• Demonstrated mastery of your subject matter?

Figure 1.19   *Headings and Questions for a Self-Evaluation Diary*

Alternatively, you might like to design a pro-forma that can be used to make a diary for each of a series of lessons. You can use the proforma to write a sentence or two about each of the aspects of your teaching. The summation of the completed pro-formas can then form a diary for the series of lessons. Such a pro-forma is shown in Figure 1.20 with some suggested headings.

Preparation:	How successful was the preparation?
Entry Behaviour:	Was the entry behaviour as expected?
Aims/Objectives:	Were the aims/objectives achieved?
Teaching Strategies:	What teaching methods were most successful?
Aids:	Were the aids successfully designed and used?
Classroom Relationships:	Why was the class climate either successful or unsuccessful?
Assessment:	What assessment techniques were most successful and why?
Subject Matter:	What was most successful in achieving the required learning?

Figure 1.20   *Pro-forma for Self-Evaluation of a Lesson*

The questions in the above example not only ask *what* but they also ask *why* and that second part is important in your self-evaluation. Whatever system you devise for yourself, it should be quick and easy to complete; if it is long and complex you will tend not to do it. However, the type of form above, when completed for, say, eight to ten consecutive classes, will form a comprehensive 'diary' of your activities, indicating what went well and what went not so well, for that group of students.

4.4.2   Evaluating a presentation

What is your first reaction when you are asked to give a presentation? For most people, even those with lots of experience, there is some anxiety. Some anxiety, or nerves, is good because you tend to be more alert and do not take the situation for granted. However, if you become too nervous, you can use deep breathing and relaxation techniques. Careful preparation reduces anxiety. Collins (1998) says if you fail to prepare then be prepared to fail.

You need to ask a number of questions as you prepare. Why are you doing this presentation? What do you want your audience to learn? Who are your audience and what do they already know? How should the audience learn? Where will the session take place and when? Experienced presenters will double-check the answers to these questions. Be clear about the aims and objectives – be as precise as you can. Keep your presentation clear and simple. Using a mind map can help you to organise the key points in the most logical sequence. Remember, most presentations have an introduction, a development and a summary. Concentrate on your opening because a good introduction helps both you and your audience to relax. You need to show the audience why they need to learn, and establish the ground rules such as when to ask questions, use of handouts, etc. Design a good lesson plan and you may use cue cards rather than using a full script.

Take care with the design and preparation of your visual aids and resources because these will have an impact for good or ill. Size of writing and careful use of space will help with the design of overhead transparencies and handouts. Do allow everyone time to read the aids rather than you reading them all aloud by saying 'Take a minute or two to read …..'.

It is usually better to stand when you present as this helps with voice projection. Establish good eye contact with all areas of the room because this helps you to look confident. Another feature which helps you to appear confident is to move into the body of your audience, if you can, as it reduces the communication barriers. Have some pauses, especially when you are about to say something important. You can use 'signposts' to assist with emphasis, such as, 'Now we come to the unique feature of this process'.

Opportunities for questions are essential to most presentations. With small groups, you may wish to take questions at anytime but with large groups, you usually ask for questions at the end of the presentation. You may avoid silences at this time by 'planting' some friends in the audience with suitable questions. Repeating the question allows you some thinking time and ensures everyone hears the question as well as your answer.

Finally, do try to evaluate your presentation by using questionnaires, such as the one shown in Figure 1.21, or by talking to members of the audience at the end as with all aspects of teaching and learning, it is not just your students who are the learners – you are, and should always be, a learner too.

In relation to your course, indicate your views on the following issues by circling the appropriate numbers or ticking the appropriate methods:

1. Are the subject aims being fulfilled?

   Fully   5   4   3   2   1   Not at All

2. Do you think that the work done in class assists you with the learning process?

   Helpful   5   4   3   2   1   Unhelpful

3. Do you feel that there are adequate resources?

   Adequate   5   4   3   2   1   Totally Inadequate

4. Are the resources used effectively?

   Effective   5   4   3   2   1   Under-used

5. Which of the teaching methods have you experienced? Tick as appropriate those experienced and those which you would like to experience.

Experienced	Method	Wish to Experience
	Lecture Group Discussion Seminar Role Play Practical Demonstration Use of Handouts One-to-one talks Other (state)	

6. Have you found the content of the subject:

   Simple   5   4   3   2   1   Difficult

7. Do you feel that your progress has been monitored:

   Adequately   5   4   3   2   1   Not at all

8. Do you feel that your progress is:

   Satisfactory   5   4   3   2   1   Unsatisfactory

9. Any other comments:

Figure 1.21 *Questionnaire for Students on the Effectiveness of their Course*

4.4.3 Feedback loop as a basis for evaluating teaching

The Basic Teaching Model gives you the basis for the evaluation of your teaching performance. Here if the feedback loop from the assessment tells you that the objectives have not been achieved by the students, you must consider: (a) if the objectives were correct, or (b) if the entry behaviour of the students was lacking, or (c) whether the teaching strategies that you adopted were inappropriate.

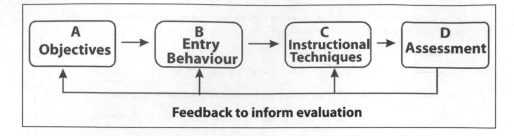

Figure 1.22   *Feedback Loop for the Basic Teaching Model*

We have already suggested that you evaluate your own teaching. As part of this process you should also involve your students in your evaluation. Students, especially adults, can provide invaluable information about your performance that cannot be collected from any other source.

Information needs to be collected from students about each aspect of the Basic Teaching Model. This information can be collected by questionnaire or through interviewing students (or a mixture of both). You need to design your own questionnaire or schedule but it is not the intention to go into questionnaire design in this chapter. However, an example questionnaire is presented in Figure 1.18.

It will be seen that this questionnaire has both open response aspects where students are invited to write their own comments, and closed response ones where students rate their choice on a 5-point scale.

In deciding the design of your questionnaire you should first consider what you want to find out. This can reflect the things that you think that you do well and things that you think could be improved. The answers that students give to the questions can either confirm or otherwise challenge these thoughts.

Achieving the LLUK Professional Standards

Standards
Domain A: Professional values and practice
AK2.2   Ways in which learning promotes the emotional, intellectual, social and economic well-being of individuals and the population as a whole.
AK4.1   Principles, frameworks and theories which underpin practice in learning and teaching.
AK4.3   Ways to reflect, evaluate and use research to develop own practice, and to share good practice with others.
AK5.2   The need for confidentiality, respect and trust in communicating with others about learners.
AK7.1   Organisational systems and processes for recording learner information.
Domain B: Learning and Ttaching
BK3.2   A range of listening and questioning techniques to support learning.
BK3.3   Ways to structure and present information and ideas clearly and effectively to learners.
BK5.1   The impact of resources on effective learning.
Domain C: Specialist learning and teaching
CK3.5   Ways to support learners in the use of new and emerging technologies in own specialist area.
Domain D: Planning for learning
DK1.1   How to plan appropriate, effective, coherent and inclusive learning programmes that promote equality and engage with diversity.
DK1.2   How to plan a teaching session.
DK1.3   Strategies for flexibility in planning and delivery.
DK2.1   The importance of including learners in the planning process.
DK3.1   Ways to evaluate own role and performance in planning learning.
Domain E: Assessment for learning
EK1.1   Theories and principles of assessment and the application of different forms of assessment, including initial, formative and summative assessment in teaching and learning.
EK1.2   Ways to devise, select, use and appraise assessment tools, including, where appropriate, those which exploit new and emerging technologies.
EK1.3   Ways to develop, establish and promote peer and self-assessment.
EK2.1   Issues of equality and diversity in assessment.
EK2.3   The principles of assessment design in relation to own specialist area.
EK3.1   Ways to establish learner involvement in and personal responsibility for assessment of their learning.
EK3.2   Ways to ensure access to assessment within a learning programme.
EK4.1   The role of feedback and questioning in assessment for learning.
Domain F: Access and progression
FK1.1   Sources of information, advice, guidance and support to which learners might be referred.
FK4.1   Professional specialist services available to learners and how to access them.

Achieving the LLUK Professional Standards

Standards	Ways in which you can show that you have achieved the Standards	See Section
AK2.2 AK5.2 AK7.1	1. It is useful to know about your students. For one of your classes ask your students questions such as: ▪ Why did you join the course? ▪ What do you expect to do on the course? ▪ What do you expect to learn on the course? ▪ What do you expect from your tutor? ▪ What qualities do you bring to the group and the course? ▪ What do you hope to do at the end of the course? Discuss with your students how they learn best and compare your findings with those in section 1.2. Devise a system for recording the information that you gain.	1
AK4.1 AK4.3	2. Applying theories or models to your own teaching is a way to develop your understanding of the learning process. For one of your classes, apply either the *Basic Teaching Model* or the *Experience-Reflection-Learning Model*. Describe the effect of using the model and how it may help you to reflect.	1
BK3.2 BK3.3 BK5.1 CK3.5	3. For at least two of the lessons that you have designed for you students explain how you have planned to: (i) Structure and present the information. (ii) Use listening and questioning techniques effectively. (iii) Select the range of resources. (iv) Use information and learning technology (ILT).	2 and 3
DK1.1 DK1.2 DK1.3 DK2.1 DK3.1	4. Select one of your lesson plans and: (i) Explain the value of the objectives and how you used them in your planning and with your students (try to cover all domains). (ii) Give a rationale for the activities included in the introduction, development and conclusion. (iii) State the resources that you have used and their value. (iv) Explain how the principles of equality of opportunity influenced the lesson. (v) Explain how you motivated your students.	2 and 3
EK1.1 EK1.2 EK1.3 EK2.1 EK2.3 EK3.1 EK3.2 EK4.1	5. For the same lesson (or another appropriate lesson): (i) Explain how you assessed the learning, why this was appropriate and how this leads to student self-assessment. (ii) Comment on the use of ILT in the assessment of your students. (iii) How have you used the principles of assessment design? (iv) Explain the role that feedback plays in the student learning.	4
FK1.1 FK4.1	6. For one of the lessons that you have given: (i) Explain how you provided effective learning support. (ii) State the specialist services available to your students and how they may be accessed.	4

For a model approach to show how you have achieved the LLUK Professional Standards see Appendix I.

Chapter 2

Learners and Learning: Principles and Practices

1. Principles of Learning

- Introduction
- Domains of Learning
- Learning Taxonomies
- Models of Learning

4. Other Theories of Learning

- The Theories
- Teaching and Learning Approaches
- Kolb
- The Learning Continuum

2. The Domains

- Introduction
- The Cognitive Domain
- The Psychomotor Domain
- The Affective Domain

3. Motivation

- Concepts Related to Motivation
- Maslow's Hierarchy of Needs
- Teaching for Extrinsic Motivation
- Deep and Surface Learning
- Learning Technologies and Motivation

This chapter discusses the ways in which your students learn and how theoretical models can inform and improve your teaching.

LLUK Professional Standards

The Knowledge and Understanding within the LLUK Professional Standards incorporated in this chapter:

Domain A: Professional values and practice

AK1.1   What motivates learners to learn and the importance of learners' experience and aspirations.

AK2.1   Ways in which learning has the potential to change lives.

AK2.2   Ways in which learning promotes the emotional, intellectual, social and economic well-being of individuals and the population as a whole.

AK4.1   Principles, frameworks and theories which underpin practice in learning and teaching.

Domain B: Learning and teaching

BK1.3   Ways of creating a motivating learning environment.

BK2.1   Principles of learning and ways to provide learning activities to meet curriculum requirements and the needs of all learners.

BK2.3   The relevance of learning approaches, preferences and skills to learner progress.

BK2.4   Flexible delivery of learning, including open and distance learning and on-line learning.

BK2.5   Ways of using learners' own experiences as a foundation for learning.

Domain C: Specialist learning and teaching

CK2.1   Ways to convey enthusiasm for own specialist area to learners.

CK3.5   Ways to support learners in the use of new and emerging technologies in own specialist area

---

1. Principles of Learning

1.1 Introduction

Learning is about change: the change brought about by developing a new skill, understanding something new, changing an attitude. The change is not merely incidental or natural in the way that our appearance changes as we get older. Learning is a relatively permanent change, usually brought about intentionally and purposefully. When we attend a course, search through a book, or read a discussion paper, we set out to learn!

Other learning can take place without planning, for example by experience, or accident. If you wallpaper a room and then paint the ceiling you could learn that you should paint the ceiling first. Some of our learning can be more dangerous; for example we might discover that a knife is very sharp by cutting ourselves. Generally with all learning there is an element within us of wishing to remember and understand why something happens and to do it better or different the next time.

This chapter is about the theoretical underpinning that is provided for us by educational psychology. It is important that we are able to relate what we do in the classroom to at least some theory. If we do not do this, then the way that we teach is likely to be done by experiment and by responding to things, without knowing why things work. Unfortunately, for every aspect of research that tells us to do something a particular way, there is another piece that suggests, not necessarily the opposite, but a different way, or a more effective way for particular students.

Educational theory has, as its base, psychology, sociology, and the study of behaviour. As teachers, it is argued, we need to know how people behave under certain circumstances so that we can optimise their learning through the provision of conditions that make it as easy a process as possible. For instance, how do we help our students to memorise the material in our subject, how do we help them understand the concepts and principles, does their attitude to both learning and the subject have a bearing on how they learn, and so on?

1.2 Domains of learning

Theorists tend to separate learning into three main groups or domains. These are the psychomotor, cognitive and affective domains. Each will be considered in turn.

Those skills which are concerned with physical dexterity, for example riding a bike, and giving an injection, fall into the *psychomotor* domain. Both of the tasks do need knowledge but, predominantly, they are physical skills which need practice.

Knowledge and knowing the 'how' and the 'why', the thinking skills, fall into the cognitive domain. Examples include 'stating the names of the major bones in the body', 'explaining why we have tides'. Both of these require thought processes to be accomplished.

The third domain, is the *affective* domain. This is concerned with attitudes. Examples in this domain include for example, 'the need to eat a healthy, balanced diet', and 'respect'. These deal with feelings and emotions and are different from the examples in the other domains.

The three domains are important in understanding the concepts of planning and assessment, especially in outcomes-based assessments. Here, if we deal with each domain in terms of what we would like our students to achieve as a result of their learning, so that in the cognitive domain, we can ask what would we like our students to know? In the psychomotor domain, 'what would we like our students to be able to do?' and in the affective domain, 'what attitudes would we like our students to display?'

Learning in these three domains often needs different teaching and learning approaches. They are often considered in isolation but in practice learning may occur simultaneously in all three.

1.3   Learning taxonomies

As teachers we tend to concentrate upon teaching our subject matter and the best or most logical order in which to teach the topics. As we see in this chapter, we teach a variety of topics at different levels and the educational literature leads us to believe we need to teach each issue in the most appropriate way. This prompts us to consider the importance of domains and levels, or degrees of difficulty, within each domain. This classification of levels is known as a 'taxonomy'. Each of the three domains needs to be considered in turn.

The levels in the cognitive domain were identified by Bloom (1960) and the levels in the affective domain by Krathwohl *et al.*, (1964). Modified versions of these are shown in Figure 2.1 and Figure 2.2 respectively. When learning is taking place at one of the higher levels, it is important that the student has the requisite lower levels of learning upon which to base the subsequent learning. This, again, shows the importance of entry behaviour, and the pre-requisite knowledge or skills that someone must have.

Levels in the cognitive domain range from the lowest level of knowledge (remembering or recall) to the more complex thinking processes required for evaluation. As you will see from Figure 2.1, to accomplish objectives at any level, objectives at the lower level need to be achieved first. For example, in order to achieve the application level the student must first possess knowledge and comprehension.

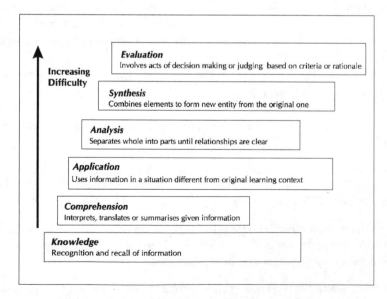

Figure 2.1   *Major Categories in the Cognitive Domain*

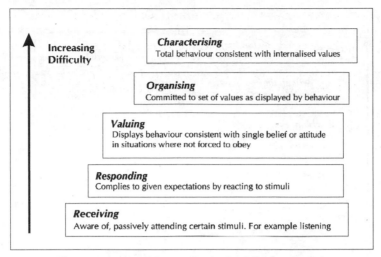

Figure 2.2 *Major Categories in the Affective Domain*

The affective domain also includes levels, but instead of the development from the simple to the complex found in the cognitive domain, each succeeding level involves more internalising of the feeling or attitude. That is, the behaviour becomes a part of our total way of responding and we become 'committed' to the feeling or attitude. In the lower levels of the domain the student is simply provided with the necessary information to know what an appropriate response is: the student is only required to *passively* attend to and be aware of the information. The highest level is only achieved when the student has *internalised* the information. At this level the feelings or attitudes have become a way of life. Thus, if this is related to, say, safety in the workshop, at the lower level the student is told about safety rules and, in order to achieve the objective, listens attentively to them. At the highest level these rules will be automatically applied without thinking about them no matter what the situation or place; they have been internalised.

Dave (1975) produced a taxonomy for the psychomotor domain and this is shown in Figure 2.3. This taxonomy is similar to that in the cognitive domain in that it progresses from the simple to the complex, in this case, skill development. A psychomotor skill consists of tasks that are integrated into a co-ordinated whole. It is developed in stages from the imitation of a model to the point at which performance becomes automatic or habitual. As can be seen from Figure 2.3 each successive level within the domain requires more complicated forms of psychomotor skills and/or a combination of several skills into a co-ordinated sequence.

The usefulness of each of these taxonomies lies in their operation in the classroom as they are applied to learning. There are three aspects of importance: (i) identifying and writing entry behaviour; (ii) writing and identifying levels of objectives; and (iii) assessing the learning of the objectives.

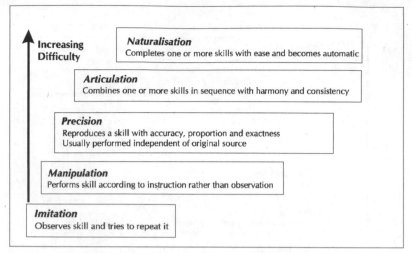

Figure 2.3   *Major Categories in the Psychomotor Domain*

In terms of entry behaviour its assessment relates to a level lower than that required by the objectives. The writing of objectives need to be at an appropriate level within the domain and the choice of methods are more applicable for some levels than they are for others. Also, the classification of objectives into levels allows you to sequence your teaching from the simple to the complex.

Finally, the assessment needs to be at the level at which the objectives have been stated. Thus, the construction of test questions needs to be at the appropriate level of the objectives.

1.4   Models of learning

There is a good deal written about, 'how to teach', and 'how students learn', which often comes from the experience of many people over many years. These books often contain theories and models which the writers feel 'work' and are useful. You need to be careful to consider the context of the model - how old were the students, what was their previous experience, how long did it take? You can try some of these models. If they help your teaching, then that is something that you can use in future. However, some models do not work well at the first attempt. You can reflect upon this and try to find out why in order to give the model another chance, or to refine it to make it applicable to your particular situation.

Blooms taxonomy in the cognitive domain forms the basis for setting more stimulating tasks to achieve analysis, synthesis and evaluation. Collins – McNaught Learning Engagement model (July 2002) identifies that students can be more engaged in learning if the task:

> Becomes more active or open ended.
>
> Or the resource is more interactive.

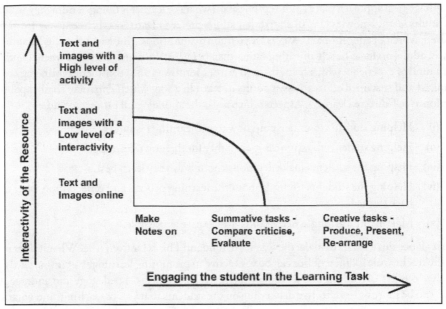

Figure 2.4   *Collins - McNaught Learning engagement Model (July 2002)*
(See: http://ferl.qia.org.uk/display.cfm?page=455, for further information)

The model shown in Figure 2.4 has two distinctive axes. The horizontal axis 'Engaging the student in the learning task' takes the student from passive tasks such as listening and making notes to the open-ended activity where the student is actively involved and has ownership of their responses. This corresponds to Blooms taxonomy analysis, synthesis and evaluation. The vertical axis looks at the 'Interactivity of the Resources'. At the lower end it is text and images while at the interactive end it is multi-sensory.

For example, making notes from the internet involves lower level skills of knowledge and comprehension. The next step is to involve the student in planning, discussion, explanation, and decision making, and these activities work well with ILT. For example:

It is easy to access a wide range of resources, text, image sound.

Assessments can be devised to give instant feedback to students so reinforcing key aspects.

It is easy to create new materials based on original materials.

1.4.1 Pedagogical vs. andragogical models

A pedagogical approach may be described as a teacher dominated learning situation. Often the teacher does all or most of the talking, dictates the pace of learning (or rather the pace of teaching!) and the students are rather passive.

The first approaches at using ILT were very much like this, in that ILT simply replaced the teacher. ILT was very much a passive activity with the students learning little more than saving work to disc, printing it out, the emphasis being on the doing, i.e. learning how to use the software.

However, the focus has moved from the technology back onto teaching and learning, and ILT now gives us an enormous toolkit to enhance learning. With imagination, it is now possible to produce learning experiences which were not practical or possible using traditional teaching methods (See Ferl/ QIA/site for further information http://ferl.qia.org.uk/display.cfm?page=86).

An andragogical approach places more emphasis on what the learner is doing. Andragogy is all about how adults learn. Knowles (1970) stated that adults prefer to learn in a different way from that of children. Much of educational theory is based upon assumptions. Knowles identified assumptions such as, adults prefer to be self-directing rather than being totally dependent on a teacher and adults have a fund of experience which helps them to learn. Mezirow (1981) considered andragogy to be an organised and sustained effort to assist adults to learn in a way which enhances their capability to function as self-directed learners. Aspects which assist the andragogical process include:

(i)   Helping students to understand how to use learning resources.

(ii)   Helping students to assume responsibility for their own learning.

(iii) Helping the students make decisions about how they learn best.

(iv)   Helping the students to think about the learning process and reflect upon what they have learned.

(v)   Making the learning as active and participative as possible.

At first glance this appears to make the teacher redundant! This is far from true. What it does mean is that the teacher role is different but can be very active in promoting learning. But importantly, there are other 'models' of teaching and learning which can utilise aspects of pedagogy and andragogy, and which can be more or less effective depending on the students that you're teaching, and what sort of subject, skill or interaction that you want them to learn. These models of the teaching – learning interaction are (Litow 1991; Joyce and Weil 1992; Pea *et al.* 2002):

    Constructivism.
    Socioculturalism.
    Transmission.
    Metacognition.

Constructivism

Teaching is about:	*Learning is about:*
Setting challenging tasks.	Personal understandings.
Observing and interviewing.	Interpreting and selecting.
Supporting learners' activities.	Actively engaging with concepts.
Creating dissonance through diversity and debate.	Constructive activity.
Helping learners to notice and reconsider.	Reviewing and integrating.

Socioculturalism

Teaching is about:	*Learning is about:*
Being a joint activity.	Social activity and understanding.
Guiding the conversation.	Assessing students' performance.
Helping joint constructions to form.	Interactivity and co-operation.
Promoting and sharing community values.	Self-regulation amongst the group.
	Evaluating and sharing values.

Transmission

Teaching is about:	Learning is about:
Giving accurate information.	Correct performance of tasks.
Being sequential and hierarchical.	Accumulating information.
Directing a one-way flow.	Receiving information.
Structuring the environment.	Taking in knowledge.
Rewarding performance.	Practising and performing.

Metacognition

Teaching is about:	Learning is about:
Explicating expertise.	Active engagement.
Modelling strategies.	Strategic management of learning tasks.
Supporting and assisting reflection.	Reflection and self monitoring.
Application across concepts.	Adapting, applying and transferring knowledge.
Providing criteria for evaluation.	Self-evaluating and being autonomous.

2.   The Domains

2.1   Introduction

Recent developments in the periods of pedagogical studies and cognitive psychology have lead to the theorisation of 'domains' of learning, meaning that teaching and learning relationships are dependent upon the dispositions, attributions and motivations of the learners.

2.2   The cognitive domain

The cognitive domain, like the other domains, as we have seen has various levels of learning. The easiest is remembering facts, relationships, laws etc. More difficult is understanding; why relationships occur, and predicting, requires concept attainment and ability to link concepts to form principles. A further step is the ability to use all these skills in order to solve problems. Perhaps the most logical approach is to consider how memory works and then move up the taxonomic hierarchy to problem solving.

2.2.1 Memory

As teachers we sometimes present our students with facts and knowledge and leave it to them to select and find a means of remembering these key issues. We should plan the learning to enhance memorability and a study of how we think memory works is helpful.

The model shown in Figure 2.5 is a simplified vision of how we think the memory system functions. Although it is simple it appears to be helpful.

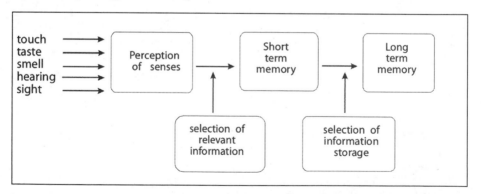

Figure 2.5 *Simple Model of Memory*

The ability to retain and recall information is called memory. Experience and experiments suggest there are three stages to the memorising process: sensory stage; short-term memory; and long-term memory. Each may be considered in turn.

The first stage is perception. The senses gather a vast amount of information and it appears that much of this is ignored. However some signals are given particular attention and active use of these signals is known as perception. Gathering of the same signals by different people leads to differences in perception because of their different experiences and abilities.

In your teaching you can help the perception process by using a variety of signals, appealing to the senses, perhaps by the use of audio visual aids. You may have to supply information, i.e. set the scene, before the appearance of the stimuli.

The short-term memory appears to retain the immediate interpretation of events. Information goes into the short-term memory quickly and is available for rapid recall. The short-term memory is a very busy area which perhaps accounts for the fact that its capacity is limited.

The long-term memory appears to have a huge capacity. If you can get information into the long-term memory – and the purpose of the first two stages is to filter material that is appropriate to long-term storage – then it may be stored almost indefinitely.

Our task then is to help students to remember. Here are some common ways to do this:

1. *Verbal Association:*   Group or pair things together e.g. bat and ball; knife, fork and spoon.
   Make unlikely associations e.g. chalk and cheese, oil and water.
   Make up a story linking things together.

2. *Visual Association:*   Group things together and visualise them in their relative positions.
   Write a list and visualise that list.

3. *Repetition:*   Write out a number of times, repeat aloud a number of times.
   Listen to a tape several times.
   Read over and over again.

4. *Self test:*   Used with repetition.

5. *Part test:*   If there is a great deal to be learned then break the material into manageable lots and remember these smaller parts.

6. *Rhyme rule:*   30 days has September, etc.

7. *First letter:*   Colours of the Rainbow –
   Red, Orange, Yellow, Green, Blue, Indigo, Violet.
   *R*ichard *O*f *Y*ork *G*ave *B*attle *I*n *V*ain

8. *Spelling Association:*   Stationery – E for envelopes.

The following conditions appear to help recall:

Errors:	Try to avoid making errors.
Recency:	You tend to remember things which have happened recently.
Frequency:	The more you make recall active, via testing, the more likely you are to remember.
Intensity:	The better the concentration the better the recall.
Importance:	You remember the most important things to you (at the time).
Feelings:	Your state of mind affects the quality of learning. If you are upset about a domestic issue then your ability to enhance recall will be reduced.
Association:	The more you can associate and relate new material to existing knowledge, the better the recall.

2.2.2 Models of teaching

A great deal is written about how students learn but not so much is written about how we should teach. Teaching, inevitably, responds to and reflects how students learn. Never-the-less it is useful to spend some time examining how we teach by reflecting upon some teaching models.

Joyce and Weil (1992) were probably the first to write extensively about models of teaching and their work has been the base for interesting work by others such as Eggen and Kauchak (1998) and Joyce *et al.* (1997). Joyce and Weil grouped a number of models into four families as follows:

The Social Interaction Family emphasises the way in which people relate to others and their role in society. Great weight is placed upon the development of the person and how they learn academic subjects. Role play and Jurisprudential models are in this family.

The Information Processing Family is concerned with the way in which we handle stimuli, organise, generate concepts and solve problems. Models in this family include: Inductive thinking, concept attainment, advanced organiser, inquiry training and synetics.

The Personal Family sees the individual as the source of ideas. The development of individuals and their emotions are crucial as they consider personality and self-image. The work of Carl Rogers and A. S. Neill would fall within this family and an example of a model would be non directive teaching.

The Behavioural Family is the fourth and final and is concerned with the careful sequencing of learning activities to shape behaviour. The work of Skinner and Bloom would fall into this family.

David Ausubel (1968) developed a model called the *advanced organiser.* This is a deductive approach in which the broader ideas are presented first, i.e. the organiser statement is presented first (the advanced organiser) which acts as a cognitive road map in order to guide the learning. The new ideas or concepts are connected to existing cognitive structures or knowledge and emphasis is placed on making relationships between existing ideas and new ideas.

The Suchman Inquiry Method as its name suggests, attempts to develop thinking skills through inquiry. Both inductive and deductive approaches are used. The process is interesting and usually follows the pattern:

> Teacher states the problem which requires the students to explain a phenomenon.
>
> Students hypothesis about a solution or exploration.
>
> Students' gather data in the form of questions to which the teacher can answer either 'Yes' or 'No'.

This last stage makes the students think quite deeply.

The *Jurisprudential* model, developed by Oliver and Shaver (1966) uses controversial topics as a basis for discussion. It is ideal for addressing problems with legal, ethical and social questions. It requires students to consider value, factual, and definitial problems. There are six phases to the Jurisprudential approach: the first three are concerned with analysis and the second three with argument. The phases are as follows:

> Orientation, where the students are introduced to the issue.
>
> Identifying the issues, where the students determine the facts, and values.
>
> Position, where the students take (or are given) one side of the case to argue.
>
> Exploring, where the teacher challenges the views of the students.
>
> Refining, where the students reconsider their position in the light of the dialogue.

Testing, where the teacher helps the students to examine their final position.

Gordon's *Synetics* model (1961) attempts to develop creativity. (Synetics is the study of creative processes). Gordon believes that we are all creative but often need help to develop that creativity. He suggests a three stage process as follows:

Personal analogy – individual students are encouraged to identify with an item in a problematic situation e.g., be a pair of pliers and imagine cutting through wire. How do you feel?

Direct analogy – individuals practice inventing relationships between two items not usually considered together. For example, consider how alike the pliers and a dish cloth are.

Compressed conflict – individual students think of opposite words (antonyms) which could be characteristic of the pliers, e.g., joining – cutting.

The process encourages students to break free of traditional approaches and can lead them to redesign the pliers with changes to shape, colour, size, materials etc.

Not included in the Joyce and Weil approach is Galperin's (1957) approach to teaching psychomotor skills. Emphasis is placed on demonstration – but demonstration in a different way. Firstly, when teaching a new skill, the teacher explains the finished performance, the component skills and how they are linked. The teacher repeats the demonstration but this time under the direction of the students. The teacher gives no commentary. The reason for this approach is that the students are freed from the physical tasks so can concentrate on the cognitive aspects i.e., tasks of 'doing'. Then the roles are reversed into the traditional manner i.e., students manipulating while the teacher directs and supervises.

2.2.3 The learning of concepts

When learning a new topic or subject, the key to understanding lies in our ability to grasp the basic concept(s). This makes teaching concepts a key skill. We probably teach many concepts without analysing how we teach them.

Before we can teach concepts we need to understand what a concept is. It is considered to be 'a class of stimuli which have common characteristics'. These can be objects, events or persons. For example a *book* is an object – there are many different varieties of books but we can differentiate between what is a book and what is a newspaper, or magazine. A *party* is an example of the 'event concept' while *teachers*, *bakers* and *doctors* are examples of 'people concepts'.

Concepts have attributes and an attribute is a distinctive feature of a concept. For example a red triangle has two attributes; colour and shape. The more complex the concept then, generally speaking, the greater the number of attributes. Some attributes are more important than others and these are known as dominant attributes.

Perhaps you are wondering why we have concepts and need to teach them. Concepts reduce the complexity of learning because we can categorise objects according to their concept rather than having to remember each individual set of attributes. Concepts also reduce the need for constant learning. We can classify new sets of attributes ourselves rather than having to be told what they are. Concepts help in communicating with each other and hence with the learning.

There are two main types of concept: concrete and abstract. Concrete concepts are often those we can see, for example, a car, a house, a book. Abstract concepts are a little more difficult and are often defined in many ways, for example democracy, poverty. Clearly concepts are important in learning and it is useful to consider how we can help our students attain them.

Concept maps are an important teaching aid, learning reserve and tool and much work has been done on them, for example, Fesmire et al (2003) and McLay et al (2003). But an early analysis of concept maps is by De Cecco and Crawford (1974).

De Cecco's Model of Concept Teaching

Step 1:   Describe the performance expected of the students after they have learned the concept.
This is what we often call the objective, the competence or the learning outcome.

Step 2:   Reduce the number of attributes to be learned in complex concepts and make the important attributes dominant.
This is part of your planning process.

Step 3:   Provide the students with useful verbal mediators.
Here we help the students by giving the names of attributes and features to ensure that they know these before we attempt to teach the concept itself.

Step 4:   Provide positive and negative examples of the concept.
This is seen as a very important step. It helps the students to discriminate among the attributes: those which form part of the concept and those which do not.

Step 5:   Present examples in close succession or simultaneously.
This process helps with contiguity and reduces unwanted learning.

Step 6:   Provide a new positive example and ask the students to identify it.
Here you are checking that students have learned the necessary attributes.

Step 7:   Provide occasions for student responses and the reinforcement of these responses.
This really takes place with steps 4, 5 and 6 and gives feedback (and praise) to the students.

Step 8:   Ask students to define the concept in their own words.
This should be done individually, and in writing, with each student using their own words to define the concept. They should not use the 'textbook' definition but should translate this into their own words.

Step 9:   Assess the learning of the concept.
This final step may not be considered as part of the formal teaching and learning of the concept attainment process but is obviously important and helpful feedback.

Figure 2.6 *De Cecco's Model of Concept Teaching*

De Cecco's model can be used in the teaching and learning of both concrete and abstract concepts. A concept has been defined as 'an idea existing in the mind' but it is associated with experience. Every concept, even the most abstract, has something to which it refers (a referent). The concept 'one' is learned through experience with one book, one ice cream, one toy. In other words it is learned through experience with things. De Cecco's steps gives us a sequence to help students with the provision of experiences. The provision of positive and negative examples provide experiences for students and this is probably better if it can be provided with real objectives (or pictures of them) to make the experiences as realistic as possible. Even abstract concepts like *viscosity* or *sibling* require referents, or examples, in their learning. If, then, the effectiveness of the learning is based on experience, it is important to provide as many and as varied a set of experiences as possible. With abstract concepts we have to make individual pictures in each of the students' minds. Much of post-16 education and training relates to processes (like the concept of work), qualities (like the concept of viscosity) or relationships (like the concept of sibling or electric current). Consequently, and in order to provide the necessary experiences for our students, we need to provide the necessary simulations. These might be actual experiences or vicarious ones that we ourselves might have had experience with.

The following list of 'rules' might be incorporated for the teaching of concepts:

Can the idea be expressed symbolically, or displayed in the form of a diagram?

If students make specific points get them to generalise and move away from the specific so as to help others understand what they are getting at.

Be ready to try a variety of teaching procedures because repetition of ideas using the same words often does not work.

Get students to think and talk *actively* about ideas and what they mean.

Encourage students to look for both similarities and differences between the new and existing ideas.

The following example of the application of De Cecco's model to teaching a concept is based on an idea in Towers *et al* (1987). Imagine we need to ensure our students need to know the new concept of a Reklaw:

Step 1	The students will be able to identify Reklaws when given a range of shapes.
Step 2	Figure 2.7a shows a range of shapes, some of which are Reklaws and some are not. The patterns and colours are not important to the teaching and learning so, before presenting to the students, we reduce the diagram to the key attributes as shown in Figure 2.7b.
Step 3	We ask the students to study the shapes in Figure 2.7b and ask them to describe what they see.
Steps 4 & 5	The students are told that Figure 2.7b contains four shapes which are Reklaws and three shapes which are not Reklaws. The students are asked to identify the four Reklaws.
Step 6	The students are shown Figure 2.7c and asked to confirm that they agree that this is a Reklaw.
Step 7	This step allows the students to check their understanding by answering questions similar to Figure 2.7d.
Step 8	The students are asked to define a Reklaw in their own words.
Step 9	Further assessment can take place now and at later dates.

Figure 2.7a   *A variety of shapes*

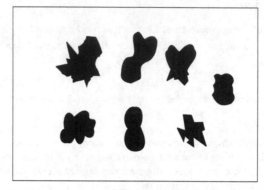

Figure 2.7b   *Shapes simplified to remove patterns and colours*

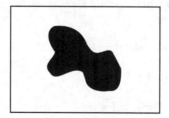

Figure 2.7c   *An example of a Reklaw*

Figure 2.7d   *Assessing or identifying a Reklaw*

Other writers have similar models. Stones (1983) stresses the importance of planning how to teach concepts. His model is based upon 12 stages which are in three phases as shown in Figure 2.8:

A	**Pre-Active**
1.	Make a task analysis of the teaching objectives to identify the key concepts involved, the subordinate concepts, specific examples, methods of presentation, students' activities and modes of evaluation.
2.	Ascertain students' prior knowledge. If this is not possible plan for diagnosis at the interactive stage.
B	**Interactive**
3.	Give a preliminary idea of the nature of the new learning.
4.	Explain terms to be used in labelling the new concepts and their attributes and call to mind existing concepts relevant to the new learning.
5.	Provide initially a series of simplified exemplars with few attributes to facilitate identification of the criterial attributes.
6.	Increase the salience of the criterial attributes to enable students to discriminate between criterial and non-criterial attributes.
7.	Provide a series of exemplars sequenced to provide a complete range of criterial attributes as economically as possible.
8.	Provide non-exemplars in counter position to exemplars to enhance discrimination between criterial and non-criterial attributes.
9.	Provide new exemplars and non-exemplars and ask the students to identify the exemplars. Provide feedback for each discrimination.
10.	Encourage the students to use their own language in explaining the nature of the concepts.
11.	Provide suitable cueing throughout to ensure that students gradually become independent in their ability to identify novel exemplars of the concepts.
C	**Evaluative** (This process is naturally much the same procedure as would be applied in diagnosing prior level of ability.)
12.	Present novel exemplars of the concepts for the students to identify and/or discriminate from non-exemplars.

Figure 2.8 *Stones' model of concept teaching*

Rowntree (1982) has a similar model but considers that there is no need to apply each step every time you teach a concept. He thinks this is too time consuming and that the model should be reserved for the more difficult concepts. This model is shown in Figure 2.9.

Isolate the concepts	-	from the facts, principles, examples, etc of our subject matter.
Define each concept	-	dictionary-type definitions to begin with, perhaps.
Examine model examples	-	to sharpen the definition by deciding which features of the examples are essential to the concept and which are incidental.
Examine counter examples	-	to further establish the essential character of the concept by identifying features that would negate it.
Examine border line examples	-	to clarify our understanding of the crucial features of the concepts by considering cases where it 'almost' applies or applies only 'in a way'.
Consider invented examples	-	testing the concept by inventing imaginary cases that might really stretch the features we have identified for the concept.
Compare personal contexts	-	in recognition that the concept will have different connotations for different individuals (which may or may not hinder communication).
Examine related concepts	-	studying one concept leads us into seeing how it fits into the surrounding network of concepts.
Elucidate the principles	-	concepts are related to other concepts in principles (rules, theorems, axioms, generalizations, statements) which constitute the message(s) of the subject matter, and the key principles need to be identified and classified (e.g. as empirical, evaluative, or semantic statements).

Figure 2.9 *Rowntree model of concept teaching*

Joyce and Weil (1990) have a three phase model (Figure 2.10) which has ten stages. Although each model has differences, they contain many similarities. It may be useful to think about a concept which you will be teaching in the near future and use one of the models to structure your teaching.

PHASE ONE Presentation of Data and Identification of Concept	PHASE TWO Testing Attainment of the Concept
Teachers present labelled examples. Students compare attributes in positive and negative examples. Students generate and test hypotheses. Students state a definition according to the essential attributes.	Students identify additional unlabelled examples as yes/no. Teacher confirms hypotheses, names concept, and restates definitions according to essential attributes. Students generate examples.
PHASE THREE Analysis of thinking strategies	
Students describe thoughts. Students discuss role of hypotheses and attributes. Students discuss type and number of hypotheses.	

Figure 2.10 *Joyce and Weil syntax of the concept attainment model*

2.2.4 The learning of principles

In the literature, concept and principle teaching are closely related because a principle is a statement of the relationship between two or more concepts. Principles are sometimes called rules, laws, theorems, or generalisations.

Some examples of principles are:

(i)   Four plus ten equals fourteen.

(ii) All men are created equal.

(iii) An object with six sides is three dimensional.

The following are statements but are not principles:

(i)   Evergreen trees.

(ii) Manchester United won the cup.

(iii) Imran made the strongest structure.

The first set of statements qualify as principles because they state relationships among concepts. The first, for example, states the relationship among five concepts: four; plus; ten; equals; and fourteen. The second relates four concepts: all; men; created; and equal. The second set of statements are not principles: evergreen trees is a concept, in the second statement Manchester is the only concept and so no relationship is stated.

It is sometimes useful to think of principles as 'if-then' statements. For example, *if* you add four to ten, *then* you obtain fourteen; *if* an object has six sides, *then* it is three dimensional. The advantage of phrasing a principle as an 'if-then' statement is that the statement then indicates the proper ordering of the component concepts. Only the proper ordering of the concepts results in satisfactory learning of the principle.

De Cecco (op cit) has the following model (Figure 2.11).

Teaching of a Principle

1.   Describe the performance expected of the students after they have learned the principle.

2.   Decide and indicate which concepts or principles the students must recall in learning the new principle.

3.   Assist the students to recall component concepts.

4.   Help the students to combine the concepts in the proper order.

5.   Require the students to demonstrate the principle fully.

6.   Require the students to give a full statement of the principle.

7.   Verify the students' learning of the principle.

8.   Provide for practise of the principle and reinforcement of the students' responses.

Figure 2.11   *De Cecco's Steps in the Teaching of a Principle*

When teaching principles in the near future you may wish to use this model as a framework for your teaching.

2.2.5   The learning of problem solving

Moving further up the taxonomy of the Cognitive domain brings us to Problem Solving. Problem Solving may be regarded as a high level activity since it usually involves using two or more principles. This separates it from lower order puzzle solving.

A similar model to those used in the teaching of concepts and principles may be used for problem solving. The steps are:

Step 1   State the learning intentions.

Step 2   Ensure students know the relevant concepts and principles and ask the students to recall them.

Step 3   Give indications or guidelines to the solution without providing the solution.

Step 4   Assess the learning outcomes.

Practice with problem solving, in a structured manner, often helps students Chapter 6, Section 4.

The following, reported in Gage and Berliner (1983) of Mager's work, are considered important principles in the solving of problems:

Habitual ways of doing things do not solve difficult problems.

Problems would not be difficult if they could be solved through habitual ways of solving problems.

A person should not stay in a rut but should keep an open mind for new meanings.

If someone fails to solve a problem, they should put it out of their mind and seek a new problem.

Solutions to problems appear suddenly and cannot be forced.

Experiments have been completed which suggest that problem solving can be enhanced through careful structuring of the teaching. The suggested sequence is:

(i)   Ensure students understand the problem completely and then get them to state it in general terms.

(ii)   Find the major solution strategies.

(iii)   List alternatives within the solution strategies.

(iv)   Evaluate the alternatives and choose the best.

Figure 2.12 is an example of the use of this sequence as suggested by Gage and Berliner (op cit).

State the problem in general terms	Find major solution strategies	List alternatives within the solution strategies	Evaluate and choose the best
Increase the attention of students in class.	Vary the methods of presentation of the subject matter.	Shout at them.	Will work if used occasionally; could frighten some students.
		Move about; create novelty and surprise; stop talking, etc.,	Must gather evidence of attitude change.
	Vary materials to be learned.	Switch texts.	Must gain approval of course team. Expensive. More exercises in new text will help.
		Add films/videos. Use programmed learning.	As above.
	Change rewards being offered.	Give consumable rewards for best test performances.	Expensive to provide sweets. May foster competition.
		Release class early. Punish when inattentive.	

Figure 2.12   *Application of Problem Solving Model*

This is only one of the models of problem solving that is suggested by educational psychologists and it is usually applied to technological problems. However, not all problems are of a technological nature, and different techniques are suggested for (a) science and (b) business studies. These models are considered in Chapter 6.

2.3   The psychomotor domain

We have all seen skilled demonstrations on the television such as 'throwing' pottery, hanging a door, and so on. We often pause and watch with much admiration. It can be motivating and we want to emulate their performance. We usually fail to achieve their high standards even when it looks so easy.

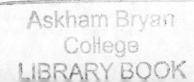

Even when we match their standards, with say home decorating, the skilled person is so much quicker. This brings us to the realisation that there are two types of performance:

> Unskilled performance which tends to lack consistency and smoothness.
>
> Skilled performance which is consistent, smooth, co-ordinated, in fact 'second nature'.

Although we tend to concentrate upon the physical part when we teach psychomotor skills, there usually is, of course, a cognitive element and an affective aspect.

A person skilled in a range of the professional tasks of, say, a nurse, a graphic designer, a carpenter, or hairdresser usually exhibits the following characteristics:

> Adaptable/flexible.
>
> Clear sense of purpose.
>
> Quick.
>
> Accurate.
>
> Professional/stylish.
>
> Consistently good results.
>
> Good condition.
>
> Smooth and rhythmic.
>
> Cool and calm.

All of the above need training, thought, effort and practice. Fitts (1967) suggests that there are three phases to achieving a skilled performance. These are:

(i)   The cognitive phase.

(ii)   The fixative phase.

(iii) The autonomous phase.

It can be argued that, in post-16 education, only the very basic skills are learned to the third of these phases. Many of the skills that we teach are only learned to the second, fixative, phase where they are correctly completed but still require thought and, in consequence, do not have the speed associated with them that are exhibited by the craftsman who can complete them without thought (that is, automatically, with all of the attributes suggested above).

The *cognitive phase* involves considering and talking about the background information. It consists of 'knowing' how to complete the skill, the nature of the steps involved, and how they might be combined.

This would include:

> Procedures.
>
> Essential knowledge.
>
> Precautions.
>
> Standards.
>
> Things to look for.
>
> Things to avoid.

This should be quite a short phase and is usually completed through a teacher demonstration. Thus, the main teaching skill in this phase involves assisting the students to memorise the information, and the conditions for this are the same as those described earlier for the cognitive domain.

The *fixative phase* involves acquiring the correct patterns of behaviour and the elimination of errors through initial practice. Thus we need to:

> Give the students an opportunity to inquire about the skill.
>
> Practise the skill.
>
> Give feedback on performance.

The *autonomous phase* is the final stage. Speed and accuracy are enhanced as the skill becomes more automatic. Speed, rhythm and concentration should increase at this stage. It may be difficult to notice when the student changes from one phase to another since the process is gradual.

Clearly, a key feature of skill acquisition is practice. Practise can be massed or distributed. Massed practise involves large blocks of time where the students practise without breaks. Distributed practise involves short practise periods, say ten minutes with breaks between each period. It is considered that distributed practise is the most effective of the two because, in massed practise, fatigue soon sets in when initially practising. There needs to be high concentration in the initial stages of practise and students find such a high level difficult to sustain. Thus, short bursts of practise are more effective.

Feedback is an important part of learning a skill. Intrinsic feedback comes from the task itself, i.e. through the senses, and is immediate. Extrinsic feedback comes from outside the task. Feedback of this nature often comes from teachers. Feedback on knowledge and skills is needed until mastery is achieved. Feedback at the mastery stage is still needed so that the learners can feel confident that they have achieved the standard.

A good deal of the literature used in the UK related to educational psychology is indigenous or from the USA. An interesting writer is the Russian, Galperin. (Galperin in Simon (1957)) He experimented with two main approaches.

The first, and traditional approach, was to explain how to perform the task, and allow the student to perform the task under teacher supervision.

The second method was the teacher carrying out the task: the student watches and helps by directing and prompting. The second method was found to produce better results, perhaps because the students concentrate upon the task elements and organisation of their own learning. Recent work on motivation suggests that it is a complex phenomenon which can sometimes have counter productive effects if linked directly to positive feedback – see Elliott et al (1999).

De Cecco discusses some useful conditions which enhance the learning of skills. He suggests that contiguity, the almost simultaneous occurrence of the stimulus and the response, is important. We may call this timing or co-ordination. This means that the proper order of sub skills is important.

Feedback, De Cecco suggests, is also of prime importance for the successful learning of a skill during student practice. Students should complete the skill correctly from the start of their practice as unlearning of incorrect movements is difficult. Hence, teacher feedback can assist in stopping these incorrect movements.

Part training is where the students receive instruction on the first subtask, then the second subtask whilst still practising the first subtask and so on. This may be compared with the whole training method where the students receive instruction and practice on the entire sequence. There is evidence to show that the whole training is more effective such as the following model shows:

Step 1   *Analyse the skill*
                At the planning stage, you need to consider body position,
                movements, sequence of movements, turning, etc.

Step 2   *Assess the entry behaviour*
                This is where you determine what the students can do
                already. It is important to look for bad practice and
                eliminate it at this stage.

Step 3   *Describe and demonstrate the skill*

Step 4   *Provide opportunity for the three basic learning conditions viz,*
                contiguity, practice and feedback

Perhaps your best approach is to select and try a range of methods, consider the outcomes and develop
an approach which you find suits you and your learners. What may happen is that one approach suits
a particular skill or task, where a second approach is more appropriate to a different skill.

2.4   The affective domain

The affective domain is perhaps the most difficult domain in which to teach and there tends to be
relatively less literature concerning attitudes. We could set out to change attitudes and in fact we are
often required to change attitudes with regard to health and safety, or alternatively we may change
attitudes unconsciously. The latter category is where attitudes are caught not taught! For example if we
are perpetually late starting our classes then we often find students late in attending; if our boardwork
is untidy then students' notes often reflect this. In these cases, the students are using us as a role model
and we need to be aware of this. Attitudes are learned and may have roots in the emotions but they
may also have a major element of knowledge.

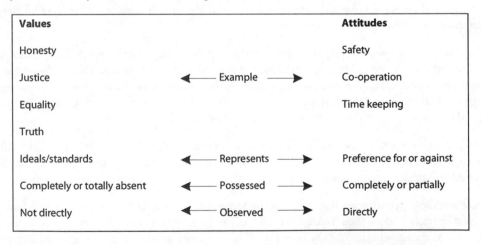

Figure 2.13 *Comparison between Values and Attitudes*

Knowledge: What the student knows.

Emotion: What the student likes or dislikes about the subject.

Action: What the student does to express feelings of like or dislike.

We all tend to have a value framework i.e. a set of standards or ideals and these are linked to attitudes. Figure 2.13 compares values and attitudes. Attitudes have three components each of which may vary in intensity. These are:

Davies (1981) believes that you cannot change attitudes before the appropriate change of behaviour but it is better to change behaviour before there is an attitudinal change. A great many intelligent people smoke or eat an unhealthy diet, and know they do so but are unable to change. However, if the behaviour is changed first then attitudinal change is more likely to take place. So, how can we plan to change students' attitudes? The following guidelines appear to be helpful:

1.   State intended learning outcomes (e.g. objective).

2.   Small group discussions.

3.   Student centred rather than teacher centred.

4.   High levels of participation by each individual. Peers can have a major influence on attitudes (Think of fashion!).

5.   Role play and simultaneous discussion.

Attitudinal change often takes a long time. You can force change by using rewards or punishments and gain what appears to be rapid results but it is usually only a short-term change. However, if you encourage participation, then this slower process tends to be long-term and to all intents and purposes – permanent.

3.   Motivation

3.1   Concepts related to motivation

Motivation is a key factor in successful learning. A less able student who is highly motivated can achieve greater success than the more intelligent student who is not well motivated. Students may come to us highly motivated and all we have to do is maintain this motivation. However most student groups tend to have some highly motivated students, across the range to one or two who appear to have no motivation. Our task, then, is to maximise motivation. To do this we need to consider the concepts related to motivation.

Interest – Students with an interest in a subject tend to pay more attention to it and study it to a level greater than we demand. Their attention and workrate is high with a correspondingly higher quality of learning. Our task is to develop and maximise this interest.

Need – There are several possible needs but the most common student needs are:

> Need for achievement e.g. success in reaching a goal.
>
> Need for affiliation e.g. friendly relationship with other persons including you, the teacher.
>
> Need for dominance, and this is attained by obtaining leadership, power or control over others e.g. getting the best results in the class.

Attitude – Emotions, and feelings are important. So if students get pleasure out of calculations then they will enjoy working with activities involving calculation, or if they get satisfaction from working with their hands, they will learn psychomotor skills well.

Aspirations – Students may have a particular aim in mind. If they pass your course then they can enter another course which will then qualify them to practise a chosen profession. Motivation can be classified into intrinsic motivation and extrinsic motivation. Intrinsic motivation may be defined as motivation without apparent reward i.e. studying for its own sake. Many writers say this is the best form of motivation. Extrinsic motivation depends upon external stimuli, which we, as teachers, may have to provide.

3.2   Maslow's hierarchy of needs

Abraham Maslow's (1962) hierarchy of Basic Human Needs is well known and is based on ensuring that lower needs are met before moving upwards in a step-by-step progression from basic physical needs to self-actualisation. Figure 2.14 is an attempt to place the five needs identified by Maslow (physical, safety and shelter, love and belonging, self-esteem and self-actualisation) into a 'classroom' setting with examples of what we as teachers might do to promote an individual's achievement of that need.

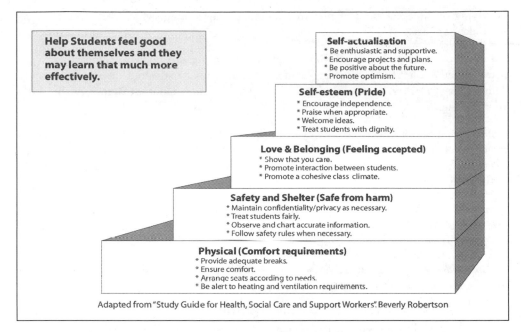

Figure 2.14   *Maslow's Hierarchy of Basic Needs as Applied to the Classroom*

3.3   Teaching for extrinsic motivation

The following guidelines for the provision of extrinsic motivation are the result of the experience of many teachers. Most of the techniques appear to be effective with most groups most of the time. They are relatively easy to use.

Verbal praise – Feedback to the students such as 'good answer' or 'that's an interesting observation' give the students social approval and such praise appears to be a powerful motivational technique. Your comments to your learners are important.

Test results/marks – Results of periodic tests and feedback on assignments are important to your students so that they can see that they are making progress. Poor results should be used to diagnose and remedy learning difficulties, not just left and ignored.

Arousal – Humans, even your students, are naturally curious and like suspense and to explore. We need to use this natural curiosity to enhance motivation. Most subjects have features which perplex and baffle students with their apparent contradictions. 'Why should that happen when I expected this to happen?' This is a powerful stimulant provided the puzzlement does not last too long and leads to frustration.

Unexpected – As teachers, we tend to have our favourite ways of teaching which allows the students to predict the style of learning. This may allow the learner to relax and feel comfortable but it is motivating to have an unexpected event so that the interest of the students is aroused. For example, if the problem-solving has previously been theoretical – introduce a very practical problem. Change the arrangement of the furniture in the room. Instead of setting the test yourself ask the students to design the test.

Surprise – This is an important concept in teaching and learning, since 'cognitive conflict' or making students think in a surprising way about concepts, often causes different learning to take place, instead of relying on 'safe' methods of preferred teaching and learning, which may even reinforce misunderstandings.

Use material familiar to the students – When students are learning, they often have problems with new material, and research shows that using examples that are familiar to the students eases the learning. This may involve you in learning a little yourself, like the current fashions so that these can be used in your teaching.

Unusual contexts – Once you feel concepts or principles are learned you can ask your students to apply them in unusual situations. For example, the law of supply and demand applied to say 'classic cars'. Note that students learn better when attaining concepts with familiar examples but applying them in an unfamiliar situation.

Games and simulations – Games and simulations motivate students to participate in the learning. Take care to ensure that the learning is reinforced and by the end of the topic the students know why they played the game.

Minimise adverse effects – There are a great many issues which reduce motivation and your job is to try to *minimise* these influences. You can add to this list no doubt:

> Listening to a dull, boring, uninteresting teacher.
>
> Tests which are too hard or too easy.
>
> No feedback on progress.
>
> Pace too fast/too slow.
>
> Sitting for too long.
>
> Poor lighting/heating/acoustics.
>
> Being told they are unlikely to understand something.
>
> Waiting for help from the teacher.
>
> Being told that the topic is difficult.

3.4   Deep and surface learning

Deep and surfacing learning are concepts linked to motivation since it is possible to understand them in terms of motivation to achieve an end result by means of using a surface or strategic approach. This means that such students sometimes can be motivated by outcomes rather than by understanding or autonomy.

We can relate to students who have done well in examinations simply because they have a good memory and have recalled facts. There is usually something wrong with assessment if it only involves the recall of facts. We want our students to think and be highly motivated learners. There is a good deal of concern, particularly in Higher Education, where students are doing little to earn their degree. Good students have been observed to be 'deep' learners whereas mediocre students have been considered to be 'surface' learners. These terms are discussed 'inter alia' by Gibbs (1992) and Ramsden (1992) and are summarised as follows.

3.4.1   Characteristics of Surface Learning Include

> Intention to recall/reproduce lecture notes.
>
> Sole aim to pass assessments.
>
> Passively accepting teachers ideas/notes.

No reflection.

No concept of overall patterns or themes – focus on elements only.

Treating assignments and reading as a burden.

3.4.2 Characteristics of deep learning are:

Relating concepts to existing knowledge and understanding, and to everyday life.

Organising and structuring new information.

An interest in understanding new materials.

Challenging new concepts and reading widely.

Examining the logic of the development.

Determining what is significant.

We can help our students to be deep learners by designing active learning experiences and placing less emphasis on detailed, passive note taking. Deep learning is encouraged by engaging in applying learning to problem-based situations, encouraging discussion and structuring reflection. These ideas have implications for our choice of teaching strategies and how we assess learning.

As an example, you may be involved in teaching aspects of time management. This can be done in the traditional way; a talk followed by handouts. However, you could ask each of your students to record a day's activities before you discuss time management. As individuals, the students could analyse how they spend their working time and decide how they can improve their time management skills. During the class, small groups could discuss their outcomes and generate some rules or guidelines. After the feedback, and discussion, you could introduce what the management experts have to say and ask the students to compare and contrast their outcomes with accepted theory. The students should be encouraged to challenge theory. One time management guideline is to delegate more work to subordinates – your students could well say they have no-one to delegate to! This approach helps the students to relate to everyday life, and to debate and discuss the key points: A much more active approach!

3.5 Learning technologies and motivation

We have already suggested in Chapter 1 that ILT is a powerful tool that can enhance motivation, improve teaching and learning for our students. Using ILT allows us to:

Create interest by using a wide variety of resources.

Use a wide range of teaching styles.

Use one to one, or small group working.

Promote problem solving.

Enable reflection – by giving immediate feedback.

Challenge – make available a wide range of materials so encouraging differentiation.

If ILT is such a motivator why then do we not make more use of it? Reasons are plenty:

Resources – they are expensive and therefore limited.

Confidence – afraid of being shown up by students.

Time – to learn new aspects and write materials.

Change – natural reluctance to change.

Even when teachers have used ILT they often find it is not the motivator that they were led to believe. Work by Jen Harvey and Nora Mogey, LTDI, Implementing Learning Technology; suggest that we need to look at how we go about making use of such technology. They offer the following advice:

> Integrate ILT - How many times have we heard the teacher say 'I use ILT to give a PowerPoint presentation'. We need to fully integrate ILT in all aspects, not just a lecture, so that students get the benefits.

> Build ILT activities into the course – dont expect students to use it just because it is there.

> Set yourself up as a role model by using ILT in class, using a wide variety of methods video, sound, images, assessment.

> Appropriate – use it where it is most appropriate. Dont create artificial scenarios to just include ILT.

> Use a combination of teaching methods, including ILT, to give a good balance.

> Give your students ownership of the materials so they can work at their own pace and from the comfort of their home or workplace.

> Make sure your students are comfortable with the hardware and software. Put on support where necessary.

> Use email for sending and receiving assignments.

> Use electronic assessments such as crosswords, multi-choice, games which give instant feedback to your students and create interest.

> Provide support groups to learn high level features of the package that will be helpful in the real world. Using Microsoft Word to create an index for a report will be useful to students at work or in higher education.

> Make ILT relevant and fun.

All of these aspects relate directly to the comments made about motivation; make it fun, engage the learners, give immediate feedback, reflect and involve. Integrating ILT with other learning methods is a vehicle for motivation of our students and therefore enhancing learning.

4. Other Theories of Learning

4.1 The theories

There is a great deal written about how we learn and there is a great range of theories emerging which shed light on the complexity of cognition. The purpose of the final part of this chapter is merely to introduce you to some theories so that you can read in those areas which appear to be most useful to you at the moment.

The five main areas are Behaviourism, Neo-behaviourism, Gestalt (Insight), Cognitive Development, and Humanists, as well as more recently theorised areas of lifelong learning or 'third age' learning, which feature principles of gerontology.

4.1.1 The Behaviourists

The origins of behaviourism are in the early 20th century. At that time it was thought that human activity or learning could be predicted and explained by studying the behaviour of animals. The essentials of the work involved animals responding to stimuli, that is stimulus-response (S - R). The learning model became more refined with the study of the effect of conditioning.

Pavlov, one of the early workers in the field, proposed the hypothesis of conditioned learning and used experiments with dogs to provide evidence to support the hypothesis. Basically, he linked a specific sound with the provision of food which, of course, caused salivation. After some time the mere sound caused the dogs to salivate.

Watson, another of the early workers in the field, thought that sensations, feelings and instinct were not a necessary part of the study of learning. The only area of interest is what the 'subject' is doing in response to the stimulus. He rejected the concept of memory. Instead, he said that responses were due to learning and we respond when we meet those stimuli again. Learning, he said, was a question of strengthening stimulus-response bonds. Conditioning, therefore, became important and habit forming was considered to be significant.

Both Pavlov and Watson have been criticised as they were considered to only think in mechanistic terms and extrapolated the results of their work with animals to predict human behaviour. Stimulus-Response, however, is quite a powerful action as we all know when we smell our favourite food cooking. The effect of conditioning is also important. We can all probably remember an unpleasant episode at school which put us off a subject for the rest of our lives.

Another early worker, Thorndike, showed in experiments that pleasurable experiences tended to reinforce stimulus-response bonds and 'discomfort' reduced these bonds. There are clear links to rote learning when Thorndike said that there was a need to maximise the strength of a bond. To do this, he suggested that the number of times and duration of the link should be maximised. Also associated with this work was the fact that an external reward was seen as being effective, whereas punishment was less important.

The behaviourist learning theory suggests that we learn by receiving a stimulus that provokes a response. So long as that response is reinforced in some way that response will be repeated. As a teacher we may direct this process by selecting an appropriate stimulus (say, teaching method) and by reinforcing the 'correct' responses while discouraging the 'wrong' responses. Behaviourists say that learning is brought about by association between the response and reinforcement.

Such a theory stresses the active role of the teacher with the student often seen as passive. Although the student is responsible for the responses, it is the teacher who controls the stimuli, who chooses the 'correct' response and who rewards it appropriately. Feedback from the teacher is largely seen as related to the reward and this part of the process is seen as separate from, and following after, the learning process.

Behaviourists do not see the theory as only applied to low level cognitive learning. They argue that stimulus-response applies at more advanced levels of learning as well. Nor is it confined to psychomotor skill learning: it is the basis of attitudinal learning as well; for example the appreciation of music. Stimulus and reinforcement, behaviourists argue, are elements of all different types of learning.

So, how can we apply behaviourist theory in the classroom? The following guidelines show potential of stimulus-response theory:

1. Use reinforcement to strengthen behaviour that you want to encourage. For example to encourage effective remembering:

    (a) When students are learning factual materials, give feedback frequently and quickly.

    (b) When students are learning to understand and apply factual information, use delayed feedback to encourage trial and error learning so assisting the understanding process.

    (c) Use several kinds of reinforcers (e.g. praise, marks, prizes) so that each keeps its effectiveness.

2. Take advantage of the different schedules of reinforcement to encourage the learning process. For example:

    (a) When students first attempt a new kind of learning, supply frequent reinforcement, but, at a later stage, supply rewards less often.

    (b) If you want to encourage spurts of activity, use a fixed-interval schedule of reinforcement.

3. Use programmed learning approaches by describing the terminal behaviour, organising what is to be learned, and finally provide feedback. For example:

    (a) In the introduction to your lessons, list and tell the students exactly what you want them to learn by the end of the lesson.

    (b) Arrange the materials to be learned into a series of steps.

    (c) Provide feedback to each of the steps so that correct responses will be reinforced and students will be aware of correct responses.

4. When students lose motivation, use special forms of reinforcement to motivate them to persevere. For example:

    (a) Negotiate a contract with a student for the work to be completed to earn a particular reward.

    (b) Use short-term, frequent, immediate rewards.

You can see that this is very much 'controlled' education with the teacher controlling what goes on in the classroom. Control is based upon the specification of behavioural, product objectives. We should be aware that there is some considerable criticism of the use of this approach and such criticisms are mainly based upon cases being made both 'for' and 'against' the specification and use of product objectives. MacDonald-Ross (1973) provides a very useful critical review of the use of behavioural objectives. The points for and against are summarised below.

Benefits Claimed	Case Against
1. The only well-worked-out method of rational planning in education.	1. No consistent view as to where objectives come from or how they are best derived.
2. Encourages teachers to think and plan in detailed, specific terms.	2. Defining objectives before the event can be limiting in a number of learning situations.
3. Encourages teachers to make their plans explicit.	3. In some disciplines criteria can only be applied after the event.
4. Provides a rational basis for assessment.	4. Objectives are inherently ambiguous and lead to ambiguity if told to students.
5. Provides guidelines for choice of teaching methods.	5. Trivial (knowledge) objectives are the easiest to operationalise.
6. Objectives communicate curriculum from designers to teachers to students.	6. Lists of behaviours do not adequately represent the structure of knowledge.
7. Objectives can be made the basis for individual programmes.	7. Can lead to teachers not thinking for themselves.

Figure 2.15 *Review of Objectives Model*

4.1.2 The Neo-behaviourists

Tolman, Skinner and Gagné are, perhaps, the best known neo-behaviourists. They provided a more human perspective in that they considered the human mind to be selective in its actions and not simply responsive to stimuli.

Tolman's work showed that he felt that humans use their beliefs and feelings when responding to stimuli and that there is a need to consider the whole rather than isolated stimulus-response incidents. In other words, humans seek a purpose and people have a 'cognitive map'. This is a set of relationships appropriate to different stimuli. So the student has to fit new learning into a pattern, that is 'what leads to what'. Motivation comes into learning theory according to Tolman. The importance of a logical learning sequence is shown and the students need to *apply* their new learning in order to test its validity.

Skinner placed great importance on 'operant conditioning' where an operant is a series of actions which a learner completes. Through reinforcement of the learning, the learning quality becomes greater. Skinner's approach was highly structured. He stated that teachers need to identify what learning they wish to take place and then select 'reinforcers' which will help to maintain the desired behaviours. Such a reinforcer may only be a nod of the head in agreement. Skinner's work showed that it is important to reward the learner frequently in the early stages of learning, then at random or at a fixed interval subsequently. In the early stages of learning, each successive step in the learning process should be as small as possible so that rewards can be given as reinforcement.

Gagné recognised that the design of the teaching had to match the type of learning that was taking place. He listed eight learner characteristics which would influence the way in which the 'instruction' would take place. His eight types of learning are:

1. *Signal Learning:* Learner associates exact response to stimuli.

2. *Stimulus-Response Learning:* Learner associates exact responses to stimuli.

3. *Chaining:* Learner acquires a number of S-R bondings as, for example, in changing a car wheel.

4. *Verbal Association:* Verbal chains are acquired.

5. *Multiple Discriminations:* Learner discriminates between apparently similar stimuli and makes the correct response.

6. *Concept Learning:* Concepts are classes of stimuli and the learner can recognise these classes.

7. *Rule Learning:* Chains of two or more concepts often called 'principles' or 'laws'.

8. *Problem Solving:* The discovering of relationships where rule learning is applied.

Gagné suggests that these eight types of learning are in a hierarchy with the lower types being needed as pre-requisites for the higher ones. He also suggests that it is valuable to have a sequence to instruction and such a sequence can usefully be based on the learning types. This, he suggests, might be:

Inform the students what they are expected to do, that is, tell them the objectives.

Question the students to determine their entry behaviour.

Use cues to form the chains of concepts or rules.

Question students so that they can demonstrate their learning.

Ask students to make a verbal statement of the rule.

This list can be compared with De Cecco's model for concept attainment.

As may be seen, the teacher designs the learning programme to ensure that students have the lower orders of learning before they progress to the higher levels. Planning for feedback is the key feature of the approach advocated by Gagné and is a characteristic of neo-behaviourism.

4.1.3 The Gestaltists

'Gestalt' comes from the German for pattern or structure. This indicates that the Gestaltists are interested in the overall perspective as opposed to the behaviourists who are concerned with a series of incremental actions. In other words, the whole is greater than the sum of the individual parts: it is the pattern which is important. Understanding, according to Gestaltists, is based upon *insight*. Insight has a particular meaning to those of the Gestalt school. It is when the student suddenly becomes aware of the relevance of the behaviour or learning. We have all experienced a sudden flash of inspiration– and this is a form of insight. The characteristics of insight are that the solution to a problem comes suddenly, the solution can be applied to similar problems in different contexts and the solution can be retained over a period of time.

Gestalt psychology has some basic laws which are of interest. They may well be evident from your own teaching.

1. *Figure-ground relationships:* Perceptions are organised into figures or features which stand out from their background. As you look at this page, the print is, as you think, the key part, but the spaces are just as important.

2. *Contiguity:* Proximity in time and space influences how we group things. The closer they are, the more likely they are to be grouped and linked together.

3. *Similarity:* Items which are similar tend to be grouped or classed together.

4. *Law of Praganz:* Figures will be perceived in their best possible pattern of form.

5. *Closure:* Figures, or items, which are incomplete, may be perceived as complete because we tend to complete the figure or 'fill in the gaps'.

6. *Transposition:* Patterns and figures may be distorted or changed to some degree but they can still be recognised.

As with all the schools of psychology, Gestaltists have their critics. The above laws have never been 'proved' and there appears to be a lack of factual or empirical evidence. Insight is also difficult to observe and measure (although this does not mean that it does not happen). Many subjects, or parts of subjects, do not need insight. For example, learning the times tables does not require a 'flash of inspiration'; rote learning is probably the most efficient way.

However, Gestalt theory has implications for us to use in our classrooms. The following techniques can be used to encourage the use of insight by our students.

1. Group similar things together so that the 'pattern' can be more easily understood.

2. Use diagrams where possible as this shows the whole at one glance.

3. Allow times for students to apply information to their own situations so that they can make their own patterns and have insight in terms of their own previous experiences.

4. Let students solve problems in their own way.

4.1.4 The Cognitivists

Behaviourists place their focus on the task and the Stimulus-Response model. The Cognitivists, on the other hand, place their focus on the students and how they gain and organise their knowledge (that is, cognise). Students do not merely receive information, but actively create a pattern of what it means to them. The implications of this are that, if you have a class of sixteen students, they probably have sixteen slightly different understandings. The students 'fit' their new learning onto their own existing mental structure.

Dewey defined learning as 'learning to think' and the process of learning is not just doing something, such as a task, but *reflecting* and learning from this. The teacher is the key to Dewey's work because, he says, the teacher must plan for reflective thinking to take place. Education being firmly linked to social growth was one of Dewey's main claims.

Bruner was insistent that students must be taught *how* to analyse problems and how to think for themselves in order to become independent learners. The implications of this include the idea that teaching a lot of factual information is unproductive since the learner forgets most of it in a relatively short time and will use very little of it. However, teaching generalities is efficient as generalities can be applied in a number of situations over a period of time. Bruner considers the learning process as the acquiring of new information, transforming that learning with regard to existing knowledge and then checking it against the new situation. So, knowledge is a process rather than a product. Models are constructed by the learner which explain the existing but can also predict what might be. Bruner sees the teacher's role as one of facilitating the student's own discovery known as 'inquiry training'.

Ausubel sees the key to effective learning as the students relating their new learning to existing cognitive structures. He advocates the use of 'advance organisers' (that is, bridges between what the students know and what they need to know). Such an organiser is a short description of the new material *before* the lesson so that the students are prepared to accept the new materials.

These theories point to the active engagement of the mind in relation to the subject matter under consideration. They stress the *processes* involved in creating responses (as opposed to the responses themselves that are the aspect of behaviourism) and the organisation of perceptions that go on in the mind. The theory is similar to behaviourism, however, because in order to learn, understanding is necessary: the materials must be marshalled step by step and then mastered. The setting of goals is related to each part of the materials, and feedback is an essential element in the process of learning, *but* not separate from it.

Cognitive psychologists argue that we are not passive receptors of stimuli when we learn: the mind actively processes the information it receives and converts it into new forms and categories. So how do we apply cognitive theories in the classroom? The following suggestions may assist you.

1.   Call attention to, and take advantage of, the structure of the subject. Stress relationships in what you present. Use advance organisers where appropriate and urge students to seek patterns of their own.

2.   Take advantage of students wanting to find answers to problems that have personal significance to them, so relating the learning to their own personal situations.

3.   Arrange the learning so that students discover things for themselves.

4.   Structure discussions by posing specific questions.

5.   Use discussions and give students themselves the responsibility for leading them.

Through the use of these techniques, which are all related to the importance of the structure of the subject, you are attempting to promote learning through insight of the cognitive structures of the subject: the concepts that are embodied within it. It is argued that students learn the best when they gain insight into, and understanding of, the underlying structure of the knowledge embodied within the subject. They need to be active in seeking new information and need to be active in participating in the teaching methods. They learn best when they discover concepts and principles for themselves.

4.1.5 The Humanists

Since about 1960, beginning with the publication of A S Neill's 'Summerhill', a new movement aimed at criticising and improving education in fundamental ways has gathered momentum. The movement has been particularly attractive with post-16 education whose students have been unhappy with their own schooling. It seemed to respond to their own resentment with the regimentation, pressure, competition, and so on. The movement has had several names: 'new romanticism', 'open schooling' and 'alternative education', but is now generally termed 'humanistic education'.

Summerhill, in southern England, is an 'open', private school where the education of the whole person is considered more important than subject matter. No pupil is forced to attend classes but go only when they want to. The school 'rules' are made through a school committee on which every pupil and staff member have one vote. Neill recounts the story of how he tried to get football stopped in the corridor outside his office through the committee. Initially he was outvoted and it was not until he had brought it up on several occasions that he managed to get it accepted. Neill argues that the apparent freedom allowed pupils to gain an education that the conventional kind of schooling was not capable of providing. Although the academic successes of the school were low, and HMI tried unsuccessfully to close the school on several occasions, Neill argued that if one of the ex-pupils of Summerhill gained an interview, they were more likely to get the job than someone from a conventional educational background.

The Humanist school of psychology, then, was developed as a reaction against behaviourism because its proponents saw behaviourism as reducing the concept of the human being. The person was seen as being worthy of dignity and teachers needed to develop qualities of worth and self-esteem. This involved helping every person to make the most of themselves that they could.

Maslow, as described earlier, is best remembered for his work on motivation. His hierarchy of human needs is well known and is a feature of many management books. Essentially, Maslow states that needs must be satisfied before effective learning can take place. If a student is tired, cold and hungry, then the quality of learning will be reduced. The student who feels threatened in the learning situation is unlikely to learn effectively. Our task as teachers is to create an environment where students feel part of a group and feel that their contribution has worth.

Rogers' thinking is similar to Maslow's. He felt the need to place the student at the centre of the learning process through active self-discovery rather than having to respond to stimuli. He stated that humans are essentially 'good' and that they have a desire to develop and grow. The job of the teacher, in his view, is to generate the conditions and environment for students to develop their own self-concept.

The key to effective, long-term learning is based upon experiential learning which has the following features: personal involvement, stimulation of feelings and thinking, self-initiation and self-evaluation. The behaviourists see the need to structure and control the learning whereas the humanists see it as essential to trust the learners to follow their own learning programme at their own pace and direction. Active learning by doing is seen as the key, but some form of reflection through evaluation is essential. More recently, Kolb has completed work in the humanist vein.

The humanist approach is quite different to what was (and, perhaps, is) the perceived way in which adults learn. Schools have always stated that they want to educate the whole person rather than train them for an occupation. Colleges tended to keep to subject matter and link their courses to specific occupational areas – in fact the recent legislation ensures that employers have considerable influence over colleges via their corporation.

The humanist learning theories are not so coherent as the behaviour or cognitivist theories. Like cognitivism, they stress the active nature of the learner. Indeed, the student's actions largely create the learning situation. They emphasise:

> The urges and drives of the personality.
>
> Movements towards increased autonomy and competence.
>
> The compulsion towards development and growth of the individual.
>
> The active search for meaning.
>
> The goals that individuals set for themselves.
>
> The social setting in which students operate.

The theories state that learning and setting goals for oneself are natural processes calling into play the persona; learning abilities that students already have and seek to enhance. Learning is largely by imitation and identification with others. Motivation for learning comes from within.

These views also stress the autonomy whereas other views stress learning in terms of 'control': that the learner is controlled by the stimuli, by the teacher or by the subject. The materials, humanists argue, on which students exercise their learning skills are less important than the goals that they have set themselves. This means that the role of the teacher is to increase the range of experiences so that the students choose how to achieve their own learning changes.

So, how do we, as teachers, apply the humanist perspective? Perhaps we could:

1. Be aware of the extent to which we control the learning and, where possible, allow students to make choices and to manage their own learning.

2. Establish a warm, positive class atmosphere so that every student believes that they can learn and that you want them to learn.

3. Act as a facilitator to learning and encourage, help and assist the learning process.

4. Consider participating as an individual in group settings.

5. Do our best to help students to develop positive feelings about themselves.

6. Use role-play and simulation exercise when they are appropriate.

7. Use the taxonomy of educational objectives in the affective domain to identify specific goals of humanistic education.

8. Provide learning activities that will lead to the development of the habits and attitudes that we want to foster.

4.2 Teaching and learning approaches

4.2.1 Inductive and deductive approaches

The differences and similarities of inductive and deductive approaches are, perhaps, best seen through simple examples.

Suppose we wished our students to gain an understanding of magnetic forces. We could give the students a magnet and a number of items made from a range of different materials. The students are then allowed to explore the use of the magnet and the various items made from the different materials. The students may then list items attracted to magnets and those not attracted. You may have to prompt this stage. The list may be as follows:

Attracted by Magnet	Not Attracted by Magnet
Pen	Plastic pen
Chair leg	Paper
Watch	Cup
Paper clip	Wood
Hair clip	Clothes
Spoon	
Zip	

You can then ask the students to make a statement which summarises their observations. It may be that they say metals are attracted by the magnet. A more sophisticated test would indicate only some metals are attracted by the magnet. The students can then be given more objects and asked to predict which items would be attracted.

An alternative approach could be to give out magnets, telling the students that magnets attract (some) metals but not objects made from other materials. Question and answer could then be used to ask the students to predict, then test, whether the magnets will attract various materials.

The two methods have some commonality. Essentially the content and equipment are the same. Both methods depend upon the generalisation that magnets attract (some) metals.

However there are significant differences. In the first case the students make observations about specific examples and then make and test a general statement. This process of moving from specific examples to generalised statement – or law is called an *inductive* approach and would be advocated by humanists. In the second case the generalisation was stated and then tested using specific examples. This process of working from a general statement and using specific examples is known as a *deductive* approach and would be advocated by behaviourists.

Both approaches have their benefits, and choice of approach may depend upon the topic under consideration. Also some students in your class will prefer an inductive approach whilst the other students may learn better with the deductive one. It could well be that the best approach is to use a mix of the two throughout the course.

Example	Deductive	Inductive
Mixing Colours.	• Teacher states "Yellow and Blue mixed make Green". • Students mix colours and test.	• Teacher "How can we make green?" • Students experiment.
Interview Skills.	• Lists process of do's and don'ts. • Practice role play interview. • Playback video and discuss in relation to do's and don'ts.	• Students interview each other. • Design guidelines. • Apply guidelines in new practice interviews. • Playback.
Needs of a Stroke Patient.	• Teacher states needs of Stroke Patient.	• Students visit Stroke Patients and their relatives. • Students meet in a group and generate the list of needs.

4.2.2 A Constructivist's approach to learning

As teachers we tend to make assumptions about the 'entry behaviour' of our students. We tend to think that the students know nothing about the topic or that they know a good deal. The truth is likely to be somewhere between the two extremes and will differ from student to student. As we saw with concept attainment, it is important that the students do not have misconceptions before they even start to learn the concept.

The constructivists' view is that we identify the students' current ideas which they may well have to modify or abandon before they can construct new meaning.

The key assumptions of this constructivist perspective [as described by Driver and Bell (1985)] include:

1. What the student currently believes, whether it is correct or incorrect, is important.
2. Despite having the same learning experience, each individual will construct an individual meaning which only they hold.
3. Understanding or constructing a meaning is an active and continuous process.
4. Learning may well involve some conceptual changes.
5. When students construct a new meaning, they may not believe it but may give it provisional acceptance or even rejection.

6.   Learning is not a passive process, but active, and depends upon the students taking responsibility to learn.

A simplified model of the Constructivist approach is shown in Figure 2.16.

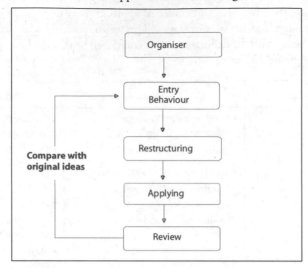

Figure 2.16   *Model of the Constuctivist Approach*

The process starts with an outline of what is going to be learned. This allows the student to prepare the way for new ideas. The teacher should then try to ascertain the entry behaviour of the students (i.e. what they think now) by, say, question and answer. This may reveal quite a high level of learning or some strange ideas which will inhibit the correct learning which it is hoped will take place. Correction of these misconceptions may then be addressed.

The restructuring phase follows and although this restructuring process is the responsibility of the student, the teacher needs to lead and facilitate this approach. The teacher may achieve this by designing appropriate practical activities and/or discussions or explorations. The students can try their ideas in new, different situations. The review stage is when the students reflect upon their ideas and how they have changed since the start of the learning.

4.2.3 Andragogy

Earlier we discussed the differences between pedagogical and andragogical models and defined andragogy as 'how adults (as distinct from children) learn'. The following provides an overview of the important facets of adult learning.

Malcolm Knowles (1983) identified six assumptions made about adult learning. These are related to:

(i)   *The need to know.* Adults need to know why they need to learn something before starting to learn it.

(ii) *Self-concept.* The self-concept moves from teacher dependence to self-direction in the learning process. Adults have a self-concept of being responsible for their own lives. Once they have arrived at this self-concept a need is developed to be seen by others, and treated by others, as being capable of self-direction.

(iii) *Experience.* Adults have a reservoir of experience upon which to draw for their learning.

(iv)   Readiness to learn. Adults are motivated to learn those things they need to know and be able to do in order to cope effectively with their real-life situations. For example ten year-olds are not ready to learn about infant nutrition and marital relations, but when they get older they will be more ready to learn.

(v)   *Orientation to learning*. Adults are motivated to learn when it will help them to perform tasks or deal with problems that they meet at work or in real-life situations.

(vi)   *Motivation*. While adults are responsive to some external motivators (like promotion) the best motivators are internal pressures (like increased job satisfaction and self-esteem).

Andragogy, says Mezirow (1981), as a professional perspective of adult educators, must be defined as an organised and sustained effort to assist adults to learn in a way that enhances their capability to function as self-directed learners. We, as teachers of adults, need to help the learning that will continue after our students have left us. Mezirow provides us with a 'Charter' which gives us suggestions as to how we may achieve this. His suggestions are outlined in Figure 2.17.

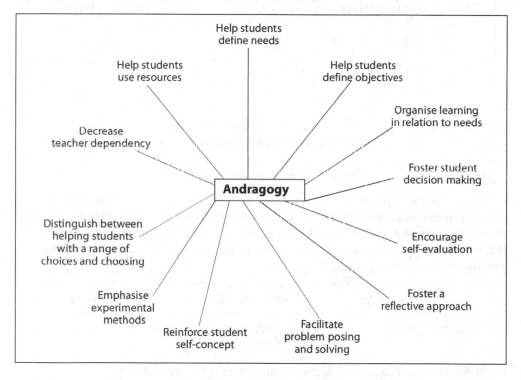

Figure 2.17   *Charter for Andragogy (Mezirow - 1981)*

It will be seen that Mezirow's Charter operationalises the assumption made by Knowles about how adults learn. As such, it provides you with a set of principles upon which to base your lesson planning. For instance, you should always tell students the objectives of the session(s); you should negotiate with students about the objectives that they are to achieve and how they, as individuals might achieve them; you should get them to make their own decisions and encourage their own self-valuation. Therefore, in order to achieve the Charter, you should treat students as individuals who will not be dependent upon you as the teacher, but help them to be self-dependent. In short, it is suggested that a move from behaviouristic principles towards the more humanistic is appropriate for adult learning.

4.3   Kolb

A very well known model of learning was devised by Kolb, (1984). As you can see from Figure 2.18, the model has four stages.

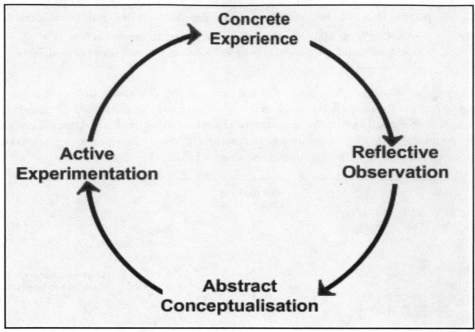

Figure 2.18   *Kolb's Four Stage Learning Cycle*

Kolb states that the sequence of the stages in the cycle are important, (i.e. it flows in a clockwise direction), reflection is a crucial feature of learning and that the cycle may be started at any of the four stages. This last point is often overlooked. One of the barriers to the effective use of Kolb's mode; is the jargon used by Kolb. The following figure may help you to understand and use Kolb with your own students:

Kolb's Terminology	Meaning	Simplified Term
Concrete Experience	Practical Activity (physical or mental)	Do
Reflective Observation	Exploring what happened	Review
Abstract Conceptualisation	Thinking about models. Theories or rules	Devise rules, laws or procedures
Active Experimentation	Testing the models in new situations	Test

Figure 2.19   *Kolb's Terminology*

The simplified terminology yields the following diagram:

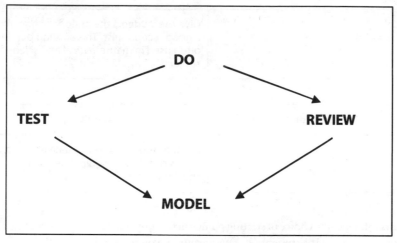

Figure 2.20 *Kolb's Model Simplified*

So, how does Kolb's model apply to your teaching? Suppose you are teaching 'Customer Care' to your students and the topic is 'Reception Duties'. The lesson could be based on:

Stage	Activity
1. Do	Undertake reception duties, (real or simulated), or observe college receptionist.
2. Review	Class discussion about what happened, what was good, not so good. How could it be improved etc.
3. Model	Draw up a checklist of good practice.
4. Test	Simulate reception duties.

Notice that we have followed the four stages of the cycle in a clockwise direction and, of course, the students can go around the cycle again so refining their learning.

Do you remember we said that the cycle may start at any point? For the other three points on the cycle we can start as shown:

Starting Point	Activity
1. Review	Ask the students to recall their experiences with receptionist say, Doctors, Hotels. Then move onto the next stages.

Starting Point	Activity
1. Model	Give the students the 'theory' of how to be a good receptionist. This starting point is often used in mathematical and scientific subjects.

Starting Point	Activity
1. Test	Ask the students to undertake reception duties by following guidelines or a checklist.

Many factors influence the choice of starting point, such as previous learning/experience, the nature of the subject, the ages of the students etc. We encourage you to experiment with your teaching by trying different starting points. They do result in different learning experiences and can enhance the level of student activity and involvement.

Honey and Mumford (1982) have identified individual preferences (Activist, Reflector, Theorist, and Pragmatist) for each stage of Kolbs model. Figure 2.21 identifies the relationship between each of the stages in Kolbs model and also looks at teaching strategies that can be used for each stage.

Stages in Kolb's Model	Honey and Mumford Learning Styles	Teaching Strategies for Each Stage
Concrete Experience – Direct practical experience.	**Activist** – Prefers doing.	Hands on approach, lab or practical session, simulation, taking notes, observation, visits – field trips, project, role play, debate.
Reflective Observation – Reflect, describe, communicate and learn from the experience.	**Reflector** – Observes and thinks about situation.	Discussion, personal development diary or log, tutorial, case study, one to one.
Abstract Conceptualisation – Use models and theories to draw conclusions.	**Theorist** – Needs to understand reasons, concepts, relationships.	Lecture, seminar, discussion, reading.
Active Experimentation – Testing those rules, apply to new learning experiences.	**Pragmatist** – Have a go, try out to see if they work.	Experiment, simulation, buzz group.

Figure 2.21   *Table Linking Kolb's 4 Stage Model with Honey and Mumford Learning Styles and Identification of Teaching Methods for Each Stage*

4.4 The learning continuum

The three main models of learning, behaviourism, humanistic and cognitivism, provide us with choice: which is most appropriate for your students and for your subject area? Should we stick to one model, or should we use different models for different occasions? If we should use different models, upon what principles do we make the choice?

Behaviourism is based on stimulus-response theory and is about teacher control. The teacher uses external reinforcement to motivate the students and uses prompting techniques. Variety of approach comes from strategies like role play and simulations but, in the main, the sessions are teacher-centred. The advantages of the approach are that the objectives are clear, it is highly specific and it is measurable. The *humanistic* approach is founded on the theory that learning is individual. The work of the teacher is to extract lessons from the students' own insight and experience and get them to reflect upon things. The theory is based on the Socratic approach where you do not need to tell students anything, just ask them the right questions so that they will find out for themselves. The teaching strategies involve discussion, with the teacher asking questions, action planning. self-assessment and guided reflection. The advantages claimed for this approach include building on individual experiences, treating people as adults and developing critical thinking and creativity. *Cognitivism* is an academic approach based on the principle that learning accrues through exposure to logically presented information. Such logic comes from the subject itself. The teaching strategies associated with the theory include videos, class presentations, readings, case studies and debates. The advantages claimed include treating people as adults (again), faster learning, and the building upon a base of information, concepts and principles to provide a rationale for action.

So how do we choose? Knowles (1983) suggests relating one's teaching approach to a mixture of topic and student analysis. The topic is related to both the type (cognitive, affective or psychomotor) and level of learning that is required. Simpler tasks, he says, are probably best learned by behaviouristic techniques, while higher level learning needs more cognitive input and humanistic insight. The student analysis depends upon the ability of the student's thought processes. Less able learners are often satisfied with behaviouristic approaches while the more able require greater cognitive information and a chance to discuss and share what they already know. It might also be argued that the stage in a course is a factor in deciding which approach to use. To begin with a behaviouristic approach can provide all with the basic levels of information before proceeding to the cognitivist approaches to provide high level information and a rationale for its existence. Finally, a humanistic approach can stimulate initiative, creativity and independent thinking which allows students to individualise the learning and apply it to their own situations.

Figure 2.22 (adapted from Kramlinger and Huberty – 1990) provides a guide to the selection of different learning strategies for each of the theories. The diagram indicates that the behaviourist methods are the most structured and teacher-centred and the humanist the least structured and more student-centred.

It is also possible to link the three models with student learning styles. Honey and Mumford (1986) describe four learning styles as theorist, activist, pragmatist and reflectivist. They also provide a questionnaire so that individuals can find their own preferred style. It is argued by Kramlinger and Huberty (op cit) that:

> The theoretical learner learns best with cognitivist methods such as reading.

> The pragmatist learns best with a mixture of behaviourist and humanist approaches such as tasks and case studies.

The reflective learner learns best with humanist approaches such as group discussion.

The activist responds to a mixture of behaviourist and humanist approaches.

Theory Type of Learning		Methods		
		Behaviourist	**Cognitivist**	**Humanist**
Knowledge	Transmit	Memory Association	Lecture Class presentation Case Study/Reading	Discussion Games
Knowledge	Assess	Question/Answer	Test	Discussion
Psychomotor Skills	Initial	Demonstration	Demonstration	Discuss action
Psychomotor Skills	Practice	Worksheets	Case Study	Project Simulation
Psychomotor Skills	Application	On-the-job	Coaching/Feedback	Action Plan/Contract
Attitudes	Transmit and Assess	Assessment Reinforcement	Vicarious experience Debate	Self assessment Discussion of beliefs

Figure 2.22   *Guide to Selection of Learning Strategies*

Kramlinger and Huberty (op cit) conclude that humanistic techniques answer the why questions; cognitivist approaches answer the what questions; and methods that are predominantly behaviourist but with some humanist techniques answer the how questions.

Figure 2.23 provides an overview of the three main models together with their prominent aspects. The implication for us is to decide which approach best suits our students and to organise accordingly. That is not to suggest that we use only one approach: at different times and with different subjects, we may use a combination. Indeed, often the curriculum materials lead us to a combination. For example Edexcel, use a mixture of process and product approaches where both the subject matter and key (core) skills require product and process learning.

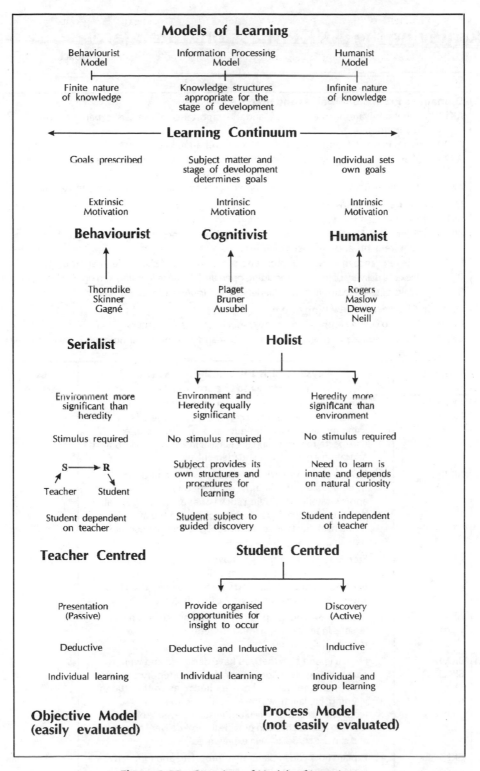

Figure 2.23 *Overview of Models of Learning*

Achieving the LLUK Professional Standards

Standards
Domain A: Professional values and practice
AK1.1   What motivates learners to learn and the importance of learners' experience and aspirations.
AK2.1   Ways in which learning has the potential to change lives.
AK2.2   Ways in which learning promotes the emotional, intellectual, social and economic well-being of individuals and the population as a whole.
AK4.1   Principles, frameworks and theories which underpin practice in learning and teaching.
Domain B: Learning and teaching
BK1.3   Ways of creating a motivating learning environment.
BK2.1   Principles of learning and ways to provide learning activities to meet curriculum requirements and the needs of all learners.
BK2.3   The relevance of learning approaches, preferences and skills to learner progress.
BK2.4   Flexible delivery of learning, including open and distance learning and on-line learning.
BK2.5   Ways of using learners' own experiences as a foundation for learning.
Domain C: Specialist learning and teaching
CK2.1   Ways to convey enthusiasm for own specialist area to learners.
CK3.5   Ways to support learners in the use of new and emerging technologies in own specialist area

Standards	Ways in which you can show that you have achieved the Standards	See Section
AK1.1 BK1.3	1. Consider the level of motivation of one of your groups of students. Experiment and comment upon the effects of using motivational techniques such as: verbal praise; unexpected events; using the familiar in an unfamiliar context; educational games; using puzzlement; etc.	3
AK2.1 AK2.2	2. Review your course documentation with regard to the three domains of learning. Comment on its appropriateness including such issues as: coverage of all three domains; sufficiency of emphasis on the affective domain; ability to identify the levels within the cognitive domain.	1 and 2
AK4.1	3. From a lesson plan that you have recently developed, covering at least two domains of learning, identify the relevant theories of learning which have been used to support the development of the learning.	2 and 4
AK4.1	4. Explain how you use theories of learning to design your lessons in terms of engaging students in active and meaningful learning.	4
BK2.1 BK2.3 BK2.4 BK2.5	5. From a lesson plan that you have designed and which covers at least two domains of learning, identify and state the conditions that you have applied to assist the student learning. Explain how these conditions: meet the requirements of the curriculum; ensure relevance of the learning approaches; can provide flexible delivery of learning; and can use students' own experiences.	4
CK2.1 CK3.5	6. Explain how you implement appropriate and innovative ways to motivate your students in your subject area. This should include the actual and possible use of ILT.	3

For a model approach to show how you have achieved the LLUK Professional Standards see Appendix I.

Chapter 3

Teaching Strategies and Learning Styles

1. Teaching and Learning: the Interaction

- Application of Teaching Strategy
- Choice of Teaching Strategy
- Teaching Strategy and Objectives
- Teaching Strategy and Student Characteristics

2. Teaching Strategies

- Large Group Strategies
- Small Group Strategies
- Individual Teaching Strategies
- ILT as an Aid to Learning for Disabled Students
- Conclusion

3. Learning Styles and Strategies

- Learning Styles
- Using ILT to Support Learning Styles
- Teaching 14-16 year-old Students

4. Evaluation of Teaching Strategies

- Deciding upon what to Evaluate
- Data Collection
- Data Collection in Practice
- Data Analysis

This chapter reviews traditional and non-traditional teaching strategies, including the importance of your students learning in an active manner. Guidelines are given to help you select the most appropriate experiences for your students.

LLUK Professional Standards

The Knowledge and Understanding within the LLUK Professional Standards incorporated in this chapter are:

Domain A: Professional values and practice

AK6.2   Ways to apply relevant statutory requirements and the underpinning principles.

Domain B: Learning and teaching

BK1.1   Ways to maintain a learning environment in which learners feel safe and supported.

BK1.2   Ways to develop and manage behaviours which promote respect for and between others and create an equitable and inclusive learning environment.

BK2.1   Principles of learning and ways to provide learning activities to meet curriculum requirements and the needs of all learners.

BK2.2   Ways to engage, motivate and encourage active participation of learners and learner independence.

BK2.3   The relevance of learning approaches, preferences and skills to learner progress.

BK2.4   Flexible delivery of learning, including open and distance learning and on-line learning.

BK2.5   Ways of using learners' own experiences as a foundation for learning.

BK2.7   Ways in which mentoring and/or coaching can support the development of professional skills and knowledge.

BK3.2   A range of listening and questioning techniques to support learning.

BK3.3   Ways to structure and present information and ideas clearly and effectively to learners.

Domain C: Specialist learning and teaching

CK3.1   Teaching and learning theories and strategies relevant to own specialist area.

CK3.5   Ways to support learners in the use of new and emerging technologies in own specialist area

Domain D: Planning for learning

DK2.1   The importance of including learners in the planning process.

DK3.1   Ways to evaluate own role and performance in planning learning.

Domain F: Access and Progression

FK1.1   Sources of information, advice, guidance and support to which learners might be referred.

FK2.1   Boundaries of own role in supporting learners.

---

1. Teaching and Learning: The Interaction

When you begin teaching, you may tend to adopt an approach with which you are comfortable and which enables you to feel in control of things. You may adopt a model based on someone whom you regard as an 'ideal', or on someone who taught you. This may mean you give out information by talking and working on the chalkboard. Perhaps there are some question and answer sessions and even a test. This is the usual way people may gain confidence in teaching a group of students.

Once you feel confident in this teaching role, you are then able to experiment with how students learn and with ways in which to improve the effectiveness of their learning. You should start to consider the range of teaching strategies available, explore them and build up your experience, expertise and confidence over a wide range of approaches. However, it is worth remembering that it may take some time to really understand the differences between the methods that you use to teach and the effect on the students' learning.

1.1 Application of teaching strategy

There are many teaching strategies; we will examine the most common or popular in this chapter. You will find considerable overlap between them and so we have grouped the strategies into those which are suitable for large groups, small groups and for individuals. Of course, you can use most of these strategies in all three situations. As usual in education, there are few answers which are totally right or totally wrong. Some strategies appear to be more effective with certain students in certain situations. Figure 3.1 shows the possible applications of various teaching strategies and relates each of them to the three domains, indicating the objectives that may be achieved by each strategy. For example a lecture will be likely only to achieve low level cognitive objectives, a demonstration will be likely to achieve low level cognitive and psychomotor objectives, and so on.

1.2 Choice of teaching strategy

Your choice of teaching strategy is often related to your own individual style and what you feel most comfortable in doing. However, there are some overall 'rules' that you might like to consider. These relate to two aspects. The first is the type of objective that you want your students to achieve. For example, you need to always ask yourself – what do I want my students to be able to do? – what do I want my students to know? The second is the number of students you have to teach. Although we describe each separately, you should consider them together in making your final choice of which teaching strategy to use.

Teaching Strategy	Domain					
	Cognitive		Affective		Psychomotor	
	Low	High	Low	High	Low	High
Lecture	✓✓✓					
Demonstration	✓✓				✓✓	
Team Teaching		✓✓			✓	
Discussion		✓✓		✓✓		
Debate		✓✓		✓✓		
Question & Answer	✓✓✓					
Video		✓✓	✓✓		✓✓	
Seminar		✓✓	✓✓			
Laboratory/Workshop		✓✓	✓		✓✓✓	
Gaming/Quiz		✓✓	✓✓			
Brainstorming		✓✓				
Buzz Group		✓✓				
Field Trip		✓		✓	✓	
Role Play		✓		✓✓		
Ice Breaker			✓✓			
Simulation		✓		✓	✓✓	
Case Study		✓✓				
Project/Assignment		✓✓	✓✓		✓✓	
Tutorial		✓✓	✓✓			✓
Open/Distance Learning		✓✓				
One to One		✓✓		✓✓		✓
Information Learning Technology (ILT)		✓✓		✓✓		✓✓

Figure 3.1   *Possible Application of Teaching Strategies in the Three Domains*

1.3   Teaching strategy and objectives

The basic teaching model that we described earlier showed us that learning and its objectives are at the heart of teaching and that all other behaviours and actions flow from them. Thus, when you come to choose your teaching strategy it is logical that you make the domain and level of objective you are seeking to achieve the basis for the choice. For example, we suggest that the most appropriate way to learn a motor skill is through demonstration and individual practice; to gain knowledge and understanding, a lecture and question and answer are appropriate; and to develop students' attitudes towards issues then you might use discussion to best achieve the objective. In Figure 3.1 we take this a stage further. The figure splits the domains into the different levels and then suggests that different strategies are more appropriate for the lower level objectives in a domain than for the higher levels. Thus a lecture might achieve low level objectives (such as knowledge and comprehension), while to achieve the higher levels (for instance, synthesis and evaluation) then you might find a debate or seminar more appropriate.

1.4   Teaching strategy and student characteristics

Let us look at another means of categorising teaching strategies; a simple category, group size. At one extreme a 'group' may consist of only one student. In such circumstances you could use methods such as projects or assignments, tutoring and individually prescribed instruction such as open learning.

Next we have small groups of between 5 and 20 students. With such a group you may find that a discussion method is suitable. The conventional classroom size for post-16 education and training is a group of between 10 and 20 students. With such groups the approach often adopted is what is traditionally called 'classroom teaching' which consists of a mixture of methods. Because this form of teaching is most frequently used you might consider it a strategy in its own right. The nature of such classroom teaching will vary considerably from one teacher to another. It will often have a short lecture, followed by question and answer, some small group discussion and some individual work.

The final group size is a group greater than 20 students. Such large groups can lead to difficulties in dealing with individuals and so you may have to use strategies such as lecture and demonstration, which can still be active and challenging methods of learning, if carried out properly.

Recent research into effective teaching (Bransford, 1999, Lampert, 2002 amongst others) indicates that there are some features of effective teaching behaviours which are common across all of the post compulsory sector. These appear to be:

> Engagement with students on a personal level.
>
> Excellent subject knowledge.
>
> Demonstrating 'care' in their relationships with students.
>
> Purposeful teaching.
>
> Attention to feedback and a commitment to keeping 'promises' (such as work being handed back on time).

We can think of choice of teaching strategy in terms of classroom management. How you choose your teaching strategy has a direct influence on how you manage your classroom. It has been said repeatedly in this book that students learn in different ways: an approach that is appropriate to one student may well be inappropriate for another. Some people learn better in a group through the interaction with both the teacher and other students. Others find interaction difficult and use the group sessions for gathering of information and only learn when they are on their own. Some learn by reading and listening, others learn through the application of the knowledge gained.

When we accept this premise we realise the importance of providing a variety of learning activities for our students. We might start off by *telling* them, next provide a group activity and finally provide an individual application activity. In this way, the coverage of the content is through a number of different strategies in the hope that one of them will appeal to all of the students and ensure that students learn in a manner appropriate to themselves.

The level of participation of the students in the learning process is an important factor. Figure 3.2 gives a general guide to participation levels, which will obviously vary depending upon the way in which the strategies are implemented.

Strategy	Level of Student Participation
Lecture	Low
Demonstration	Low/High
Team Teaching	Low
Discussion	High
Debate	High
Question & Answer	Medium
Video	Medium
Seminar	Medium
Laboratory/Workshop	Medium
Gaming/Quiz	Medium
Brainstorming	High
Buzz Group	High
Field Trip	Medium
Role Play	High
Ice Breaker	High
Simulation	High
Case Study	Medium
Project	High
Assignment	High
Tutorial	High
Open/Distance Learning	High
One to One	High
Information Learning Technology (ILT)	High

Figure 3.2   *Teaching Strategy and Level of Participation*

We often find very early on in our teaching careers that students learn in different ways. The differences may be slight, but also may be significant. You may have experienced a lesson and thought, 'That was really good. I learned a lot from that'. However, some of your friends may have said, 'That was useless. What a waste of time'. This may indicate, many things, such as the way that the subject touched you, your prior understanding of the topic, and not least, your learning style. This may indicate your *learning styles* are different. Honey and Mumford (1986) published the Manual of Learning Styles which identified four main learning styles. Briefly, they said:

Activists enjoy the present, like the immediate experience and respond to short term issues.

Reflectors prefer to think about things and explore all aspects before coming to a conclusion.

Theorists like principles, theories, models and systems. Logic rules!

Pragmatists look for new ideas and are keen to experiment.

You can use Honey and Mumford's book, which contains a student questionnaire, to ascertain the preferred learning styles of your own students.

This leads us to think about what teaching strategies our students prefer. Many students often say they prefer 'lectures' because they are passive and few demands are made of them. However, our own research which is on-going, gives a different view. The 'top ten' teaching strategies are shown in Figure 3.3

The Top Ten Teaching Strategies
1. Group work
2. Games
3. Simulation
4. Self directed (including open learning and ILT)
5. Assignments
6. Discussions
7. Buzz groups
8. Lectures
9. Case study
10. Field trips

Figure 3.3 *Teaching Strategies: Student Preferences*

One method that you might use when considering your choice of teaching strategy to meet students' needs is to negotiate with them. You might ask, from a range of options, the type of strategy they prefer and use this along with other aspects before you make your final choice.

However, there are other 'inventories' to assess learning styles and preferences, and it would be a very good idea to assess yourself to give you a better idea of the diversity in learner attributes. Examples are:

AVK (Audio, Visual, Kinaesthetic modes).

'Relational'styles (Individualistic, social, passive, controversial).

Multiple intelligence theories (Gardner's 7 Multiple Intelligences, Sternberg's Triarchic theory).

There is a range of research material which looks at the importance of all these inventories in teaching and learning – see for example Gardner (1992), Sternberg (2002), Grasha (2000).

1.4.1 Choice of teaching strategies related to ability of students

Your classroom management needs to be related to the ability of your student group and your choice of teaching strategy. It is no good lecturing to students and expecting them to take their own notes if they are either not able to do this or not used to it.

The ability of students relates to their temperament and special aptitudes. When choosing a teaching strategy you need to consider the attention span of the students and the ability they have to cope with the adopted approach. More mature students will be able to cope with the use of a similar method for a more protracted period while the less mature will need to benefit from more changes in approach. It may be that the less mature, or less able, will have an attention span of not more than ten minutes. If this is the case, changes in approach will have to be considered for each time span.

1.4.2   Choice of teaching strategies related to motivation of students

There is no doubt that the choice of teaching strategy can have an effect upon the motivation and interest of the student. The manner in which the teacher approaches the teaching strategy will have an effect upon motivation: an enthusiastic approach is more likely to motivate than a dull approach and in truth, all of us like to be stimulated in some way – through an action, an example, a manner of speech, a type of presentation. In consequence, to encourage a positive attitude to learning, you should not yourself appear to be disinterested either in the content or the approach.

Some students enjoy working with others. If this is the case, group teaching approaches might give you better results than individual approaches. This could be particularly important in the achieving of affective domain objectives where the use of discussion groups, role play or seminars might be effective.

Figure 3.4 gives an overview of some of the aspects that you might consider in making your choice of teaching strategy. Added to this, of course, is your own personal preference and your ability to cope with specific methods.

Aspect Related to Choice	Points to Note
Objective to be achieved.	Both the domain and the level in the domain need to be considered.
The size of the group.	Different methods are more appropriate to different sizes of class.
The needs and characteristics of students.	Student needs and the characteristics of students need to be considered. This might involve negotiation.
The ability of the student.	Ability and 'intelligence' need to be considered.
The motivation of the student.	Appropriate strategies can motivate an individual to learn.

Figure 3.4   *Aspects to be Considered when Choosing Strategies*

2.   Teaching Strategies

In order to make the choice of teaching strategy it is important that you are familiar with each and know where they might best be used. The following pages give you a description of each of the strategies, where they might be used, guidelines relating to preparation and presentation and, finally, the merits of each. For ease of reference the methods are divided into the three group sizes to which they are most applicable: large groups, small groups and individual. The sub-division is shown in Figure 3.5.

Group Size	Appropriate Strategy
Very large group > 50	**Lecture (passive or interactive)**
2.1 **Large Group** **(N = > 20)**	2.1.1 Lecture. 2.1.2 Demonstration. 2.1.3 Team Teaching. 2.1.4 Discussion. 2.1.5 Debate. 2.1.6 Question and Answer. 2.1.7 Video.
2.2 **Small Group** **(N = 5 – 20)**	2.2.1 Seminar. 2.2.2 Workshop. 2.2.3 Gaming/Quiz. 2.2.4 Brainstorming. 2.2.5 Buzz Groups. 2.2.6 Field Trip. 2.2.7 Role Play. 2.2.8 Ice Breaker. 2.2.9 Simulation. 2.2.10 Case Study.
2.3 **Individual** **(N =<< 5)**	2.3.1 Project/Assignment. 2.3.2 Tutorial. 2.3.3 One-to-One (Coaching). 2.3.4 Open/Distance Learning. 2.3.5 Information Learning Technology (ILT).

Figure 3.5   *Teaching Strategies Related to Group Size*

2.1   Large group strategies

The strategies that are appropriate to large groups are lecture, demonstration, discussion/debate, question and answer and video.

In 1992 PCFC published an interesting resource pack called 'Teaching more Students'. Some of the problems it identified were students just being overwhelmed by the size of the campus, the number of people, everywhere being full, not knowing anyone and the problems of getting to know people. Lack of opportunity to discuss issues and to gain feedback were also highlighted.

Brown (1987) found that students wanted 'good notes'. Symptoms of barriers to this included lecturers saying too much, too quickly, no summaries, lack of stress of major points, no mention of reservations, no time to copy diagrams, poor organisation and so on.

There are two main avenues of approach to the problems of large groups. We can:

Develop lecturing skills.

Take a more active and interactional approach.

We advise that it is beneficial to explore both of these avenues.

Lectures need to be planned carefully and delivered to a high standard. Let your students have an overview of the whole series of lectures at the outset, and if possible, give them the lecture notes in advance. Students like to see a structured approach as it helps them to organise themselves. You also need to share, with the students, the structure of each lecture, and emphasise to them in advance, that the classes are not going to be a repetition of the notes, but an area in which the notes are going to be argued, reinterpreted or discussed.

You need to be heard. There is a limit to your voice projection, you may need a microphone. (Speak more slowly to give emphasis, use pauses and give cues.)

Your visual aids need to be seen by everyone. Larger writing, less content and better use of colour is helpful.

Always start on *time*, never over-run and, if possible, have short breaks in the lecture. *Moving* about indicates you are confident, relaxed and in control. Don't forget to smile.

Look at the students and try to detect when they are interested, bored or tired. Visual clues are always central to understanding how well your class is going!

Students like examples. They bring the topic to life. However, it is beneficial to give negative examples because this helps with concept attainment and understanding.

Verbal signposts can help the students to make notes as they listen:

> *'Today I will ...', 'First we shall look at ...'* help the students to prepare for new materials.

> *'Now let's turn our attention to ...', 'So that's how ...'* help the students to see the material in 'sub sets'.

> *'Now this is crucial ...', 'The key aspect is ...'* help the students to identify main points.

> *'Similarly, ...'* helps the students to make links to other aspects.

All lecturers have views about handouts. Our view is that handouts should be given at the start of the lecture or event the week before. Trying to give them out during the lecture is too disruptive. They should be bound or stapled otherwise there could be total confusion. You want your students to *use* the handouts so give skeletal, framework, structured or gapped handouts. In other words, the handouts are incomplete and the students need to listen, *actively*, for the crucial points. This means that the handouts are useless unless they attend, and attend to, the lecture. Diagrams, key proofs or formulae can be given, saving valuable time. Students could then, say, complete a graph diagram, label a given diagram, list assumptions. Obviously, you need to indicate these activities at the appropriate times. You should ensure that all handouts are produced to a good standard, perhaps with coloured paper and your own 'house style'.

Jenkins (1992), Habeshaw *et al.* (1992), Brown and Atkins (1988) all suggest that the one hour lecture is too long without a break of some kind. You can introduce a number of mini-breaks of two/three minutes in your lectures but remember that you might have to 'train' your students who are unused to this technique. Establish ground rules such as switching the OHP on and off when you are ready to restart.

You might also say some of the following:

> Review your notes for two minutes.
>
> Swap notes with someone near you and compare.
>
> Write down a question you want to ask in the next seminar.
>
> Try to solve this problem.
>
> Try to answer these five multiple-choice questions.
>
> Write down some aspect you want to know more about.
>
> Discuss for two minutes.
>
> Complete the following sentence.
>
> Who agrees with x?

You could ask the students to work in pairs, to snowball, pyramid, rainbow or syndicate. Walk around as the students talk and gain some feedback on the quality of the discussions. The groups could then make a contribution.

You could undertake formal evaluation using questionnaires. Indeed, this may be a departmental procedure. However, you can get more useful feedback, on a more frequent basis, by issuing 'postcards' and asking students to make constructive suggestions or to state any unresolved questions. This will reduce the feeling of (academic) impotency and help you to become a more effective lecturer.

2.1.1 Lecture

What it is:
- A lecture involves the teacher talking to the students about the subject.

When is it used:
- Either in the classroom or workshop to pass information to the class in a cost-effective manner (i.e. to a group of students in a short time by one person).

Example:
- Explaining a concept to a group of learners.

Guidelines:

  (a) Preparation:
- Extract key points from the topic;
- Prepare visual aids (OHP transparencies, handouts, chalkboard) to supplement the verbal material.
- Consider how to introduce and conclude.

  (b) Presentation:
- Avoid monotone voice and be loud enough for the room.
- Emphasise (by repetition, visual aids etc.) key points.
- Assist learners in their note taking.
- Avoid words that learners will not understand and be sure to define technical words.
- Include an introduction and a summary.

Advantages:
- A teacher can reach a large number of students.
- Conveys a large amount of material in short time.
- Teacher has complete control (unless listeners rebel!).

Disadvantages:	• Little opportunity to question teacher.
	• Little or even no feedback regarding the effectiveness of the learning.
	• Need for a large, comfortable perhaps purpose built room.
	• Need to be a communication expert.
	• Large group could be off putting to teacher.
	• Students are often passive.
	• Little use of teaching skills.
Summary:	• Lecturing skills are an essential part of your teaching repertoire. The lecture is often completed without the preparation needed to ensure success. It must have a beginning, middle and end, (introduction, development and conclusion) and must be supported by other strategies in order to both consolidate and assess the learning which has taken place.

An interesting description of a lecture is: "You tell them what you are going to tell them, you tell them, and you tell them what you have told them." In other words, the lecture has an introduction to the content, the detail is then presented, and finally there is a summary of the lecture. The word lecture comes from the Latin word '*letcare*' meaning to read aloud.

The period of concentration of students is not very long. Some authors tell us that ten minutes is the maximum amount of time that an individual can concentrate. To assist this, the development of a lecture should be carefully structured. For instance, if your topic is 'fishing' you might structure it as shown in Figure 3.6. Such an organisational breakdown into sub-topics allows breaks to be made so that the topic is divided into manageable 'chunks' of information which will cope with different concentration spans. The sub-topics need to be sequenced in such a way that students can follow the flow of information.

Making a case for active learning is especially relevant for lecturing. The case for having an incomplete handout, encouraging students to make their own notes, or asking questions even when the group is large, is easily made.

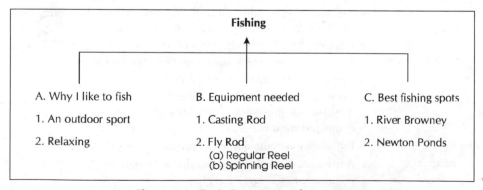

Figure 3.6 *Topic Organisation for a Lecture*

Other techniques that can be associated with the lecture so that you maintain attention include (a) showing enthusiasm for the topic; (b) ensuring vocal inflection, gesturing and maintaining eye contact; and (c) adding a touch of humour (but not too much).

2.1.2 Demonstration

What it is:
- The technique is usually associated with demonstrating a practical skill. It often introduces the skill; its point and importance. The skill is demonstrated after which the students practice the skill.

When is it used:
- In the practical situation to introduce a new skill to a group of students to rectify faults with individuals.

Example:
- Giving an injection; changing a car wheel; wallpapering.

Guidelines:

(a) Preparation:
- Identify key points.
- Relate theoretical underpinning to key points.
- Rehearse to ensure all equipment is working and that you can use it.
- Ensure all students can see even small equipment and processes.
- Time your demonstration. If it is more than, say 10 minutes, consider sub-dividing into a series of demonstrations.
- Consider how to make the students active (e.g. helping, completing a handout, answering questions, predicting the next step, noting results).
- Consider how to emphasise safe working practices.

(b) Presentation:
- Clear introduction.
- Name of tools/equipment.
- Check entry behaviour.
- Do not show how not to complete the skill.
- Stress key points and show links between them.
- Monitor safety aspects.
- Check learner understanding.

Advantages:
- When performed well, the demonstration can be highly motivating – better than a verbal description.
- Theory and practice can be linked.
- Pace of demonstration can be varied.
- Students usually enjoy actively doing things.
- Expert demonstrations may be available via the video.
- Key points can be stressed and repeated.
- Three dimensional, even sounds and smells.
- Students see the sequence and build-up.
- May allow students to ask questions.

Disadvantages:
- A poor demonstration can be frustrating for the students.
- Can be too fast or too slow for the learners.
- No permanent record.
- May be difficult to see.
- May be too long leading to loss of concentration.
- Students may learn bad habits/techniques.
- Can be expensive in terms of material costs.
- Teacher needs to rehearse.
- Students can be passive.

Summary: • The first stage in learners acquiring a skill. It must be well
prepared, key points identified, learners involved and must
be followed by individual learner practice and feedback.

A skilled demonstration is characterised by its speed and dexterity. Some skills are difficult for you to slow down because when you do, you lose the 'flow' (the links in the chain of stimulus-response relationships). A golf swing, slicing an onion, and plastering a wall are all difficult to slow down.

In order to overcome this problem of speed a useful sequence to follow is:

(i)   Complete the demonstration at normal speed without commentary.

(ii)   Repeat the demonstration with commentary stressing the key points, asking students questions (what comes next? can you hold this? will you fill that?).

(iii) Ask a student to repeat the demonstration with all of the students watching.

(iv)   Ask another student to repeat the demonstration with a third one giving a commentary.

Interestingly, recent research (Bransford 2000) illustrates that great advantages can accrue when an 'expert' teaches a specific skill to students, because we often don't stop to analyse our own behaviour or skills unless we have to teach them. This can often cause us to improve our own subject-related skills directly as a result of teaching them.

You do not need to complete all of the above stages of course but they are possibilities. Remember that you are helping the students to *verbalise* (to remember in their own minds) the stages or steps involved in the skill. And, as you will remember, repetition is helpful in helping students to remember.

Points (iii) and (iv) above are useful because, when you are not directly involved in demonstrating the skill, you can concentrate more upon the teaching aspects: you can more easily identify the key points and tell students to expect them, to watch out for them, or ask them what they are, without having to stop the student who is completing the demonstration.

Also getting students to demonstrate is useful for highlighting the problems that exist in the completion of the skill. You should *not,* in your demonstration, show students the wrong way of doing things. They may remember only the wrong way and think that it is the correct one. However, when a student is completing the demonstration with the others watching, it is likely to be done incorrectly, and you can immediately point out any mistakes.

The above strategy has linked the method to the initial stages of skill learning but it can also be used for the teaching of concepts. If you are able to visually demonstrate the concept, then all of the above benefits of the strategy can be maintained. For instance the teaching and learning of Pythagoras Theorem can be better achieved by a demonstration showing that, on a right angled triangle, the hypotenuse is visually an equal area to the sum of the squares on the other two sides. Thus the principle can be conceptualised.

Figure 3.7 shows the relative merits of handouts when used with demonstrations. As you can see, the limitations of one approach may be balanced by the advantages of the other.

Demonstration	Handout
Advantages Can be highly motivating; Students can see development/progress; Students can be supervised and errors prevented; Students can ask questions; Three dimensional; Students use same tools/equipment as the teacher.	**Advantages** Permanent record; Words and diagrams; Can be trial tested and hence error free; Can be designed by an expert; Accessible to teacher and student; Inexpensive; Work at own pace; Step by step.
Limitations No permanent record; Pace suits teacher and not individual students; All students may not be able to see easily; Students may not understand; Students must practise; Some skills (e.g. chopping an onion) cannot be slowed down; Students can be passive for too long; Costly in terms of teacher time, materials, room. etc.	**Limitations** Needs to be clear and unambiguous; Cannot see real product/tools; No supervision; No-one to ask; Vocabulary may not be suitable; Must be error-free; Two dimensional.

Figure 3.7 *Comparison Between Demonstrations and Handouts*

2.1.3 Team teaching

What is it:	• Two or more teachers co-operating in the planning, presentation, assessment and evaluation of a course, but mainly in the presentation.
When is it used:	• Where there are large groups of students and the teachers can take responsibility for parts of the course or where special expertise is needed.
Examples:	• Communications in science. • Nurse teacher training.
Guidelines:	• The course team need to prepare very carefully to avoid duplication of topics and to ensure contiguity. Tutorial or seminar support may be needed.
Advantages:	• Reduces preparation time for each teacher. • Teachers work to their strengths. • Teamwork can produce a better course. • Curriculum development enhanced.
Disadvantages:	• Communication breakdown. • Talking to large numbers of students can be daunting. • Large teaching room(s) needed. • Can be seen by the students as disjointed. • Variation in teaching quality.
Summary:	• A well co-ordinated team teaching approach can lead to a high quality course.

2.1.4 **Discussion**

What it is:	• The students are actively involved in talking to each other about an issue of mutual concern. Your job is to manage the situation so that learning takes place.
When is it used:	• Discussion is often used to help solve problems, or to explore issues and take decisions. It is a useful way of exploring attitudes and to help change unhelpful or antisocial attitudes.
Examples:	• Treatment of Young Offenders; preventative medicine.
Guidelines:	• Discussion must be carefully planned. A clear intention or objective is needed and ground rules need to be established. Timing is a crucial issue as is the need to reduce your own involvement whilst trying to ensure all can participate. The topic should be easily understood by all students. Ensure that the room layout is conducive to a discussion.
(a) Preparation:	• Must be relevant to an objective.
	• Do learners need to research the topic?
	• Consider size of group and room layout so that all participate (i.e. small groups and intimate areas).
	• Consider if a semi-structured handout will assist coverage of topic.
(b) Presentation:	• Tell students how long they have for discussion.
	• Tell the students how the results are to be fed back.
	• Your role is (a) to provide information and not answers; (b) to monitor the discussion: and (c) to try to ensure that all participate.
	• Assist learners to summarise the main points as a conclusion, and finally you must summarise the main issues.
Advantages:	• Can be used following a video or lecture in order to reinforce the learning.
	• Very useful for changing attitudes.
	• Involves the students – and quiet members of the group can emerge as leaders.
	• Can be very creative.
	• Needs a summary.
	• Can encourage students to become more articulate.
	• Students can criticise each other's views and not the person.
	• Broadens views.
	• Does not feel like hard work.
	• Provides interesting feedback on students knowledge of the topic and their social skills.
	• Encourages 'deep' learning.
Disadvantages:	• Students and teachers need to develop discussion skills.
	• Can be risky.
	• May take a relatively long time.
	• You must not dominate.
	• Have something else prepared in case discussion is ineffective.

- May be difficult to keep to the point.
- May be noisy.
- Can degenerate into an informal chat.

Summary:
- High learner participation but you need to develop the necessary management skills.
- Remember to arrange the furniture in the room so that the communication in the discussion is enhanced.

The seating plan is very important for discussion. Figure 3.8 shows an ideal situation where desks have been removed and students are seated so they can both see and hear each other. The 'network' has been decentralised so that there is no focal point – the students are seated in a circle.

If there is a focal point (for example, someone sitting in the middle) some students are likely to look to this person for a lead and will not participate as an 'equal partner'. If it is not possible to remove the desks, then they should be arranged in a square or circle so that all of the students can see and hear each other and, again, there should be no focal point. However, desks can provide a barrier behind which the more introvert students might hide.

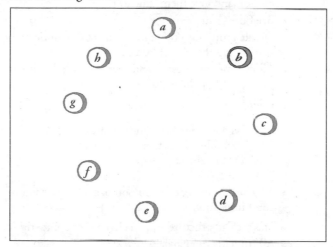

Figure 3.8 *Decentralised Student Seating for a Discussion*

Often the results of the discussion will need to be fed back to either the whole group or to you as teacher. This needs to be made clear at the start and it is useful to let students decide who is to do this. However, it is useful that they make this decision at the start of the discussion period so that the chosen individual can make the necessary notes and preparation (or ensure that another student does it for them).

2.1.5 Debate

What it is:
- A debate is very similar to a discussion but tends to have more rules regarding procedure.

When is it used:
- Where there is no right answer and where both sides of the argument would benefit from exploration. To enhance formal communication skills in the presentation of an argument.

Examples:
- The use of nuclear power to generate electricity; bring back corporal punishment; the National Lottery.

Guidelines:
(a) Preparation:
- Nominate/elect a chair from the students to ensure rules are followed in an impartial manner.
- Select a topic which will stimulate debate and allow argument for and against.
- Select a main speaker for the motion and one against the motion and give them time to prepare.
- Brief the chair.

(b) Presentation:
- Divide group into those in favour of the motion, those against and those uncommitted.
- Allow time for research and preparation of arguments.
- Arrange debate in steps:
  (a) Proposer for.
  (b) Proposer against.
  (c) Seconder for (to argue against (b)).
  (d) Seconder against (to argue against (a)).
  (e) Open debate;
  (f) Vote.
- Teacher summary of main points and assessment of communication skills.

Advantages:
- Has a clear structure and an element of competition;
- All students can participate.
- Students can take the leading roles.
- Good for contentious issues.
- Students can enhance their presentation skills.
- Increases teamwork.
- Both sides of the argument are exposed.
- Students can enjoy the process.

Disadvantages:
- Students may find the rules and procedures difficult to understand.
- A minority of the students may do most of the work.
- Students must prepare thoroughly which may take some time.

Summary:
- Student centred, structured technique for learning communication skills and extracting key points of a topic.

2.1.6 Question and answer

What it is:
- Posing a series of questions to students in order to promote thinking and understanding.

When is it used:
- It is an informal assessment technique which is used with groups of up to 30 students. It is a way of ascertaining the existing level of learning or entry behaviour in the introduction to a lesson and/or, assessing the learning that has taken place at the end of a lesson (or during it).

Example:
- Building concept attainment (e.g. a tourist).

Guidelines:
- Questions need to be carefully considered so that the learners supply their knowledge and do not simply answer yes or no.
- Ask simple questions first and then move to more complex ones.
- Spread the questions so that all learners respond.
- Ask the questions, allow thinking time and then ask students to respond. This may involve setting rules to avoid chorus answers.
- Praise a correct response, praise the correct part of a partially correct response and explore the reason for an incorrect response. Always accept the students' answers to ensure future participation.

Advantages:
- Students are involved and feel they are contributing to learning.
- Misconceptions may be identified at an early stage.
- Can build from simple to complex.
- Key questions can be pre-planned.
- Feedback on quality of learning is gained.
- Maintains concentration.
- Can stimulate students.
- Gives feedback on quality of teaching.

Disadvantages:
- You need to be able to respond quickly to the students answers.
- Careful planning may be needed.
- May use too many closed questions.
- A minority of students may participate.

Summary:
- You need to develop this useful skill. Question and answer may last a few minutes or be developed into a longer session. The feedback showing misconceptions is very valuable. Encourage all answers and build upon wrong or partially correct answers.

When discussing lesson planning in Chapter 1 it was suggested that 'key questions' should not only be planned but be stated as part of the teacher activity in the body of the plan. This means that you need to plan the questions related to the level of the objectives. Figure 3.9 gives an indication of questions at the different levels. Each level in the Cognitive Domain has been included but only up to 'valuing' in the Affective Domain. You might want to combine the higher three levels in the cognitive domain into 'invention'. The reason that the higher levels in the affective domain have not been covered is that post-16 education and training tends not to go higher in this domain.

You will see that, not only do the levels of question get harder to answer the higher they go up the domain, but the length of the responses is also likely to increase. Those questions that warrant a one word answer are termed 'closed' questions: those that require a sentence or more to answer are 'open' questions.

Domain	Level	Example Question
Cognitive	Knowledge	What city is the capital of Algeria?
	Comprehension	Explain, in your own words, the meaning of pollution.
	Application	Now that you have studied energy, if you leave a refrigerator door open and switched on in a sealed room, will the temperature rise or fall?
	Analysis	Why do you think that Democrats after the Gulf War, said that the Republicans were a party of warmongers?
	Synthesis	Now that you have studied static electricity, how could you stop getting a 'shock' when you slide over the plastic seat covers of a car?
	Evaluation	Describe the fallacies in reasoning in the statement "All cats are mammals. All dogs are mammals. Thus, all cats are dogs".
Affective	Receiving	How interesting was your visit to the museum?
	Responding	How did you feel after reading "Catcher in the Rye"?
	Valuing	What actions if any, would you take with a friend who wrote a 'Letter to the Editor' of a local newspaper?

Figure 3.9 *Questions at Different Levels in Different Domains*

It is useful to have both types in a lesson but it is often the case that closed questions will elicit a 'chorus' response as many will know the answer and want to show that they know.

When you use the question and answer technique, you will want as many of the class to respond as possible and you will want them to answer both low and high level questions. The type of questions that you ask are not only classified into levels but also into whether you *'nominate'* a student to answer or whether the question is *'un-nominated'* (any student in the class can answer). Consider the response pattern to teacher questions shown in Figure 3.10 which gives an overview of a question and answer session with 9 students siting in a semi-circle. From this you can see that the teacher has asked equal numbers of nominated and un-nominated questions. This is generally useful in that, if you want all of the students to respond, you can nominate individuals to get them to think, involve them in the session, and so on. You will also see that the total of teacher initiated interactions is 36 and the total student initiated interactions (them making comments and asking questions) is 16. Thus a third of the interactions are student initiated which is a good proportion: it is generally useful to get students to talk to you as well as you talking to them. Often this is very difficult and you may find in your classes a very small proportion of the interactions are student initiated.

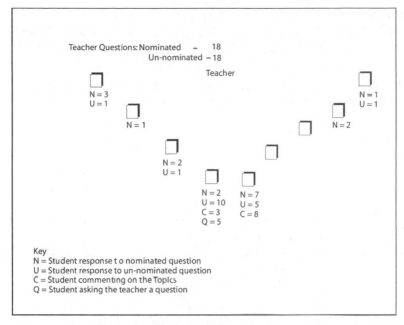

Figure 3.10   *Response Patterns to a Class Question and Answer Period*

However, when you look at the positions of the responses around the class, you will see that a total of 40 of the 52 interactions (77%) were from two members (22%) of the class: a very uneven distribution. Also, three members of the class (33%) did not interact at all or only interacted once. Thus 33% of the class were involved in only 2% of the interactions. The questions that need to be answered associated with this type of analysis include:

(a)   Did it matter that some students did not respond or make any contribution at all?

(b)   If it does matter, what might be done to ensure that they participate?

(c)   Does it matter that 77% of the interactions came from 22% of the group?

(d)   If it does matter, what might be done to make them respond less?

(e)   Does seating have any influence on the response pattern?

(f)   What response pattern would be ideal?

The answer to question (a) depends upon the respective abilities of the students who did not respond. If they are bright students in your subject and they are not introvert, then perhaps it does not matter that they do not answer. They might not like question and answer and learn in spite of the use of this technique. If, on the other hand they are not concentrating and/or do not do very well in your subject, then a series of nominated questions to them will be an advantage. If they are introvert, then nominated questions will have to be handled carefully – you will need to make sure that they are easy questions that they should be able to answer and make sure that you give praise when they respond.

The two who answered so many questions obviously need consideration and action: they have over-dominated the session. They should not be asked nominated questions and you might have a quiet word with them to ask them to let others participate more. Perhaps the seating has an effect: they are sitting directly opposite the teacher and together. Perhaps dividing them and sitting them at the edge of the vision of the teacher so that not so much eye contact is maintained could be useful.

2.1.7 Video

What it is:
- A method of bringing realism into the classroom or workshop.

When is it used:
- Can be linked to a range of other teaching strategies as a means of providing variety and realism.

Examples:
- Loading nuclear fuel rods; a surgical operation.

Guidelines:
  (a) Preparation:
- Preview video and identify main points. Pre-select appropriate scenes if entire programme is too long.
- Plan an associated activity for the student to be completed during or after viewing.
- Book necessary equipment (video, tape, room etc.).
- Know how to operate the equipment.

  (b) Presentation:
- Introduce the video and the activity and alert students to the key points.
- After viewing assess the learning.
- Stop for questions or replay any important points.

Advantages:
- Can bring a well known expert into the classroom.
- Students can see dangerous or one-off situations.
- A permanent record.
- Can provoke thought used as a trigger.
- Relatively cheap and very convenient.
- Can be taken home by (some) students.
- Helps the students to visualise.
- Freeze-frame and slow-motion available.
- Movement, colour, sound.
- Can choose to view small extracts.
- Modern medium which is popular.
- Video tapes may be hired or borrowed.
- An alternative to 'teacher-talk'.

Disadvantages
- May disrupt class.
- Class handed over to 'another'.
- May be perceived as merely entertainment.
- Can induce sleep.
- Can be seen as an easy option for the teacher.
- Technical problems.
- Availability of resources.
- Video from an 'authoritative' source may be biased and bias the students.

Summary:
- Video used with care can be a stimulating part of a lesson.

Used properly, the video can be an excellent addition to the classroom or workshop teaching of a large group of students. However, there is a danger when using a video to pass the responsibility for the teaching entirely over to the programme: to the voice on the TV and the picture on the screen. The 'good' use of a video, like so many other teaching strategies, must ensure that the students are *active*.

We have suggested that you preview the video and highlight the main points: the key features that it exhibits. Either before or after the showing of each main point, you can stop the recorder, emphasise the point, make a note of it on the chalkboard and ask students to note it before going on with the viewing.

You can also prepare an incomplete handout for the students which invites them to take notes under the main headings as they are viewing. If you consider that they have insufficient time to make the necessary notes you can again stop the recorder for the activity to take place. Another advantage of such a handout is that your students also have a permanent record of what they have watched.

2.2 Small group strategies

Just as large group strategies are appropriate for certain educational purposes, there are times when you should use strategies that are appropriate to small groups. Students are likely to work in small groups in industry and commerce and, in consequence, we have a moral obligation to use such approaches in our controlled environments.

Industry and commerce are continually telling us of the importance of 'key' skills to be associated with our subject specialism skills and one of these relates to the ability to work 'as an effective group member'. This, generally, means the ability to work in small groups; to be an effective leader as well as an effective follower; to learn to cope with other people's idiosyncrasies; to be able to present a logical argument and analyse others' arguments; to co-operate with others and adopt a variety of roles when working co-operatively.

As educators have become dissatisfied with the conventional classroom, its basic assumptions, and its effectiveness, so the strategies associated with small group work have gained momentum. Such strategies include seminar, role play, case study, a simulation. These often employ different aspects of small group discussion where students are able to think things through for themselves without having the direct control of the teacher. Of course, this means that you automatically lose some of your control over what is being said and what is being done. You become more a manager of the situation as opposed to the purveyor of information. You need to set up the situation and take more of a 'back seat' and let the students proceed more at their own pace. This means a very different perspective for you and one that some teachers find, at least initially, very difficult to cope with. You become a more 'humanist' teacher with the concentration upon the need of the student as well as the need of the subject. Students learn from each other.

Because of the different approaches that you have to adopt with a smaller group, the range of objectives that you can achieve is greater. The higher level cognitive and affective domain objectives are more applicable to these methods. It has been argued that in some subjects the major concepts, principles, and methods are so well established that no competent person raises any doubt about them. At the introductory levels in such subjects like science, engineering and mathematics there is much agreement about what is important. In other subjects there is not such a consensus. In the social sciences – in history and economics, political science, psychology, literature, music and art, we do not agree nearly so readily about what is important, good, true, valid or significant. Consequently, in these low consensus subjects, discussion methods may be necessary. Similarly, the discussion method may also be better suited to the changing of attitudes and behaviour. During the discussion, students make public decisions committing themselves to a given course of action.

As with all forms of teaching, you need to be well prepared. Arranging the learning environment to suit small groupwork is important. Often just simply moving the chairs to form circles is sufficient.

You may want to identify the small groups in order to engineer some facet of the learning e.g. a good gender mix, or age mix. At other times, you may be content to give the students a free choice. Experience shows that a group size of four is ideal. This allows all to participate and reduces the chance of 'passengers'.

The students need to be clear about the activity and be clear about what they are learning. Giving written specification of the task, perhaps OHP, flipchart or hand-out, helps students to keep to the point. It is important to negotiate some ground rules. This may include time for task, mode of reporting outcomes, acceptable behaviour and so on.

A very important role for you when the students are busy is to monitor progress after ensuring that all of the groups are clear about the task. Give them a few minutes to discuss the task and to get started. Then join each group in turn. Sitting at the same level, rather than standing over them, encourages discussion to continue. Listen to the students. If they are progressing well, give some encouragement and positive feedback. If the students are having problems make a few suggestions and before the reporting-back stage, ensure all groups have something good to contribute even if it is really your own thoughts. Remind students about the time: when to start summarising: when to start writing and so on.

One of the problems with small group work is the time taken to feedback the outcomes. It is important to value the outcomes and to emphasise the key points. You have set time limits when you have lots of small groups or flipchart presentations can be typed, photocopied and distributed to all at a later date.

Do not destroy the feedback sheets when the students are in the room. Take the sheets away with you and, if they are not needed, put them in the waste bin in your own room! Some students resent seeing the results of their labour being destroyed and rightly so.

The final part of your role is to link the work done to the learning objectives. This demonstrates to the students that their work has been fruitful and you were not opting-out of 'proper teaching'.

Your role, when dealing with groups, is demanding and adaptability, flexibility and responsiveness are key themes. In order for the students to gain the maximum benefit from the group activity and interaction, you could consider the following:

> Ensure students understand the objectives of the task and have a record of them.
>
> Answer questions regarding the purpose, procedures and limitations.
>
> Check progress and summarise progress made.
>
> Monitor timekeeping.
>
> Encourage contributions/diplomatically restrain the dominant.
>
> Reward contributions.
>
> Resolve internal conflicts.
>
> Keep the groups 'on track'.
>
> Defuse emotional aspects.
>
> Delegate as many tasks to the groups themselves as possible so that, over a period of time, your role is minimised.
>
> See that the group has all that it needs – e.g. pens, paper, flipchart, OHTs, clear (written) guidelines.

2.2.1 Seminar

What it is:	• A student researches a topic, presents the findings to other students and leads the ensuing discussion.
When is it used:	• Widely used with mature students to explore specified topics.
Examples:	• How to deal with problem students; the causes of World War II.
Guidelines:	• A student should have time to consider relevant readings, view videos, listen to lectures etc. before the seminar. Some questions may be posed in advance. At the seminar, each student should be encouraged to share their views so that the range of issues can be explored.
	• Students should be encouraged to use OHP, flipcharts, etc. You need to monitor the proceedings and avoid cross-talking, dominant individuals and unrelated discussion.
Advantages:	• Students involved in the preparation.
	• Students know what is to be discussed and that they will have the opportunity to participate.
	• Opportunity to ask questions of their peers and teachers.
	• Seminars are student led.
	• Ideal for very specialised topics.
	• Responsibility given to students.
	• Builds confidence.
	• Can link theory and practice.
Disadvantages:	• Students may be reluctant to participate at first.
	• Need to summarise the main issues at the end of the seminar.
	• Can be dull.
	• Students may not respect their peers.
	• May be time consuming.
	• Student may be reluctant to criticise their peers.
	• May be difficult to assess.
Summary:	• A different way for learning and, if the group is small, then opportunities easiest for effective interaction.

The aims of the seminar method include the key skills of 'the ability to find information' and 'the ability to present an argument'. Often discussions take place in class without students having all of the facts and understanding the topic. The advantages of the seminar are that students are involved themselves in finding the information prior to giving a short input, and they then discuss its implications and sustain an argument through the answering of questions on it from their colleagues.

Thus, the phases in a seminar are:

(i)   Finding information.

(ii)   Presenting the information to their colleagues.

(iii)   Answering questions from colleagues.

The assessment of the work, therefore, can give feedback on the subject matter; the ability to find information; the ability to present the information, and the ability to answer questions from their fellow students.

2.2.2 Workshop

What it is:
- An opportunity to develop practical skills in a simulated situation and link the theory with practice.

When is it used:
- In the development of skills.

Examples:
- Using a CNC lathe; making a dovetail joint.

Guidelines:

(a) Preparation:
- Ensure all equipment available and ready.
- Consider how to introduce and conclude each session.
- Prepare an assessment schedule related to key points.
- Prepare worksheet to indicate task schedule and associated assessment points.

(b) Presentation:
- Often starts with a demonstration.
- Manage individuals working at their own pace (question, feedback, rectify faults).
- Overtly link theory with the practical aspects.
- Monitor safety aspects.
- Allow time for a conclusion so that students can see/critically analyse others' work/progress.

Advantages:
- Can take place before or after theoretical aspects.
- Can be a good basis for problem solving.
- Teacher can talk with the learners on a one-to-one basis.
- Reinforces learning in a realistic and meaningful way.
- Students work at own pace.
- Students can work using a variety of skills.
- Students can work in groups.
- A non-threatening environment.

Disadvantages:
- Can be seen as tedious or boring.
- Expensive in terms of time, equipment and rooms.
- Implications for Health and Safety.
- Teachers may lose control of learning.

Summary:
- A valuable, if not essential part of many courses. Usually enjoyable for the students as it often appears to be real and exciting.

2.2.3 Gaming/quiz

What it is:	• Games are a learning situation with an element of competition and/or co-operation.
When is it used:	• Can stimulate and involve learners when they interact with other students and/or the game.
Examples:	• Team building; effects of an oil spillage, healthy diet.
Guidelines:	
(a) Preparation:	• Try out and test game prior to use with students.
	• Ensure rules are clear and understood by students.
(b) Presentation:	• Introduce the game in its learning context.
	• Monitor programme and assist only when essential.
	• Summarise and consolidate the learning outcomes.
Advantages:	• Can be fun.
	• Compete against a machine or situation rather than another student.
	• Immediate feedback.
	• Teacher has time to observe students.
Disadvantages:	• May have to make your own game.
	• Game may not work.
	• Immediate feedback.
	• May not be taken seriously.
	• Be difficult to control.
Summary:	• Can be a different type of learning which the students generally enjoy.

The Quiz is a particular form of gaming. Teams or individuals may participate and an element of competition may be introduced. It can be an interesting way of obtaining feedback on the quality of learning and motivating students to revise and study their notes.

2.2.4 Brainstorming

What it is:	• A problem solving technique used to generate a number of ideas (solutions) in a short time e.g. 5 to 15 minutes.
When is it used:	• When a problem, real or manufactured, exists, the students are invited to generate possible solutions. Often used in management courses or with problem solving.
Example 1:	• Warm-up – uses of a paper clip.
Example 2:	• Problem – how to prevent strikes.
Guidelines:	• The 'problem' should be stated as 'in how many ways can we .....'. Restatements can be suggested by students to ensure that they understand the problem. The students may then be 'warmed up' using a trial brainstorm. The students are encouraged to shout out key words – these are all written down without criticism or censure. If the participants dry up, there can be an enforced two minutes silence. Then the brainstorm continues. The key words are then categorised and discussed. Possible solutions are then identified.

Advantages:	• Unusual solutions may be identified.

Advantages:
- Unusual solutions may be identified.
- All can participate.
- Needs few resources.
- Seems to be part of the creative process.
- Uses students experiences.
- Encourages teamwork.
- No-one looks foolish.

Disadvantages:
- Group needs to learn and obey rules.
- Warm-up sessions may be needed.
- Can be demanding and can only be used for short periods.
- Some students can opt out.

Summary:
- A challenging and active learning situation.

2.2.5 Buzz groups

What it is:
- A relatively large group of students are divided into smaller groups of about 4 to 6, usually to discuss a problem/situation for a short time, say 5 minutes. The buzz of the several simultaneous discussions gives the strategy its name.

When is it used:
- With large groups where you want the students to interact with each other.

Example:
- Merits of an integrated transport system.

Guidelines:
- Make sure the groups know what they have to discuss and how long they have. Nominate a leader or tell each group to appoint one. State the manner of feedback e.g. oral from the leader, OHT, flipchart etc.

Advantages:
- Introduces student activity into what could be perceived as a teacher-centred situation.
- Gives a change of activity and allows the students to express themselves.
- Can be used in a large, formal lecture theatre.
- Gives feedback on the learning.
- Gives teacher a break.
- Can be used to recap.
- Can be a safety valve.
- Helps problem-solving.
- Develops teamwork.

Disadvantages:
- Sometimes can be difficult to nominate groups.
- Feedback could take some time (try a maximum of 60 second feedback from each group).

Summary:
- Small groups discussing giving a 'buzz' of conversation.

2.2.6   Field trip

What it is:	• Usually the students are taken out of their normal learning situation to a 'real-life' situation.
When is it used:	• Where realism is essential, or very helpful, in reinforcing the learning.
Examples:	• Study of rock formation; a food processing plant.

Guidelines:

(a) Preparation:
- Plan links with the theory/learning intention.
- Consider safety and make allowances for delays.
- Prepare handouts and activities.
- Plan for inclement weather.
- Consider insurance and parent/employer permission.
- Brief students before the visit.
- Plan follow up activities.
- Follow your organisations guidelines.

(b) Presentation:
- Ensure adequate supervision at all times.
- 'Visit' students, use question and answer.

Advantages:
- Students can see the real situation.
- Realistic and lifelike.
- Motivating.
- Clear links between learning and visit.

Disadvantages:
- Time consuming for planning and visit.
- May be costly.
- Legal/safety problems.
- Supervision of students on visit.
- Heavy responsibility.

Summary:
- Can be a very valuable and rewarding experience but may turnout to be a nightmare.

2.2.7   Role play

What it is:
- Students acting a part or a role in events before a situation, during the situation and after the situation.

When is it used:
- Helping the students to feel the influences and pressures in their role. It is suggested that role play is particularly effective with attitudinal issues.

Examples:
- Conflict in the workplace e.g. receptionist and 'difficult' customer.
- Conflict within the team in the workplace.
- Situation where people are disadvantaged due to race, gender, disability etc.

Guidelines:

(a) Preparation:
- Have role cards for participants.
- Plan activities for those students not in role, i.e. observers for feedback; NB. players should not see each others' role-play cards.
- Set up physical environment to enhance realism.

(b) Presentation:
- Introduce the role play and indicate its function in the learning, i.e. why you are doing it.
- Monitor the role play and only step in if things go badly wrong, i.e. a student is going to be embarrassed.
- Debrief the students so that they are no longer 'in role'.
- Ensure that the role play is analysed and related to the intended learning outcome.

Advantages:
- A good way to address attitudinal issues.
- High degree of student participation.
- Brings learning to life.
- Realistic.
- Emotions can be felt.
- Students can teach their peers about their feelings in their role rather than the teacher telling them.
- Usually a safe environment.

Disadvantages:
- Can be threatening – especially for the shy participants.
- Needs careful preparation.
- Needs careful managing.
- Essential to debrief the students.
- Can take some time.
- May be difficult to manage.
- Some students hate role play.

Summary:
- Once written and tested, the role plays can be used many times with different classes. High student involvement with the difficult area of attitudinal change.

2.2.8 Ice breaker

What it is:
- A technique used to get the student to feel part of the group and part of the learning process.

When is it used:
- Often used with the first meeting of a group or when a student or students join an established group.

Examples:

Example 1:
- Ask the group to go into pairs; one person interviews the other and asks their name, their interests etc. (Nothing too personal). The roles are then reversed. The students then introduce each other to the whole group.

Example 2:
- Each student writes their first name on the board and tells as much as they know about it e.g. its origin, its meaning, how they feel about their name, famous people with the same name.

Example 3:
- Prepare a brief questionnaire which asks, what qualities do you bring to the group? What are you looking forward to? What are your concerns? Display the results and ask the students to look at the responses of the others in the group. N.B. the questionnaires need to be anonymous.

Guidelines:	• The balance between helping a group to get to know each other and causing embarrassment is a delicate one. Care needs to be exercised and judgment made so that the student is allowed to develop but is not threatened.
Advantages:	• Can help discussion and small group work to achieve maximum effectiveness very quickly.
	• Students feel part of a group.
	• Builds trust.
	• No long silences.
	• Students pose more questions to the teacher earlier in the course.
	• Relieves tension.
	• Can be fun.
Disadvantages:	• Can take a long time.
	• May not be perceived as being 'useful'.
	• Some students may hate it.
	• Can be over-used.
Summary:	• Used with care and in a non-threatening way, icebreakers may help establish a group identity in an hour rather than weeks or months.

2.2.9 Simulation

What it is:	• The simulation of a real or a possible situation.
When is it used:	• In situations where it is not possible or desirable to undertake learning in the actual conditions.
Examples:	
Example 1:	• Computer simulation of the economy.
Example 2:	• Flight simulator.
Example 3:	• Managers trying to see own skills in prioritising and time management in a simulated situation.
Example 4:	• Job interview.
Example 5:	• Handling customer complaint.
Example 6:	• Running a reception desk.
Guidelines:	• The simulation needs to be made as realistic as possible. Supervision of all students is essential at all times in order to avoid reinforcement of errors.
Advantages:	• Can be used where the real situation is dangerous, costly, 'difficult' or too time consuming.
	• Can be repeated until desired level of learning is achieved.
	• Can be stopped at any stage in order to inject concepts, principles etc.
	• Students are active and take responsibility for their own learning.
	• Can be a good introduction to the real thing.

Disadvantages:	• Can be time consuming to set up.
	• May be difficult to supervise all students all of the time.
Summary:	• May be the only way to learn in some situations, with the students being able to stop and ask questions.

2.2.10 Case study

What it is:	• It is an examination of a real or simulated problem which is structured so that learning can take place or be reinforced.
When is it used:	• Often used on management and business study courses to analyse what went wrong in a given situation and to consider how failure could be avoided. It tends to be used in situations where rules or laws cannot be applied or where there is some ambiguity.
Examples:	• Why a particular company collapsed.
Guidelines:	• What happened to the British Motor Cycle Industry.
	• The situation needs to be as realistic and as accurate as possible. As much information as possible needs to be given and often superfluous information is given as in real life.
Advantages:	• Can be an individual or group activity.
	• Can be in class or at home.
	• Real, including current, situations can be studied.
Disadvantages:	• The case study needs to have clear learning intentions.
	• The aftermath of the study needs to reinforce learning.
	• Needs to be well structured.
	• May seem unreal.
	• A good deal of preparation may be needed.
Summary:	• Takes a good deal of preparation but can bring realism into the learning situation..
	• Problem based learning.
	• Learning logs and diaries.

2.3   Individual teaching strategies

Just as some strategies are appropriate to large and small groups, there are times when you need to provide opportunities and activities for students to work on their own. What are these? When is a student best left alone with an assignment, a set of printed materials, a set of programmed instruction materials, or a broad mission to be carried out through independent effort and study?

The individualisation of instruction has gained momentum in recent years. Some educators have become dissatisfied with the conventional classroom, its basic assumptions and its effectiveness.

2.3.1 Project/assignment

What it is:	• The students are usually given an individual topic for an in-depth analysis. They often have to work independently, do research and report either in writing or verbally to a group. The project could involve a group of students working together on different facets of the same problem.
When is it used:	• Often used in advanced courses for training in research techniques but now used in a wide variety of situations including practical work.
Examples:	• Research the incidence of AIDS in the UK (individual).
	• Design and build a wind tunnel (individual).
	• Build a house (group project).
Guidelines:	• Students may need help with the study skills involved, particularly when working on their own. The project and assignment has to be realistic in terms of time and cost. Clear learning intentions are needed.
Advantages:	• Realistic situation for students.
	• Can promote independent learning.
	• Student feels in command.
	• Tutorial links may be on a one-to-one basis.
	• Can be highly motivating.
	• Enhances study skills and key skills.
	• Cross curricular.
	• Useful end-product.
	• Some unpredictable aspects.
	• Can develop practical skills.
	• Could involve groupwork.
	• Active learning.
	• Students find their own level.
Disadvantages:	• Supervision can take up a good deal of time.
	• Some students need a lot of managing.
	• Can be costly.
	• Resources, library, need to be available.
Summary:	• A recognised and realistic alternative to traditional examinations.

2.3.2 **Tutorial**

What it is:
- The teacher usually sets the student a task and the tutorial is a means of preparing the student for the task, assisting in the process and then discussing the quality of the learning outcomes. It is essentially a strategy to support and enhance the quality of learning.

When is it used:
- Used in all spheres of learning but may not be called a 'tutorial'.

Examples:
- Supporting work on an assignment.
- Checking progress on the course as a whole.

Guidelines:
- It is important to listen to students to see what they know and what they do not know. Positive outcomes should be planned. Tutorial could be on a one-to-one basis but when students have similar tasks a small group approach can generate valuable discussion and peer support. Students and teacher should prepare for tutorials.

Advantages:
- Individual attention.
- Opportunity to see the quality of learning.
- Valuable support to progress.
- Opportunity to establish a rapport with students and improve communication.
- Confidential aspects can be discussed.
- Individual concerns addressed.

Disadvantages:
- Costly because of one-to-one relationship.
- Student may feel pressurised.
- Finding a suitable room.

Summary:
- In widespread use and students should find tutorials to be of great value.

The following checklist (Figure 3.11) may be a useful framework for both the planning and evaluating of tutorial work:

| Observer: _____ | Person Observed: _____ | Date: _____ |
| Course: _____ | Subject: _____ | No of Students: _____ |

Make comments upon the following aspects

	Aspect	Comment
Methods of Supervising	Quick tutorial start to ensure that all know what to do.	
	Spend time with students who need help rather than those who demand it.	
	No students left waiting for assistance for too long.	
	Quick problem solving to identify and overcome student problems.	
	Mixture of teacher and student initiated visits.	
	Allow time for students to get on with the task(s) themselves.	
	Asking questions to help students solve their problems as opposed to doing things for them.	
	Praising students as appropriate.	
Timing and Number of Visits	Length of specific visits OK (not too long/short).	
	Optimum time between visits (not too long/short).	
	Number of visits and length related to ability.	
	Appropriate time spent with each student.	
Other	Others (please state)	

Figure 3.11   *Checklist for Tutorial Supervision*

2.3.3 One-to-one (coaching)

What is it:	• The teacher and the student working together on a one-to-one basis which may be the full teaching strategy, say on a ward, or part of another teaching strategy, say demonstration followed by individual practice.
When is it used:	• In all spheres of learning.
Examples:	• During lessons, IT, in a workshop as part of a practical.
Guidelines:	• It is tempting to be unplanned for one-to-one work. You need to consider the learning objectives, likely stumbling blocks, what to assess, when to give feedback, how to record progress, encourage reflection.
	• Mentoring.
Advantages:	• Individual attention.
	• Opportunity to observe individual problems.
	• Chance for student to question you about their concerns.
Disadvantages:	• Time consuming.
	• Expensive.
	• May be intimidating for shy students.

In a one-to-one situation the teaching is tailored to meet the individual students needs and abilities and to accommodate the difference between students. The following checklist (Figure 3.12) provides a framework for the leading of a tutorial one-to-one session and for its evaluation.

Observer: ——————   Teacher Observed: ——————   Date: ——————
Course: ——————   Subject: ——————   No of Students: ——————

Make comments upon the following aspects. Other aspects to be added as necessary.

		Aspect	Comment
Preparation		Setting goals for individuals	
		Planning work at correct level (not too easy/difficult)	
		Task sheets provided with attractive layout	
		Relevance of work to individual needs	
		Planned week-to-week progression	
Implementation	**Introduction**	Goals communicated to individual(s)	
		Student(s) motivated appropriately	
		Negotiation with student(s) regarding how to achieve goals	
	Development	Appropriate time spent with student(s)	
		Asking questions as opposed to answering them	
		Ensures that an acceptable result is achieved	
		Variety takes place for the student	
		Progress regularly reviewed	
	Conclusion	Feedback provided for student(s)	
		Records completed kept as appropriate	
		Appropriate goals set for next session	
Feedback		Appropriate praise provided for students(s)	
		Student(s) clear about performance achieved	
		Student(s) knows how to improve	
Others		Other (please state)	

Figure 3.12 *Checklist for a one-to-one Coaching Session*

2.3.4 Open learning/distance learning

What it is:

- This is usually where the teacher and student meet infrequently (if at all). It may include videos, broadcast materials, audio tapes, written material, etc.

When is it used:

- Useful for students who cannot attend due to work commitments, or because of distance to travel.

Examples:

- Open University, Open College, Nursing up-dates.

Guidelines:

- The materials used must be tried and tested, unambiguous and interesting. Carefully consider the existing materials. If planning your own materials, build in as much activity and feedback as possible.

Advantages:

- Helps students who cannot attend a given location at a given time.
- Student proceeds at own pace.
- Large number of students taught simultaneously.
- Convenient.

Disadvantages:

- May be seen as a cheap alternative 'to proper teaching'.
- Can be expensive to design and produce.
- Teacher feedback could be infrequent.
- Can be difficult to maintain student motivation.
- Feeling of isolation and lack of peer group support.
- May be regarded as 'second-best'.
- Students may need access to a computer.
- Poorly designed materials.

Summary:

- The only option in some situations but tutorial support is often needed.

2.3.5 Information Learning Technology (ILT)

What it is:

- Using technology in the teaching and learning environment.

When is it used:

- Can be used in just about any learning situation be it theory, practical, distant, individual or with large groups.

Examples:

- Making handouts, worksheets, assignments etc. Using Word.
- Using PowerPoint presentations.
- Encouraging students to word process assignments.
- Setting tasks for students which involves them using the Web.
- Communicating with students using email.
- Using text messages via mobile telephones.
- The European Computer Driving Licence (ECDL) designed for those who wish to gain a qualification in computing to develop their IT skills. It can be taken in the traditional tutor-led manner or can be studied through flexible learning using computer-based materials through a virtual learning environment (VLE) from material on the web.

- Cert Ed/PGCE using a flexible learning approach where interaction between student and tutor is via email, chat lines and forums.

- Using Microsoft Producer (PowerPoint and Video). PowerPoint is a useful presentation package and, used in conjunction with a lecture, forms a useful learning method. Placed on a VLE, its use loses impact because the teacher is not explaining key points and adding additional material. Microsoft Producer incorporates PowerPoint with video, enabling teachers to create, edit and incorporate rich-media productions.

- Using a VLE outside the classroom.
  The VLE can be used as somewhere to store your learning materials (e.g. notes, schemes of work, practical work, assignments, etc.). Also, you might place a document/article on a VLE and ask students to critically evaluate posting their ideas on the VLE forum.

Guidelines:

- There is a need for good **interactive** materials which take into account your students, the subject, the environment in which the learning will take place and the outcomes to be achieved. The materials can be designed so that they can be used independently. They can be very effective when they are integrated or 'blended' with traditional learning methods. Using email, chat lines, video-conferencing assists the learning process.

Advantages:

- Students can dip into the learning programme at any time or place.
- Enhances interaction between tutor and student(s).
- An expert can deliver a lecture, demonstration or discussion which is broadcast over the web (Web Cast) to a large audience in any location, allowing students to be involved through electronic questions (using email or chat lines).
- Increased motivation by making use of a VLE which provides variety
- Being able to see a demonstration over the web or listen to a guest speaker without having to travel to a distant location.

Disadvantages:

- High quality materials have high set-up costs.
- The creation of good interactive materials is time consuming.
- Keeping student motivation whilst working on their own.
- Reduced interaction between students.
- Careful planning required.
- Knowledge of technology is essential.
- Good technician support essential.

2.4   ILT as an aid to learning for disabled students

Here, disability is defined as:

> '*having physical or mental impairment which has a substantial and long-term adverse effect on the ability to carry-out normal day-to-day activities*'
>
> Special Educational Needs and Disability Act (SENDA), 2001

All students may:

> Have varied listening and learning skills.
>
> Need a flexible learning environment.
>
> Need different time scales to absorb different learning.
>
> Require different teaching approaches.
>
> Have varying levels of motivation.

In the past integrating learners with a disability has, in the past, meant 'fitting-in' with the organisations existing structure. The 2001 Disability Act (op cit), makes it the responsibility of the college to respond to the individuals' learning requirements.

The benefits of ILT for disabled learners are listed below:

> Flexible learning approaches.
>
> Access to materials at their own pace.
>
> Materials available prior to the session.
>
> Electronic materials can easily be adapted (e.g. font size, colour of background, screen reader accessible, etc.
>
> Contact between staff and student can be improved with use of e-mail, discussion forums, etc.
>
> Allows for greater differentiation.

It could be argued that these benefits apply to any student. However, it is even more important that these benefits are available to disabled students in order that they help overcome their own disability. For example, the VLEs and intranets may use fonts, colour and text size which are difficult to read. Now the student may change the magnification of the screen quickly and easily to meet their own requirements.

Examples of good practice in the use of ILT to help disabled learners include:

> Email and chat lines for on-line discussions.
>
> Use of VLEs to allow access to materials at a time convenient to the student.
>
> Structuring of a VLE to break down tasks into small bite-sized chunks which are readily achievable.
>
> Use of digital camera, video, audio to demonstrate and record materials as well as allowing assessment.
>
> On-line assessment screen readers for document reading.

To maximise accessibility for all students you should consider the following:

> Ensure that the learning environment is suitable for all students or potential students.
>
> Identify learning disabilities and implement solutions.

Involve support staff at an early stage.

Use suitable teaching methods that enhance inclusion.

Ensure all students are confident using the hardware and software.

Provide feedback on spelling and grammar to **all** students.

2.5 Conclusion

There are unique differences in the way people learn and we must recognise this and not regard individuals as one group or body of students.

It is important to look for differences which affect learning. Sometimes these differences can be grouped into categories of a similar nature, e.g. experience, knowledge and skill but recognising the variety and range of individual differences is more important than categorising them. Being aware of them means that we can try to accommodate them in our teaching.

2.5.1 Individual differences between students

Using words: students differ in their abilities to use words with understanding and fluency. Verbal ability affects understanding of how to set about a task.

Using numbers: number skills vary in accordance with ability to use numeric rules and with mental capacity.

Remembering: varies in both ability to recall and reorganise material. Some students are better at remembering what they see, others at what they see and hear.

Reasoning: often there are great variations in students capacities to solve problems and make decisions.

Being creative: students have not only to solve problems, but the way in which they create original solutions by flexible thinking varies greatly.

Achieving: students achieve at different rates.

Studying: no-one studies in exactly the same way. Students all have styles of learning which they prefer and so use their own techniques to study.

Using skills: apart from mental skills, students show great differences in mechanical abilities, in dexterity, in speed, precision and manipulative capacity, in co-ordination, in reaction times and in spatial ability, or the capacity to deal with relationships in different dimensions.

Having interests: patterns of interest vary and are reflected in differing interests shown in training.

Showing maturity: large variations are shown in the way in which students see themselves with objectivity, accept and show responsibility, believe their own worth, are active and curious, behave consistently with predictability and stability.

Developing and holding attitudes: an important area especially in variations of students attitudes towards the value of the learning and behaviour in groups.

Having motivation: probably the most important area of all, especially the degree to which students are self-motivated, rather than motivated by the teacher. Without adequate student motivation, little can be achieved.

Showing perception: a lot of variation in individuals is shown in the area of differing student perception of the learning and the degree to which they attend to and select information.

Seeing themselves: there is a wide range of personality variables, such as self-concept, need to achieve, a degree of self-discipline, measure of conformity and compliance; all affect learning. There are marked differences between younger and older students who are more anxious, fearful of failure, self conscious and cautious, more careful and resistant to changes. Older students are more demanding of effective learning and often more critical of the teacher.

Having different backgrounds: variations in social background, parental attitudes, previous experience, create differences in values and beliefs and can radically affect learning.

Persisting: the amount of time students are prepared to work is important in deciding their likely degree of achievement. Perseverance is only one part of personal psychology which affects the potential of students. There are others, all significant in themselves and including such aspects as the degree of introversion or extroversion, neuroticism or stability, need for affiliation, desire for certainty, dogmatism, etc.

Having needs: establishing needs through Needs Analysis is perhaps one of the first actions to be taken when designing learning programmes. Students may have needs in common with others but will also entertain varying personal goals and this affects their motivation.

The possible variations of individual differences can be enormous and in any one situation they can vary across a wide range but it is likely that the teacher will become sensitive to the individual's learning style as the teacher-student relationship develops.

3.   Learning Styles and Strategies

We have already introduced the concept of learning styles in section 1.4 of this chapter when discussing the work of Honey and Mumford (1986). Here we considered the importance of the preferences that students have with teaching strategies. This section considers some of the concepts of basic 'learning style' theory or learner preferences based on the work of Felder-Silverman (2001), Kolb (2003) and Myers-Briggs (2003) and how different learning styles may enhance student learning (FEDA, 1998; Felder, 2003).

The underpinning concepts are:

> Students are intrinsically different and have different preferred learning styles.

> Teaching is a purposeful activity which aims to promote learning and cause learning to take place.

3.1   Learning styles

3.1.1 Visual/verbal learning style (verbalisers)

This style suggests that students learn best when information is presented visually and in a written language format. In a classroom setting, students benefit from teachers who use a board (whiteboard, OHP, flipchart) to list the essential points, or who provide them with an outline to follow. They benefit from information obtained from textbooks and class notes. They tend to like to study on their own in a quiet room. They often see information 'in their minds eye' when they are trying to remember something.

The following are suggested approaches for using this style:

> To aid recall, make use of colour coding when presenting information in notes. Encourage the use of highlighter pens, highlighting different kinds of information in contrasting colours.

> Encourage this type of student to write out sentences and phrases that summarise key information that they have obtained from either their lesson or their reading.

> When information is presented in diagrams or illustrations, write out explanations for the information.

3.1.2 Visual/non-verbal learning style (visualisers)

This style suggests that students learn best when information is presented visually, in a picture or design format. In a classroom setting students who prefer this style prefer teachers who use visual aids such as diagrams, maps, charts, film, and video. They benefit from the information obtained from the pictures and may not like to work in groups. When trying to remember something, they can often visualise a diagram in their mind. They may have an artistic side and so enjoy activities to do with the design and drawing of diagrams.

The following are suggested approaches for using this style:

> When learning mathematical or technical information, make charts to organise the information. When a mathematical problem involves a sequence of steps, draw a series of boxes, each containing the appropriate bit of information in the sequence.

Use the computer to assist in organising material that needs to be memorised. Using word-processing, create tables and charts with graphics that help student to understand and retain what is to be learned. Use spreadsheet and database software to further organise material that needs to be learned.

3.1.3 Tactile/Kinaesthetic learning style (activists)

This style suggests that the student who prefers this style learns best when physically engaged in a 'hands-on' activity. In the classroom these students benefit from a laboratory setting where they can manipulate materials to learn new information. They learn best when they can be physically active in the learning environment. They benefit from teachers who encourage in-class demonstrations, hands-on learning experiences, practical work and field-work outside the classroom.

The following are suggested approaches for using this style:

Encourage these students to sit near the front of the room and take notes throughout the lesson. Do not worry about spelling or writing in complete sentences. Let them jot down key words and draw pictures and charts to help them remember.

Think of how to make their learning tangible i.e. something that they can put their hands on. For example, make a model that demonstrates a key concept. Spend time in a practical setting to learn an important procedure. Spend time in a practical setting to provide first-hand experience of the subject matter.

3.1.4 Auditory/verbal learning style

This style suggests that the student learns best when information is presented in oral language. In the classroom they benefit from listening to lectures and participating in group discussions. They also like to obtain information from audio tape. When trying to remember something they can often 'hear' the way someone told them the information, or the way that they previously repeated it aloud. They learn best when interacting with others in a listening/speaking exchange.

The following are suggested approaches for using this style:

Encourage these students to study in a group to help them to learn the course material. Or, working with a 'study buddy' on an on-going basis to review key information and prepare for exams. When studying by themselves, encourage them to talk out loud to aid recall.

When learning mathematical or technical information, get them to talk their way through the new information. State the problem in their own words. Reason through solutions to problems by talking out loud to them or with a study partner. To learn a sequence of steps get them to write them out in sentence form and read them out loud.

3.2   Using ILT to support learning styles

Lockett, W (2004) suggests that a combination of learning styles based on an understanding of learning strategies supported by appropriate ILT within a flexible, supported environment will produce a learning experience that suits individual styles and maximises the student's potential. He further suggests that teachers should take an holistic view of learning when developing resources and environments. Figure 3.13 identifies preferred learning methods and shows how ILT can support different learning styles. The suggestion here is that, for each of the three main styles, specific resources and strategies are more appropriate as an aid to learning. At the start of this third section we mentioned that Honey and Mumford provided us with a questionnaire to find the preferred learning styles of our students. However, he used activists, reflectors, theorists and pragmatists. If we use such a questionnaire and want to link this to methods we need to link the four styles with the three headings in Figure 3.13. Perhaps activists are the same (Kinaesthetic), verbalisers are both reflectors and theorists and prefer auditory prompts and visualisers are the pragmatists who prefer diagrams and pictures.

Auditory (Verbalisers)	Visual (Visualisers)	Kinaesthetic (Activists)
Audio tape	Video, film	Note – taking
Radio, MP3 player	Images	Hands-on, Discussion
Mobile phone	OHP transparency	CD ROM, DVDs
Lecture, discussion	Multimedia materials	Internet, Intranet
	CD ROMs, DVDs	Interactive
	Electronic and printed	resources/assessment,
	handouts	simulation, discussion, chat
	Compute Software e.g.	lines, forums, VLE
	Word, PowerPoint	

Figure 3.13 *Preferred Learning Methods*

3.3 Teaching 14-16 year-old students

The (IFP) Increased Flexibility Programme has enabled FE colleges to form partnerships with schools and training agents to attract 14-16 year-olds into vocational, and work-related courses. For example, 14 year-old students might study construction at an FE College for one or two days a week as part of their school curriculum. Popular vocational courses for 14-16 year-olds include engineering, construction, catering, hairdressing and beauty therapy. Similarly, an FE teacher might teach vocational programmes in school.

The programme has led to some criticism by FE teachers in that '*we did not come into FE to teach school children*'. Other criticisms are on the qualification and pay factors when comparing school teachers to their FE counterparts. An article in the *Times Educational Supplement* (TES 2006) highlighted concerns in that training was inadequate to cope with 14 year-olds, and that worries related to:

> '*classes were large and with semi-vocational subjects it became a nightmare to supervise. Also, lack of interest by students and constant disruptions completely destroyed any learning by the group*'.

This leads to the question '*are there differences in teaching such young students in an FE environment*' when, after all, we have always taught 16 year-old and older students. A project from Learning and Skills Development Agency (LSDA 2004), cites that 14-16 year-old students should be:

> Treated like an adult.
>
> Treated with respect.
>
> Allowed to have an opinion.
>
> Listened to.
>
> Helped with their work, when necessary.
>
> Given feedback on how their work is progressing.
>
> Called by their first names.

Allowed to talk about other things than their work, when appropriate.

Also, the project reported that the students who were on work-related programmes enjoyed both the relevance of their learning to the workplace, and the practical aspect of their programmes. This, it would appear, provides the 14-16 year-old age range with a viable alternative to the academic stream in schools and might overcome some of the problems that have existed for so long in schools with some pupils dropping-out (or switching-off) from their studies at an early age. Relevance can be an excellent motivator.

The LLUK Project (op cit) identified a number of key factors for success. These include:

> Identifying the preferred learning styles of individuals. Some organisations use a system of accelerated learning which makes use of visual, auditory and kinaesthetic learning styles.

> Identifying an Individual Learning Plan (ILP) for each student so that they know what they need and how to identify success.

> Operating an induction programme which identifies:

> - The health and safety procedures that are necessary and important.

> - Codes of conduct.

> - Equal opportunities policy and practices.

> - Specific requirements of the programmes chosen by the young learners/trainees.

> Ensuring rapport with students that is built upon mutual respect, some humour and strong leadership.

> Having additional support staff available within the practical environment to ensure that health and safety requirements are followed as well as helping to support youngsters with problems.

> Using a wide range of teaching and learning methods including the use of ILT to allow for simulation, wider range of learning styles and to promote assessment opportunities.

> Creating tasks that will give the young students skills, attitudes and behaviours that will be found in a real-work situation such as working in teams, communication skills, decision-making skills, leadership and co-ordination skills, research skills, risk-management awareness, economic and business understanding.

> Involvement of business organisations to reinforce what skills are required.

Although this seems a long list, many of the points that are made are the same as those that are required for any vocational student. In short, what the project is suggesting is that 14-16 year-olds should be treated like any other vocational student in the FE environment but they may also need some additional help and guidance.

It is worth considering that many 14 year-old students are used to a very structured and rigid system in their schools. Suddenly coming to an FE College can be bewildering, frightening and also disruptive. Allowing students to wander round the college aimlessly at break is a recipe for disaster. Hence the need to implement a somewhat more structured regime while the students are within the college which identifies a code of conduct of what is, and what is not, acceptable behaviour. Setting the rules is often the first step with these young students.

Perhaps the next stage is to consider the teaching and learning. As already identified, the need to discover each student's preferred learning styles comes high on the list of priorities. The use of ILT is a strong contender when working with younger students. They are happy when using ILT having often been taught from primary level with interactive whiteboards, computers and, possibly now, the use of e-mail and chat lines. Unlike working with adults, ILT offers little fear for the younger students. We need to re-examine our teaching methods with these aspects in mind.

School sessions are often shorter than those in FE. This means that there is a need for a wide range of strategies including practical and hands-on activities to keep motivation and interest high through variety. Breaking a session down into smaller aspects, which are achievable, should be considered. Sessions with clear objectives help the students to identify what they are doing and why they are doing it.

A key motivating factor seems to be in giving students the skills that they need in the workplace. A powerful response when challenged by a student with 'Why are we learning this?' is when you can demonstrate that these skills lead to employment or higher education.

4.   Evaluation of Teaching Strategies

Improvement in your use of teaching strategies can come from better preparation but this is only a small part of the process. Your effectiveness in the use of the strategies can be achieved through (a) introspection involving you thinking about what you have done after the event, (b) asking a colleague to sit in with you and comment on your approaches, (c) using 'micro-teaching' where you teach a topic to a group of colleagues and they critically analyse what has taken place (this is often video recorded), or (d) asking students what they think of your approaches. Each of these will benefit from some sort of preparation; preparing a questionnaire for the observer(s) to complete; asking specific questions at the end of the lesson; or recording through either sound or video tape, what has taken place. This preparation will provide you with evidence or data upon which you can make judgments and decisions about what changes you might make. This, then, is the process of evaluation.

4.1   Deciding upon what to evaluate

It is all too easy for you to say that you want to improve your teaching and to look at too many things all at once. It is important that you decide the particular aspects that you want to improve and to concentrate upon those particular aspects at a specific time. You might want to improve a particular teaching strategy such as question and answer, or an introduction or conclusion to a session. You then need to prepare an instrument to ensure that you collect the information, or data, that you require in order that you can make the appropriate evaluative judgments.

The questions that you might want to find answers to include:

(i)   How can I improve my technique with ... (a specific teaching strategy)?

(ii)   How can I improve the interaction of my students?

(iii)   What is the effectiveness of my introductions/conclusions to my sessions?

(iv)   How well do my students learn?

4.2   Data collection

One of the easiest methods of collecting data is to audio-record, say, a question and answer part of your lesson, or an introduction to a lesson or a conclusion. The recording will give you specific data upon which to work. For instance, for a question and answer session you can find the following:

(a)   The total number of questions that were asked.

(b)   The number of questions that were open to all the class to answer and the number of questions that nominated a particular student to answer.

(c)   Whether you nominated a student to answer either before or after asking the question.

(d)   The number of knowledge and the number of thinking questions.

The recording provides the evidence for finding out answers to the questions that you have planned. It might be useful to assist with the analysis of the data to make a transcript of either the whole or part of the recording.

The Explanation guide (Figure 3.14) uses the principle that every explanation should have an introduction and conclusion and that the key aspects of the explanation should be stated and easily identified. It requires the students to answer yes or no (or not observed) so it is easy and quick to complete.

The Explanation Guide

Please mark each aspect below with a 'Yes' or a 'No' or 'Not Observed'.

1. Introduction
- (a) The opening gained and held my attention.
- (b) The opening established rapport.
- (c) The opening told me what was to follow.
- (d) The opening said what was to be expected of me.

2. Key Points
- (a) The key points were clearly expressed.
- (b) The examples amplified the key points.
- (c) The examples added interest to the explanation.
- (d) The timing enabled me to understand the points.

3. The Summary
- (a) The summary brought together the key points.
- (b) The conclusions were clearly stated.

Figure 3.14 *Explanation Guide for Student Completion*

4.3   Data collection in practice

Questionnaires to students can also form useful data upon which to make your judgments. Figure 3.14 gives an example of a questionnaire to be given to students to evaluate your explanations, Figure 3.15 your discussion, Figure 3.16 your demonstration, and Figure 3.17 your lecturing. The design of each of the questionnaires is slightly different and you should decide which you prefer and which will most likely give you the type of information that you require.

Instructions to students:

Think back to the discussion we have just had and try to recall the role of the teacher in it. Examine each of the following statements and rate each one from 1 to 6 in terms of truthfulness. If you think that the statement is completely true then ring (1). If you think that it is completely untrue then ring (6). Ring numbers in between if you rate the statement as being somewhere between these opposites.

Student Rating Schedule

1.   The teacher explained the discussion task clearly.   1 2 3 4 5 6

2.   The teacher asked questions which encouraged group members to talk   1 2 3 4 5 6
     freely.

3.   The teacher did not interrupt constantly but listened.   1 2 3 4 5 6

4.   The teacher did not try to appear to be superior to the views expressed.   1 2 3 4 5 6

5.   The teacher encouraged the group to describe their own experiences when   1 2 3 4 5 6
     appropriate.

6.   The teacher attempted to involve each group member.   1 2 3 4 5 6

7.   The teacher did not show irritation with a particular viewpoint.   1 2 3 4 5 6

8.   The teacher did not force own views on the group.   1 2 3 4 5 6

9.   When desired, the teacher gave information/shared experiences.   1 2 3 4 5 6

10. The teacher allowed unpopular as well as popular views to be expressed.   1 2 3 4 5 6

11. At the end, the teacher gave members of the group the opportunity to   1 2 3 4 5 6
     offer their own conclusions.

Figure 3.15   *Student Rating Schedule for Teacher's Role in Discussion*

Rating Scale for Demonstration

Name: Group:

Topic: Date:

Key: T = Transmission
         E = Emphasis
         V = Variation
         M = Meaningfulness

T1	Skilful performance by demonstrator.	Good	1 2 3 4 5	Poor	
T2	All equipment available.	All	1 2 3 4 5	Some	
T3	Equipment visible to all students.	All	1 2 3 4 5	Some	
T4	Clarity of commentary.	Clear	1 2 3 4 5	Poor	
E1	Attention directed at specific points.	Clear	1 2 3 4 5	Confusing	
E2	Well paced step by step procedure.	Good	1 2 3 4 5	Too	Fast Slow
E3	Use of Q & A for emphasis.	Effective	1 2 3 4 5	Poor	
V1	Variation in student activity.	Good	1 2 3 4 5	Too	much little
V2	Variation in teacher activity.	Good	1 2 3 4 5	Too	little much
M1	Integration of demonstration with other subject matter.	Good	1 2 3 4 5	Disjointed	
M2	Involvement of students with other subject matter.	Good	1 2 3 4 5	Too	much little
M3	Best method of teaching the topic.	Suitable	1 2 3 4 5	Not suitable	
M4	Use of Q & A or other method to evaluate the learning.	Effective	1 2 3 4 5	Poor	

Figure 3.16 *Rating Scale for Demonstration*

Feedback from Students
Lecture Rating Schedule

This questionnaire has been designed to inform me of your opinions concerning my presentation. They will be useful to me when giving future presentations. Please indicate your present thoughts by means of a mark on the 5 point scale below. For example, if you found the lecture quite interesting, you will show this as follows:

Interesting   1 ② 3   4   5   Boring

Use the reverse side of the sheet for additional written comments

The Lecturer

Clearly audible	1 2 3 4 5	Inaudible
Lively	1 2 3 4 5	Monotonous
Too fast	1 2 3 4 5	Too slow
Pleasant Manner	1 2 3 4 5	Unpleasant Manner
Well organised	1 2 3 4 5	Muddled
Interprets ideas clearly	1 2 3 4 5	Leaves me confused
Stressed important point	1 2 3 4 5	All points seem the same
Good use of examples	1 2 3 4 5	Examples were confusing
Is up to date with subject	1 2 3 4 5	Not aware of latest developments
Explanations clear	1 2 3 4 5	Incomprehensible explanations
Lectures confidently	1 2 3 4 5	Not confident

Subject Matter

Difficult	1 2 3 4 5	Easy
Too much material	1 2 3 4 5	Nothing much in it
Vocationally useful	1 2 3 4 5	Waste of time
Interesting	1 2 3 4 5	Boring
I will do further study	1 2 3 4 5	I will not pursue it

Use of Audio Visual Material

OHP Transparencies easy to read	1 2 3 4 5	Illegible
Sufficient time to read transparencies	1 2 3 4 5	Insufficient time to read

Activity

Too many different lecturer activities	1 2 3 4 5	Not enough
Too many different student activities	1 2 3 4 5	Not enough

Figure 3.17 *Student Lecture Rating Schedule*

The design of each of the questionnaires is based on the questions that are required to be answered. The data is provided by the students in answering the range of questions.

4.4   Data analysis

The summation of the data can be achieved by taking a blank questionnaire and, on it, placing slash marks beside each question as to how the individuals have responded. Summation of the slash marks will give the overall response of the group.

The data from the questionnaires can be analysed by looking at the summation of all of the responses and finding those aspects that are very positive and those that are very negative. These, then, give the good aspects, those that should be kept, and the poor aspects, those that should be changed.

Using ILT you can create your questionnaires using electronic voting (described in detail Chapters 7 Assessment of Learning and Achievement and 8 Evaluating and Improving Professional Practice). The main advantage is that it can be used in a lesson in conjunction with the interactive whiteboard. The students are invited to vote on a particular point and, after a given time limit, the software analyses the responses and feeds back directly (or it can be hidden for later use). If given as an immediate feedback, it allows the teacher to question the result from the students and get a more in-depth understanding of the issues.

Achieving the LLUK Professional Standards

Standards
Domain A: Professional values and practice
AK6.2   Ways to apply relevant statutory requirements and the underpinning principles.
Domain B: Learning and teaching
BK1.1   Ways to maintain a learning environment in which learners feel safe and supported.
BK1.2   Ways to develop and manage behaviours which promote respect for and between others and create an equitable and inclusive learning environment.
BK2.1   Principles of learning and ways to provide learning activities to meet curriculum requirements and the needs of all learners.
BK2.2   Ways to engage, motivate and encourage active participation of learners and learner independence.
BK2.3   The relevance of learning approaches, preferences and skills to learner progress.
BK2.4   Flexible delivery of learning, including open and distance learning and on-line learning.
BK2.5   Ways of using learners' own experiences as a foundation for learning.
BK2.7   Ways in which mentoring and/or coaching can support the development of professional skills and knowledge.
BK3.2   A range of listening and questioning techniques to support learning.
BK3.3   Ways to structure and present information and ideas clearly and effectively to learners.
Domain C: Specialist learning and teaching
CK3.1   Teaching and learning theories and strategies relevant to own specialist area.
CK3.5   Ways to support learners in the use of new and emerging technologies in own specialist area
Domain D: Planning for learning
DK2.1   The importance of including learners in the planning process.
DK3.1   Ways to evaluate own role and performance in planning learning.
Domain F: Access and Progression
FK1.1   Sources of information, advice, guidance and support to which learners might be referred.
FK2.1   Boundaries of own role in supporting learners.

Achieving the LLUK Professional Standards

Standards	Ways in which you can show that you have achieved the Standards	See Section
AK6.2	1. List the teaching strategies that you currently use and, for each of them, state: • Whether they are teacher or student-centred. • The dominant domain with which you use them. • Whether they are used with large groups, small groups or individuals. Explain how the statements are in accordance with the statutory requirements of your subject and how they promote equality?	1 and 2
BK1.1 BK1.2 BK2.1 BK2.2 BK2.3 BK2.5	2. Select one of the teaching strategies that you presently use and justify its choice (including a detailed lesson plan). Important factors could include type of intended learning outcome, domains of learning, size of student group, meeting curriculum requirements, student needs, using students' own experiences, how you divide your time equitably and fairly with students, the way you structure motivation and the provision of a safe environment.	1 and 2
BK2.2 BK2.5 BK3.2 BK3.3 CK3.1	3. Identify an aspect of one of your lessons where you use a Socratic (questioning) approach. Explain how the use of the approach can (i) be structured and (ii) support learning.	2
BK2.1 BK2.2 BK2.3	4. Identify the preferred learning styles of a group of your students. Explain how the results influence any changes in your approach to teaching them.	3
BK2.2 BK2.3 BK2.4 CK3.1	5. Explain how you use the theories of learning to plan your lessons in terms of choice of strategies and motivation of your students.	2
BK2.4 CK3.5 DK2.1 DK3.1	6. Identify aspects where ILT can be used with your students and explain the advantages of their use.	3
BK2.3 BK3.2 DK2.1 DK3.1	7. Design a questionnaire for your students to evaluate a specific aspect of your teaching. Give the questionnaire to a group of students, collect and analyse the data and draw conclusions about (a) what are the good aspects that you would accentuate and (b) the poorer aspects that you might change.	4
BK2.2 FK1.1 FK2.1	8. For one of your classes show how you: • Provide an effective induction programme. • Develop a rapport with your students. • Ensure health and safety requirements (using support staff as appropriate). • Use a range of teaching strategies and learning styles; • Use ILT. • Relate your teaching to the real-work situation. • Provide an inclusive, equitable and motivating learning environment.	2

For a model approach to show how you have achieved the LLUK Professional Standards see Appendix I.

Chapter 4

Resources for Teaching and Learning

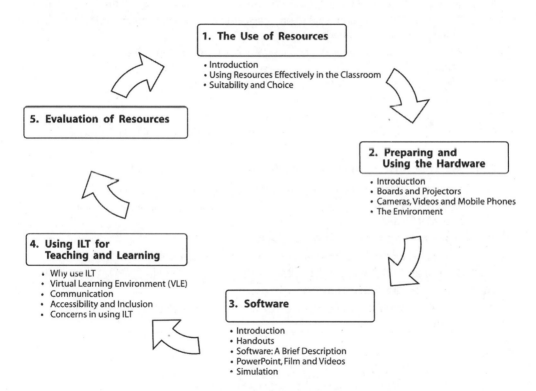

1. The Use of Resources
- Introduction
- Using Resources Effectively in the Classroom
- Suitability and Choice

5. Evaluation of Resources

2. Preparing and Using the Hardware
- Introduction
- Boards and Projectors
- Cameras, Videos and Mobile Phones
- The Environment

4. Using ILT for Teaching and Learning
- Why use ILT
- Virtual Learning Environment (VLE)
- Communication
- Accessibility and Inclusion
- Concerns in using ILT

3. Software
- Introduction
- Handouts
- Software: A Brief Description
- PowerPoint, Film and Videos
- Simulation

This chapter deals with the design of active and engaging learning experiences for your students, with particular reference to individual learning styles and the use of ILT.

LLUK Professional Standards

The Knowledge and Understanding within the LLUK Professional Standards incorporated in this chapter are:

Domain A: Professional values and practice

AK6.2   Ways to apply relevant statutory requirements and the underpinning principles.

Domain B: Learning and teaching

BK1.1   Ways to maintain a learning environment in which learners feel safe and supported.

BK1.2   Ways to develop and manage behaviours which promote respect for and between others and create as equitable and inclusive learning environment.

BK2.1   Principles of learning and ways to provide learning activities to meet curriculum requirements and the needs of all learners.

BK2.2   Ways to engage, motivate and encourage active participation of learners and learner independence.

BK3.3   Ways to structure and present information and ideas clearly and effectively to learners.

BK5.1   The impact of resources on effective learning.

BK5.2   Ways to ensure that resources used are inclusive, promote equality and support diversity.

Domain C: Specialist learning and teaching

CK3.1   Teaching and learning theories and strategies relevant to own specialist area.

CK3.5   Ways to support learners in the use of new and emerging technologies in own specialist area.

Domain D: Planning for learning

DK2.1   The importance of including learners in the planning process.

DK3.1   Ways to evaluate own role and performance in planning learning.

Domain F: Access and progression

FK1.1   Sources of information, advice, guidance and support to which learners might be referred.

---

1.   The Use of Resources

1.1   Introduction

In Chapter 1 we defined a teaching strategy as a 'combination of student activities supported by the use of appropriate resources ...' and we discussed the basic resources (or aids) needed by the novice teacher to supplement their teaching strategies. Now we are going to consider some more sophisticated resources and then discuss how we select and evaluate them.

Learning aids use all of the five senses. They use 'hearing' through audio aids (like the cassette recorder), 'sight' through visual aids like charts and posters, websites and printed resources like handouts and books, 'touch' through resources like specimens and models, and also, to a lesser extent, 'taste' and 'smell' in, for example, cookery. Also, more than one sense can be combined in a visual aid such as a film, a tape-slide presentation or a web-based presentation which combine both hearing and sight. So, anything that you use to augment your teaching or learning strategy, or anything that you get your students to use, can be termed a learning aid or a resource. For example, a drawing on a whiteboard can simplify a complicated wordy explanation and a video clip or newsreel can bring a more interactive and 'real life' dimension to a lesson.

There is a great range of resources available to you as a teacher. Some are indicated in Figure 4.1. You should consider (a) those that you have used, (b) those that you have not used and (c) those that you would like to use.

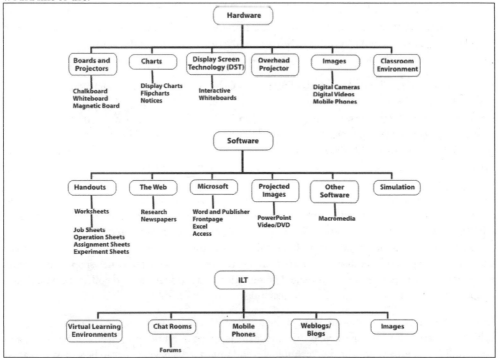

Figure 4.1 *Range of Available Resources*

Perhaps the most influential resource of modern times is the computer. Coupled to a projector, it is a device for showing a PowerPoint demonstration, a DVD for showing a clip, but linked to the internet it is a means of taking the classroom to the student, and an effective means of communicating with the student.

There are resources which ultimately will make the computer outdated. For example, the mobile phone which is now inexpensive, allows communications in the form of voice, image, text and, linked to the internet can send email, search the web, and receive lessons from the classroom — it is a force to be reckoned with. The mobile phone is making use of ILT, that is the use of communication networks coupled to technology thereby putting the learner at the centre of learning.

Effective use of ILT can really enhance your students' learning experience. Inspection reports, like those produced by OFSTED, are a rich source of advice and these reports often link poor learning with the failure to use learning technologies and similarly link effective learning to the professional use of well designed ILT. For example, The Annual Report of Her Majesty's Chief Inspector of Schools 2004/05 documents (http//www.ofsted.gov.uk/publications/annualreport0405/):

> English language and communications
>
> *Increase and improve the use of ILT in teaching and learning*
> Although the use of ILT has improved, too few lessons make enough use of it to improve and enhance teaching and learning. Although colleges are often well-equipped, many teachers do not use the available resources effectively.
>
> Health and Social care and public services
>
> The contribution of information learning technology (ILT) to developing students' research skills has improved, but colleges make insufficient use of ILT to improve teaching.
>
> Humanities
>
> The use of information and communication technology (ICT) as a key learning resource for humanities remains underdeveloped in many colleges.

There is little doubt that use of more than one sense, for example both sight and sound, enhances understanding and memory. As long as you do not overload your students' sensory input, then the more senses you use the better.

If you consider the traditional methods of teaching, the lecturer standing in front of the class talking, then the main sense the students are using is hearing. Psychologists tell us that only about 12% of what we learn comes in this way. In comparison, they also tell us that 75% of what we learn comes through what we see. Thus, six times more of what we learn is through sight than through listening. This has implications for the range of teaching strategies that you use. Do you provide six times the opportunity for learning by sight as you do for learning through listening? Do you use visual pictures to accompany what you say? Do you give opportunities for using other senses, such as touching and using equipment and other artefacts? The television news is a good example of the use of pictures to associate with the spoken word. During the news there are invariably either picture stills associated with the news item, or, more often, video recordings of what is being talked about. Rarely do we only see the newscaster alone on the screen. Even when we do, there is often a still picture depicting the story in the background. Because of media such as the Internet, television, radio, newspapers, magazines etc., students are used to more sophisticated presentation and productions and you, as a teacher, have to compete with this, or at least offer your teaching through more diverse means.

It is said that all good learning aids start in the mind of the teacher with the idea of putting over the subject matter in the most effective way to make the learning easy and interesting for both you and your students. Audio-visual learning technologies and multimedia in general, can be very stimulating to students and provide the often necessary variety to your teaching.

How many words per minute do you speak? If you speak very quickly you might reach 200 words per minute but the average is much less than that – usually around 150 words per minute. Compare this with the number of words per minute that you can think. Psychologists tell us that the average thinking time is around 800 words per minute. So, there is an important *differential* between *speaking time* and *thinking time.*

Consider one of your students listening to you when you are having a good day. You are talking to your students about a topic which has particular interest and relevance to them: they are motivated. They are listening to you talking at 160 words per minute but their minds can think much faster than that. So they are filling the differential between *your* speaking speed and *their* thinking speed by trying to anticipate what you are going to say next, by thinking how they can apply what you are saying in their projects or at work. The outcome of this is that your students are eager to imagine what is the *next* concept you're going to teach. That is a good day!

Now consider a day that is not so good. You are talking to them, for too long perhaps, about a topic which holds little interest to them and it is approaching lunch time, it is hot and they are hungry and thirsty. They start to listen to you but then say to themselves 'What use is this to me? I will never use this topic.' So they listen for a minute then their minds wander. 'What shall I have for lunch? Shall I go to the canteen or just buy a sandwich at the snack bar?' They tune back in to you and realise that you are still on with the same boring topic. Their minds start to wander again. 'What shall I do tonight. Shall I go to the cinema? What shall we do after we have been to the cinema?' This is a voyage upon which there is no return. The next thing that they hear is you saying 'Thank you very much. I will see you next week' and the other students are putting their books together and leaving, and you have made very little impact on their minds at all.

People *can* do two things at once. They can listen to you *and* they can do something else while they fill the differential between speaking and thinking speeds. The skill in teaching requires that you fill that differential for your students in a meaningful manner so that they are using the differential to further concentrate upon the topic. This is the place for using other media both to reinforce what you are saying and to stimulate them towards learning and thinking in different ways. You can provide students with a handout which they can relate to whilst you are talking or, even better, provide them with an incomplete one which they can fill in whilst listening to you. You can get them to take their own notes, draw a diagram during a demonstration or some other activity which will allow some of the differential between the two speeds to be filled.

1.2   Using resources effectively in the classroom

Well designed resources should:

1. Enhance perception: By involving more than one sense there is a greater likelihood that the learner will perceive what is intended. For example, the touch and smell of a piece of wood can be more effective than reading about it.

2. Promote understanding: With greater perception there is likely to be greater understanding.

3. Help reinforcement: When you use learning aids to supplement your spoken words, there is more likelihood of repetition and reinforcement. The reinforcement can be both during the teaching (for example with a chalkboard) and after it has taken place (for instance reading from a handout).

4. Aid retention:

An important aspect of memory is repetition (remember learning your telephone number?). So, repetition leads to retention.

5. Motivate and arouse interest:

As with the idea of changing the learning methods to create interest, so using a wide range of resources can create a similar effect. Repetitive use of PowerPoint in every lesson will quickly lose the interest of your students.

6. Provide variety in learning:

The use of visual aids not only provides repetition, but repetition using a different medium. Hence the provision is more varied.

7. Make effective use of time:

As students are more motivated and show greater interest, then more effective use will be made of the time they spend learning.

Resources should be:

1. Simple.
2. To the point.
3. Interesting.

An excellent visual aid is the map of the London Underground:

It is simple.

It makes good use of colour.

It is not accurate (in a geographical sense) but *representative*.

One point can not be stressed enough — keep it simple. Making resources can be time consuming and costly. Because we are more aware of images through the media of television and computers, we often try to compete, indeed, our students expect us to. However, think before you go down this road. After all, is it necessary to go to this length when a simple slide or tape recording can do the same job more effectively? The simpler the resource the easier it is to use it.

It does take time to make a good learning resource, if the resource can be used for other lessons then it becomes more valuable.

1.3   Suitability and choice

Having identified a range of resources it is necessary for you to select resources for specific purpose. Unfortunately, like so many aspects of teaching, there are no definitive answers for the selection of a particular aid. The design of aids starts in your own mind. A good aid is one which does a particular job to assist in the learning of a particular topic for a particular group of learners. But all learners are different. So, what works for one group does not necessarily work with another. However, there are some general rules that you can use as a guide.

1.3.1   Factors affecting choice of resources

Some of the factors affecting the choice of visual aids are shown in Figure 4.2. First, the choice of a particular teaching strategy will often dictate (or at least limit), the choice of aids. Using a simple resource such as an overhead projector you could manage without a screen, by projecting onto a wall.

Not the ideal but it works. Giving a presentation using PowerPoint you will need a computer, screen, possibly speakers for sound. You could manage with just your laptop but what about the screen? Manipulating 30 students around a 14 inch screen is not ideal! You have put a sound clip onto the computer but you forgot your speakers. It becomes useless.

You need to consider the practicalities of how and where you are going to use the resource at the point of making it. And before you say 'You did not have this problem with the overhead projector, think how many times has the bulb failed on it prior or during the lesson. It appears reasonable, therefore, to consider:

> Teaching strategies.
>
> Learners.
>
> Type of learning.
>
> Practical considerations.
>
> Decisions about visual aids, multimedia.

Perhaps one further factor should be added to the list – and that is yourself. You may either love or hate using the overhead projector. If you hate it, you are unlikely to use it. Also you may have no training in its use and be afraid of it. Thus, you must have the skills to be able to use it properly.

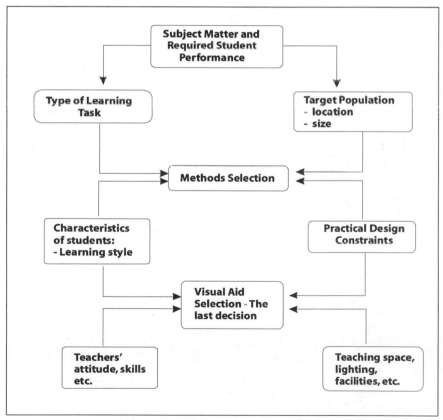

Figure 4.2 *Factors Affecting the Choice of Visual Aids*

Most of us can write on a whiteboard. What about using an interactive board? What about using the computer in the lesson as a demonstration or play a DVD? We need new skills to make use of these resources effectively. There is nothing worse than trying to find the delete key on the computer in front of a group of students who can all use the computer to a far higher level than yourself. Find out how to use them by asking colleagues or enrol on staff development courses and practise — practice does make perfect.

2.   Preparing and Using the Hardware

2.1   Introduction

In this and the next section we begin to examine the role and use of resources. Throughout we have made use of the computer terms 'hardware' and 'software' to differentiate between the 'hard' resources such as projectors, and cameras and the 'soft' resources of handouts and computer software. We start by examining the environment you are going to use with your students.

2.2   Boards and projectors

2.2.1   Boards

Boards are probably the most popular and most used of all visual aids. The are quick and easy to use and are available in 99% of teaching accommodation. However, they are probably the most *misused* as well. It is all too easy to jot hurried notes on them; complete a quick sketch; or to place student responses to questions on them. To use them well, however, you need to plan carefully and be neat when using them.

There are several types of board in use: Chalkboard, Whiteboard, Feltboard, Magnetic board, Flipchart, and Electronic Whiteboards.

Boards are in widespread use because of their advantages:

> Always available.
> Easy to alter and amend work.
> Versatile – suits any subject.
> Colour is able to be used.
> Simple.
> Cheap (depending on the type of board in use).
> Students can see the build-up of diagrams.
> Easily cleaned.

The disadvantages are few:

> Many people have a tendency to 'talk to the board' as they write.
> You cannot see the students as you write.
> Your writing needs to be larger than normal.
> If your presentation is unplanned it can be untidy.
> Your notes on the board do not provide a permanent record, unless you have an electronic whiteboard.
> Electronic whiteboards can be costly.

You should remember that what you put on the board tends to go into your students notes in the same form. If your writing or drawing is untidy, if you have not drawn parallel lines when they should be parallel, if you have got half incomplete rubbing out, you cannot expect your students' work to be neat and accurate, and of high quality.

At various times during the lesson, it is useful to go to the back of the room to make sure that your writing and drawings are visible to all of the class, that your writing does not drop towards the right hand side and that you have no spelling mistakes. It is only really from the rear of the class that you can get a true indication of the worth of your board work.

Chalkboard

Chalkboards have in the main been superseded by whiteboards or interactive whiteboards. However, if you look carefully most colleges have at least one chalkboard hidden away. The chalkboard dated back to an era of writing up notes on the board for the student to copy — facilities such as photocopying being unavailable or expensive to use. With more inexpensive copying facilities and the use of computers to disseminate class notes through, chalkboards have become increasingly unfashionable.

The major drawbacks of chalkboards are that they are slow to use and you end up covered with dust. However, one advantage especially in using the rollerboard against the fixed board is that you can write at your own level and then push the board up to reveal the notes clearly for all students. For clarity green boards and yellow chalk are the easiest for students to see.

Whiteboard

Whiteboards are very popular and have tended to replace chalkboards in most learning environment – although there are some exceptions. They are used for exactly the same purpose as a chalkboard and the principles of their use are the same. However, they are clean and bright. They have better visibility than the chalkboard especially when you use colour as they are more like a book with dark print on a white background. Additionally the white background gives the classroom a brighter atmosphere. But beware! you must use a drymarker – that is a non permanent pen. You can also use whiteboards as OHP screens but you must be careful of any glare that might be produced from the bright light. Many whiteboards have a steel backing which means they can be used as a magnetic board as well and we will discuss their use later. Writing on whiteboards tends to be more difficult than on chalkboards because there is less surface resistance. You will find that the pens tend to 'flow' over the surface of the board. 'Poor' writers therefore tend to be even poorer when using a whiteboard. If you have not used one before, have a practise before you use it in front of a class of students.

Magnetic board

The great advantage of magnetic boards is that you can use them to depict movement. For instance, consider teaching a group of naval students how to dock three or more navy ships in harbour. What better way than making models of ships and sticking magnets to them, drawing the outline of the coast and harbour on a magnetic board, showing the movement of the ships in formation and the required docking procedures.

You should not just use the magnetic board when you want to show movement. You could cut out pictures from magazines or outlines could be cut from coloured card. Stick magnetic tape to the undersides, for display on the board. For example consider the concept formation of herbs in a horticulture class. You could cut out magazine pictures of basil, dill, parsley, rosemary, thyme, and marjoram and display them randomly with lettuce, tomato, cucumber and turnip. You can then ask your students to classify them into herbs and non-herbs.

2.2.2 Charts

Charts make an attractive display in a teaching base room. You can cover all of the walls with materials which are of interest and are informative to the students. You can make changes regularly depending upon the stage of the course you have reached. As the topic changes, the charts change. Charts form a useful, often colourful display.

Figure 4.3 shows a different type of chart; notices to be placed at strategic points to indicate the location of the class for the first meeting. You can make these colourful and with interesting shapes so that they catch the eye of the passer-by.

We have already said that charts should be regularly changed so that they maintain impact. They need therefore to be stored until they are required for the next class. Ideally they need to be kept flat and out of sunlight. Alternatively, roll them up and place them safely in a cupboard.

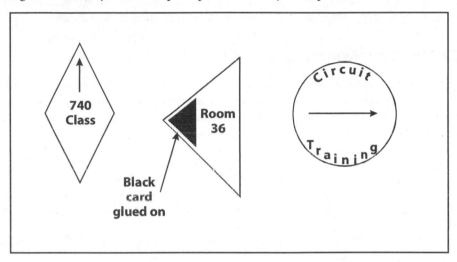

Figure 4.3   *Notice for the First Class Meeting*

Flipcharts

Flipcharts are essentially large pieces of paper placed on a stand and used instead of a white, or chalk, board. After the initial investment in the easel/stand, the flipchart:

> Is low cost as you only need the paper and pens.
>
> Is simple to use, and when one piece of paper is full, you just take another sheet.
>
> Is easy to transport from one location to another.
>
> Is unlikely to go wrong as there are no working parts or electricity required.
>
> Can be used with charts, diagrams, etc., or whatever you wish to draw.
>
> Is suitable for use with photos or colour pictures as 'stick-ons'.
>
> Allows you to use the reveal technique by sticking pieces of paper over the parts that are not to be seen straight away and then peeling them off as required.
>
> Can be prepared before the lesson so that you can take your time over neatness.
>
> Can be semi-prepared so that you can complete it during the lesson. You can prepare using feint pencil (blue is best) and rule feint guidelines to help keep your writing level.

The disadvantages are that flipcharts are:

> Bulky to transport (depending upon make).
>
> Difficult to store.
>
> Much smaller than a whiteboard.
>
> The A1 pads of paper that you can use on a flipchart are expensive and can be quickly used up.

However, it is a very flexible tool and especially useful if working away from your usual teaching environment. With a prepared flip chart pad, you may find the writing on the next sheet showing through. If this is the case, have a blank sheet which you can place underneath the display sheet. It is this flexibility that makes the flipchart a useful resource. Having three or four flipcharts available in a lecture theatre allows you to encourage participation by asking the students to write notes on the boards, or put 'stickit' notes on the board. For group work each group has their own flipchart. They can then make notes/presentations on their own board before feeding back to the other groups.

2.2.3   Display screen technology (DST)

Display screen technology includes interactive whiteboards or whiteboard emulators such as mimio, plasma screens or other large television monitors or screens and data projectors. Display screen technologies used in the classroom give a much more focal point which can be interactive and can be used with software.

At present, there is a large range of products on the market, varying in price from a few pounds for a cable connecting a computer to a large television screen, to thousands of pounds for the latest technology. The less expensive options tend to produce a lower quality display but are nevertheless useful in situations where high resolution is not essential. Some options, for example the purchase of an interactive whiteboard, are currently more expensive and may also involve related costs such as room alterations, modified lighting and acquiring a data projector that can operate effectively with the whiteboard.

The use of DST has increased considerably over the last three years, although this growth has mainly been in schools and colleges and may not be currently reflected in the Adult and Community Learning (ACL) sector. Anecdotal evidence of the impact of DST on the student includes the following benefits:

> It captures the attention of students.
>
> It makes the curriculum area come alive.
>
> Students show increased motivation.
>
> Students enjoy the interaction the technology offers.
>
> Teachers can use software, multimedia resources and the internet with large groups of students.

However, for teachers, it is still early days in the development of resources and activities for use with DST. Although many organisations are using the technology, they have not yet fully exploited its potential for learning.

Interactive whiteboards

Interactive whiteboards were used initially as a large screen for teaching 'computer science' so they became located in computing and multimedia rooms. Now they are gradually being adopted by many teachers across the curriculum.

The interactive whiteboard needs a computer, a projector and sound speakers as well as the whiteboard in order for it to operate. The board has all the features of a computer screen but allows you to work on a larger format in front of the class. The board comes in various sizes and with a number of features. Most of the boards are controlled by a 'pen', but some are touch sensitive so that drawing with your finger becomes possible. There are portable versions of the equipment that turn your existing whiteboard into an interactive board.

The basic use of a whiteboard allows you to display your PowerPoint slides on a big screen. The simple interactivity features built into most of the boards allow you to control the slideshow from the screen. Additionally, many boards will allow you to play DVD, video and music through its sound system. A big advantage is the ability to save and print the work that has been completed on the board so that students can have a copy in the form of a handout.

Electronic voting systems are available with some boards. Here, each student is given an electronic voting pad which has numbered buttons on it. You present a question on the board and ask your students to vote on whether they agree or disagree with a statement or question or comment. When all students have answered you can then reveal the results and analyse the voting patterns.

However, there are disadvantages to using the interactive whiteboard which include:

> They are expensive and need a computer, projector speakers and a board.
>
> The running costs are also expensive. For instance, a projector bulbs costs in excess of £100.
>
> Due to the costs, colleges are reluctant to install interactive whiteboards in every room. This restriction means careful planning becomes essential.
>
> Skill is needed in order to use the boards effectively. It is important to practice before using the board with your students and continue practising frequently in order to become proficient.
>
> So many features are available that some important ones are overlooked e.g. the 'count-down clock'. This can be placed on the board for all students to see. Setting a time limit for a group task can help motivate and focus a group of students.

A comment from OFSTED inspectors, suggests that they seldom see evidence of students using interactive boards in lessons. Obviously, and sadly, this reduces the degree of 'interactivity'. You encourage your students to write on an ordinary whiteboard, so why not on an interactive whiteboard?

A number of reports have been published on the use of interactive whiteboards. For example please refer to the following: Becta *What the Research Says About Interactive Whiteboards* (http://www.becta.org.uk/page_documents/research/wtrs_whiteboards.pdf) and *JISC TechLearn Briefing paper: Interactive whiteboards in education* (http://www.jisc.ac.uk/uploaded_documents/Interactivewhiteboards.pdf)

2.2.4 The Overhead Projector (OHP)

The OHP has been in widespread use for many years. It is inexpensive, found in most classrooms, portable simple to use and can be set up with minimal problems, excepting the possibility of the bulb blowing. It has more recently been superseded by the advent of the interactive board and PowerPoint as a presentation device. Both the interactive board and PowerPoint offer all of the features of the OHP, and are now readily available (laptop computer and portable projector will allow you to present a slide show).

However, OHPs still have a use in the classroom and many of the ideas in use and creation of slides can be applied to the modern equivalent Word or PowerPoint.

When to use

OHPs have a number of uses in the classroom:

As a means of presenting information, such as images and maps. Maps can be in outline or partially completed allowing the students to complete if the image is projected onto a whiteboard.

In group working, students can write and then present their findings or comments to the rest of the class using slides. This is simple, quick and, used with a time constraint, gets the students working to deadlines.

It simple to use and can be used effectively for individuals or groups with limited computer skills. Also students don't need to have access to computers which can be disruptive and time consuming in a lesson.

Speed — slides can be created simply and quickly.

Does not need expensive equipment to show the slides.

Very effective as a reveal or silhouette effect, (reveal is where a number of transparencies are placed on top of each other to build up a complex picture, whereas for a silhouette effect, light shines and creates a shadow from an object such as a leaf or X-ray).

Limitations

The fan can be noisy. It is advisable to switch the OHP off after use as it can distract students.

Keystoning effect — this is where the image on the screen is wider at the top than at the bottom. This can be avoided by using a screen which allows adjustment. Modern projectors with electronics have adjustment built in.

The students vision can be impaired by the projector blocking the screen. Set the projector up to the side of the room rather than in the middle of the room or failing this when finished with the projector move it out of the way (wait until it cools down or you will find the bulbs fail quickly).

The bulb can fail (normally at a crucial point in your lecture). Carry a spare and know how to change it. Be aware of college health and safety issues in handling electrical equipment.

Using the OHP

Check that all equipment works prior to the lesson. Set it up properly: ensure it is focused. It becomes a distraction for the student if you do this during the lesson.

Ensure students can see the board and the projector does not get in the way.

Switch off after the slide show. If you intend to have a discussion switch off the projector and then when finished switch it on again. The hum of the fan can be distracting and also, for students with hearing disabilities, even mask out the discussion.

Stand to one side when delivering. Read from the OHP slide rather than the board. The OHP allows you to stand in front of the board, facing your students.

Keep your slides to a minimum, you are showing only the key points. Use handouts for the detailed content.

Involve your students through the use of questions or a discussion.

Where you have a number of points to make, reveal all the points before masking them out with a sheet of paper. Then, reveal only one point at a time. This helps the students to understand what is coming and hence be able to organise the materials.

Many of the points made here also relate to the use of PowerPoint. However, the projectors used for the interactive whiteboard or attached to your computer are much more complex. You will need time to set them up before your lesson as you have to access the computer, which in turn has to load the software. It is not so easy to switch them off and restart if the bulb is still hot, as you would with the OHP. The bulbs in projectors have a much longer life but are very costly and need a technician to fit. So failure in a remote classroom without technician support can lead to a ruined lesson. Have a back up plan.

2.2.5 Design principles

The use of computer and software like Word or PowerPoint has taken over from transparencies, removing the need for many processes such as the use of Letraset, pens, colour film etc. Letraset (a process for transferring letters to the transparency). By using such software packages such as Word and PowerPoint, you can quickly and easily create stunning slides and just as quickly and easily, change them. Slides can be printed directly to a photocopier, laser and/or ink jet printers using special transparencies. You must use a special quality transparency which is heat resistant for laser and photocopier, otherwise the slides will melt. Ink jet printing also needs special transparencies otherwise the ink will rub straight off them.

Designing attractive and effective transparencies/slides is one of the more straightforward aspects of teaching. We are often reminded of the need to be more prudent with resources and to save the organisation money so we tend to 'cram' information onto handouts and transparencies. This is false economy as the impact of the message is often ineffective. Figure 4.4 suggests some useful guidelines when designing transparencies/slides.

> - One main point per slide.
> - Use space effectively.
> - Maximum of eight words per line.
> - Maximum of 8 lines per transparency/slide.
> - Headings, 24pt minimum.
> - Text, 18pt minimum.
> - Lower case rather than upper case.
> - Keep it simple in terms of colour effectiveness.

Figure 4.4   *Design Guidelines for Transparencies/slides*

When using packages such as PowerPoint do not simply accept the default settings; instead, explore what is available and change the settings of typeface (Ariel and Helvetica are easy to read typefaces), font sizes, bullet points etc. to your own preference; engage the bold setting in order to project a dense image and remember, even in a power failure your transparencies/slides can become excellent handouts.

2.3   Cameras, videos and mobile phones

As with OHPs the advent of the digital camera and digital video camera has replaced traditional 35mm cameras and large format video camcorders. With a digital camera, no longer do you have to wait for the film to be developed or in the case of the digital video, handle a bulky video camera with wires trailing everywhere.

2.3.1   Digital cameras

Digital cameras are now small, inexpensive and allow for photographs or video clips to be imported directly to the computer. Software on the computer allows you to edit photographs to a sophisticated level while similar editing software allows for the editing of video and sound.

Digital cameras come in all shapes and sizes with starting prices of £50 to £500. For general purpose work cameras around £250 are adequate. Cameras save their images to disc, floppy, CD/DVD or to a memory card. This is then transferred to the computer at a later date. In the main the cameras are simple to work. However if you are going to use them in a lesson be sure that the cameras are charged or you have batteries and consider how you will transfer the images to the computer. This last aspect can be time consuming, especially if you have a large group of students.

Once the material is on the computer it becomes an easy matter to move it to Word, PowerPoint or other software for viewing.

Using digital cameras

One of the great advantages of using digital cameras is that they appeal to a wide range of both age and abilities. Because they are inexpensive they tend to be used in group working. For example: for a project involving studying your locality; groups can quickly go out and take digital photographs. Once the images are transferred to computer they can quickly be built into a slideshow or newsletter. A project on 'mobile phone masts' allows for students to create editorial and include local images of phone masts. Students studying horticulture can take digital photographs of trees, shrubs, flowers and transfer these images to a database. Using email allows images to be shared between groups of students in different locations.

2.3.2   Digital videos

Digital videos have similar appeal to students being used in the same manner as digital cameras. The cameras are inexpensive coming with a built in microphone and either saving to mini-tape, DVD or flash card systems. Transferring and editing the images can be time consuming depending upon the quality and use required of the video.

Using digital video cameras

The video camera is effective in recording group work as it is small and unobtrusive. Observations of teachers on teacher training courses can be used to give feedback. Induction assignments such as health and safety issues and finding your way around the college can be recorded by groups of students and fedback to all.

2.3.3 Mobile phones

Many new mobile phones have a built-in camera allowing still and video images to be recorded and emailed. Although the quality is poor at the moment, it is still a useful source of evidence when students undertake project work. For example, hairdressing students can collect evidence of styles they have created with their mobile phone, sending their evidence to their teacher or recording it for their portfolio.

2.4   The environment

2.4.1   Room requirements

Having made and designed appropriate learning aids, it is necessary to show them to their best advantage, through the appropriate positioning of tables, chairs, desks and equipment.

In order to motivate your students and allow them to concentrate upon their subject matter, you need to have a room that is:

> Comfortable and as quiet as possible.
>
> The right size for the number of students you have.
>
> Adequately ventilated.
>
> Acoustically good.
>
> No direct sunlight.

To apply these principles you should be able to move desks and tables about, have curtains or blinds at the windows, some covering on the floor, and chairs that are comfortable.

Your organisation of the room should depend on the number of students that you have. Figure 4.5 shows an optimum arrangement for up to 20 students, Figure 4.6 for between 20 and 30 and Figure 4.7 for more than 30.

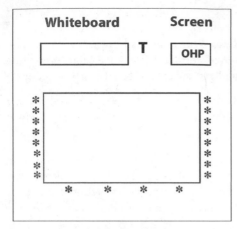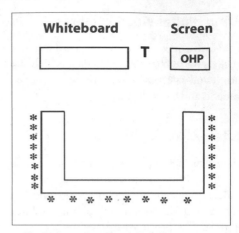

Figure 4.5   *Rectangular Table for up to 20 Students*   **Figure 4.6**   *U-Shaped Arrangement for up to 30 Students*

The arrangements shown in Figures 4.5 and 4.6 have the advantage that students have eye contact with each other. Consequently, with a relatively small class size, you can easily use question and answer and whole group discussion and the students will be able to see and hear what others are saying.

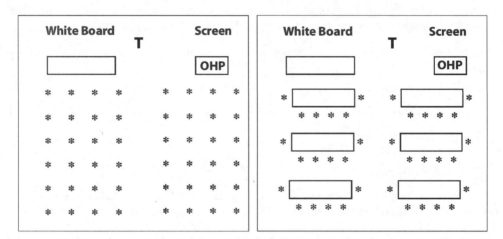

Figure 4.7   *Theatre or School-Type Seating for Larger Audiences*

The arrangements shown in Figure 4.7 are, in effect, for lectures when the passage of information is principally from you, the teacher, to the students and there are limited possibilities for interaction.

Each of the room layout diagrams have shown 'formal' arrangements. However, you will realise that many rooms are used as multi-functional accommodation, requiring a formal setting on one occasion and an informal one on another. Usually, desks or tables are capable of being moved and there are great advantages in the less formal arrangements shown in Figures 4.5 and 4.6.

You need to be careful when siting your whiteboard and screen. Students must be able to see both of these aids clearly and so your position must not obscure their vision of either. This means that you should stand slightly behind the overhead projector, as we show in the diagrams.

This leads us to consider your ability to move about the classroom. It is important, when you move furniture, to consider your ability to move freely about the whole of the room as opposed to just standing at the front. Moving to the back of the class allows you to have a 'student's eye view' of the resources that you use.

Many rooms now have an interactive whiteboard and computer, replacing or duplicating the overhead projector, screen and whiteboard. The same considerations for positioning are relevant.

A newer development of classroom layout involves the inclusion of actual computers. All colleges now have computer rooms where computers are laid out either around the outside of the room, or in rows (see Figure 4.8).

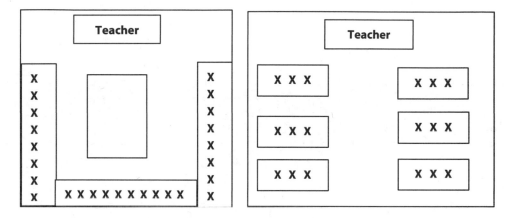

Figure 4.8 *Showing Computers Arranged Around the Room and in Rows*

Both of these layouts pose problems to teaching and maintaining your students attention. Rooms arranged with rows of computers and desktop screens allow students to hide behind their screens and ignore the teacher. A temptation is for students to write up and try out what the teacher is talking about rather than listen, the computer forming a convenient barrier.

With computers arranged around the back walls of the classroom, the student sits with their backs to the teacher – not a particularly engaging layout for the student or the teacher.

In both cases, the teacher should encourage their students to leave their computers and move nearer to the board to listen and make notes, returning to their computers to carry out their tasks. A benefit from this is that it also reduces eye strain by giving the students a break from looking continuously at the screen.

A further development is to take computers directly into the classroom, as opposed to a separate computer room. In many classrooms a number of computers are positioned to one side, allowing for research, individual and group working. The idea, essentially good, is that the students can instantly research or write up notes on the computer without the need to move to specialised computer rooms or resource centres. However, in most cases there are limited computer resources available. As a teacher in such a room you need to be able to have a range of activities for the non computer users to carry out, as well as ensuring that all students at some point during the lesson get access to the computers.

2.4.2 Learning resource centres

In many colleges the library has been replaced with a learning resource centre, containing traditional library facilities such as books, periodicals, video, and films and incorporating computer facilities and appropriate working environment. Many also house specialised sections covering key skills, literacy and numeracy support.

For the teacher, the learning resource centre, can become an extension to the classroom, offering an informal but productive work environment, an area where research can be carried out, written up and desks arranged to allow for discussion. At the same time, you are also developing your students life skills by enabling them to use a research environment with suitable supervision before they go of to university and have to undertake this kind of research independently.

3. Software

3.1 Introduction

In this section we will look at how software can be used to support student learning. The computer, with its access to the web, has not only improved our range of resources but given us new ways of presenting the information we gather.

3.2 Handouts

Teachers vary in their views about handouts from 'essential' to 'the students file them and never read them'.

Copying notes or diagrams from a board or OHP transparency is not usually an effective use of class contact time. Class contact time is valuable and handouts are one means whereby this time can be saved. With the advent of the word processor, the laser printer and high speed photocopier, handouts can be made easily and quickly. The use of 'cut and paste' allows the teacher to copy materials from one document and place it effortlessly into another document. This same point is also true for students, who can copy and paste someone elses words into their own documents. (See Chapter 7, plagiarism, for further comments).

However, what we will see later in this section is that handouts need not be on paper (they can be on disc or on screen) and it is the screen that is important in helping us overcome our students reluctance to read handouts. The screen allows us to make handouts *interactive* by engaging the students and encouraging their participation.

Also, you need to make them visually attractive and include some form of activity (for example incompleteness) so that your students have to use them. They should be 'user friendly' through the use of language and vocabulary that the students can understand. Sketches and drawings can replace a relatively large number of words. If you give instructions, ensure they are clear and correct – trial test them! If you have ring binder holes punched into the handouts, it will save a lot of noise and disruption as students try to borrow a hole punch in the lesson.

Handouts tend to be used a good deal. They can be used in a variety of ways:

> Directly related to lesson content.
>
> Supporting – to introduce the lesson.
>
> Contain relevant (complex) formula.
>
> As a reading list.
>
> As a worksheet/jobsheet/operation sheet.
>
> As information sheets – presenting rare or hard-to-find information.

There are different types of handouts but all have one thing in common: they should help the student. *Information handouts* are used to provide students with data and facts. There are three main types:

> *Notes:* These are directly related to the lesson content, for example the main points of a lesson.
>
> *Supporting:* An introduction to a topic, definitions, complex formulae, graphs, tables and diagrams.
>
> *Reading lists:* Which can be related to the course as a whole or to an individual topic.

A *worksheet* is an incomplete handout which the student is expected to complete during or straight after the lesson. They can be used by individual students which economises the teacher's time allowing time for individual attention. They allow students to work at their own pace, in an independent manner.

Worksheets:

(i)   Can save you repeating yourself especially if the students are working at different rates.

(ii)   Need to be foolproof or have been tried and tested.

There are several types of worksheet:

(i)   *Job Sheets*: These contain instructions or a specification so that a student can complete a piece of work. An example of a job sheet might be a specification for making a skirt or other articles of clothing. Here the instructions are given so that students can complete the article on their own.

An alternative which can be completed by students is shown in the example in Figure 4.9. Completion can be achieved through inserting words in spaces left for the purpose for homework, through exposition as the lesson proceeds or by having an associated OHP transparency on which you can write in the appropriate words in the spaces as you go through each of the steps.

(ii)   *Operation Sheets*: Used to explain a process or series of operations such as how to take blood pressure, how to operate a photocopier, or the 'Decorative Bottle Wrapping' shown in Figure 4.10.

The example shows how each step is highlighted with both pictorial and verbal instructions associated with each of the steps. This seeming repetition ensures that the instructions can be followed where some students (the 'visualisers') will follow the pictures, others (the 'verbalisers') will follow the words, while most will use both the pictures AND the words to ensure understanding. The layout is clear with good use being made of 'white space'. So after a demonstration (or even without one) students can work on their own to complete the Bottle Wrapping.

(iii) *Assignment Sheets*: Usually consisting of a number of questions, problems or tasks to be performed.

(iv)   *Experiment Sheets*: Frequently used in laboratory work although the 'recipe' approach should be avoided.

Whatever type of handout is used, they should be well designed and checked for errors.

Plant Propagation
Hardwood Propagules

Significant points to be considered when preparing propagules.

1. Select only .... of the previous season's growth to form propagules.

2. Select wood where possible of about ..... thickness, preferably from the basal region.

3. Prepare the propagule by cutting it flat across the bottom ...., and at the top a slopping cut ....
Ensuring that any unripened wood is removed.

4. Each propagule should be about ...-... mm (20 cm) in length but try to make cuttings of equal size.

5. Dip the bottom end of the propagule in the ...., and tap gently to shake off any excess.

6. Make out a label in the prescribed way

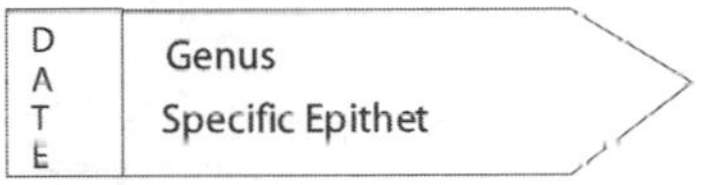

D A T E	Genus
	Specific Epithet

7. Collect the propagules together and tie in bundles of ...... together with the label.

8. Insert the bundles of propagules in ...... where they can remain until the following spring when they can be lined out or inserted straightaway.

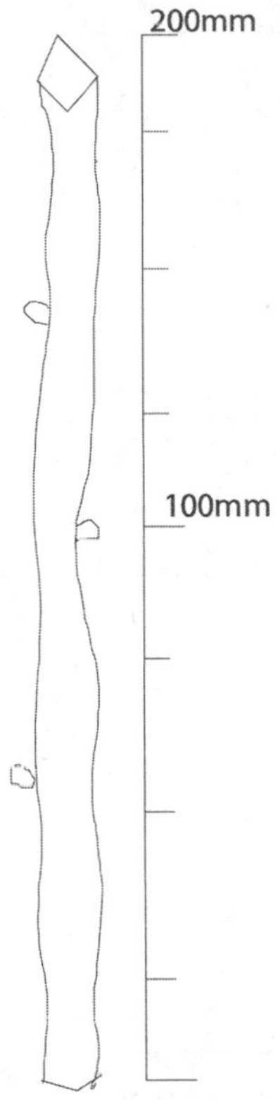

200mm

100mm

Figure 4.9   *Example Jobsheet – Incomplete Handout*

Step 1: Lay bottle of wine on its side on wrapping paper With approx 2 - 4 cm overlap at bottom of bottle and approx 9 cm at the top.

Step 2: Fold the paper around the bottle and secure it with sticky tape.

Step 3: Fold paper at base of bottle and secure with tape.

Step 4: Stand bottle upright. Fold down excess paper in a fan like manner.

Step 5: Secure folded layer centrally with tape. Take top layer of side A and top layer of side B to meet each other and secure with tape.

Step 6: Complete with self adhesive bow. Ribbon may also be added for further decoration.

Figure 4.10   *Example Operation Sheet Showing Step-By-Step Instructions*

The danger of handouts is that they are distributed and the learner never reads them. To overcome this, the handout should have some learner activity included, for example:

Leave blanks – students have to listen for or find key facts/words etc.

Give the learner time to read and then ask for a summary.

Or use questions and answers.

Follow with a test.

A valuable use of an incomplete handout is to issue it at the start of the lesson. You can then use it as a test of entry behaviour. Completion of the handout can form the focus of the learning. The student then uses the handout and has a permanent record of the issues discussed.

Copyright law

There is a tremendous amount of printed, web-based and recorded material available and some of it is ideal for teaching purposes. The use of photocopiers, video recorders, and the Internet have made it easy and cheap to make copies of these works. However, the need to protect copyright is important. Copyright law is a specialist area of law and, before making copies, you need to be clear about your right to do so. If you work for a college or training organisation you should be able to seek guidance from your management colleagues.

Briefly, copyright is a right given to or derived from work and not a right in the novelty of ideas. The types of materials included under copyright include:

Literary works, written and including written tables or compilations.

Music works.

Dramatic works.

Artistic works.

Sound recordings.

Films.

Broadcasts.

Published editions.

An exception to copyright is 'fair dealing' which in this case means research or private study. You are allowed to make one copy of anything which is protected under copyright so long as it is only for your own research or your own private study. Also, you are allowed to copy part of a document, so long as it is *not a substantial part* of the work. This, however, is not very helpful to us as the definition of a 'substantial part' is open to interpretation. A substantial part could be 'the most vital part' of a book, the main thesis, even though in terms of volume it is not a large proportion.

However, many colleges and institutions, through their Local Education Authorities, have a CLA (Copyright Licensing Agency) Licence which allows them to copy 'for immediate use in no more than one course of study in any academic year:

up to one chapter or (if greater) 5% of a book

up to the number of copies required for the personal use by each member of the class plus the teacher ...'

Clearly this scheme is of major benefit to us but, before using this process, you should ensure that your organisation is a member of the scheme and you should read the conditions very carefully.

Copyright is very clear when you use the web. All items on the web text, image, video or sound are copyright and pasting them to your own document is breaking the copyright. For example copying an image and placing it in your word document is a breach of copyright unless it is stated that you can officially make a copy.

3.3   Software: a brief description

Previously (see section 2.1) we have drawn the distinction between hardware and software. We defined 'hardware' as the machines and 'software' as the aspects that you put into or get out of a machine. An example of hardware would be the computer and an example of the software would be the programs that you put into the computer. We now look at the design and use of computer software.

There have been massive changes in the computer software available to enhance learning. For example we have the World Wide Web, search engines, general software packages like PowerPoint, and subject specific packages. The following indicates the types of software generally available which, if used effectively, have a major impact on the quality of your students' learning.

3.3.1   The Web

The World Wide Web (www), or Web is a major resource for teachers and students. A computer attached to a telephone via a modem (or increasingly more likely, Broadband) can access information from a variety of sources. These sources include Government, Universities, business and commerce, as well as individual sites world wide and they can be accessed at any time and with little cost. The web can be used in two main ways:

(i)   for researching and retrieving information;

(ii)   creating your own web pages;

(iii)   sharing information and content; and

(iv)   communicating with others in exciting and stimulating ways.

Research

Using the web as a research tool is straightforward. In order to search the web you need to access a 'search engine'. These are web pages that allow you to enter key words from which the search engine will produce a list of websites that incorporate your heading. Probably the two most commonly used search engines are Google (www.google.co.uk) and Yahoo (www.yahoo.co.uk).

Let us suppose that you are collecting evidence to show that you can 'use appropriate assessment methods' and you are unsure of the concept of *reliability*. In order to research this topic you need to enter keywords such as 'reliability of assessment methods' in your search engine. Once that you have done this, the search engine will identify for you a number of web sites that might provide the information that you need. The problem is that for a general topic there are too many web sites that are identified. The more specific that you can be with your keywords, the more specific are the web sites that are identified. So, you might make the keywords 'reliability of assessment methods in post-16 education and training'. Searching the web effectively is a skill and once these simple skills are developed, much more targeted research can be achieved.

Newspapers

Newspapers and periodicals have always been a good teaching resource. They can be particularly useful when encouraging students to look at job specifications, styles of writing, types of photograph, and so on. Now that newspapers and periodicals gather their stories electronically, it has meant that electronic copies can be kept of current and back issues. A search on the web will give access to many local, national and international newspapers. For example http://www.guardian.co.uk/ gives access to today's issue of the Guardian newspaper, while http://education.guardian.co.uk/egweekly/ takes you to the Guardian's weekly education magazine.

Not many sites allow you to electronically search their back issues. In order to do this you have to take out a subscription. For instance Thompson Learning – InfoTrac offers such a service. This allows both teachers and students to search a wide range of newspapers and periodicals going back over the last ten years. To do this you use a search engine similar to the web search engines which allows you to search for a headline, sentence, specific paper, and so on. Having found an article you can read it and/or print it out. The main advantage of such a catalogue is the quality and authenticity of the information.

An example of using Infotrac while teaching the Key Skill of Communication with students who are asked to research the 'fears of radiation from mobile phone masts' is given below. Part of their research is the use of online newspapers and periodicals. Figure 4.11 shows the initial page of the search engine where the student has typed in, 'mobile phone masts and radiation' as the aspect to be searched. Figure 4.12 shows a sample of three results that have been found out of the 120 articles that the search engine located. Each result shows the headline that was used by the newspaper, the date that it was published, the page on which it appeared and the length of the article. From this information students can select the articles to read and/or print.

Basic Search

Find: Mobile phone masts and radiation | Search

Search for words in: ○ Subject ● Keyword ○ Full text
Limit the results:

☑ to documents with full text

☐ to document with images

by publication date(s) : ● All Dates ○ Before ○ On ○ After ○ Between
        "None" ∨   "None" ∨   "None" ∨   and
        "None" ∨   "None" ∨   "None" ∨

by publication title: [   ]   Browse Publication Title

Figure 4.11 *The Initial Page of a Search for Newspaper Articles Relating to Radiation from Mobile Phones*

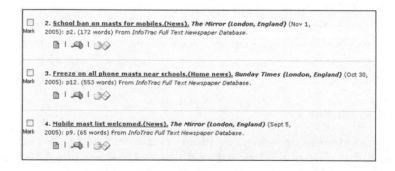

☐ **2. School ban on masts for mobiles.(News).** *The Mirror (London, England)* (Nov 1,
Mark 2005): p2. (172 words) From *InfoTrac Full Text Newspaper Database*.

☐ **3. Freeze on all phone masts near schools.(Home news).** *Sunday Times (London, England)* (Oct 30,
Mark 2005): p12. (553 words) From *InfoTrac Full Text Newspaper Database*.

☐ **4. Mobile mast list welcomed.(News).** *The Mirror (London, England)* (Sept 5,
Mark 2005): p9. (65 words) From *InfoTrac Full Text Newspaper Database*.

Figure 4.12 *Some of the Results from the 'Mobile Mast' Search*

Many educational institutions are now buying, or taking out annual subscriptions, to electronic books where once they would buy the traditional printed version. For example, Encyclopaedia Britannica is available on a CD or Online. This electronic copy is not expensive, it is up-to-date and can easily be searched compared with the traditional volumes. Additionally, maps and dictionaries are appearing in an electronic format.

Creating a website

An increasing number of students have their own websites where they post information about hobbies, games information, exchange information, and so on. In order to do this they purchase a web hosting account and a domain name for their site. Many teachers have also started to use the web to post resources (such as copies of their lesson, assessments, handouts) on their own website or by using their college's intranet (their internal website) or extranet (their external website often restricted by password). If you do this, your students will have access to the resources at any time and from any web access point. Packages such as Microsoft FrontPage and Macromedia Dreamweaver can create a website quickly and easily. An alternative approach to creating your own website would be to make use of the College's Virtual Learning Environment (VLE) to post your materials (see Section 4.2).

3.3.2   Microsoft Office

Microsoft Office is a suite of software which include:

> Word –a word processing package;
>
> Excel – a spreadsheet;
>
> Publisher – for publishing documents; and
>
> FrontPage – for creating web pages.

Although many competitors have similar systems, almost everyone uses the Microsoft versions. Microsoft has also a wide range of ideas and resources including lesson plans available from http://www.microsoft.com/education.

Microsoft Word

This is by far the most used of the software. Teachers use it to write their lesson plans and handouts and students use it to create and complete their assignments. However, many of the features that are included in Word are not greatly used. For instance you could:

> Save your documents and put them on the intranet so allowing students to access them.
>
> Place an incomplete handout on the intranet and ask students to complete it online.
>
> Create a form and use it as a multiple-choice quiz.
>
> Use comment boxes allowing you to annotate an electronic assignment rather than writing upon it.

Microsoft Publisher

This is another word processing package but with many additional features. These feature consist of a large number of templates that are created through the use of on-screen wizards, or helpers, which you can use to create all kinds of high quality publications. The publications include:

> greetings cards;
>
> business cards;
>
> brochures;
>
> calendars;
>
> certificates;
>
> newsletters;

and so on. Used in conjunction with a digital camera, Publisher allows the creation of a storyboard, linked to the web it allows research ideas and images to be published as a newsletter, or a discussion document, or as a poster. These ideas allow you easily to integrate Key Skills into both your lessons and assignments.

Microsoft FrontPage

This is a web authoring package. It allows you to create simple web pages or a multiple page website.

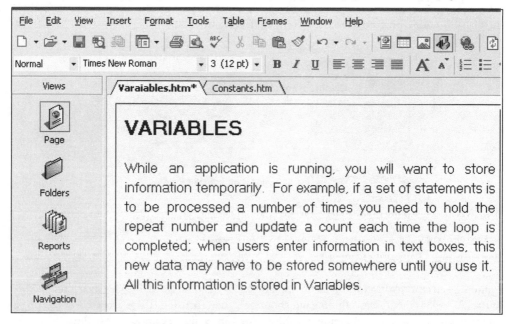

Figure 4.13 *An Example of a Handout using Microsoft FrontPage*

Figure 4.13 shows FrontPage being used for a handout. It was originally designed in Word, but has been posted into FrontPage. FrontPage has changed both the format and the presentation of the handout to improve its readability. The finished document is then saved as a web format (Hyper Text Markup Language – HTML). It can then be stored on the local network or made available for the web. This simple format allows students and teachers to access documents from college, work or home. The format of FrontPage allows the user to import texts, images, links to files and the web very easily.

A more detailed understanding of FrontPage can lead to the creation of interactive documents such as an interactive questionnaire. You could use a questionnaire developed in this way to gather your student's opinion of the course that they are completing.

Microsoft Excel

This is a powerful spreadsheet which is used extensively in the work place and primarily in business and financial arenas. This is due to its ability to perform mathematical functions, report statistics, handle and manipulate data in a number of ways and by presenting data graphically and dynamically. As a teaching tool it opens up a number of pathways. It can be used very effectively to teach theories in mathematics and sciences where teachers can set up spreadsheets to illustrate theories and its dynamic formulas can be used to test 'what if' scenarios. However, its potential to teachers in any subject area is its ability to create informal assessment opportunities. By simply setting up a spreadsheet with a set of questions and leaving areas for students to either choose an answer or input an answer, spreadsheet formula can be used to evaluate answers and respond with set feedback. This feedback can be summarised and marks reported to students and teachers. Questions are not limited to numerical questions and answers but can include text, pictures and multimedia as with all Microsoft applications.

Microsoft Access

This is a database which can be used to both organise and investigate information. For example you can use it to produce a profile of the students in one of your classes by setting up a database of their entry qualifications, progress in each subject, attendance, and so on.

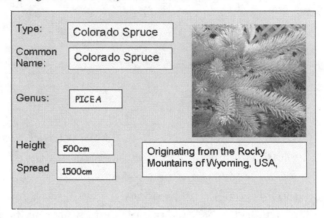

Figure 4.14 *An Example of a student database collecting facts and images*

Figure 4.14 an example of a student database collecting facts and images of trees for their arboriculture course. As well as the students finding out about trees they are using ILT as a *key skill* in creating a database, and finding the images either on the web or using a digital camera to take them.

3.3.3 Other software

There is a wide range of other software available. Companies such as Macromedia produce graphics software, Dreamweaver for creating web pages and Flash for creating animation and integrating video and sound. Although both Dreamweaver and Flash are specialist packages they can be used with a wide range of students at different levels. At one level they are simple drawing packages but at a much higher level the still drawing of an aeroplane becomes, through a series of animated drawings, the flight of an aeroplane.

Another specialised package is that of computer aided draughting (CAD). Such packages allow you to draw at varying levels of accuracy from very simple to very complex shapes. Coupled to engineering components, computer-aided manufacture (CAM), you can turn drawings into actual components.

3.4 PowerPoint, film and videos

3.4.1 PowerPoint

PowerPoint, at its simplest level, allows you to easily make and edit slides, bring in colour and text, and use bullet points and reveal methods. It is the modern OHP – a tool for supporting a lesson and ultimately creating a handout for your students at the end of that lesson.

Due to its usefulness, it can often be 'over-used' hence the term 'Death-by-PowerPoint'. However, used properly this can be avoided, particularly if you vary the slides and make them interesting. For example you could incorporate:

Images taken from a digital camera.

Music and voice. For instance, recording a discussion and playing it back to the group.

Simple animation. For example, bullet points appearing when you click on the mouse button.

Links to other software packages or the web.

'User buttons' (Figure 4.15). Where the buttons allow students to choose what they want to see next.

As an assessment tool. A question can be raised on one slide with the 'user buttons' indicating a choice of answers. Choosing the correct button takes the student to the answer and the next question. Whereas an incorrect choice takes them to an explanation of why they got the question wrong.

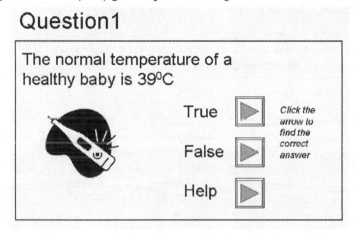

Figure 4.15 *How Buttons can be used to Navigate a Document*

You do not need to be an expert in the use of PowerPoint to construct effective slide presentations but merely need to be able to search the Web for ideas. A useful starting point is the Ferl/Becta site (http://ferl.becta.org.uk/) which identifies many teaching resources which use PowerPoint (and other software packages). It is free to download to use in your teaching.

PowerPoint can be used in exactly the same way as the OHP:

As an introduction to your lesson to, say, introduce the aims and objectives and/or identify the main points to be covered.

During the lesson to provide a visual representation of the main points.

At the end of the lesson, with questions to assess the main points, or to provide a summary from the aims and objectives.

After the lesson, on a website, as a focus for discussion for the next session.

This last aspect is important. It changes from the activities that have been used during the lesson, which may have been teacher-led, to one that is used after the lesson and has a student focus.

3.4.2 Video and DVD clips

Video and DVD clips can be used to:

> Promote critical thinking by asking students to analyse situations from different perspectives.
>
> Discuss the issues raised in the clips.
>
> Explain procedures that would be difficult to show in the classroom. For example dangerous experiments, or the operation of equipment.
>
> Demonstrate how to perform a task or procedure.

When you use the clips you want your students actively involved in the lesson: not passively watching a 15 minute video. You might involve your students by one or more of the following:

> Setting tasks relating to the content of the clip.
>
> Giving different tasks to different groups to complete whilst they are watching.
>
> Stopping the clip at key points and asking questions or for comments.
>
> Recapping a point by stopping and replaying the point.

A major problem with a video or DVD lies in their availability. You need to order it well in advance. For those clips which are heavily used, consideration might be given to their purchase. ILT has improved this by allowing you to download clips quickly and easily – but beware of copyright limitations.

Two important areas to visit are:

The Joint Information Systems Committee (JISC) (www.jisc.ac.uk) houses a number of resource collections specifically aimed at further and higher education. One such collection is the Moving Image Gateway (MIG) (www.jisc.ac.uk/index.cfm?name=coll_mig&src=alpha). The websites listed at MIG provide guides to recommended moving image and sound resources suitable for educational use. The websites are classified by subject area. Registration is required before you are allowed to download resources. Access to news reports from Pathe News (www.britishpathe.com) and ITN (www.itnarchive.com/britishpathe) are also available (Figure 4.16). The BBC, Open News Archive, (www.bbc.co.uk/calc/news/content_intro_results.shtml.) have just made a number of resources available.

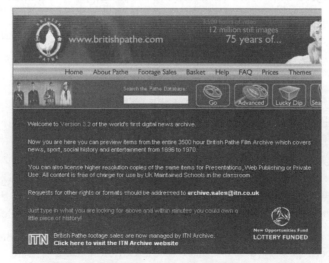

Figure 4.16   *Home page of British Pathe News*

For further education and adult education the National Learning Network (NLN) website (www.nln.ac.uk/?p=Dist) gives you access to multimedia resources relating to most of the subject areas within further education (Figure 4.17). These resources cover from catering, hairdressing through to construction and travel and tourism at levels 1 to 3. The materials are of a high quality and often include interactive assessment. The resources are professionally made and all involve input by subject specialists. However, you need to register before you can access materials.

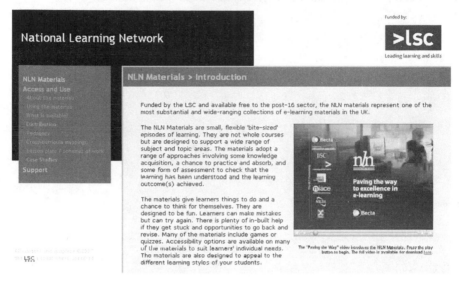

Figure 4.17   *Part of the NLN Site relating to Materials*

As with all resources, you should try them prior to using them with your students. You also need to check which equipment, both hardware and software, you need. For example, all the resources above need speakers and most need Macromedia, Flashplayer. This is readily available from downloads at the Macromedia site (http://sdc.shockwave.com).

3.5   Simulation

The main goals of simulations are to help students learn design and experimentation, both of which are key skills for many forms of inquiry (such as case studies, trials, projects and research) and all kinds of subjects (such as art and design, engineering, science, amongst others).

Simulations themselves can range from complex software-based programmes which can allow input of data and which allows you to see the response, to fairly simple design programmes. An example of the first might be in changing the values of current and voltage in an electric circuit and measuring changes in impedance or resistance. A more simple simulation might be to do with having various design options so that an impression of different visual impact can be gained. An example of this type of simulation is interior design software, where furnishings and wall colour can be altered.

A far more complex application is the computer controlled flight simulator which is used to train pilots to cope with situations that are too dangerous to undertake in a real aeroplane.

Other examples of simulations are:

> Engineering students testing a structure to destruction.

Business studies students in order to maximise profits by simulating sales and purchases over a given number of years. The software can easily and quickly simulate unexpected changes (as happens in real life) making the students rethink their strategies.

Beauty therapy students can use different hair colours and styles to see how they affect people with different weights, skin colours or complexions.

4. Using ILT for Teaching and Learning

So far in this chapter we have discussed different types of resources, their uses, related and, recent innovations (mainly the involvement of computer technology). This section takes a step further by combining computers and communications to enhance the learning of our students.

4.1 Why use ILT

The term information learning technology (ILT) describes the way we make use of computers and communications. In the previous sections we have used the word computer or information technology. In the main we have replaced one resource with a new resource. For example, the overhead projector has been replaced with the interactive whiteboard and PowerPoint, the camera with the digital camera, the handout with the electronic handout: the old technology being replaced with the new.

But once we connected to the web and started using communication technology there were additional changes. We did not need to use the library so much but simply went to the web and searched for the information that we required. As a teacher, we can now save our lessons on a disc, edit them and put them on the college intranet or extranet. Also, our students can access the intranet or extranet to get their notes whenever they like from wherever they happen to be.

No longer are we confined to the classroom but we now have opened up our teaching and learning to anytime and anywhere. We are no longer restricted to traditional teaching methods. Using electronic communications such a email, forums and chat rooms, you can communicate with your students and they can communicate with you. When this happens we realise that this new technology, ILT questions much of what we have previously learned about teaching. It challenges us to look at our teaching methods, their associated resources and the assessment. ILT encompasses all of these issues.

At its simplest level you could put class notes on the web so allowing your students to access them. However, ILT gives you so much more scope than this. It allows you to bring learning to life using the resources of text, images and sound.

So, why should you use ILT? To turn your back on it will only hinder your students. Today students of all ages are driven by image and sound and the younger of your students have been surrounded by technology from an early age through both their school and home lives. You must not only continue this familiarity with technology, but should take it to higher levels. In terms of the skills, you need to give your students the skills that they will need in business and commerce, higher education and life in general.

4.2 Virtual Learning Environment (VLE)

The Quality Improvement Agency (QIA) website (http://excellence.qia.org.uk) provides us with a definition of a Virtual Learning Environment: 'a VLE refers to a specific piece of software that enables students and staff to interact and includes content delivery and tracking'. They provide a diagram (see Figure 4.18) of a Managed Learning Environment (MLE) where VLE is a part of the MLE. The VLE covers both the teaching delivery and assessment functions whilst the MLE includes the VLE and the management functions such as quality assurance, student records and other valuable data.

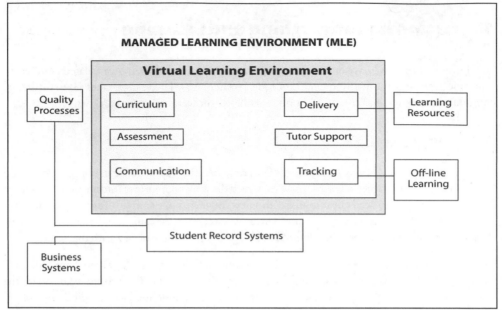

Figure 4.18　*Aspects of VLE as part of the MLE*

The diagram indicates that a MLE is a software system which is designed to help teachers manage their courses and students. A VLE, which is part of the MLE, consists of a set of teaching and learning tools designed to assist a student's learning by including computers and the internet in their learning situation. The component parts of a VLE are:

Curriculum mapping	breaking the curriculum into manageable 'chunks' that can be learned and assessed.
Student tracking	online support for both teacher and student.
Electronic communication	email, conferencing, chat lines, web publishing.
Tutor support	Via email, chat, blogs, etc.
Assessment of learning	different types of e-assessment (see Chapter 7).
Delivery	using e-resources and e-communication

Many educational establishments have invested heavily in VLEs. There are a number of popular VLE products including Blackboard, Moodle, and Fronter. Although these are different products, they are very similar in their working. They all allow you to upload resources to a website either hosted internally or externally. All allow communication through chat lines, forums and emails. They permit you to assess your students using multiple choice questions to the more traditional assessment methods which your students can either complete online or forward to you electronically for marking.

Figure 4.19 shows a screen shot from the VLE. The left hand side of the screen shows a student's diary and the tasks that they have to do. The right hand side shows the communication systems that are available e.g. notices, forums and chat. The centre shows the student's course.

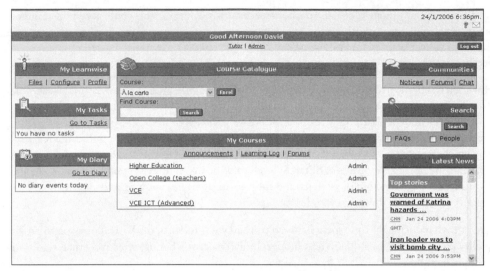

Figure 4.19 *A Screen Shot of the VLE 'Learnwise'*

Although often expensive to either purchase or lease and dependent upon teachers or support staff to upload materials to the web, VLEs are gaining in popularity. The advantages of using a VLE include:

Secure area to upload resources and notes.

Easy access via the web.

Students can have access to the learning environment when it suits them.

Enhances communication between teachers and students.

The system is password protected.

Allows students to access resources from any web-enabled computer.

Can be used to conduct assessment.

Tracks students' usage.

Some disadvantages of a VLE system include:

Costs of purchase and running.

The need to continuously update resources.

Cost required to create materials.

Hardware costs.

Students expect it to be available at all times for all courses.

4.2.1 Use of VLEs

VLEs have replaced the old style mail order, distance learning approach where students received a set of notes and assessment tasks which they returned to their tutor for assessment. Discussions within this system were both difficult and time consuming. VLEs have revolutionised distance learning. The materials, not just written materials but images (including video and sound), can all be made available on-line. Assessments including multiple-choice and traditional methods, are easily made available. With 'instant' support to a tutor through email, assignments can be discussed quickly. Forums and chat lines to other students offer a chance to discuss problems, which overcomes the 'you are alone' feeling which was often associated with traditional distance learning. Coupled with the facility that all of this can be tracked, VLEs provide the proof necessary for assessment.

A VLE was initially thought of as a repository for materials. Your students could access the resources, which saved you time in creating and photocopying handouts. It also allowed students who had been absent to collect their own handouts. They could also collect their notes, PowerPoint slides and, perhaps, watch a video of the session.

However, it is in the traditional lesson that VLEs can be used with great success. A VLE allows you to make available a wide range of resources, including video and photo, which helps to accommodate many of your students' learning styles. As *a teacher-led session*, your students can be supervised as they use the resources. In a *student-led approach*, your students can choose which resources to look at and when to look at them. As a *vehicle for differentiation* between your slower and faster students you can create a wide range of resources at different levels of difficulty. Different communication channels allow discussion, in and out of sessions, and the tracking methods allow you to identify who needs support as well as the ability to provide that support.

Rather than reducing the time spent between you and your students, the VLE allows you to provide quality learning to many students and support individuals, much more effectively than traditional teaching methods.

One further advantage of using a VLE as part of your teaching is that it can make learning more accessible for students with disabilities. A visually impaired student can read using a screen-reader (many VLEs have this facility built-in without the need to purchase further equipment). Additionally, the colours, text size and fonts can be changed to further improve readability.

4.3   Communication

4.3.1   Chat rooms and forums

Chat Rooms provide opportunities for real-time, unstructured conversations between students and between you and your students. Chat Rooms can be dropped in and out of at times and places to suit individuals, and students can catch-up with work they have missed. It is a mechanism which can provide peer support both inside and outside of classroom time. Session times can be agreed, where you are available to give tutorial support out of normal class time.

Multiple Chat Rooms can be organised for students to collaborate on a specific task. Chat Room conversations can be archived into text files which can be used for assessment evidence.

Similar to Chat Rooms, *Forums* (or Bulletin Boards as they are sometimes called) can be accessed at times and places that suit both the teacher and the students. However, as they are not real-time discussions, they give the opportunity, for both teachers and students, to take their time to formulate answers or contributions and, unlike chat rooms where short answers are the norm, give fuller contributions. Discussions can be developed and customised in the following days or weeks. For example a discussion on the concepts involved in motivation could be explored at the beginning of the week, a summary be put together by the teacher later in the week and explored again at the end of the week.

Participation in Chat Rooms and Forums are at the individual's convenience. No travelling is required and there are no rigid time demands.

4.3.2   Mobile phones and text messaging (SMS)

Mobile phones have the potential of becoming a teacher's ally instead of the scourge of the classroom that they have sometimes become.

Mobile phones and text messaging can be effectively teaching tools, and they are in a medium that students willingly accept. You can use them to contact students, to pass-on key information (including change of classroom or timetable and exam dates) and reminders or even delivery of course materials, direct to them. As technology in this field is advancing almost daily, it is accepted that it is only a matter of time before students will be able to download subject information from on-line databases held at the college, directly onto their mobile phone.

4.3.3   Weblogs and blogs

Weblogs, or blogs as they are now commonly called, are personal internet journals that are frequently updated and written in a personal tone. In other words, a blog is a diary or journal where the writer, or 'blogger', will write their observations and sometimes provide links to subject specific websites.

Due to many easy-to-use programs and websites, almost anyone can set up their own blog and due to this, you can usually find blogs on any subject on which you are working, or in which you have an interest. Their value, however, is often questionable as you may have no idea about the authenticity of the materials.

4.3.4   Podcasts

Podcasting has become another buzzword of the internet and is often mistaken as something that can only be used with an iPod. This could be due to the fact that the word 'podcast' is a combination of the words 'iPod' and 'broadcast'. However, a podcast is simply an audio, or video, file that you can download and listen to where and when you want, on any media that can use an MP3 file, including a PC.

Podcasts are usually subscribed to and the user downloads the file to listen to or view offline and when convenient. The potential of podcasts in education is vast. Any lesson could be recorded, either with sound only or with video, and then made available for students to download.

4.3.5   Rich Site Summary (RSS) feeds

RSS is a format for delivering regularly changing web content. RSS feeds are becoming widely available and although originally were found mainly on news-related websites, they are now found on numerous websites that update key information.

RSS feeds keep subscribers informed by retrieving summaries of the latest content from sites in which they have an interest. To view RSS feeds you need a Feed Reader or News Aggregator software. This will allow you to 'grab' the RSS feeds from various sites and display them for you to read and use. A variety of RSS Readers are available and can be found on the internet through a search for 'RSS Feeds'. Once you have the Feed Reader, it is a matter of finding sites with content of interest to you and setting up a link to them. A good starting point can be the BBC website as they have a number of content specific sites in one place. You can help your students by indicating a small number of sites which they may find valuable.

4.4   Accessibility and inclusion

ILT can be used to enhance accessibility for your students. Simple things like being able to change the print font and size, the print colour and the background colour of electronic documents allows you to improve the readability of your resources either on a handout, on a computer screen or on the interactive whiteboard. Key points to remember when creating these types of documents are:

> Font should be at least 12pt.
>
> Typeface should be non serif, for example, use **'Arial'**.
>
> There should be clear contrast between text and background.
>
> Use 1.5 line spacing to make the print clearer.
>
> Avoid centering headings so that the eye does not have so far to move.

A set of guidelines called Web Content Accessibility Guidelines is available for users placing resources on the web at http://www.w3.org. Here guidance is given on font sizes, colour, styles and content. As well as keeping navigation consistent, it encourages you to ensure that your images have captions to allow screen readers to identify them for their users. Many sites are dynamic in that they allow you to choose the size, colour and format of the resources that suits your needs best.

A guide to the legislation and more precise information can be found at Techdis at http://www.techdis.ac.uk, which is a leading educational advisory body in accessibility and inclusion.

4.4.1   Hardware

There is a wide range of hardware available to support students with disabilities. Many of the devices allow networked computers to be adapted quickly for the disabled student, so avoiding the issue of being singled out to work on a stand-alone machine. Some general examples of hardware available for students with a variety of disabilities are:

> Keyboard with large keys that are:
> - in alphabetical order rather than the traditional QWERTY keyboard arrangement,
> - with overlays to prevent the student striking two keys at the same time.

More specialised keyboards have different shapes to reduce the hand and eye movements:

> Mice with large buttons or roller balls to reduce movement.
>
> Monitors which allow split screens or touch screens.
>
> Platforms to lower or raise the working height, allowing wheel chair access.

4.4.2   Software

Microsoft has a range of *accessibility* software built into its operating systems such as Windows XP (look under Programmes, Accessories, Accessibility). A Wizard takes through customising your screen, keyboard and speakers. At its simplest level, you can set the mouse keys for left handed users or set the response rate faster or slower for mouse or key strokes. For students with poor hand control making use of 'Stickykeys' or 'Filterkeys' allows the student to hold down one or more keys in sequence rather than all at once, or filter out repeated keystrokes due to holding down the key for too long.

For students with *sight* difficulties there is a wide range of software available. This ranges from screen readers where information from the screen is read out aloud, to packages such as 'Jaws' which have more sophisticated devices including Braille printing.

For students with *dyslexia* there is a range of predictor software available. This, after putting in the first few letters, suggests possible words so speeding up the writing process. Speech recognition software such a 'Microsoft Speech Recognition', 'Dragon', and 'NaturallySpeaking8' make use of the microphone to translate the spoken word intro electronic text. These, however, take time to set up and often require the student to read a number of documents so that the software can learn the pronunciation of key words.

4.4.3 Training

For the hardware and software to be used effectively the student, teacher and support worker need to be familiar with its working and its limitations. Where the student uses the same equipment at home or in their workplace, they will use it more effectively and are better equipped for the classroom. You, as the teacher, need to be aware of the limitations in the software as well as how to plan your teaching incorporating new software. For example, in using magnification software, although the student sees the screen, they are often restricted to just a fraction of the full screen, so slowing down their movements. For students with sight or hand movement problems, giving them alternative key strokes such as CTRL + P to print a document can be more effective than using the main menus. As you can imagine, teachers, support workers and students need to discuss the hardware and software which is going to be the most effective.

4.4.4 Alternatives

Not all support needs to be hi-tech. Large text or use of coloured paper can be just as effective for some sight problems as a sophisticated screen reader. A tape recorder can be made available to a student to record a lesson or discussion, either being played back after the session or typed onto a computer.

4.5   Concerns in using ILT

As we have seen in this chapter, ILT is a major contributor not only to resources but to the way teaching and learning takes place. However, there are some concerns in using ILT: these are as follows:

> *Confidence* — Many of the IT resources, when used properly, demand the teacher to not only learn new skills but also to keep abreast of new developments. For example, using the interactive whiteboard requires practice not only to learn the many aspects of its software but also to use it proficiently for the students. There is no simple way of learning these skills. You can know the manual backwards but time is required in the classroom in using the resource. Working with an experienced teacher or using staff development will help you to overcome most problems.

> Not having the *hardware or software* in your classroom — Many new FE and HE institutions are equipped with ILT resources in their classrooms but this is not much help if you do not have them in your teaching rooms. Putting time and effort into a PowerPoint presentation only to find that you do not have a projector or speakers to show it tends to put you off using ILT in the classroom. Good planning, changing rooms with colleagues, and asking managers for more equipment goes some way to overcoming a shortage of equipment.

> *Time* is a major factor — We have discussed the amount of time needed to learn how to use the hardware and software correctly. A further aspect is the time required in developing the software for your students. Creating a set of handouts and a PowerPoint presentation are time consuming. However, once they are in an

electronic format, they can be used and changed quickly. This last concern is, perhaps, the most important in that all resources should be made to be easily changeable so that they can be used for a wide range of classes.

These concerns are nothing new and have always related to the making and using of resources; the same comments were true of making slides for the OHP. However, there are further concerns in the way that ILT is changing teaching and learning. They are as follows:

There are some teachers who believe that ILT in the classroom takes control away from the teacher. Using new methods such as interactive resources and VLEs means students can learn when they like and, in many cases, without the need for a teacher. However, for many, it is the interaction with other students that they need. With the use of ILT, the teacher, rather than losing control, now takes on the true role of facilitator directing the students to the learning materials. It is in this way that we are increasing the amount of student-led learning in our classrooms.

Following on from 'loss of control', it is believed that the reality of placing materials on the web and the videoing of sessions, will eventually result in the loss of teaching posts. However, for most this will not happen as the teachers' role changes to that of facilitator and to that of directing the students' learning. By having such banks of materials, we can concentrate on the students who are having problems or who want to go in a different direction.

Using electronic communications results in students communicating when they choose and demanding an immediate response. In this instance there is a need to set standards of response times such as how quickly can a student expect a reply to an email. For instance, within two hours during a normal working day. Whereas more complex requests may require some problem solving, and the response time could be extended 24-36 hours.

For those who are considering on-line teaching, you should look at 'Learning to Teach Online (LeTTOL) at http://weblearn.sheffcol.ac.uk/lettol/.

5.   Evaluation of Resources

As with all of your teaching, it is important that you consider how to evaluate the aids that you use.

The checklist shown in Figure 4.20 on the next page will help you in considering the aspects that you might use to evaluate your design and use of aids. It should be completed through answering all of the 18 questions with either a 'YES', 'NO' or 'NOT APPROPRIATE'. If you have any answered with a NO, you should reconsider that aspect of the design, use, etc.

An alternative way to evaluate your aids is to ask students questions about their suitability, whether they assisted the learning, whether they appreciate them, and so on. Students are the ones for whom the aids are designed – they have to suit their needs.

Also you might ask colleagues what they think about your various aids. Indeed, it is useful in a department to have a pool of aids so that you can use each others' and file them in a central place. In this way the time taken in their design and production is shared.

Evaluation of Aids			
Preview	**YES**	**NO**	**N.A**
1. Have you checked in advance:			
(a) That you have not used too many aids?			
(b) That you have not used too few aids?			
(c) That your aids work?			
Presentation			
2. Can the aid be seen/heard?			
3. Is it used for too long/not long enough?			
4. Is it clear (does it aid learning)?			
Design			
5. Will it work (blackout, bulbs, leads)?			
6. Is there a logical sequence?			
7. Is the time for use about right?			
8 Can it be misinterpreted?			
9. Is there enough/too much variety?			
10. Is there enough/too much colour?			
11. Is it well made?			
Use			
12. Have you invited co-operation of the students?			
13. Does it attract attention?			
14. Have you decided how it will be introduced?			
15. Does it supplement verbal information?			
16. Does it hold attention?			
17. Is it challenging for the students?			
18. Does it consolidate learning?			

Figure 4.20   *Checklist for the Evaluation of a Learning Aid*

Achieving the LLUK Professional Standards

Standards
Domain A: Professional values and practice
AK6.2   Ways to apply relevant statutory requirements and the underpinning principles.
Domain B: Learning and teaching
BK1.1   Ways to maintain a learning environment in which learners feel safe and supported.
BK1.2   Ways to develop and manage behaviours which promote respect for and between others and create as equitable and inclusive learning environment.
BK2.1   Principles of learning and ways to provide learning activities to meet curriculum requirements and the needs of all learners.
BK2.2   Ways to engage, motivate and encourage active participation of learners and learner independence.
BK3.3   Ways to structure and present information and ideas clearly and effectively to learners.
BK5.1   The impact of resources on effective learning.
BK5.2   Ways to ensure that resources used are inclusive, promote equality and support diversity.
Domain C: Specialist learning and teaching
CK3.1   Teaching and learning theories and strategies relevant to own specialist area.
CK3.5   Ways to support learners in the use of new and emerging technologies in own specialist area.
Domain D: Planning for learning
DK2.1   The importance of including learners in the planning process.
DK3.1   Ways to evaluate own role and performance in planning learning.
Domain F: Access and progression
FK1.1   Sources of information, advice, guidance and support to which learners might be referred.

Achieving the LLUK Professional Standards

Standards	Ways in which you can show that you have achieved the Standards	See Section
AK6.2 BK5.1 BK5.2	1. List the types of learning resources (visual aids) that you currently use. Explain how their design and use is influenced by factors such as: ▪ Teaching strategy. ▪ Learning styles. ▪ Type of learning. ▪ Number and type of student. ▪ Practical considerations. ▪ Equality of opportunity. ▪ ILT.	1 and 2
BK1.1 BK1.2 BK2.1 BK2.2 BK3.3 BK5.1 BK5.2	2. Design and produce three different resources and show how the design principles discussed in this chapter have informed the design process.	1
BK1.1 BK1.2 BK2.1 BK2.2 BK3.3 BK5.1 BK5.2	3. List the types of learning resources that you do not use but would like to. Explore the barriers that prevent their use and design an action plan to overcome these barriers.	1
BK1.1 BK1.2 BK2.1 BK2.2 BK3.3 BK5.1 BK5.2	4. For one resource that you use explain how you provide effective learning support to your students within the boundaries of your teaching role.	2
CK3.1 CK3.5	5. Explain how the use of ILT can enhance either the design or the use of resources for your students and your subject area.	4
CK3.1	6. From the list of hardware and software provided in this chapter, identify those aspects of ILT resources which are particularly appropriate to your students and your subject. Explain how each would be used to promote student learning.	4
DK2.1 DK3.1	7. Evaluate the effectiveness of one of your visual aids by the completion of the checklist in Figure 4.20. Draw conclusions from the completion to identify, with reasons, the effectiveness of the aid.	5
DK2.1 DK3.1	8. Review your teaching and identify any topics where you could encourage your students to make and/or use learning resources. Explore the value to both you and your students in employing this approach.	1, 2 and 3
FK1.1	9. Identify sources of information that might be used by your students where they might get advice, in the use of ILT, in their own work.	4

For a model approach to show how you have achieved the LLUK Professional Standards see Appendix I.

Chapter 5

Curricula, Courses and Lessons: Planning and Design

Overview

1. Curriculum Development

- Introduction
- Analysing a Syllabus

4. Lesson Planning

- Designing Plans
- Examples of Lesson Plans
- Negotiation
- Classroom Management

2. The Process of Specifying Learning Outcomes

- Course and Subject Aims
- Intended Learning Outcomes
- Product Objectives
- Process Objectives
- Competences

3. Schemes of Work

- Defining Topics
- Sequencing Topics
- Topic Analysis
- Planning Schemes

This chapter examines design and planning techniques to ensure efficient and effective learning. It explores the processes from the course aims and objectives through to detailed schemes of work and lesson plans.

LLUK Professional Standards

The Knowledge and Understanding within the LLUK Professional Standards incorporated in this chapter are:

Domain A: Professional values and practice

AK6.1   Relevant statutory requirements and codes of practice.

AK6.2   Ways to apply relevant statutory requirements and the underpinning principles.

Domain B: Learning and teaching

BK1.1   Ways to maintain a learning environment in which learners feel safe and supported.

BK1.2   Ways to develop and manage behaviours which promote respect for and between others and create an equitable and inclusive learning environment.

BK2.1   Principles of learning and ways to provide learning activities to meet curriculum requirements and the needs of all learners.

BK2.2   Ways to engage, motivate and encourage active participation of learners and learner independence.

BK3.3   Ways to structure and present information and ideas clearly and effectively to learners.

BK5.1   The impact of resources on effective learning.

BK5.2   Ways to ensure that resources used are inclusive, promote equality and support diversity.

Domain C: Specialist learning and teaching

CK3.1   Teaching and learning theories and strategies relevant to own specialist area.

CK3.5   Ways to support learners in the use of new and emerging technologies in own specialist area.

Domain D: Planning for learning

DK1.1   How to plan appropriate, effective, coherent and inclusive learning programmes that promote equality and engage with diversity.

DK1.2   How to plan a teaching session.

DK1.3   Strategies for flexibility in planning and delivery.

DK2.1   The importance of including learners in the planning process.

DK2.2   Ways to negotiate appropriate individual goals with learners.

DK3.1   Ways to evaluate own role and performance in planning learning.

Domain E: Assessment for learning

EK3.2   Ways to ensure access to assessment within a learning programme.

---

1.   Curriculum Development

1.1   Introduction

Educational institutions are fundamentally about learning. It follows that one of your duties as a teacher is to review your curriculum at regular intervals. This involves you in reviewing what you teach, what your students learn, how that learning is organised and with what success. Any changes resulting from these reviews can be called curriculum development.

You will need to ask three interlocking questions.

(a)   What is it that I want my students to learn?

(b)   How can I get them to learn it?

(c)   How will I know when they have done so?

Although you are generally presented with some form of syllabus upon which to base your teaching, the answer to these questions falls firmly upon your shoulders, not upon those of the syllabus designer. In order to find answers to questions, you must look at the aims and objectives of what is intended to be learned, sequence the objectives and choose appropriate teaching strategies and assessment methods. This is what curriculum development involves.

Your 'syllabus' document may be stated in terms of the aims of the subject, a list of objectives, a list of competences, a list of topics, or a mixture of some or all of these. It may also indicate the common themes to be developed and assignments that are to be completed by the learners. This document is the official guide to the course of study which is often prepared by an examining or validating body or by yourself.

The following are characteristics of a syllabus:

(a)   Aims of the course of study.

(b)   Pre-requisites/entry behaviour expected of the learners.

(c)   Expected outcomes (objectives, competences, etc.).

(d)   Major topics.

(e)   Time allocated for the coverage of the course.

(f)   Suggested teaching/learning methods.

(g)   Assessment procedures to be used.

(h)   Recommended textbooks and references.

However, not all syllabii have all of these features which means that the curriculum developer – you, the teacher – have to interpret them for your students.

1.2   Analysing a syllabus

Documentation for courses tends to be brief, ambiguous or lacking sufficient detail or guidance. You could use the following suggestions to minimise the effects of these weaknesses:

No.	Syllabus Deficiency	Possible effect on Teaching/Learning Process	Measure to minimise the effect
1.	Absence of depth of treatment.	Previous exam papers become the only guide. The effect being that teaching becomes based on recall of factual information.	Convey thoughts to syllabus designers and decide, with colleagues and industry, what depth is required.
2.	Absence of indication of ability and skills expected of student.	As (1) above.	As (1) above.
3.	No indication of teaching strategies to be used.	Most teaching strategies revert to what has been used before and to the needs of the examination/assessment.	List all teaching strategies and show how often they are used.
4.	No indication of 'best' resources to be used.	As (3) above.	List all necessary resources for 'best' coverage of the topics and ensure that they are available when needed.
5.	Not enough information on testing procedures.	The classroom testing may be done with little thought to remedial and enrichment teaching.	Review with colleagues how best to test and how best to use the results of testing.
6.	Absence of logical sequence of topics and content.	This is likely to lead to a serious discontinuity in the learning process.	Plan a logical sequence and make any additions/changes necessary.
7.	Absence of indication of useful links with other subjects.	Compartmentalisation of teaching can also lead to repetition of topics.	All teachers, to share their individual schemes of work.
8.	Absence of indication of links with industry.	This is likely to lead to inadequate and inappropriate learning experiences.	Review tasks required of course graduates in industry and build these into the course.
9.	Absence of abilities, skills and attitudes to be developed.	This can lead to teachers developing different abilities, or ignoring some important ones.	Write objectives for knowledge, skills and social abilities that are needed in industry.
10.	Absence of lesson plans.	As in (9) above.	Teachers to write lesson plans and to share them with colleagues.

2.   The Process of Specifying Learning Outcomes

Before considering the details of course planning and design, it can be helpful for you to consider the totality of the process and what is involved in the specification of learning outcomes. The diagram, Figure 5.1 shows the various components of the curriculum development process.

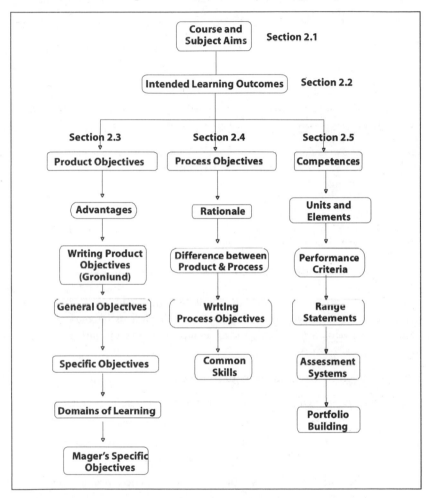

Figure 5.1   *Specifying Learning Outcomes*

This diagram shows us two main things:

(a)   That the development process is *sequential* starting with the aims of a course and progressing, with increasing detail, to more specific outcomes.

(b)   That there are *alternative ways of specifying* of learning behaviours. These are:

  (i)   Product objectives which concentrate upon what the student will be able to do as a result of learning; i.e. the end product

  (ii)   Process objectives which specify the use and application of knowledge and skills that are required for work; i.e. the way in which learning takes place.

Statements of competence which specify the knowledge and skills required in the workplace for a particular occupation.

gram suggests that you need to choose one of the three models. This is sometimes true. However, you can choose to use a mix of the above three models as appropriate.

The next sections of the chapter expand upon each aspect in the diagram.

2.1 Course and subject aims

Courses often consist of a number of 'subjects' or 'units' (for example Business Studies may include accounts, law, word-processing etc.). The development of courses and subjects, can be considered at course and subject levels.

Course Level – development at this level is concerned with the whole of what the student is intended to learn. It is sometimes, but not always, carried out by awarding bodies.

Subject Level – a subject is sometimes called a module or a Unit. Quite often a subject is the responsibility of one member of staff and the development is the responsibility of that member of staff. The subject is broken down into lessons.

Often teachers are required to complete development work at subject and lesson levels. Most of the external bodies like Edexcel, OCR as well as GCSE Examination Boards are placing more responsibility for the development work in the hands of the teacher.

The starting point for development work lies with the course aims. Course aims are fairly general and describe the overall purposes of the course. Davies (1971) describes these as 'ultimate goals' – goals that are to be reached by the learner at the end of the course in all of the subjects and all of the lessons. A course aim is a general statement which gives both shape and direction to the course. Aims are a starting point for curriculum development and are necessary in order to mould the more precise decisions that are to be taken.

The aims of a Civil Engineering Technician course might be to:

> Develop accuracy in measurement and methodical scheduling of quantities.
>
> Comprehend the factors which affect the cost of buildings.
>
> Develop knowledge of contractual procedures concerned with construction.
>
> Develop the ability to work as an effective member of a team.
>
> Develop the ability to prepare working drawings, sketches, specifications and planning data.

You will see that the aims are all related to the course of civil engineering and are requirements of the industry. The course will consist of a number of subjects (i.e. surveying, maths, services, building science, drawing) and each of these subjects will require its own aims. The course aim 'to develop the ability to prepare working drawings and sketches' suggests a drawing subject. This will have its own aims and these might be:

> Develop skill in the use of formal drawings as a means of communicating technical information.
>
> Understand architectural and working drawings.
>
> Show skill in the production of simple working drawings of plant rooms and their associated equipment.
>
> Etc.

It is important that you are able to differentiate between aims and the more detailed forms of learning outcome – objectives.

Product objectives and competence statements have 'rules' or procedures which help to make them unambiguous. There are no rules to assist with writing aims but the following gives some characteristics of aims which may help you to formulate your own course or subject aims.

Characteristics of aims

Are broad ranging and often cover several subjects or topics. They are general statements.

Often cover more than one domain of learning, perhaps encompassing all three domains.

Are long-term. The aims of a degree course may take three or more years to achieve.

Often contain more than one verb.

Are difficult to observe directly.

Give a sense of direction and 'flavour' of the course.

The list shown in Figure 5.2 can be useful when you are writing your own course aims.

Cognitive	Affective	Psychomotor
Identify Develop knowledge Give an understanding Apply Enable Provide a foundation Equip students with	Develop confidence Give an appreciation Assist flexibility Promote a positive attitude	Develop skill Develop competence

Figure 5.2 *Useful Terms for Writing Course or Subject Aims*

The following examples of aims illustrate the broad nature of aims and how they relate to a range of subject areas. You may find some of the phrases useful when you write aims for your own courses. A tip which we find helpful is to think about your course-leaflet, or how you advertise your course. The course aims should 'sell' your course to the students. They should give an idea of what the students should be able to do at the end of the course. They should be realistic and not misleading.

Examples of course aims

Develop road sense, driving skills and a mature and safe attitude to driving.

Develop the necessary knowledge and skills of a good bar manager and instil confidence in both colleagues and customers.

Increase the knowledge and skills needed to decorate a home.

Develop a creative and mature attitude to their work and customer relations.

Develop practical skills and confidence in handling cash and credit card sales.

To be able to apply a range of materials, colours and techniques in order to create a suitable decor in a variety of situations.

To provide a foundation for practising as qualified accountants in both the private and public sector.

Give an understanding of the world of work.

To prepare students to be able to budget their grants/loans appropriately, and develop confidence in cooking meals which are quick, cheap and nourishing.

You can use the checklist shown in Figure 5.3 for writing your own aims.

	Yes	No	Not Required
1. Do the aims cover: (a) knowledge required? (b) skills required? (c) attitudes required? (d) personal development?			
2. Do the aims identify priorities or are they all inclusive?			
3. Do the aims identify competences to be developed as well as topics or subject areas?			
4. Are the aims of practical use to the teacher or just decorative?			
5. Can the aims be used to write objectives?			
6. Are the number of aims about right to be useful (not too many or too few)?			

Figure 5.3   *Checklist for the Evaluation of Aims*

Not all of the aspects identified in the checklist will be required for all courses. Consequently, when completing the checklist for a specific set of aims, you will tick one of the columns 'yes', 'no' or 'not required'. For a well written set of aims, none of your ticks should appear in the 'no' column. If they do, the aims should either be re-written or modified.

2.2   Intended learning outcomes

In the previous section we discussed the aims of a course. These aims, however, are insufficient to convey to the teacher (or the students) the intended learning. More specific intentions, in other words objectives, will be needed. As we can see from the examples shown in Figure 5.4, an objective is a mixture of a *student behaviour* together with an element of *subject content*. Consider the three different categories of objective shown in Figure 5.4.

Objective Type	Example
Product objective **Process objective** **Competence**	Define raising agents in a recipe. Prepare a window display. Demonstrate competence in laying a table for guests.

Figure 5.4   *Examples of Different Types of Objective Statements*

It is important that you understand and can write objectives. Each type of objective will now be considered in isolation but you should remember that, in practice, a mix of types might be appropriate.

2.2.1 Learning behaviour

As a teacher, your concern is that your students should learn aspects which are considered desirable or educationally important. When we use the words 'learn' or 'learning' they can often have many meanings. To be useful, we have to agree upon an operational definition of the terms.

Suppose the students mentioned below were observed on two different occasions: before and then after teaching. There will be a difference between the two observations such as:

> Alan can read music.
>
> Cindy can solve equations.
>
> Kalo can turn a table leg on a lathe.
>
> Ram can recite a poem.
>
> Jane observes laboratory safety precautions.
>
> Ali can ride a bicycle.

Between the period of the two observations something must have occurred so that these students can now do what they could not do earlier.

You will see that what the students have learned is very different – each of them involved different behaviours. In educational terminology *behaviour* is used to represent any act that is performed by a person – physical, mental or emotional. We must remember that this use of the term behaviour is different from the one used in everyday language when it is normally used to describe the *good* or *bad* behaviour of a person.

If we agree that the term behaviour is used to denote any activity, it can be said that students are displaying a behaviour *after* learning that they did not display *before* their learning. In other words, the process of learning has resulted in a *change of behaviour*.

Therefore, if we can observe a change in the behaviour of a person, we may conclude that learning has taken place. In education, learning could be defined as:

> 'a relatively permanent change in behaviour as a result of experience, training or practice'.

2.3 Product objectives

2.3.1 The advantages of product objectives

Product objectives were the first of the three types of learning behaviour shown in Figure 5.4. Earlier in the book we suggested that objectives were useful for:

> Communicating intended learning outcomes.
>
> Teachers.
>
> Students in learning.
>
> Assessing the learning that has taken place.
>
> Improving teaching.

We should also have noted that objectives should be written in terms of **intended learning outcomes** that are expected after instruction.

The second point to note is that as objectives are used by so many people (such as students, teachers and examiners), in order for them to be effective they must convey the same meaning to everyone who reads them. In other words, they must be unambiguous.

Consider the following statement written as a product objective:

'This lesson is intended to demonstrate the blood circulation system to the students'.

What is wrong with this? You will notice that it describes the method of instruction but it does **not** specify the intended learning outcome. What does the teacher expect the learners to learn? What changes in behaviour will the students display? If the teacher does not know this, how can the learning be verified? Technically speaking the objective will be achieved as soon as the teacher completes the demonstration, irrespective of whether the students have learned anything or not.

Now consider the following objective:

'At the end of instruction, the student will understand the working of a petrol engine.'

Note that in this case the objective is stated in terms of *learning outcome*; in other words that at the end of learning, the student will *understand*.

But, does it convey the same meaning to everyone? What does the term 'understand' mean? What will the students have to do to demonstrate that they actually understand? Will they have to describe the petrol engine? Will they have to draw a sketch of the parts? Will they have to identify the working parts? Or will they have to complete all of these?

Although the understanding of the working of the petrol engine may be a desirable learning outcome, the use of the word 'understand' does not clearly communicate the intent of the objective and therefore it is not useful in guiding the teaching and testing. The term has to be less ambiguous.

There are many verbs similar to the verb 'understand' which are open to many interpretations: for example, such words as 'know', 'appreciate', 'enjoy', 'believe', 'think critically' and many others The main reasons for the different interpretations is that these verbs attempt to describe what goes on in the mind of the student. Since an observer cannot enter the mind of the student, a teacher does not know when students understand or when they appreciate.

What is required is a statement of some observable behaviour which can be accepted as proof or indication of the student's understanding or appreciation. In other words, a product objective should specify what the student should be able to do which can be observed by an outsider. For instance, if it is agreed that a learner can do the following, it should be accepted that they understand Newton's Laws:

1. *States* Newton's laws in own words.
2. Gives *examples* where each law is applicable.
3. *Distinguish* between the situations where each law is applicable.

Note: Each of the words that are written in italics describe actions which could be observed and indicate specific behaviours which could be measured (tested) to find if the objective had been achieved.

When the objective is written using a verb which specifies an *observable behaviour* it is known as a *product objective* (or sometimes called a behavioural objective, or specific objective).

Verbs such as 'write', 'state', 'identify', 'classify' or 'draw' describe actions which can be observed and, therefore, **can** be used when writing product objectives. Verbs like 'know', 'understand', 'appreciate' or 'think' do not describe observable action hence they cannot be used in specific product objectives.

There has always been a tension in education regarding detailed specification of learning outcomes and more generalised statements. The debate will go on. You may have a choice or you may be constrained to follow a certain model. Whichever, you need to be aware of the benefits and limitations of product objectives. Figure 5.5 gives a summary of the main points.

Product Objectives	
Advantages	**Limitations**
• gives students a clear target	• limits student learning
• gives teachers a clear framework	• constrains teacher
• communicates to third parties e.g. employers	• can be too detailed
• informs assessment	• may be perceived as trivial
• informs selection of teaching strategies	• may not help achieve overall aims
• provides clear standards	• are time consuming to write
• encourages planning	• may be given undue status
• gives a reliable system	• may be perceived as too narrow
• are unambiguous	

Figure 5.5 *Product Objectives: Advantages and Limitations*

2.3.2 Writing product objectives – Gronlund's approach

In the previous section we defined Product Objectives as a statement which uses a verb specifying observable behaviour and we identified the difference between observable and unobservable behaviours. There are situations where the teaching of specific observable behaviours is very useful; particularly for knowledge level objectives. However, much education is directed to the more complex behaviours of understanding and applying knowledge. Employees need not only to know the principles of their vocation, but they need to understand them so that such principles can be applied to specific situations. Earlier, we noted that verbs like 'understand' and 'apply' do not describe an observable behaviour. Hence they cannot be used for the writing of product objectives in behavioural terms. If we sought to specify all of the learning outcomes, the number of objectives required for a subject/topic would be too great. Too many product objectives may restrict the scope of teaching.

In an attempt to ensure that (a) the totality of the subject matter for teaching purposes is covered and (b) the specific behaviours are suitable for the formulation of assessment, Norman Gronlund (1970) suggests writing product objectives at two levels. These are:

1. *General objectives,* and
2. A sample of *Specific objectives* corresponding to and representative of each general objective.

Gronlund further suggests that *teaching* should be directed towards the achievement of the general objectives whereas the specific objectives should form the basis of *assessment*.

An example of the Gronlund approach is shown in Figure 5.6

General Objective:	1.	Understand Newton's Laws of Motion
Specific Objectives:	1:1	State Newton's Laws of Motion.
	1:2	Define force, momentum, action and reaction.
	1:3	Explain the units of force.
	1:4	Derive the relation F = m.a
	1:5	Etc.

Figure 5.6 *Example of Gronlund Style Objectives*

Note that verbs like 'know', 'understand' 'apply' and 'appreciate', which we considered unsuitable for stating behavioural objectives, may now be used for stating general objectives. The general objective describes a general learning outcome which, by itself, is not observable. It is, however, further clarified through a representative sample of specific behaviours.

2.3.3 General objectives: guidelines

Guideline 1.   Objectives should be stated in terms of student performance.

Consider the following two objectives:

1.   To teach Faraday's Laws of electro-magnetic induction.
2.   Understand Faraday's Laws of electro-magnetic induction.

The focus of the first of the objectives is on what the teacher does, whereas the attention of the second one is on what the student does; in this case what the student understands. Objectives should always be stated in terms of student behaviour rather than in terms of teacher behaviour.

Guideline 2.   Objectives should be stated in terms of the learning outcome and not in terms of the learning process.

Examine the following statement:

'The student gains knowledge of Bernoulli's theorem'.

The statement emphasises the gaining of knowledge (the learning process) rather than the type of behaviour that provides evidence that learning has taken place. Words like 'gains' 'acquires' and 'develops' generally indicate the learning process rather than the desired outcome of the learning experience.

Guideline 3.   Statements of objectives should be an amalgamation of subject matter and the desired behaviour.

Examine the following:

1.   Armature reaction.
2.   Understands armature reaction in a D.C. machine.

The first statement is merely subject matter and contains no verb or student behaviour. The second tells the general outcome of learning with the addition of the desired student behaviour; it is an amalgamation of the subject matter and the student behaviour.

Guideline 4.   Avoid the use of more than one verb in each General Objective.

Read the following objectives:

1. Uses appropriate experimental procedures in solving problems.
2. Knows the scientific method and applies it effectively.

The second objective includes both 'knows' and 'applies' as possible learning outcomes. It is better to have a separate statement for each because some students may 'know' the scientific method (that is be able to state it) but may not be able to 'apply' it effectively.

The checklist shown in Figure 5.7 can be helpful when writing your own general objectives.

Aspect	Yes	No
1. Does the general objective indicate an outcome appropriate to the subject?		
2. Does the general objective include desired outcomes such as knowledge, skills, attitudes, etc?		
3. Is the general objective attainable, taking into account the ability of the learners, facilities, time, constraints, etc?		
4. Is the general objective relevant to the course aims?		
5. Does the general objective begin with a verb?		
6. Is the general objective clear, concise and well defined?		

Figure 5.7   *Checklist for Evaluating General Objectives*

2.3.4 Specific objectives: guidelines

The following guidelines should assist you to write specific objectives which will expand upon the general objective and give a representative sample of behaviours showing how the general objective could be assessed.

1. State the general objective.
2. Begin each specific objective with an action verb which indicates what the students have to do.
3. Write the specific objectives so that they explain the general objective.
4. State the objective including conditions and criteria, where possible, in order to reduce ambiguity.
5. Do not omit complex objectives (e.g. appreciation) simply because they are difficult to state in behavioural terms.
6. Write a sufficient number of specific objectives for each general objective so as to adequately describe the student behaviours for achieving the general objective.
7. Write a specific objective to communicate each learning outcome.
8. Sequence the specific objectives in such a way that the learning outcome of one becomes the pre-requisite for achieving the learning outcome of the next.

A checklist is shown in Figure 5.8 which is similar to the one for General Objectives. It, again, provides the important aspect for writing specific objectives.

Aspect	Yes	No
1. Are the specific objectives relevant to the general objective?		
2. Does the specific objective contain a verb which is an observable behaviour?		
3. Is the specific objective stated in terms of student behaviour as opposed to teacher behaviour?		
4. Does the specific objective communicate only one learning outcome?		
5. Have the specific objectives been arranged in a logical sequence?		
6. When seen as a whole, does the list of specific objectives reflect what is intended by the corresponding general objective?		

Figure 5.8 *Checklist for Evaluating Specific Objectives*

Writing general and specific objectives must be within one of three domains and at a specific level within that domain. The process relies upon the specification of the *verb* which is relevant to both domain and level. The lists shown in Figures 5.9 and 5.10 are adapted from Gronlund (1970) and give an indication of the verbs that might be considered for writing general and specific objectives. Notice that some of the verbs appear in more than one domain and more than one category in the cognitive domain. The reason for this is that the verbs are only *illustrative* of the domain and level and the specific level depends upon the context within which the verb appears. For instance the verb 'solve' (a specific objective cognitive verb) can be at three levels.

'Solve two times two' is recalled as 'four' and is *knowledge*. 'Solve a problem' by putting numbers into an equation is *comprehension*. 'Solve the height of a building' by devising an equation for the first time is *application*. Thus, the verbs given in the lists are to assist with writing objectives: there are many others and the ones given are only an indication of those that you might use.

Level	Illustrative General Objective	Illustrative Verbs for Specific Objectives
Knowledge	**Knows** common terms. **Knows** specific facts. **Knows** basic concepts. **Knows** principles. **Knows** basic procedures.	Defines, describes, identifies, labels, lists, names, outlines, reproduces, selects, states.
Comprehension	**Understands** facts. **Understands** how to interpret charts and graphs. **Understands** how to translate verbal material to maths formulae. **Understands** how to estimate future consequences from data.	Converts, classifies, compares, contrasts, defends, determines, distinguishes, estimates, explains, extends, generalises, gives new examples, infers, justifies, paraphrases, reviews, suggests, summarises.
Application	**Applies** concepts and principles to new situations. **Applies** laws/theories to practical situations. Constructs charts and graphs.	Changes, computes, demonstrates, discovers, manipulates, modifies, predicts, prepares, produces, relates, shows, solves, uses.
Higher than Application (Analysis, synthesis & evaluation)	**Recognises** unstated assumptions. **Integrates** learning from different areas into a plan for solving a problem. **Judges** the logical consistency of written materials.	Breaks down, discriminates, infers, outlines, relates, separates. Categorises, combines, devises, designs, modifies, plans, rewrites, summarises. Appraises, compares, concludes, justifies.

Figure 5.9   *Illustrative Verbs for Specific Objectives in the Cognitive Domain*

Domain	Illustrative General Objective	Illustrative Verbs for Specific Objectives
Affective	**Appreciates** the need to show sensitivity to human needs and social problems. **Appreciates** the need for class discussion. **Appreciates** safety rules. **Appreciates** a healthy diet.	Asks, chooses, selects, answers, assists, complies, practices, follows, forms, initiates, influences, shares, studies, works on own volition.
Psychomotor	**Shows skill in** writing. **Shows skill in** operating. **Shows skill in** typing. **Shows skill in** preparing food. **Shows skill in** cutting hair.	Assembles, builds, calibrates, changes, cleans, connects, composes, creates, designs, hammers, makes, manipulates, mends, paints, saws, sews, sketches, starts, stirs, weighs.

Figure 5.10   *Illustrative Verbs for Specific Objectives in the Affective and Psychomotor Domains*

2.3.5 Domains

Selecting the domain

You should note that few objectives are purely cognitive, psychomotor or affective. The major criterion that we use in selecting the domain in which the objective belongs is the *primary behaviour* called for: if it relates primarily to 'knowing' about the subject, it is cognitive; if it relates primarily to physical 'skill behaviour', it is psychomotor; and if it relates primarily to 'feelings' or 'attitudes', it is affective. The checklist shown in Figure 5.11 can be used for writing your own product (general and specific) objectives.

Aspect	Yes	No
1. Does each objective have an observable verb?		
2. Does each objective contain only one behaviour?		
3. Does each objective in the cognitive domain deal with intellectual skills?		
4. Does each of the objectives in the psychomotor domain deal with physical skills?		
5. Does each of the objectives in the affective domain deal with attitudes, feelings or emotions?		

Figure 5.11   *Checklist for Evaluating Product Objectives*

Precision in classification into levels within a domain

In many instances you can classify a given objective as belonging to one level from one point of view and to another level from a different point of view. In such cases, particularly for psychomotor and affective objectives, it may not be advisable for you to classify them as strictly belonging to one level or another. For most occasions you will find it acceptable if the following simplification of the levels is used for operational purposes:

1.   The levels in the cognitive domain are classified as:

    (a)   Knowledge.   (b)   Comprehension.

    (c)   Application.   (d)   Higher than Application.

You should note that level (d) includes the levels of Analysis, Synthesis and Evaluation. This level is sometimes called 'Invention' and this is descriptive in that it is a high level cognitive behaviour which involves the learner in doing something new. Very little of many syllabuses will contain a high percentage of this level and some, particularly in the initial years of a course, may not contain any at all.

2.   No sub-division of the Psychomotor and Affective domains need be used.

Uses of taxonomic Levels

You will notice that classifying product objectives into the different levels in domains will assist you in your teaching in the following ways:

1.   To *sequence* objectives for teaching so that learning progresses from known to unknown and simple to complex.

2.   To include objectives at *all* of the required levels within a domain. This ensures that you emphasise the different levels required by the overall aims of the course.

3.   To construct appropriate *assessments* in order to measure desirable changes in behaviour at the required levels.

Taxonomic levels in teaching/learning programmes

You may not find it possible or desirable within the time available to develop all cognitive, psychomotor or affective abilities to the highest level in each domain. For example, some motor skills may be developed to a naturalisation level (done automatically and with ease), but it would not be possible or even realistic to expect all skills to be developed to this level. Similarly, in the affective domain you will find it likely that most of the objectives may not go farther than the valuing level and it has already been indicated that the higher than application level in the cognitive domain is a high level skill with only small amounts in any one year of a course. The tasks which students have to perform determine, to a large extent, the taxonomic levels to which they have to be developed during the educational programme.

2.3.6   Mager's approach to writing product objectives

In the previous sections we described Gronlund's approach to writing general and specific objectives and we identified the taxonomic levels in the three learning domains. Gronlund's approach to writing objectives has much to commend it. However, you will find that the specific objectives are often open to interpretation due to their lack of specificity. Robert Mager (1970) suggests a method of overcoming this problem.

The intention is to make specific objectives unambiguous so that everyone who reads them gets the same meaning. There are two ways in which we can achieve this:

1. Write all product objectives using terms which describe only the specific observable behaviours as intended learning outcomes.

2. Use non-observable terms to describe the intended learning outcomes and then add a sample of specific behaviours.

The first method of writing product objectives is the one favoured by Robert Mager while the second one is the one that we have already described as suggested by Norman Gronlund. As a teacher you will find both methods useful. You will find some situations in which the Mager type objective is useful and others where the Gronlund approach helps. Mager suggests that objectives should be written which specify what the learner should be able to perform (or do) to demonstrate mastery of the subject/topic. As many statements as necessary should be written to describe all of the learning outcomes.

He further recommends that to make the objective more specific, it should contain three elements. According to Mager it is, however, not always essential to include all three elements in every objective. The three elements are:

1. *Terminal Behaviour* (behaviour to be demonstrated by the student at the end of instruction).

2. Important *conditions* under which the terminal behaviour is expected to occur.

3. *Criteria* of acceptable performance.

Terminal behaviour

The terminal behaviour describes what the student will do or perform after instruction. It is essential that it should specify observable behaviour like 'repair', 'state', 'write', 'select'. Verbs like 'know', 'understand' and 'appreciate' which are not observable behaviours do not qualify to describe terminal behaviour in Mager's approach.

Conditions

Conditions refer to what the learner will be given, for example, with the help of 'handbook', 'tools', 'references'. It can also specify what the learner will be denied, for example 'without the use of a calculator', 'from memory'.

Criteria

Criteria refer to the extent or standard of attainment. They may specify speed or efficiency, for example, 'within 40 minutes'. They may make reference to quality or quantity, for example 'to the second place of decimals', 'eight out of ten correct'.

The following **example** shows the three elements in use:

Given a 7.5 kW DC motor, that contains a single fault and given a standard kit and references, the student must be able to repair the motor within 45 minutes.

In the above objective:

1. *Repair* communicates the desired terminal behaviour.

2. *Given a 7.5 kW DC motor that contains a single fault and a standard set of tool and references* communicates the conditions under which the behaviour is expected to occur.

3. *Within 45 minutes* tells us the criteria of acceptable performance.

A simplified approach to this is to ask yourself three questions:

What do you want your students to be able to do?

How do you want your students to demonstrate that they have learned?

How well do your students have to perform?

An example of this approach is as follows:

What: Swim 50 metres,

How: in a swimming pool, wearing outdoor clothes,

How well: within ten minutes.

Figure 5.12 illustrates some examples which may help you. But please bear in mind that it is not always possible to stipulate the conditions and/or the criteria.

What (Behaviour Performance)	How (Conditions)	How Well (Criteria)
Lay a table for 20 places.	Given a menu and 30 minutes.	Correctly.
List the sequence of steps needed to change a circuit in a P.C.	Without reference to notes or manual.	Correct sequence without error.
Identify O.S. signs.	Given an O.S. map.	With 9 out of 10 correct.
Change a car wheel.	On a drive, observing safety precautions.	Within 10 minutes.

Figure 5.12   *Examples of Objectives with Conditions and Criteria*

2.3.7 Examples of product objectives

We have discussed several guidelines which are intended to help you to write objectives. You may feel overwhelmed! This section gives examples of general and specific objectives which cover a range of subjects. We hope these may give you some ideas and some encouragement. A range of styles is used and you are encouraged to adopt your own style.

Example 1: resuscitation

1.0   **Know basic anatomy and physiology of the heart.**

    1.1   State the main functions and components of the heart.

2.0   **Understand the need and procedure for basic life support.**

    2.1   Describe the method for carrying out cardio-pulmonary resuscitation (CPR).

    2.2   Explain the procedure of CPR using appropriate medical terminology.

    2.3   List 3 causes of cardiac arrest.

    2.4   State the signs and symptoms of cardiac arrest.

    2.5   Explain the role of the nurse during and after a cardiac arrest.

3.0   **Show skill in carrying out basic life support.**

    3.1   Perform basic life support unaided and with assistance.

    3.1   Carry out immediate post resuscitation care.

Example 2: music

1.0   Know composers and compositions.

    1.1   List five composers.

    1.2   State at least two works of the above composers.

2.0   Understand concepts which influence musical sounds.

    2.1   State the effect of rhythm

    2.2   State the different keys

    2.3   Explain how minor keys influence the mood.

Example 3: food hygiene

1.0   Know the correct storage conditions for all raw materials.

    1.1   State 3 storage conditions for raw meats given four examples.

2.0   Appreciate the importance of correct procedures.

    2.1   Choose to follow correct procedures.

3.0   Show skill in raw food preparation.

    3.1   Prepares two items of raw food to prescribed standards within specified time.

Example 4: driving

1.0   Know the Highway Code.

    1.1   State 90% of road signs correctly.

    1.2   State correct braking distance on wet and dry roads.

2.0   Appreciate the importance of road sense.

    2.1   Choose to drive with safe distances.

    2.2   Choose to comply with speed limits.

3.0   Show skill with driving techniques.

    3.1   Complete an emergency stop safely.

    3.2   Use gears correctly.

Example 5: bar management

1.0   Know the law relating to bar management.

    1.1   State opening hours.

    1.2   State age limits.

2.0   Appreciate the need for good customer relations.

    2.1   Choose to engage customer in conversation.

Example 6: painting and decorating

1.0   Understand the importance of thorough preparation of surfaces.

    1.1   State how to prepare a surface.

    1.2   Explain the implications of poor preparation.

2.0   Appreciate the importance of safety.

    2.1   Choose to ensure adequate ventilation.

3.0 Show skill in painting.

   3.1   Paint a door to a smooth surface with total coverage.

Example 7: information technology

General Objectives	Specific Objectives
Know the basic components of a computer.	• Name the parts of a PC.
Show skill in the use of the component parts of the computer.	• Manipulate the appropriate keys of the keyboard.
	• Manipulate the mouse correctly.
	• Use diskettes correctly.
	• Manipulate the floppy disk drive correctly.
Appreciate the need for safety whilst using a computer.	• Choose not to eat or drink whilst working on a computer.
	• Choose to adopt a correct posture and position whilst working.
	• Choose to take breaks away from the computer at 2 hour intervals.
Understand the concepts of how to store and retrieve files.	• State the correct commands for saving files.
	• State the correct commands for loading files.
	• Explain the rules governing the naming of files.
Understand the concepts of disk drives and directories.	• Explain the difference between the hard drive and the floppy drive.
	• Explain the structure of file directories.
Appreciate the need to organise files and disks.	• Choose to organise his/her files correctly and logically.
	• Choose to store diskettes safely.
	• Choose to use appropriate file names.
	• Choose to back up files regularly.
Understand the basic WINDOWS concepts.	• Name the various parts of the WINDOWS screen.
	• Explain the principles of multiple windows.
	• Define 'icons'.

2.4   Process objectives

2.4.1 Rationale for process objectives

In the previous section, we concentrated upon writing product objectives and we suggested that general and specific objectives were a useful method to convey their meaning. We further suggested that this type was useful for the acquisition of knowledge and skills. However, apart from knowledge and skill, a workforce needs to be adaptable and flexible due to the rapid changes in technology. The knowledge and skills associated with product objectives do not necessarily give us this required flexibility

– hence the need for process objectives which concentrate upon the use and application of knowledge and skills that are required for work.

Traditional examinations are characterised by:

> A dependence on memory and speed.
>
> A judgment made on a single occasion.
>
> A judgment made by someone remote from the learner.
>
> The need for contrived problems to suit designated examination times.
>
> A lack of acknowledgement of transferable skill development.
>
> A likelihood that they are norm referenced.

We can identify two major problems with product objectives:

(a)   There is a likelihood for curriculum developers to (over) concentrate on the low level skills because these are the easiest product objectives to write and assess.

(b)   Teachers tend only to teach to the behaviours stated in the specific objectives and ignore the more all-embracing general objective which precedes them.

Work-based assessment is characterised by:

> A need to investigate, inquire and be reliable.
>
> The fact that assessment is continuous.
>
> Judgment being carried out by oneself and peers, providing feedback.
>
> Real-life problems.
>
> Skill development being continuously demonstrated as circumstances change.
>
> Being criterion referenced because a certain level of competence is required.

If our courses are to reflect the needs of the workplace then the objectives should reflect processes or competences that are important at work.

The addition of process objectives to a course specification is an attempt to ensure that students not only acquire knowledge but, also, apply it. Such activities are more likely to lead to learning which is flexible and durable as it will allow our students to change to meet the needs of a changing technology. Additionally, the inclusion of such process objectives is likely to lead to increased student motivation when they realise that the competences are relevant to their work.

Justification for the process model is given by Cole (1982) where he suggests that promotion of process education 'stems from the realities of a satisfying and productive life in the present world'. He suggests the following eight justifications:

1.   The world is changing so fast that it is impossible to predict what knowledge individuals will need in the next few years.

2.   The state of knowledge is so vast that only a small proportion can be taught to students.

3.   The acquisition of processes ensures an individual who can solve problems.

4.   Processes are more widely applicable than knowledge and information.

5.   Processes are more permanent than other types of learning.

6.   Information is easily obtained when needed but processes cannot be 'looked up'.

7.   An emphasis on processes is needed to prevent academic isolation and social irrelevancy.

8.   Processes are required for learning to occur through formal education.

2.4.2 Differences between process and product objectives

The key features of the process model are:

(a) A focus on student activities.

(b) The teaching and assessment of transferable skills which are common to a number of subject disciplines.

These key features mean that process-based curricula focus on a clear description and identification of the learning activities like the following:

> Communication skills.
>
> Problem solving skills.
>
> Self appraisal and evaluation.
>
> Working as an effective group member.

As you will see, these activities are common to all work personnel and are required as life skills. Of course, they need to be aligned to relevant subject content and it is suggested that this is completed in one of the two ways shown in the next section.

The Product and Process models may be better understood by comparing and contrasting key features as shown in Figure 5.13.

Product Model	Process Model
Concentrates on the output i.e. the end or terminal behaviour, the end product.	Concentrates on the learning experiences and student activities.
Students tend to learn very similar things.	Students may learn very different things because the experiences are individually interpreted.
The teaching and learning are seen as a means to an end.	The teaching and learning activities are seen as inherently worthwhile.
Learning is observable or measurable.	Learning may not be observable or measurable.
Outcomes are predictable.	Outcomes may be unpredictable.
Content important and dominant.	Content not so important.

Figure 5.13 *Features of Product and Process Education*

The examples given in 5.14 will serve to illustrate the main facets of the models. First, you should notice the difference between product and process types and see that product objectives concentrate upon student terminal behaviours whilst the process type concentrate upon student activities.

Product Objectives	Process Objectives
State the principle of movement.	• Establish the effect of a force rotating about a point.
Draw a histogram from specific data.	• Collect, tabulate and summarise statistical data.
List at least 5 reasons for planning lessons.	• Participate in a discussion on lesson planning.

Figure 5.14 *Examples of Product and Process Objectives*

2.4.3 Writing process objectives

You will remember from the previous section that process objectives concentrate upon student experiences. Process objectives should:

1. Reflect the general learning that the subject/course aims to achieve.

2. Blur the boundaries between topics and often make reference to personal qualities, skills, attitudes and practical knowledge.

3. Rely more on the generalised process skills of analysis and problem solving, personal qualities such as resilience and responsibility, the ability to transfer knowledge and skills acquired in one context to other problems and situations.

4. State them in terms of the experiences that students will undergo.

BTEC (1988) suggest two methods of writing process objectives. Both of these employ what they call principal objectives, the bases of learning, and these are supported by either indicative objectives or indicative content. The methods are outlined below:

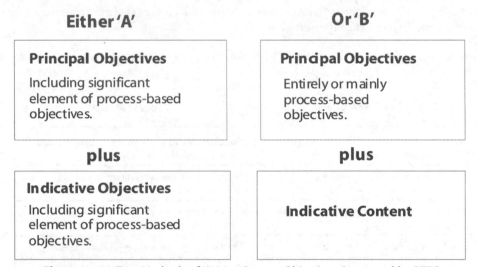

Figure 5.15 *Two Methods of Writing Process Objectives Suggested by BTEC*

You can see that principal objectives are like the general objectives discussed earlier. However, these contain a significant amount of process-based objectives. Associated with these principal objectives are either *indicative objectives* or *indicative content*. The word 'indicative' is obviously important in that the principal objectives may be achieved in a number of different ways. The indicative content or indicative objectives are just some of the ways in which this might take place. The main difference between the two methods of specification is that 'A' has fewer process-based objectives than 'B'. If indicative content is given as in 'B', then more of the principal objectives are required to be process-based.

To illustrate the use of **principal objectives and indicative objectives and indicative content**, the following examples are given:

Principal objective

Obtain information on basic financial accounting procedures used in a variety of offices.

Indicative content

The principal objective might cover items such as:

> Invoices, order forms, credit purchases and sales, delivery notes, statements of accounts.
>
> Methods and procedures used to record transactions and verify payments.
>
> Documenting, recording and valuing stock.
>
> Payroll operating.
>
> Computer-based and manual systems.

Here, you will see that the principal objective concentrates upon the process of obtaining information; students are required to find their own information on financial accounting procedures as opposed to it being given to them. The content is only indicative and covers a variety of aspects that might be obtained by the students.

An example of **principal objective followed by indicative objectives** is related to workshop safety and shown below.

Principal objective

Simulates the appropriate procedures which should be adopted in the event of workshop accidents.

Indicative objectives

The principal objective might cover items such as:

> Giving mouth to mouth resuscitation using a simulated patient.
>
> Describing the effects of various types of fire e.g. oil, electrical, chemical.
>
> Bandaging various types of physical injury.

Here the process involves the simulation of procedures in the event of workshop accidents. The indicative objectives are of the process type except for the describing of the effects of fire – this is a product type.

You can use the checklist shown in Figure 5.16 for writing process objectives.

Aspect	Yes	No
1. Are the principal objectives written in terms of processes?		

2. Are the process objectives written to:
    (i)   Reflect the general learning of the course?
    (ii)   Blur boundaries between topics?
    (iii)   Rely on process skills?
    (iv) State experiences that the learners will undergo?		

3. Do the indicative objectives include a significant element of process-based objectives?		
4. Are the student learning experiences explicitly defined?		

Figure 5.16   *Checklist for Evaluating Process Objectives*

2.4.4   Key (common or core) skills

The term skill denotes cognitive (or thinking) skills as well as the more purely technical or manipulative (psychomotor) abilities. Thus, we see that there are two kinds of skill:

> *Vocationally specific*, that is those applying to a particular vocational area.
>
> *Common*, that is those general or transferable skills like the ability to acquire new knowledge or to cope with problems of an unpredictable character.

We previously suggested that the key features of the process model are the transferable, common, key or core skills and that these are based on competences that are common to a number of subject disciplines.

The term 'key skill' is to be used in this book but synonyms for it are often used such as 'transferable skills', 'general skills', 'core skills' or 'core competences'.

Definition of key skill

A key skill can be defined as:

> The possession and development of sufficient knowledge, appropriate attitudes and experience for successful performance in life roles. This includes employment and other forms of work; it implies maturity and responsibility in a variety of roles; and it includes experience as an essential element of competence.

The QCA (Qualifications and Curriculum Authority) place great importance on these key skills, as do awarding bodies.

Initially, key skills were seen as transferable skills which play an essential role in developing personal effectiveness in adult and working life. Workers with such skills are able to adapt and respond creatively to change.

Originally, these common skills were: managing and developing self; working with and relating to others; communicating; managing tasks and solving problems; applying numeracy; applying technology; applying design and creativity.

Common skills should help the students to apply knowledge and understanding to real situations, to cope with problems of an unpredictable character, and to acquire new knowledge.

There are 6 key skill units. These are:

> Application of number.
>
> Communication.
>
> Information communication technology (ICT).
>
> Working with others.
>
> Improving own learning and performance.
>
> Problem solving.

Each of these units are available at levels 1 (GCSE grades D-E) through to level 4 (higher education work). They are all assessed by creation of a portfolio of work but the first three units (Application of number, Communications and ICT) are also assessed by examination. In some cases students can claim exemption from the key skills tests when they have successfully completed similar examination such as GCSE or A level English or Literature. They must, however, complete the portfolio of work.

The six key skills are as follows:

Application of number	This skill involves interpreting information associated with numbers, calculating and presenting findings. Such skills can be addressed by: • Measuring. • Calculating amounts and sizes. • Using charts to present and interpret information. • Analysing and interpreting complex information presented in a variety of ways.
Communication	This skill covers reading, writing and listening skills. Such skills can be addressed by: • Taking part in a discussion. • Reading materials. • Presenting information in a variety of ways. • Completing forms and writing a report. • Analysing and interpreting information and complex information.
ICT	This skill covers using a computer to find and present information in a variety of formats. Such skills can be addressed by: • Finding specific information using a computer. • Presenting information in a variety of formats. • Writing letters and reports.
Working with others	This skill involves carrying out team activities. Such skills can be addressed by: • Working in a team to carry out a task. • Carrying out a group project. • Organising an event.
Improving own learning and performance	This skill involves managing your own personal learning and development. Such skills can be addressed by: • Setting targets to improve your own performance. • Organising your approach to learning. • Reviewing and reflecting on your progress.
Problem solving	This skill is about recognising and solving problems. Such skills can be addressed by: • Working out how to solve problems at home, at work or as part of your studies. • Using a variety of methods to solve problems. • Reflecting on how well you have solved the problem.

Teaching key skills can be either as a specific subject or, more effectively, integrated into the student's vocational subjects. For example Working with others can be addressed by the organisation of event, such as an exhibition of work completed in a vocational subject. Here the students as a group decide on the major aspects such as when, venue, aims, costs and individuals are given specific tasks. It might be one student is given the task of sending out letters to perspective exhibitors, another organising and pricing the venue or catering costs. Information is recorded for each meeting, the work undertaken and forms the basis for the students' portfolio of evidence.

Additional skills such as Application of Number and Communications can also be integrated into such an event. Application of Number for example can be used to identify the floor space of the exhibition and so decide on costs charged to exhibitors. Discounts could be offered for local clubs, charities and education establishments so introducing percentages. Writing letters, invitations and recording of minutes brings in communication skills.

Although hard work to organise, such events tend to interest the students. Ideas should be planned well in advance and the pitfalls identified. It does promote teamwork among teachers and is a good way of bringing together a variety of subjects into a more meaningful and realistic set of a assignments.

A simple example is the construction of a web site by students. This type of activity can incorporate most if not all of the key skills subjects. Students working in groups decide on the purpose of the web site, identify individual working tasks and time limits. More realistic events involve bringing in outside companies so that the students get the realism of discussing with a real client, creating artwork which will be criticised by real client and the students have to communicate effectively. Such a scenario is much more effective for a group of second year or higher level students who have the subject knowledge and can therefore offer a realistic solution to the problem.

2.5   Competences

2.5.1   Units and elements of competence

A competence is defined as the 'ability to perform an activity within an occupation'. Competence is a wide concept which embodies the ability to transfer skills and knowledge to new situations (Bloom's application level in the cognitive domain and a high level ability) within the occupational areas and includes aspects of 'key' skills. In order to receive a qualification, candidates need to accumulate the *units* of the competence which make up that qualification. Each unit is usefully subdivided into appropriate *elements*. The relationship between the qualification and its units and elements are shown diagrammatically in Figure 5.17.

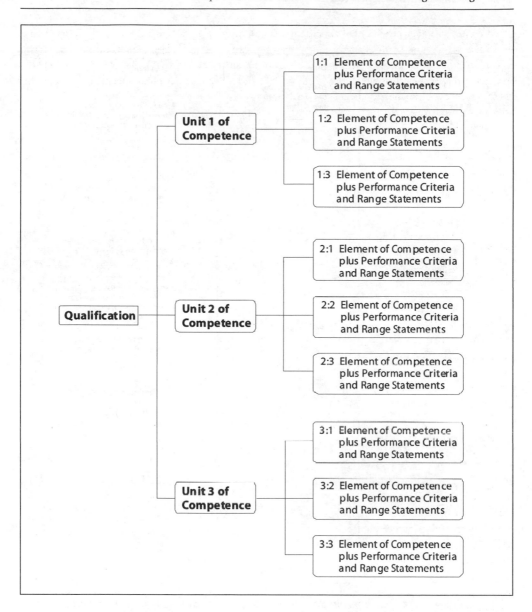

Figure 5.17   *Relationship Between Units and Elements*

Figure 5.18 shows how the units and elements have been applied by the Training and Development Lead Body to one of their areas (Provide Learning Opportunities, Resources and Support) with its two elements and associated units.

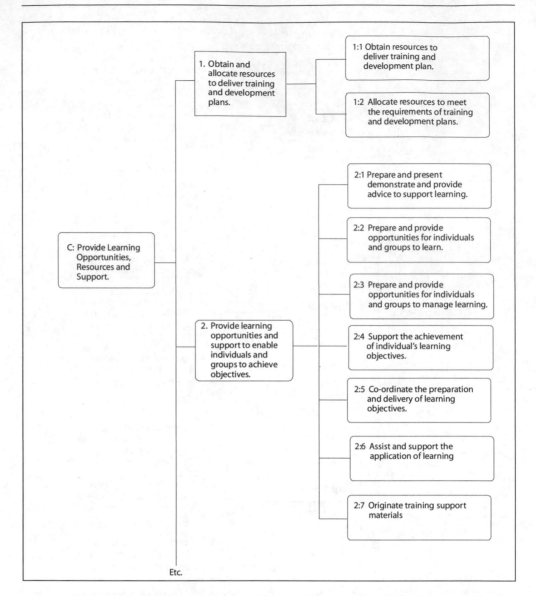

Figure 5.18   *Relationship Between Units and Elements from TDLB Standards*

Units of competence

The qualification is made up of a number of Units and each Unit consists of a number of Elements of Competence (with associated Performance Criteria and Range Statements). Examples of Unit titles from different occupational areas are:

> Establish ornamental borders (*from Horticulture*).
>
> Design posters (*from Design*).
>
> Handle power – aerated doughs (*from Bakery*).
>
> Filing (from Business Administration).
>
> Devise a Scheme of Work (*from Teacher Training*).
>
> Manage Learning Activities (*from Teacher Training*).

Units of Competence should be written in terms of what an employee must be able to do to achieve the overall competence for the qualification. Units are a mechanism for sub-dividing the qualification into manageable parts for both learning and assessment.

The writing of a unit should conform to the general guidelines for all statements of competence. It should: refer to outcomes rather than activities, tasks or skills; follow the structure of action verb followed by object.

The following example from Business Administration illustrates the component parts of a Unit of Competence:

action verb: process

object: petty cash and invoices

The following checklist Figure 5.19 can be used for written units:

Checklist for Units of Competence	Yes	No
Is each Unit:		
(a) Expressed in a language which is precise, and is an acceptable and distinct work role, within the industry or occupation?		
(b) Composed of elements, performance criteria and range statements which have a coherent relationship with each other and which describe outcomes, achievements, or results of activity?		
(c) Of sufficient size and scope to recognised as a creditable achievement in its own right?		
Do the Units taken as a whole:		
(a) Identify all the work roles within the occupational sector?		
(b) Identify emerging as well as current work roles?		

Figure 5.19 *Checklist for Units of Competence*

2.5.2 Elements of competence

The purpose of Elements is to make units manageable for the purposes of assessment and learning design. The element title should be a precise description of what somebody should be able to do, but still phrased as an outcome rather than a specific task or activity. For example:

Maintain reception area.
as opposed to:
Reception duties.
Display boards and publicity materials.

An element is a precise description of what someone should be able to do as a necessary part of the unit. Elements are expressed in functional form; that is, they are expressed as outcomes rather than processes. This is shown in the examples below from *horticulture*:

Unit	Establish ornamental borders.
Elements	• Build the border with attractive shapes.
	• Create colour matching schemes.
	• Choose plants which flower in succession; etc.

and from *Teacher Training*:

Unit	Assist and support the application of learning.
Elements	• Assist individuals to apply learning.
	• Provide advice to support the application of learning.
	• Monitor and assess the effectiveness of the learning process.

Alternatively an element may describe knowledge and understanding which is essential if the performance is to be sustained or extended to new situations. An example of this from *Information Processing* is:

Unit	Process records in a database.
Elements	• Define styles and formats of organisations.
	• Describe security and back-up procedures.
	• State relevant aspects of Data Protection Act.

Performance criteria

One or more performance criteria apply to each element. Each criterion defines a characteristic of competent performance of the element. All criteria attached to an element *have to be met* for the performance to be considered competent. Thus, the criteria discriminate between satisfactory and unsatisfactory performance: the assessment criteria give an answer to the question 'how should I know that a candidate is competent in ...?' Performance criteria are precise descriptions which are used as a specification to guide and structure assessments. As with elements, the results may be tangible products or nontangible results of processes. The example below gives an indication of the type of performance criteria expected:

Element: Promote the sale of products to potential customers.

Performance Criteria:

Appropriate and accurate information about the product/service is offered.

Potential needs and status of customers are identified accurately and politely.

Options and alternatives are offered where products and services do not directly meet potential customer needs.

Customers are offered the opportunity to make a purchase.

Potential customers are treated in a manner which promotes goodwill.

Thus, in the example, the main outcomes which are reflected in the criteria are the quality of the information given *plus* the treatment of the customer. They give a clear indication of what must be assessed and how it will be assessed.

An example from the Training and Development Lead Body (TDLB) is:

Element: Provide advice to support the application of learning.

Performance Criteria:

> Appropriate advice and support is given to those who support the application of learning.
>
> Information about the learning needs of individuals and groups is provided for those who support the application of learning.
>
> Opportunities and facilities for giving and receiving feedback are given to those who support the application of learning.
>
> Etc.

Checklist for elements and performance criteria

Elements, performance criteria (plus range statements, see below) indicate the 'content' of units for those involved in the design of learning or in the writing of competences. The following checklist Figure 5.20 can be used for the writing of competences to ensure that they are acceptable, or for you as a teacher if you do not find given competences acceptable for your design of learning sessions, to adapt or modify them.

	Checklist for Elements and Performance Criteria	Yes	No
1.	**Does each element:**		
(a)	Use precise language to indicate a distinct work role within the industry or occupation?		
(b)	Describe outcomes, achievements or results of activity rather than activities or procedures themselves?		
(c)	Describe outcomes that can be demonstrated and assessed?		
(d)	Possess appropriate associated assessment criteria?		
2.	**Do the elements taken as a whole:**		
(a)	Identify, within appropriate limits, critical aspects of work?		
3.	**Is each performance criterion:**		
(a)	Given as a clear evaluative statement?		
(b)	Expressed in a manner which facilitates a mode of assessment?		
4.	**Do the criteria, taken as a whole:**		
(a)	Describe only those outcomes which are essential for successful performance?		

Figure 5.20 *Checklist for Elements and Performance Criteria*

Range statements

A range statement is a description of the range of application to which the element and performance criteria apply. They give suggestions of the range of situations where the competence must be assessed.

An example of the need for a range statement is for the competence to 'drive a motor vehicle'. Does it only apply to cars or will it include lorries? Is it only in UK or on mainland Europe as well? The range statements can help clarify these matters for the candidate and the assessor. Thus, the range in which the driving certificate applies might be:

> All vehicles up to 3 tonnes.
>
> All road conditions (light/dark, wet/dry).
>
> All roads including motorway.
>
> All European countries (on left or right).

An assessor would have to make the judgment as to whether a 30 minute driving test in one vehicle provided adequate evidence of competence. Generally this is supplemented with oral questions to give an assessment of other driving abilities as well as to assess the underlying knowledge and understanding.

An example of an assessment criteria with associated range statements from the TDLB Standards is:

Element: Originate visual display and support materials

Performance Criteria:

(a) Visual and written materials are developed which are relevant to the learning outcomes to be achieved.

(b) Visual display materials are legible, accurate and conform to display conventions.

(c) Equipment used to produce visual materials is operated according to manufacturer's instructions.

(d) Written support material is in a language, style and format which is appropriate to the learning needs of the target audience.

(e) Materials from external sources are appropriate to the content and are adapted and used within the constraints of copyright law.

Range Statements:

1. Display media: OHPs; flipcharts; whiteboards.

2. Written materials: tutor notes; participants' brief; summaries; handouts.

3. Equipment: computer based; OHP material; production equipment.

A range statement describes significant categories in order to expand upon the scope of the performance criteria. Such categories are shown in Figure 5.21. They are not assessment options. They are assessment sampling categories so that each should be sampled. The particular instances within the categories which should be sampled are identified when the assessment system is in place, not in the specification.

Category	Example	Sample Range
Tools, equipment, machinery, plant.	Visual aids.	Flip charts, white boards, video recordings, OHP and slides.
Products and services.	Lending services.	Mortgages, further advance, personal secured loans, unsecured loans, credit cards.
Methods, processes and procedures.	Information.	Oral, computerised and paperback sources.
Clients and customers.	Customers.	Minors, teenagers, 16+, middle aged, pensioners, professional contacts, non residents.
Physical constraints.	Health.	Normal, ill health, early and late retirements.
Environments.	Where assessed.	On-the-job, in a simulated situation.

Figure 5.21   *Example Categories of Range Statements*

The following checklist Figure 5.22 can be used to assess the effectiveness of written range statements.

Checklist for Range Statements	Yes	No
Does the range statement:		
(a) Describe both existing and emerging practice?		
(b) Specify classes and categories (not each individual instance) in sufficient detail to enable an assessment schedule to be developed at a later stage?		
(c) Only include categories where a difference in application is significant?		
(d) Set specific boundaries of application, each of which MUST be included in an assessment sample?		
(e) Act as a reminder of specific instances which might be missed?		

Figure 5.22   *Checklist for Range of Statements*

2.5.3   Designing assessment systems for competence schemes

The basis of assessment is the generation of evidence by individuals to show that they can achieve the assessment criteria associated with units of competence. The evidence is judged and verified by assessors as to whether it is sufficient to merit accreditation. National awarding bodies' certificates are awarded to individuals on the basis of accredited achievement of the competences. This system is shown diagrammatically in Figure 5.23.

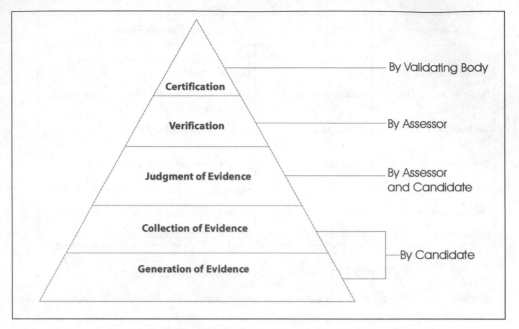

Figure 5.23 *Assessment System*

The requirements of the assessment system are, therefore:

(i)   The generation and collection of evidence by individual students which is relevant to the elements of competence, the performance criteria and the range statements. They also need to judge whether the evidence that they have collected is sufficient and relevant.

(ii) The assessor then needs to judge whether the collected evidence is sufficient and relevant and, if so, to verify this fact.

(iii) Finally, the Awarding/Validating Body provides a certificate to indicate achievement of all of the units and elements.

The different layers of the pyramid are discussed separately below. In reality, however, they all interact together. The overall objectives of the system are:

(i)   The units and elements, and their associated performance criteria must be assessed. The assessment must cover, but be limited to, the units which make up the certificate.

(ii) The evidence should relate clearly to the elements.

(iii) The evidence should cover the range of contexts for the element.

(iv) The assessment must be open to verification by an assessor.

Generation of evidence

As shown in Figure 5.24, there are three basic sources of evidence that can be used to assess the ability of an individual.

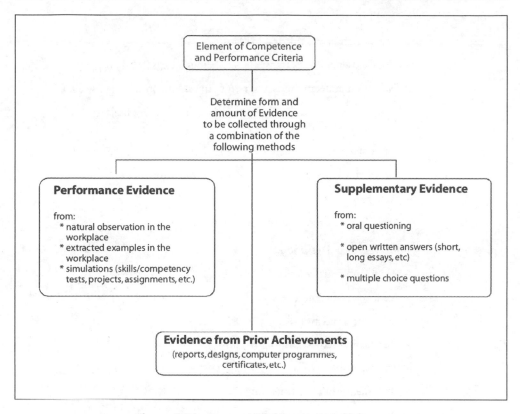

Figure 5.24 *Sources of Evidence of Competence*

Evidence from prior achievements results from activities which have been undertaken in the past. The evidence may be clearly available, e.g. articles that have been made or designed or, even, qualifications previously gained. Alternatively, candidates may need to generate the evidence in terms of, say, written reports of work that has previously been completed but which has no tangible evidence e.g. from being a member of a working party or from working on a project.

Performance evidence can result from observations of individuals completing tasks as part of their normal work OR from specially set tasks and simulations. Again, the evidence may already be available e.g. from the individual's employer's normal work records, or it may be generated while the individual works. Both the process of work and its outcomes may be considered as evidence. The specially set tasks can be skills/proficiency/competency tests or projects or assignments. Traditionally this has been the most commonly used method of collecting evidence for accreditation.

Supplementary evidence relates to all forms of questioning (both oral and written). This is often required, as suggested in the range statement example of the driving test above, to assess the individual's underpinning knowledge and understanding of applications which might otherwise be difficult to assess.

The evidence can be built into a portfolio which might, for a teacher, include, for example:

Direct evidence: – Artefacts: photographs, models.

　　　　　　　　　　 – Video recordings.

　　　　　　　　　　 – Audio tapes.

       – Teaching materials.

       – Plans: schemes of work, lesson plans.

       – Visual aids: handouts, transparencies, slides, charts.

       – Evaluation materials: tests, test results, questionnaires, interview data.

       – Development work: papers from working parties, proposals for new programmes/courses.

       – Reports: meetings, conferences, visits, discussions with colleagues.

       – Summaries: books, articles, radio or TV programmes.

       – Projects or assignments.

       – Analysis of classroom and other activities.

Indirect evidence: – References and testimonials.

       – Reports on practice.

       – Feedback from employers.

       – Certificates and awards.

Reflections: – On learning activities during a course.

       – On development of competence.

       – On someone observing teaching.

       – On a project or an assignment.

Collection of evidence

Assessment must cover every element. The amount of coverage depends upon both the element, the performance criteria and the range required. In some cases it is not possible to collect evidence for all of the activities: there is not time and it would be too expensive. The individual needs to make this judgment. However, this sufficiency of evidence is crucial. Imagine collecting evidence which suggests that a candidate has only a 50:50 chance of being judged proficient. More evidence can then be collected using the same assessment method, or a different one might be used to provide the additional evidence. For example a test can be supplemented by oral questioning.

In deciding the frequency and spacing of assessments there are three variables which you should take into account:

(i)   Assessment should be more frequent the closer one gets to being judged competent.

(ii)   If there is some doubt as to the competence, it may be necessary to continue assessment after the student is first judged to be competent.

(iii) If the assessment is particularly large, it is practicable to subdivide it into smaller component parts.

Portfolio building

Why portfolios?

With the advent of National Vocational Qualifications, there has been a need to produce evidence related to the competence. The assessment for an NVQ consists of three stages:

(i)   Planning what to do to meet the standards.

(ii)   Collecting together the evidence.

(iii) Judging of the evidence against the standards by an assessor.

The second of these stages, the collection of evidence, is at the heart of the NVQ process. Carrying out the job whilst being observed by a qualified assessor is the best source of evidence that can be used. However, where this is not possible, candidates may perform in a simulated environment, or present a product of their work, or carry out an assignment, or answer questions, or present a statement by a colleague detailing their performance.

Generally at levels 1 and 2, the presented evidence is typically as a result of assessor observations. At the higher levels of 3 and 4 candidates are operating in a more complex environment and direct observation is not always possible or appropriate. It may be suggested in the assessment requirements that the evidence could be based on observation by an assessor or other sources such as reports, designs and other forms or written work. This mixture of evidence from diverse sources is typically gathered in a **portfolio** of evidence.

A portfolio is an organised 'folder' of evidence compiled by a candidate in relation to an element of competence. It should contain evidence that the candidate has reliably demonstrated the skills, knowledge and understanding to be given recognition of competence.

The National Institute of Adult Continuing Education (1991) suggests that a portfolio is not only useful for qualification purposes, but is also useful for gaining employment and for personal development. In terms of gaining employment the portfolio can provide a systematic overview of past learning and achievements through its lists of verified competences which can be used as evidence for interview purposes. In terms of personal development it can encourage self-assessment as well as increasing self-confidence and self esteem through it completion.

What might be in a portfolio?

City and Guilds (1994) suggest that a portfolio should contain the evidence that the candidate is competent in relation to the element of competence. The key features of a portfolio are shown below:

A portfolio is a 'folder' which contains details of:

> Skills.
>
> Knowledge.
>
> Understanding.
>
> Achievement.

which may arise from:

> Observation of employment tasks.
>
> Products resulting from performance.
>
> Documentary evidence of completed tasks.
>
> Written accounts of activities.

The source of evidence should include:

(i)   Notes from an assessor detailing what has been observed and how the performance criteria and ranges were covered.

(ii)   Products of candidates performance at work such as letters, memos or reports produced as part of normal work. For teachers this may be lesson plans, schemes of work, assessment plans, test instruments, or audio visual aids.

(iii) Evidence from others about the individual candidate's work and abilities. These may be letters, reports or appraisals from managers, colleagues, clients or others involved in the work process. These types of document are sometimes referred to as 'witness testimonies'.

(iv)   Evidence produced from supplementary activities. To ensure coverage of the standards it may be necessary to write about activities that have been completed. This may be in the form of a project or assignment that has been suggested by the assessor.

Criteria for a good portfolio

The assessment process is much easier if the evidence is presented in an orderly manner. The main criterion is that the portfolio should be easy to follow with the different pieces of evidence easy to locate. It should have a clear structure which makes it easy to follow. This means that the candidate needs to be logical in the design of the portfolio and have an index and cross reference system which relates the evidence to the elements of competence and performance criteria of the NVQ.

The aspects that should be included within the portfolio are:

(i)   Autobiographical account indicating name, address, date of birth, job description and any other relevant details.

(ii)   A list of the competences, performance criteria and range to be covered (i.e. a copy of the standards which are subdivided in the format that is to be followed).

(iii) An index for the evidence (i.e. where the sections are located);

(iv)   An indication of how the elements are covered (i.e. where each of the pieces of evidence is located).

(v)   Evidence (probably best divided element by element).

(vi)   Supplementary written evidence to show how range has been covered (again element by element).

These are indicated diagrammatically in Figure 5.25. The indexing system presupposes that each of the pages are numbered for ease of location and some sort of dividers are used to separate each of the elements. This will further facilitate understanding of the materials.

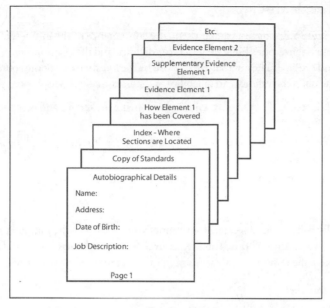

Figure 5.25 *What might a Portfolio Look Like?*

Portfolio checklist

All portfolios must follow the four basic rules of evidence. These are:

(i)   Validity: That the evidence is directly related to the standards.

(ii)   Authenticity: That the evidence relates to the candidates own abilities.

(iii) Currency: That evidence is up-to-date.

(iv) Sufficiency: That there is enough evidence (and not **too** much) to demonstrate competence.

Figure 5.26 may provide further indications of what to do when completing portfolios. Each of the aspects should be ticked with 'Yes', any ticked with a 'No' need further consideration.

	Aspect	Yes	No
1.	Does the evidence cover the performance criteria?		
2.	Does the evidence indicate how the range of situations is covered?		
3.	Is the evidence relevant to the requirements of the element(s)?		
4.	Is the evidence clearly your own work?		
5.	Is there variety of types of evidence to show competence?		
6.	Have you shown reasoning why particular evidence has been chosen?		
7.	Is all of the evidence relevant?		
8.	Have the pages been numbered?		
9.	Is the indexing system and subdivisions logical?		
10.	Does the standard of presentation lead to easy location of evidence?		

Figure 5.26 *Portfolio Checklist*

Judgment of evidence

The pyramid in Figure 5.23 suggests that judging the competence of the individual with respect to performance criteria is the responsibility of both the individual and the assessor. The assessor will likely be both internal and external. The internal assessor will be the line manager or the course tutor and will need to concentrate upon the validity and reliability of the assessment. Assessors need to guard against:

(i)   Lack of direction. They need to know what is being looked for and base their judgment on this.

(ii)   Halo effects where, because the individual has generally worked well, he is expected to continue to do so.

(iii)   Assessing progress and effort rather than achievement.

Verification

The awarding body will appoint an external examiner who will verify the judgments of the internal assessor. The primary purpose of this is quality assurance: ensuring that individuals from different centres are assessed in the same way with a common interpretation of the performance criteria.

External assessors must be:

(a)   Available to carry out assessments. Meaning, that they must be in a position to observe performances or outputs.

(b)   Able to interpret the performance criteria with specialist knowledge in order to recognise when it has been met.

(c)   Able to manage the assessment process and be aware of the pitfalls and know how to avoid them.

(d)   Willing to undertake the work involved.

In some instances it is only possible for the external assessor to sample some of the range of assessments that have been made. This, however, is not ideal and means should be found to make any sampling as effective as possible.

Certification

Individuals' achievements are recognised by the certificates of the Awarding Bodies. Once the external assessor is satisfied of the achievement of an individual or group of individuals, they will inform the Validating Body and certificates will be awarded accordingly.

The Validating Bodies have a central data bank which records credits over time. The issue of certificates depends upon the flow of accurate, timely information from the assessors. Each system will have its own appeals procedures. The first line of enquiry for this procedure is generally through the internal assessor. If this is not satisfactory then the second line is through the Validating Body who will, in turn, refer it to the external assessor.

e-Portfolio

It is worth mentioning that many examining boards are now accepting electronic portfolios (e-portfolios). E-portfolio allows the evidence to be collected, submitted and assessed electronically. For example a report is submitted as a word processed document, a form is scanned electronically and then submitted. The comment above relating to portfolio building equally apply to electronic portfolio building.

The advantages of an e-portfolio is that feedback tends to be much faster with tutors and students sending and returning evidence when they want rather than when the teacher or student is present.

The external verifier can similarly access portfolios making judgements and feeding back to the teacher. Rather than a yearly visit to view such portfolios this can be done as frequently as required so ensuring quality of the evidence. Examples of e-portfolio are given in Chapter 7, section 5.2.4 (page 377).

Perhaps the most useful aspect of the e-portfolio is the constant electronic communications between teacher, student and external verifier. All are able to communicate with each other, problems can be quickly overcome and additional support given when necessary. In many cases the student completes the portfolio much faster and to a higher standard.

Summary and inter-relationships of learning outcomes

Once you have understood how to write various styles of learning outcomes, it is interesting to compare the methods and see how they inter-relate. Figure 5.27 gives a unique variable guide. Figure 5.28 may help you to select the most appropriate model at which you can base your intended learning outcomes.

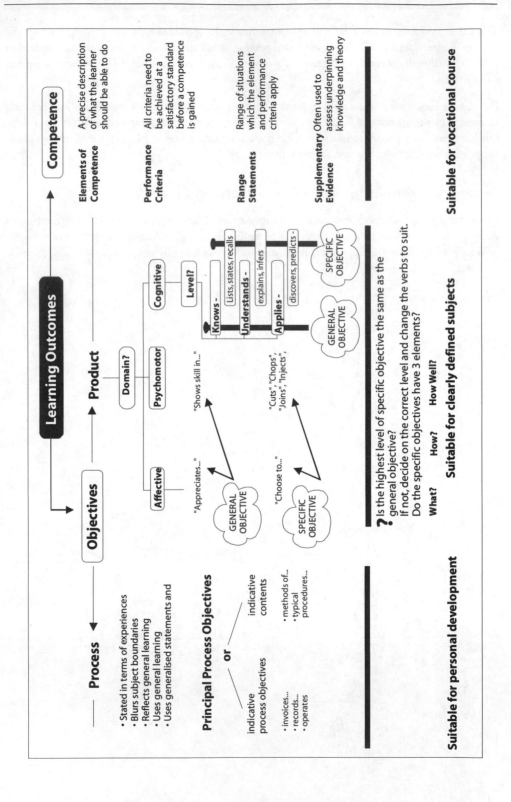

Figure 5.27   *Inter-Relationship of Learning Outcomes*

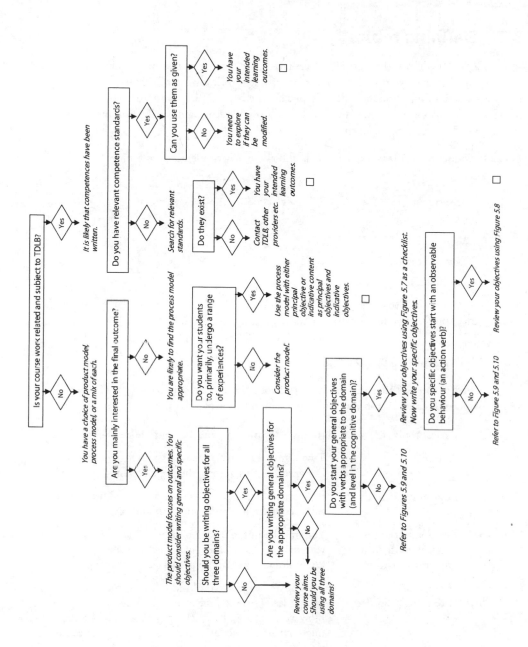

Figure 5.28 *Writing Intended Learning Outcomes*

3.   Schemes of Work

3.1   Defining topics

At the start of a course, as the teacher, you are faced with the task of planning a series of topics and learning experiences for your students. This plan is sometimes known as a Scheme of Work. There are many ways of deciding upon the order of topics but, perhaps, difficulties occur in the identification of the word 'topic'. There is no fundamental definition of the term 'topic' (in the educational literature) as it is applied to a learning experience.

For an Introduction to a Teaching Course the following may be identified as topics:

> Lesson Plans.
> Assessment.
> Memory.
> Motivation.
> Law and the Teacher.
> Profiling.

Topics like 'evaluation' 'psychology' and 'preparation for teaching' are all too large to be usefully considered as topics. So, a topic is part of a subject.

3.2   Sequencing topics

The sequence of topics is often derived from a syllabus or list of issues to be taught. There are several ways in which you can establish your order of teaching. Some of these are:

1.	Easiest topics first:	In this way you can gain the confidence of students.
2.	A theme:	Two or more themes make-up the scheme of work. For example Parliament: theme, elections.
3.	Logical sequence:	In mathematics there is a need to learn addition and subtraction before multiplication and division.
4.	Begin with the topics that you as the teacher are familiar with:	You may be in the position of being familiar only with part of the syllabus, and teaching what you know allows you time to prepare the other topics.
5.	Historical/ chronological order:	The causes of the First World War are taught before the battles. This is a logical and natural order. However, starting the teaching with a major battle, might create impact and the interest to see the causes.
6.	Normal/abnormal:	Start with the normal situation and move toward the abnormal or unusual.
7.	Seasonal:	Many topics are influenced by the seasons, e.g. cooking – availability of vegetables.
8.	Anatomically:	Start at the feet and move up towards the head.
9.	Fear/apprehension:	With an antenatal class, first-time mums are concerned about labour pains – so deal with this first.

10.	Sensitivity:	If dealing with a healthy lifestyle, perhaps smoking should be one of the final issues – otherwise students may leave early in the course!
11.	Most helpful:	If your students' course is related to their work, then start with topics which are most relevant to them, hence creating maximum impact.
12.	Controversial:	Starting with the least/most controversial topic.
13.	Theory/practice:	You may wish to integrate/mix theoretical issues with the practice or may wish to keep them discrete.
14.	Geographical:	This is a way to link social issues or natural resources.
15.	Negotiation:	Set out the issues and agree a sequence with the student.
16.	Availability:	Of resources, e.g., video, workshop, laboratory, computers.
17.	Group confidence development:	In order to discuss sensitive issues e.g. child abuse or to use challenging teaching strategies e.g. role play.
18.	Demands of other subjects:	Scientific or technological subjects may need to be preceded by certain mathematical topics.
19.	Opportunistic:	Responding to the latest political news as part of the lesson on politics.
20.	Must know, should know, could know:	Many syllabuses are overcrowded so the essential topics are addressed, then the next most important and so on. For example, with a driving and car ownership course.

Must know:
Know position of controls; switch on and start engine; change gear and brake; drive in a safe manner.

Should know:
Check oil and water levels; change wheel; tyre pressure.

Could know:
Change light bulbs; change windscreen wiper.

21.	Order of the textbook:	Rarely written with sequence of teaching in mind.
22.	Safety:	Health and safety concerns may dictate certain issues are addressed at a very early stage in the course.
23.	Evaluation:	Previous cohorts when evaluating the course may suggest a different sequence of topics.

A **Scheme of Work** may be defined as:

> a series of planned learning experiences, sequenced to achieve the course aims in the most effective way.

The scheme of work may include subject content, teaching strategies, student activities, assessment, evaluation and resources. The decision making process you go through in designing a Scheme of Work is complex and may be influenced by such aspects as:

> Student entry behaviour.

Course aims.

Course content.

Time available for learning.

Teaching strategies to be used.

Assessment techniques required.

Resources available.

3.3   Topic analysis

Having used the course aims, identified the main topics and organised the sequence for teaching, your next step in the planning process is to consider how you can present each of the topics to the students to make learning as simple and easy as possible. Some teachers go directly from the identification of the topic to the intended learning outcomes, for example by writing objectives or competences. If you wish to adopt a more rigorous approach, then you would include Topic Analysis which assists you in the identification of the main components of the topic (the sub-topics). Then proceed to order the sub-topics into a learning sequence which you will use in your lesson plan.

There are four main models of Topic Analysis which we will consider and these are ascribed to Davies (1971), Rowntree (1974), Gagne (1975) and Stenhouse (1975). Each model has its own advantages and limitations. Some subjects lend themselves to analysis by one (or more than one) of the models. Equally important is your preference for a model. If the model helps you to plan, then it serves a need. It is a valuable exercise to try each of the models in order to find which is the most helpful to you. You might find that you could use a combination of models for part of the subject (for example cognitive domain) and then use another for a different part (for instance affective domain).

3.3.1   Davies' model of topic analysis

Davies suggests that you should ask five questions for each topic:

1.   *What do you expect the students to demonstrate in order to show that they have learned the topic?*

This concentrates your mind on the objectives to be achieved through the learning of the topic.

2.   *What questions do you expect the student to be able to answer?*

The questions that are to be answered by the students give an indication of the sub-topics that are required from the topic.

3.   *What tasks, procedures and techniques should the student perform?*

Your response to this question forces you to concentrate upon the student activities required in the learning of the sub-topics.

4.   *What discrimination must be made?*

Here a comparison is made between what has already been learned and what needs to be learned.

5.   *What total change in behaviour do you expect and how will this be observed and measured?*

Your response comes back to the objectives and gets you to add criteria of acceptable performance.

Your responses to these five questions provide you with a framework for Topic Analysis and a series of prompts. It is a useful exercise in identifying sub-topics and objectives but is less helpful in the formulation of a learning sequence (that is the ordering of the sub-topics). Figure 5.29 shows how the five questions might be used to analyse the topic 'painting a door'.

Davies Question	Response
How will students demonstrate that they have learned the topic?	The students shall show skill in the application, of undercoat and gloss paint to a door, by brush.
What questions must the student answer?	The students must answer questions about: - need to protect surroundings from paint splash; - application of undercoat; - between coat procedures; - application of gloss paint; - the cleaning of tools, equipment and surroundings after each process.
What tasks, procedures and techniques must the student perform?	Skill of preparation. Skill of application of paint by brush. Working with others. Ability to work tidily.
What discriminations must be made?	Students should understand the difference between undercoat, gloss and emulsion paint. They should know how to avoid runs, misses, curtains, nibs, etc.
What total change in behaviour is expected?	The learner shall show skill in painting a door to a professional standard in a real or simulated environment.

Figure 5.29 *Application of Davies Topic Analysis to Painting a Door*

3.3.2 Rowntree model of topic analysis

Rowntree's model uses a two dimensional perspective to Topic Analysis which allows you to use a chart or diagrammatic approach. The horizontal analysis shows you the 'component behaviours' while the vertical one shows you the 'contributory' or 'enabling behaviours'.

In the example given by Rowntree (Figure 5.30) the cognitive domain is on the left-handside of the diagram with the right handside concerned with psychomotor abilities.

The horizontal aspects show the various components (that is the type of charts available). The vertical view shows what is needed to achieve the components (for example for a pie chart – draw a circle, divide the circle using a protractor, and so on). Thus, the horizontal analysis provides you with the sub-topics and the vertical provides you with the sequence with an indication, perhaps, of the required entry behaviour. This required entry behaviour is shown in italics at the bottom of each of the lines in the figure.

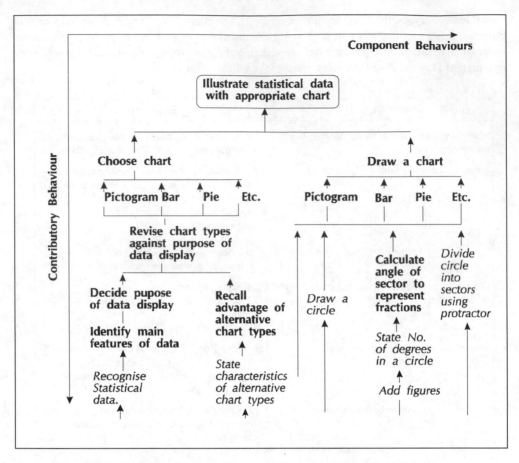

Figure 5.30   *Application of Rowntree Topic Analysis to Chart Drawing*

The Rowntree analysis can also be applied to 'Basic Graphics Techniques' and this is shown in Figure 5.31. Clearly this is a large topic but the analysis yields valuable insights which will enable you to identify the intended learning outcomes (that is the objectives and competences).

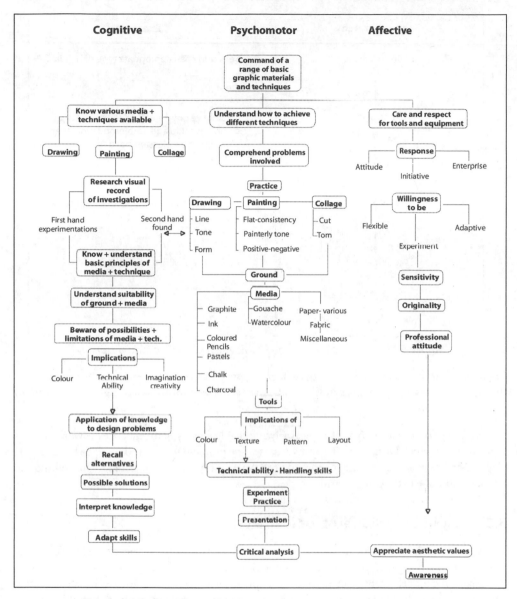

Figure 5.31 *Application of Rowntree Topic Analysis to Basic Graphics*

3.3.3 Gagné Model of topic analysis

The Gagné model is based on a hierarchy of learning; that is the student must learn simple things before learning complex ones. An example of the use of the model is shown in Figure 5.32 with each of the Gagné stages identified for solving the problem 'How to Select an Appropriate Type of Holiday'.

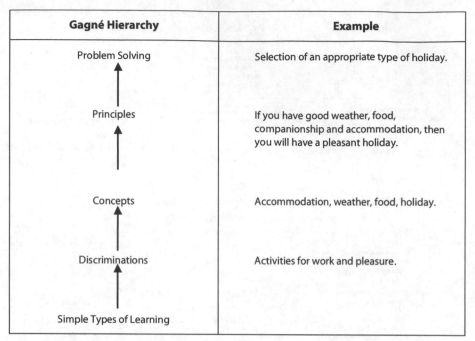

Gagné Hierarchy	Example
Problem Solving	Selection of an appropriate type of holiday.
Principles	If you have good weather, food, companionship and accommodation, then you will have a pleasant holiday.
Concepts	Accommodation, weather, food, holiday.
Discriminations	Activities for work and pleasure.
Simple Types of Learning	

Figure 5.32   *Application of Gagné Topic Analysis to Selecting a Holiday*

In this way, learners start with simple types of learning (stimulus-response) leading to discriminations, through concepts and principles until, finally, they can use all of this learning in the solving of problems; the most difficult type of learning.

The advantage of the Gagné-type of Topic Analysis is that it allows you to sequence the work in terms of the order in which learning naturally takes place. The problem for you is that, in order to use the Gagné Model, you must be able to identify the types of learning with accuracy. Indeed, not all teachers subscribe to the Gagné learning types.

3.3.4   Stenhouse model of topic analysis

The Stenhouse Model suggests that some course aims may be difficult to achieve merely by using the teaching topics. It suggests that you can use some aims directly to formulate the sub-topics and that you can use the model to achieve them. In the example given in Figure 5.33 'To Develop an Enquiring Mind and a Scientific Approach to Problems', learning may be achieved incidentally, but Stenhouse believes the analysis will help you structure teaching to ensure that activities take place which make the achievement of such aims more likely.

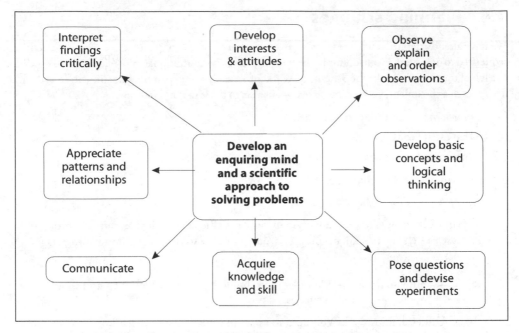

Figure 5.33   *Application of Stenhouse Topic Analysis to Problems*

You will find that the Stenhouse Model is particularly useful with 'creative' subjects. It allows you to 'map' the various elements of the topic. The example (Figure 5.34) shows the key elements in a first course in 'playing the violin'.

Note that you may use the Stenhouse Model to brainstorm the various elements involved in the topic. You may find it useful, however, to consider each of the three domains of learning (Cognitive, Affective and Psychomotor) in turn during the brainstorming so that you can be sure that you are being comprehensive in your coverage.

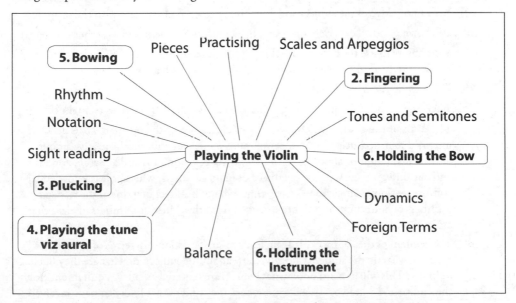

Figure 5.34   *Application of Stenhouse Model to Violin Playing*

3.4   Planning schemes

We have already defined a scheme of work as 'consisting of a series of planned learning experiences sequenced to achieve the course aims in the most effective way'. Additional information can be added to each of the topics to make the Scheme of Work into a really useful planning document. In order to design such a document, you need to arrive at answers to three major questions:

(i)   For *whom* am I planning the scheme?

(ii)   What must I consider *before* planning?

(iii) What must I consider *when* planning?

Answers to these questions might be:

(i)   For whom am I planning the scheme?

This must be mainly for the students to increase the efficiency of their learning. In order to increase this efficiency students progress from ignorance to efficiency through three stages of:

(a)   Wanting to learn   - Consideration should be given to both long and short -term goals.

(b)   Understanding   - You need to assess the students' initial level of understanding and assist them to find this level.

(c)   Practice   - There is a need for students to be involved in the learning of their subjects and the amount of involvement will likely differ between vocational and non-vocational subjects.

(ii)   What must I consider before planning my course?

Prior to such planning you need to consider your own personal ability and the type of course which you are planning. Your own ability relates to:

(a)   Your knowledge of the subject and your ability to keep up-to-date with the subject.

(b)   Your own personal experience of the subject both as a student and a teacher.

(c)   Your ability to use the range of teaching strategies in terms of your knowledge of the range, and the facilities that you have available to use such a range.

(iii)   What must I consider when planning my course?

This, of course, is the main question that you must ask yourself. The answers might be:

(a)   The **aims of the course** which give you an indication of the ultimate goals and the intended course participants. Well written aims should also indicate the relative amounts of time that might be allocated to the cognitive, psychomotor and affective domains and the different levels in the cognitive domain required (whether it is knowledge, comprehension or application). Such time will not be direct in terms of the respective numbers of hours but this might be gauged from the different numbers of aims that are indicated.

(b)   The **content** of the course. This again leads to sub-questions. In terms of the required content, what do the students already know about the subject, or what are they likely to know? This will depend upon what courses are required as entry requirements for the course and what vocational experiences the students are likely to have received from their employment.

Additionally, there will likely be a difference between the various topics of content. The topics might be subdivided into what students *must* know and what they *should* know. In other words there are some topics that are basic to the understanding of the course while others are more peripheral.

(c)   The **duration** of the course. The length of the course has a direct influence on, as indicated above, the content that will be covered and the manner in which that content is presented to the students and the activities that you are able to plan; a teacher-centred approach will take less time than a student-centred one. Thus, the available time has a direct influence on the teaching and learning methods that you use. Also, the time has a bearing on both the type and number of assessments that you are able to plan.

(d)   The **teaching strategies** to be used. In your scheme of work you need to consider whether (and where) to use teacher and student-centred approaches. The teacher-centred approaches are more applicable for the knowledge aspects, whereas the student-centred ones are more applicable for higher levels in the cognitive domain and the psychomotor and affective domain learning. Thus you need to consider the domains of learning that are involved and whether formal or informal approaches are to be used. It is also important to obtain variety of approach across the syllabus.

(e)   The **methods of assessment** to be used. As a 'rule of thumb' you need to plan not more than 10% of the total time to be allocated to assessment and feedback to the students. You need to decide the place of formal and informal assessment procedures and the place of phase tests, question and answer, examinations, assignments, practical tests, observation and self-assessment.

(f)   The **use of ILT**. To get the most out of ILT it should be considered at the planning stage of the course. By careful planning, ILT becomes a key aspect of the course rather than a bolt on idea or afterthought. Consideration should be given to the wide ranges of uses of ILT and not just as a presentation method.

Aspects to consider when planning are:

> When should be used? E.g. specific times during the course, every session, Key lectures.
>
> Availability of ILT resources.
>
> How it should be used? E.g. presentation, video, assessment, simulation, outside the classroom, backing up lessons.
>
> Advantages for using it for my students.
>
> Consider how it could be used outside the lesson.
>
> Could it improve communications between students and teachers.
>
> As an assessment tool.

All of these key points need to be considered to get the maximum benefit for your students.

When planning the Scheme of Work, apart from the aspects outlined above, you particularly need to consider the needs of the students. These are the people for whom the Scheme is designed and, unless they have priority, you may be involved in much work that is not worthwhile. The following checklist gives the type of questions that you might ask yourself in order to ensure that you do place them high on your list of priorities when designing your Scheme.

3.4.1   Checklist of student characteristics

What are the details of the group involved?

How old are they?

What is their educational background?

Where do they live?

What is the social bias of their various communities?

What moral standards are they likely to have?

What things stand high in their list of values?

What are their interests?

What is their employment category?

What are the details of the type of job that they have?

What experience of the subject are they likely to have?

It is, of course, unlikely that you are able to answer all of these questions for all of the students in your group. You are going to have to make general responses to many of the questions and you may not be able to obtain the information on others. However, the consideration of answers to the questions is a useful guide to the design of your Scheme of Work. Answers to them can assist you to answer other questions which you, as teacher, need to consider, as indicated in the following teacher checklist.

3.4.2   Teacher checklist for the scheme of work

How long is the course?

Are there any basic and necessary subjects to be included in the Scheme?

What is the likely reaction of the students to the course?

What type of teaching method will be appropriate to their abilities?

What tutorial arrangements will have to be made?

What resources, including ILT, are at my disposal?

What assistance will I have whilst working on the course?

How can I best assess progress being made towards achieving the aims of the course?

What, if any, summative assessment is in place?

An example part of a scheme of work is shown in Figure 5.35 The basis of the Scheme is the list of *topics*. The *content*, has been added for each topic and, for each of the topics the *teaching activity, student activity and resources* have been added. The completed scheme thus provides the teacher (and the students if it is decided to present the scheme to them) with a comprehensive overview of the programme and an excellent basis for the design of individual lesson plans. It allows the teacher to consider the course as a whole, which is often difficult when considering the design of the individual lessons.

The Internet provides us with example schemes of work and one of these is shown in Figure 5.36. This was taken from the DfES website, Raising Standards – sample scheme of work. It includes introductory information and in the body of the scheme, 'learning outcomes' which provide an overview of the topic.

Lesson No.	Topic	Content	Teaching Activity	Student Activity	Resources
1.	Personal Hygiene.	Cleanliness - importance of good hygiene habits: social effects of good personal hygiene. Fashion sense: Making the most of yourself; Make-up and hair care.	Exposition, drawing together information from students' lists. Collect pictures or draw latest fashions (asked to bring them in next week). Discuss pros, cons, of fashion today. Plan fashion show (for a later date).	List all of the advantages of good personal habits. Discuss in groups. Discussion.	Film "Looking Good". Unilever Fashion magazine for discussion with student pictures.
2.	Personal Relationships.	Peer group relationships: Relationships with opposite sex; Sex Education: Birth Control; Sexually Transmitted Diseases.	Exposition and Discussion. Opportunity for students to air views and problems.	Discussion after exposition of facts and distribution of leaflets and booklets for guidance.	Health Education leaflets and booklets.
3.	Smoking Alcohol and Drugs.	Social and Personal effects; Cost: Emotional Problems.	Factual exposition followed by film, supported by discussion and guidelines for preparation of project.	Start a project working in groups of 4: (a) collecting information on effects of smoking (b) on drinking and (c) on effects of drug abuse.	Film: "Abuses" Health Education Council.
4.	Etc.				

Figure 5.35   *Example Scheme of Work for a Subject 'Healthy Living'*

Centre: Utopia Name(s):J. Bloggs Subject: Communication Course Aims:		Year: 2006/7 Course Title: Duration: 1 Year		Course Code: Qualifications Aim:			
Week No.	Learning Outcomes	Session Contents	Student Activities	Resources	How Learning will be Assessed	Curriculum Ref.	
1	Be able to name some elements involved in effective communication.	Introduction to the course learning.	Brainstorming, discussion.	Folders, pens, info charts.	Observation and records of discussion.	SLD L11-3	

Figure 5.36 *Example Scheme of Work*

It is from a document such as this that an overview of both teacher and student activities can be gauged. If, for instance, there is too much teacher-centred activity, then a topic can easily be seen where a more student-centred approach might be chosen. An omission in this example is that no outcomes are indicated. When using this approach, the objectives or competences would have to be written on a separate sheet.

An alternative approach might be used where each topic is written on a separate 'card' which we have termed a 'Topic Card'. An example card is shown in Figure 5.37 with the general information related to the topic on the front side of the card and the specific information relating to content and teaching and learning approaches detailed on the reverse side.

It will be seen that there is much more information when the Topic Card approach is adopted but it has the disadvantage that not all of the course is detailed on one sheet. Thus you are not able to see the whole of the course at a glance.

Whichever approach you use, its purpose should help you to plan the best sequence of topics. It is highly likely that as you gain experience, you will develop your own particular style of planning a Scheme of Work.

TOPIC CARD

Subject	Total No. of Lessons	Total Duration _____ Hours
Topic	Lesson No.	Duration: _____ Hours

Entry Behaviour:

Outcomes:		Domain		
		C	A	P
1.				
2.				
3.				

Reverse side of Card

Lesson Content

Teaching Method(s)
Student Activities
Assessment Method(s)
Aids/Resources
Evaluation of Lesson

Figure 5.37   *Topic Card Approach to Scheme of Work Design*

4.   Lesson Planning

4.1   Designing plans

If you observe experienced teachers you may find a wide variation in practice with regard to their approach to lesson plans. Some teachers have very detailed plans while others 'appear' to have little at all in the way of a plan. What is important is that the lesson is always planned with care. What follows is a guide to some ways in which you may plan. You should experiment with planning until you find the method which works best for you. When you are planning a lesson you will find that a range of factors influence you. Figure 5.38 gives a brief overview of the process you could use. The student, of course, is at the centre of the process.

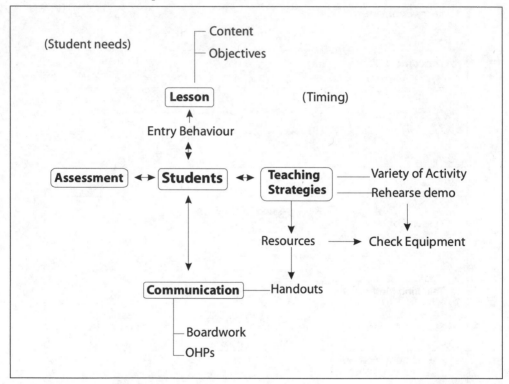

Figure 5.38   *Factors which Influence the Lesson Planning Process*

You need to consider several strands. Begin with the intended learning outcomes (objectives/ competences). In this case you need to identify the entry behaviour of the students – it could be that they know (a) too little and you have to start at an 'easier' level or (b) too much so that they do not need instruction. You should plan your communication with the students and aim to encourage communications between them. Use a variety of activities to maintain interest which will, in turn, influence your timing and your use of a range of teaching strategies and resources. When you use resources, check that the equipment does work and that you know (or remember) how to use it. For example, with demonstrations, check before you start that all of the equipment that you require is working. How long will it take to complete the demonstration?

At this stage you may wonder how you might plan all of this. The key features for a lesson plan include:

(i)   Initial information:

Topic.

Class details.

Expected entry behaviour.

Objectives of the session.

Time available.

(ii)   In the Body of the Plan:

Student activity.

Timing.

Teaching strategies.

Resources/aids.

Assessment.

(iii)   At the end of the lesson:

Homework activities to consolidate what has been learnt and additional supporting activities e.g. section in book to read and comment on for the next lesson.

One method of organising these variables is shown in Figure 5.39 with the initial information at the top of the plan and its body in a column format.

Topic	_____
Class	_____
Time available	_____
Expected Entry Behaviour:	_____
Objectives	_____

Key/Time	Teacher Activity	Student Activity	Resources

Figure 5.39   *Sample: Possible Layout for a Lesson Plan*

It is usual to consider the lesson in three stages:

(i)   Introduction.

(ii)   Development (the main body).

(iii)   Conclusion (summary).

We have said of the lecture that the good lecturer 'tells students what is going to be told', 'tells them' and then 'tells them what they have been told'. This, in effect, corresponds to the three stages of a lesson.

In a student-centred lesson, your first phase may be to outline the activity to your students and check what they should know in order to complete it (the entry behaviour). Follow this by getting the students to attempt the activity. Finally, ensure that the learning has taken place through question and answer or a test or activity that makes the required check or, alternatively, review the main points of the session (the conclusion).

Consider the following scenario:

> An inexperienced, young teacher, who works for St. John's Ambulance, has been asked to complete a 2 hour session on resuscitation to a group of twelve adults from an industrial background. He is nervous of the group because he has not met them before and realises that they have considerably more life experience than he has. He has planned a set of product objectives to cover basic anatomy and a set of procedures for carrying out resuscitation. He has put both of these (the objectives and the procedures) onto overhead transparencies. Additionally he has prepared transparencies for the main functions of the heart together with the causes of cardiac arrest and procedures for carrying out basic life support. He wants all of the group to practice the skills before the end of the two hours. He walks into the class with the twelve students there and they are all talking to each other. The introduction consists of showing the OHP of the objectives and briefly going through them. He then has a forty-five minute input about the heart, causes, signs and symptoms of cardiac arrest and the procedures for basic life support. The remainder of the session is spent with individuals practising life support on a dummy with others watching. Suddenly he realises that he has gone 5 minutes over the time and calls the end of the session.

So, how can we critically analyse this lesson? There has been only a very brief introduction and no conclusion at all. The session has had a 'sudden' start with very little preparation of the students for the main part of the lesson. Also, he has no specific idea of what they already know about resuscitation and does not know specifically what their interests are or why they have attended. To make matters worse there is no conclusion which means that he has little idea of what has been learned and has not summarised the main points of the session for them. What might he have done during these two important phases, the introduction and the conclusion, of the lesson?

The **introduction**, as a general rule, should be about 10% of the overall time available – in the scenario above this means about 10 minutes. It should gain both the attention and interest of the students and begin to build rapport with them. At the end of this phase students should look forward to what comes next. It needs to be informative about the session itself so that students have some idea of what to expect both in terms of the subject matter and how it is planned to be dealt with. Aspects for this first phase of the lesson that he might have chosen from include:

> Introducing himself.
>
> Reviewing the previous lesson by asking questions about it (from the previous lesson's objectives).
>
> Assessing the entry behaviour by asking questions about the topic.
>
> Describing the importance of the topic and how it might subsequently be used.
>
> Showing objectives.
>
> Describing an overview of the session.
>
> Informing students about the style of the lesson (make your own notes, there will be a test, there will be opportunity to practice for yourself).
>
> Showing end product.

Choosing three or four of these should settle the class, get them thinking (about what has gone before and about what is to come) and set the scene.

The **conclusion** phase of a lesson is just as important. A lot has gone on during the session and much has been both said and done. It is important, for the sake of memory recall as much as anything, to highlight the main points from all that has gone on during the lesson: students need to be able to sort the important aspects from those that are less important. So, you need to condense the lesson into a few basic points that can be quickly presented to the students to make sure that they have understood the lesson and achieved its objectives. The summary should be brief but sufficient time should be allowed to answer any student questions which may arise. As with the introduction, about 10% of the overall time should be allocated to this part of the lesson so that in our scenario above, with 15 minutes to go, the teacher knows that he must finish the development phase and start the conclusion.

As a review, the conclusion is a way of reinforcing the lesson and drawing it together. At the same time you can obtain feedback from the students as to whether they understood the lesson. You should not think of the summary as an add-on to the end of the lesson which serves only to repeat the main points that you have covered. It should be more than a review, it should extend the lesson, rather then merely restate it. You can make suggestions to the ways that students might apply what they have learned to previous learning. It should further the students' understanding by allowing them to reflect upon what they have learned and look forward to what they will learn. Additionally, you should always include opportunities to obtain student feedback. This is needed for you to have some indication whether the students have understood the materials that you have presented in the lesson.

One method that is often used at the end of a lesson is to ask if students have any questions of their own about the topic. This is probably not the best time to ask such an open question. It is likely getting near a break time and students, even adults, do not want to hold back their colleagues to ask something that others may already know. It is probably better if you ask more specific questions that require students to answer with statements that summarise the main points covered in the lesson. You might do this by making reference to the objectives of the lesson. If you have put these onto an OHP transparency, you might show this again and pose specific questions related to each of the objectives. An informal quiz, based upon the objectives, is another good way to end a lesson. Students can exchange papers and mark each other's quizzes, or students can mark their own as the answers are discussed and explained.

If you get your students to take their own notes, you might want to ask them to refer to their notes and summarise the lesson themselves for the rest of the class. Two other ways of ending a lesson is to make a transparency of the major points and project it for the class, or to prepare a handout covering the main points and distribute it at the end.

These main ways of concluding a lesson are summarised as:

> Revisit the objectives.
>
> Assess the learning either by question and answer or by a quiz.
>
> Review the main points either with a transparency, or the whiteboard.
>
> Suggest how students might apply what they have learned.
>
> Students to review the main points from their notes.
>
> Prepare for the next lesson by giving homework or reading.

4.2   Examples of lesson plans

4.2.1   Lesson plan for a psychomotor skills lesson

Topic:	Temperature Measurement
Class:	10 Student Nurses
Time Available:	60 Minutes
Expected Entry Behaviour:	State the components of a mercury-in-glass thermometer.
General Objective:	Show skill in the procedure for body temperature measurement.
Specific Objective:	Measure a person's temperature using a thermometer. Accurately record results.

Key/Time	Teacher Activity	Student Activity	Resources
Recap last lesson 5 min.	Q. Normal readings of blood pressure?	Answering.	OHP Transparency.
Introduction 5 min.	Need to take temperature. Thermometers. Use of records.	Listening.	Thermometer.
Development Temperature 30 min.	Q. Why take temp? Q. How gain/lose heat? Use a thermometer. Body Temperatures.	Answering. Watching/Listening. Practise on each other.	OHP 1. Mediwipes. List on Chalkboard.
Conclusion 10 min. 5 min.	Recap main points. Question. Objective Test.	Answer.	Test No 6.

4.2.2 Lesson plan for the teaching of attitudes

Topic:	Simulation of meeting.
Class:	15 communication students (Bus Stud).
Time Available:	70 Minutes.
Expected Entry Behaviour:	State the procedures of formal meetings.
General Objective:	Appreciate the relative merits of meetings as part of the decision making process.
Specific Objective:	Listen to others. Contribute to decision making process. Support other members of the class.

Key/Time	Teacher Activity	Student Activity	Resources
Introduction 5 min. 5 min.	Purpose of simulation. Issue/allocate roles.	Listening. Reading.	Suitable room. Role cards.
Development 30 min. 20 min.	Agenda Item 1. Agenda item 2. Agenda item 3. Debrief – questions.	In role. Feedback/discussion.	Agenda items.
Conclusion 10 min.	Summary of key learning issues.	Note taking.	OHP. Transparency.

4.2.3　Lesson plan related to indicative content

Topic:	Making a video 'Interviewing Consumers' Lesson 1.
Class:	10 Personnel Officers.
Time Available:	3 hours.
Expected Entry Behaviour:	Explain the components required in planning.
Objective:	Participate in the making of a video. Observe reactions of the interviewer and interviewee.
Indicative Content:	Use of camera. Team work. Planning work.

Key/Time	Activity
9.00	Meet class　– discuss overall task. 　　　　　　 – distribute duties to students 　　　　　　　　e.g. collect camera, etc.
9.45	Meet at 'scene'.
9.50	Confirm/discuss duties with individuals.
10.10	Coffee.
10.30	Questions.
10.35	Record interviews.
11.15	Adjourn to room to see tape.
12.00	Lunch (p.m. editing, etc.)

4.3　Negotiation

The needs of students clearly vary enormously and this is particularly true of adult learners. Using a standardised course you cannot hope to meet the range of abilities, expectations and temperaments of all of your students, but can only hope to meet some of their needs for some of the time.

If you negotiate an individual programme with a student, there is a greater likelihood that it will suit the needs of that individual. However, the system is not without its problems and in Figure 5.40 we outline some advantages and limitations.

Advantages of Negotiation	Limitations of Negotiation
- Increased motivation. - Course seen as 'right for me'. - Students active in the learning process. - Closer relationship with teacher. - Early identification of learning problems. - Increased opportunities for pastoral counselling. - Good for social skills. - Highlights (unknown) student skills.	- Can be difficult to manage. - Can be bureaucratic. - Students may not want to take on role. - Lack of rapport leading to lack of agreement. - Unrealistic goals may be set. - Practical considerations (e.g. laboratory availability) may cause difficulties.

Figure 5.40 *Advantages and Disadvantages of Negotiation*

4.3.1 The process

The process of negotiation may be seen as a five stage model:

(i)   Preparing for negotiation.

(ii) The first session(s).

(iii) The contract.

(iv) Monitoring the learning.

(v)   The review.

Preparing for negotiation

Before entering into the negotiation process, you should have a very clear idea of what your student is to achieve. The limiting factors, or constraints, that you need to establish are, for example, whether the assessment is to be determined by a third party, if the institution has constraints such as 'supervision' at all times, what is the time scale (not only the end dates but, also, regular reviews). Unplanned difficulties arise and you need to build in some contingency for them. The student may be unfamiliar with negotiation and your planning needs to take this into account. Finally, decide the best place for the first and subsequent meetings.

The first session(s)

Students often find negotiation difficult, if only because they may be adolescents dealing with an adult in a new situation. It is important, therefore, that you quickly establish a rapport. Perhaps a useful way to start is to find out more about the students as people by asking about their interests and ambitions. Establish the framework and limits or boundaries of the negotiation before the process begins properly. One approach that you could use is to start from details and proceed to agree detail by detail. This involves great expertise and time. You may find it more useful to secure a broad, wide ranging agreement and then explore area by area. Your role is to listen to the students, confirm beliefs and agreements by repeating them, and then to probe a range of issues. You will find that sticking points do occur. It is often useful not to spend too much time on these but to refer to them at a later stage.

The contract

At some stage you will need to 'firm-up' or agree the proposals. You can do this in the form of a contract or agreement. This is best in writing and needs to be in a language that the students understand – in fact, get them to draft the contract. From the contract, your students should be clear about what is the intended learning, what is to be done, how it is to be done, what resources are available, what is the time-scale, how the outcomes are prescribed and, finally, what are the assessment criteria. Regular reviews need to be a feature of the contract.

Monitoring the learning

It is important to have regular reviews to monitor progress. In this way you will set the student a series of deadlines in which to work thereby giving a structure to the process. You can identify progress, or lack of it, so that the final outcomes should be no surprise to you. The student should do most of the talking at the reviews. You can achieve this by posing questions such as 'How is the project going'? 'Have you any problems'? or 'What problems have you had'? 'What are you going to do next'? You might find it useful to note some of the outcomes in the contract itself.

The final review

Your final stage is to review what has been done and learned. Your ultimate question is 'Has the student achieved the intended learning outcome'. This may include a discussion of a formal assessment. What is also important is 'What would you do differently?' and 'What have you learned in other (negotiated) learning?'

4.3.2 Summary

As you can see, the negotiated curriculum places very different demands upon both you and the student. The benefits for the student have been discussed. The benefits for you come when you can see your students working on their own initiative and discussing, in an adult or even enthusiastic manner, their work. You need to have, or develop, the skills of a negotiator, manage several different learning activities and, very importantly, manage your own time to ensure all students have sufficient support.

4.4　Classroom management

What is classroom management? It seems to beg the question to define it as 'managing the classroom situation'. However, management is about control, about directing affairs, and about coping with uncertainties. Classroom management relates to the following:

> Controlling the learning situation.
> Directing the learning for the students.
> Coping with the individual student differences.

So classroom management can be defined as:

> ...managing the classroom situation to ensure that an **atmosphere** is generated where the most effective learning takes place for all of the students.

You will know when the right atmosphere has been achieved in a classroom because the students will have drive (be keen to master the new knowledge), self-enhancement (strive to have esteem and satisfaction from a job well done), and affiliation (be eager to gain the approval of you as teacher and of other members of the class).

Much of the literature suggests that there are four main areas of importance in classroom management:

(i)   **Arousal**   To ensure that students are motivated and ready to learn.

(ii) **Expectancy**   Making sure that students know what is required of them and what they will be able to do after learning.

(iii) **Incentive**   Ensuring students know how achievement will be rewarded.

(iv) **Disciplinary** Ensuring that the work of a group is not disrupted.

We agree that these four are important for classroom management purposes, but we would add to this list a fifth area which is equally important. This is:

(v)   **Employment**   Ensuring that students are gainfully employed in a variety of activities.

It is thought that now, not only is this list comprehensive, but it is also in order of priority with 'arousal' probably the most important in terms of learning and, especially with adult learning, discipline being the least important.

The first of these factors, **AROUSAL**, relates to attention: to individuals paying attention to the learning and committing themselves to the task in hand. There are both external and internal factors that are associated with and influence arousal. The **external** factors are the ones that the teacher influences and the **internal** ones are the physical and mental dispositions of the individual.

External factors include:

(i)   The **intensity of the stimulus** that is being presented to the student can have an effect on attention. Loud noises, bright colours and strong odours are compelling stimuli. So, how can we use these in the classroom? You can ensure that your voice is heard and present whiteboard or OHP presentations in a colourful way.

(ii) **Novel** stimuli attract attention. The reason for using *italics* in a textbook is to draw your eye to key concepts by printing the words in an irregular way. Similarly, using different teaching and learning methods which are novel to the student can assist arousal and commitment to the task.

(iii) A **variable or changing stimulus** can demand our attention. As a teacher you quickly discover how to use your voice by frequently changing the intonation. Wall charts and aids should be changed regularly, otherwise they no longer attract attention.

(iv) **Spatial and temporal irregularity** affects attention adversely. Irregular presentation of stimuli improves attention. The spatial regularity of handouts can be improved by the use of sub headings and capitals to emphasise key points. Colour and underlining can also be used for this purpose. Variation in speed of speech is more likely to maintain attention than speech which has a temporal or tonal regularity.

Internal factors include:

(i)   **Interest** is clearly a factor that can cause differential influence. Events that have relevance to the needs of an individual are more likely to attract attention. Attitudes and prejudice also affect the extent to which we are drawn to pay heed to events and ideas. You must, always, try to make topics and their application, relevant to the needs of the class.

(ii) **Fatigue** has a detrimental effect on attentiveness. The implication here is to have frequent breaks, ensure that there are frequent changes of activity between ones requiring high concentration (like brainstorming) and those which do not.

(iii) **Over arousal** can have an adverse effect on performance. Drive theory states that performance improves with increased arousal up to a point. Beyond this point, performance begins to deteriorate until, at high levels of arousal, performance is extremely poor. Attention is thought to operate in a similar way as the arousal level increases. The moral here is to ensure that individuals do not become overexcited, or that discussion becomes overheated, in a classroom.

(iv) **Personality characteristics** have a differential influence. Many behavioural distinctions exist between extroverts and introverts. Extroverts need more rest pauses while performing tasks requiring great attention. Consequently, their attention suffers in comparison with introverts. Extroverts do not like repetitive tasks and cannot concentrate consistently like introverts. So extroverts are more likely to wilt and become distracted during long periods of attentive activity.

The second factor, **EXPECTANCY**, relates to students knowing where they are going and also knowing, when they get there, that they are there. This can be used in the introductions to lessons by you telling your students what they are expected to learn. Telling them (in plain language) the objectives of the session. This, together with a brief overview of the main parts of the lesson, will provide them with an 'advance organiser' and set up an aspect of expectancy in their minds.

A second aspect of expectancy lies with having high expectations of individuals. An important experiment (Rosenthal and Jacobson 1968) involved **randomly** dividing students into three and telling one group that they were the worst, another group that they were the best, and telling the third group (the control group) nothing. They were then taught and tested. Who did best in the tests? The group who were told that they were the best. Who did the worst? The group who were told that they were the worst. A group of students will invariably live up to your expectations of them. So, always inform the class of your high expectations of them. Never tell your students that something is hard – always suggest that they are capable of doing well.

A final aspect of expectancy relates to the use of a behaviourist approach for consistency. Telling students of the objectives is the first part of behaviour modification and this should be continued in using other approaches especially with regard to **reinforcement**. Praise is usually preferable to punishment as the latter will often lead to avoidance and not the 'correct' behaviour. You should reinforce student achievement constantly and, especially with extroverts, publicly. You should avoid the use of sarcasm – it is the lowest form of wit. Also, always set a good example.

The third factor is **INCENTIVE**. No one becomes highly committed to a task when there is nothing in it for them (or for other people). Behaviourism is all about stimulus-response and advocates that responses that are rewarded (or reinforced) will be repeated. Thus, reinforcement (as indicated above) is important and students should know how achievement is to be rewarded. When an activity is set, or an assignment given, it is important that they also know how it will be assessed. Along with an assignment sheet, a **marking scheme** should also be given so that students know exactly how they are going to be assessed, what marks (or grades) are going to be used for which aspects of the work, and then they have an incentive and know where to place the effort for the work to be completed.

A second aspect of incentive relates to **relevance**. All the work that the students are asked to do should be relevant to their needs. If, for instance, the task is to learn theory for its own sake, then learning will not be as effective as it might be. It is important in the introduction to a session that you tell students **why** they are studying a topic, **how** it will help them, and **why** it is important to them.

The fourth factor, the **DISCIPLINARY** aspect of classroom management associated with adult learning, is less important than it is with children. Teachers of adults do not necessarily expect to have discipline problems like fighting or shouting at each other, or not doing as requested. The discipline problems associated with adult learning are of a more subtle nature. There can still be threats to your authority, there can still be disruption, there can still be poor time keeping, and so on. Such disruptions can lead to other members of the class being disrupted, with them finding it difficult to concentrate. An example of this is during group work when one member of the group wants to talk about something that has nothing to do with the topic. This makes it difficult for the other members to get on with their work.

The sensible teacher never allows a discipline problem to develop: it is much easier to deal with the initial stages of trouble than it is to deal with mass dissent. The problem comes with being able to recognise the signs and this is where personality can be a problem. So, how should we deal with this type of discipline problem? You will find it useful to establish effective **rules for class conduct**: getting to class on time; telephoning about any absences; and those related to effective team work like ensuring that everyone has their say, offering only constructive criticism, and so on.

Dealing with adults is very different to dealing with children – even though, at times as adults, we all act like children. It is important that you **show concern** for individuals and treat them like colleagues. It is very helpful to find out student interests (as well as their problems) as this can be effectively used during class contact time. Even if you do not like a student, try hard not to let it show. If you are rude to an adult it will be a long time, if ever, before it is forgotten. When discipline problems do occur it is beneficial for you to **address the management problem** rather than making an attack on an individual student.

The fifth and final factor related to good classroom management is **EMPLOYMENT**. It is important to adult learners that, at the end of a session, they feel a sense of achievement: that they have learned something. If adults do not feel a sense of achievement, then the atmosphere that you generate will not be one of effective learning. If they are not fully employed they will not look forward to coming to your classes. An important aspect of this lies with variety of activity. The more variety of different teaching and learning methods that you can employ, the more likely the concentration span of the students will be increased. Also, however, the **variety** must relate to effective activities. You should try to provide activities that are directly relevant to the achievement of the lesson objectives.

Achieving the LLUK Professional Standards

Standards
Domain A: Professional values and practice
AK6.1   Relevant statutory requirements and codes of practice.
AK6.2   Ways to apply relevant statutory requirements and the underpinning principles.
Domain B: Learning and teaching
BK1.1   Ways to maintain a learning environment in which learners feel safe and supported.
BK1.2   Ways to develop and manage behaviours which promote respect for and between others and create an equitable and inclusive learning environment.
BK2.1   Principles of learning and ways to provide learning activities to meet curriculum requirements and the needs of all learners.
BK2.2   Ways to engage, motivate and encourage active participation of learners and learner independence.
BK3.3   Ways to structure and present information and ideas clearly and effectively to learners.
BK5.1   The impact of resources on effective learning.
BK5.2   Ways to ensure that resources used are inclusive, promote equality and support diversity.
Domain C: Specialist learning and teaching
CK3.1   Teaching and learning theories and strategies relevant to own specialist area.
CK3.5   Ways to support learners in the use of new and emerging technologies in own specialist area
Domain D: Planning for learning
DK1.1   How to plan appropriate, effective, coherent and inclusive learning programmes that promote equality and engage with diversity.
DK1.2   How to plan a teaching session.
DK1.3   Strategies for flexibility in planning and delivery.
DK2.1   The importance of including learners in the planning process.
DK2.2   Ways to negotiate appropriate individual goals with learners.
DK3.1   Ways to evaluate own role and performance in planning learning.
Domain E: Assessment for learning
EK3.2   Ways to ensure access to assessment within a learning programme.

Achieving the LLUK Professional Standards

Standards	Ways in which you can show that you have achieved the Standards	See Section
AK6.1 AK6.2	1. Identify and list the aims of one of your courses. Review these aims indicating their value to you as you plan your teaching programme. Highlight any shortfalls and rewrite the aims indicating the benefits of your changes.	1 and 2
BK1.1 BK1.2 BK2.1 BK2.2 BK3.3 BK5.1 BK5.2	2. For a scheme of work and a lesson plan for one of the courses that you teach, show how you have achieved: • A learning environment where students are motivated. • An equitable and inclusive learning environment through the approaches that you adopt. • The chosen strategies are varied to meet the needs of all of the students. • The chosen resources promote effective learning and promote equality and support diversity.	3 and 4
CK3.1	3. Select a topic and write intended learning outcomes in the form of: • General and specific objectives. • Mager-type product objectives. • Process objectives. • Competence statements with performance criteria and range statements. Review each type of intended outcome and justify which is most appropriate for your students and your specialist area.	2
CK3.5 DK1.1 DK1.2 Dk1.3 DK2.1 DK3.1	4. Design a scheme of work for one of your classes and justify your decisions with regard to: (a) Sequence of topics. (b) Use of course aims. (c) Design of intended learning outcomes. (d) Range of teaching strategies and resources (including ILT) used. (e) Equal opportunities.	3
CK3.5 DK1.1 DK1.2 Dk1.3 DK2.1 DK2.2 DK3.1	5. Select one of your lesson plans from the scheme of work in 4 (above) and justify your decisions within it with regard to: (a) The design model adopted. (b) How the methods used allow for flexibility in planning and use. (c) Any negotiation with students that has been adopted.	4
DK2.1 DK2.2	6. Design a pro-forma which could be used as a basis for a contract for your students to negotiate effective learning. Critically analyse the design of the contract.	4
EK3.2	7. Using the scheme of work in 4 (above), explain how you have ensured that access to assessment is appropriate to the needs of your students and your subject.	3

For a model approach to show how you have achieved the LLUK Professional Standards see Appendix I.

Chapter 6

Communication, Teaching and Learning

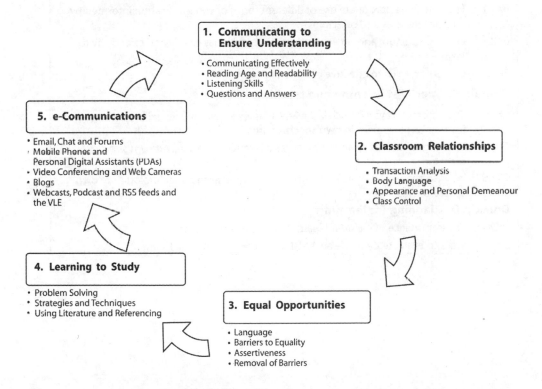

1. Communicating to Ensure Understanding
- Communicating Effectively
- Reading Age and Readability
- Listening Skills
- Questions and Answers

5. e-Communications
- Email, Chat and Forums
- Mobile Phones and Personal Digital Assistants (PDAs)
- Video Conferencing and Web Cameras
- Blogs
- Webcasts, Podcast and RSS feeds and the VLE

2. Classroom Relationships
- Transaction Analysis
- Body Language
- Appearance and Personal Demeanour
- Class Control

4. Learning to Study
- Problem Solving
- Strategies and Techniques
- Using Literature and Referencing

3. Equal Opportunities
- Language
- Barriers to Equality
- Assertiveness
- Removal of Barriers

This chapter is concerned with creating a just and secure learning environment for your students. Effective communications and appropriate relationships in relation to fruitful learning are discussed.

LLUK Professional Standards

The Knowledge and Understanding within the LLUK Professional Standards incorporated in this chapter are:

Domain A: Professional values and practice

AK3.1   Issues of equality, diversity and inclusion.

AK5.1   Ways to communicate and collaborate with colleagues and/or others to enhance learners' experience.

Domain B: Learning and teaching

BK2.2   Ways to engage, motivate and encourage active participation of learners and learner independence.

BK3.1   Effective and appropriate use of different forms of communication informed by relevant theories and principles.

BK3.3   Ways to structure and present information and ideas clearly and effectively to learners.

BK3.4   Barriers and aids to effective communication.

Domain C: Specialist learning and teaching

CK3.3   The different ways in which language, literacy and numeracy skills are integral to learners' achievement in own specialist area.

CK3.4   The language, literacy and numeracy skills required to support own specialist teaching.

CK3.5   Ways to support learners in the use of new and emerging technologies in own specialist area.

Domain D: Planning for learning

DK2.1   The importance of including learners in the planning process.

DK3.1   Ways to evaluate own role and performance in planning learning.

---

1.   Communicating to Ensure Understanding

1.1   Communicating effectively

Communication is essentially about one person who sends or transmits a message which is received by a second person. Some form of channel, or means of communication is needed. This channel could be sound, it could be movement, it could be smell.

The simple model of transmitter-receiver is satisfactory for most situations, for example, speech, non-verbal communication, reading; but in practice the situation is more complex, because there are factors which distort the message or signal. This is called 'noise' and it is a barrier to good communication. If your classroom has a poor layout, the students may not be able to see or hear you. The lighting may be poor or there may be excessive sunlight. 'Noise' could be from traffic or people outside the room or it could be from the students themselves. Noise could be more difficult to identify, like pitching the level of the learning too high or too low for the learners. The vocabulary you use could be too difficult for the learner or use too much unfamiliar jargon. We have to do our best to minimise noise and make our message clear. Non verbal signals – or even verbal signals, from the students should give us valuable feedback on the quality of communications.

1.1.1   Are you sure you are communicating?

You are explaining to your students, they are responding and the body language is good. So everything is fine. But is it?

You can use the following game (see Figure 6.1) with your own students. Most teachers find a great variation in the answers given. Some students do not put 100% for 'Always'. This shows that even if the students think they understand the message – they may be understanding something which is not your message!

The game may be used as follows:

(i)   Give each student a copy of Figure 6.1 and ask them as individuals to allocate a percentage to each of the descriptors.

(ii)   Ask the group for their answers in order to find the lowest, and the highest percentage scores for each descriptor.

(iii)   For each descriptor, write the lowest percentage and the highest percentage.

(iv)   Discuss the variation within the group for each item.

What percentage of the time does something occur if it happens:	
	Percentage
Frequently	
Occasionally	
Rarely	
Sometimes	
Usually	
Never	
Now and Again	
Always	

Figure 6.1 *Percentages*

We all have knowledge and skills and have formed attitudes, and many of us will even admit to some prejudice. All of these factors may have a significant impact on the effectiveness of the message. Figure 6.2 attempts to show some of the influences on communications and some of their complexities.

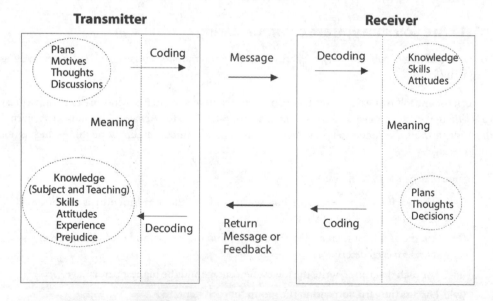

Figure 6.2 *Influences in Communications*

These complexities are involved with both the sending and the receiving of messages. Of particular importance are the affective domain aspects of the transmitter and receiver of a message. If we assume that you, the teacher, is the transmitter you have your own motives and thoughts associated with the message which influences the way that you encode (for example whether it is verbal, or done on whiteboard or a handout, or a mixture of these) the message. This is then passed on to the students who decode it in terms of, not only their knowledge and skills, but also in terms of their attitudes. Then there is the feedback element from the students back to you as the teacher. This is particularly important when you, as the teacher, decode the feedback message and your attitudes have a direct effect upon the process.

1.2   Reading age and readability

Almost all the students with whom we come into contact, will have attended school until they were at least 16 years old. We make assumptions about that experience and, in particular, we often assume that students have the ability to read the information we present to them. We give the students handouts, we write on the board, we do presentations, and we recommend textbooks. But how often do we really consider the difficulty of the reading and the ability of the students to read well? Difficulties in learning may not be caused only by the way in which we teach, or the lack of intelligence of the student but may be the result of a reading problem or a learning disability or difficulty, such as dyslexia. Consequently we should now look at how we can determine the reading age of a student and the readability of written materials.

Reading age is related to the reading age of the average child. So a reading age of 14 is the ability to read at the standard of the average 14 year old. *Readability* on the other hand considers the degree of difficulty with particular reading materials. Consider 14 year old pupils. If they are presented with material requiring a reading age of 16 then there could well be problems. However if the material has a reading age of 12 then there should be no problem. Problems with reading are not confined to students. Many people, for example, experience problems with official forms for example, legal documents, although progress has been made in making such forms more easily understood. There is now a 'diamond mark' for clear English to recognise clarity of documents and which acts as a regulator to ensure that people are not being disadvantaged by the use of difficult language. Official jargon is often called 'Gobbledegook' and this word is used in the title of two of the techniques we will now look at.

Remember that calculating readability (or the reading age required to understand a text) is an inexact science. So, two of the techniques used, the FOG index and the SMOG index, and the results they produce, should be seen only as guidelines.

1.2.1   Readability

The FOG index

The FOG index is one of the indices used to calculate the required reading age of written materials. You can use it on your handouts to give an indication of whether you are writing at an appropriate level for your students.

FOG is the *Frequency Of Gobbledegook* and may be calculated as follows:

1. Select a passage of 100 words.
2. Count the number of complete sentences.
3. Count the words in each of the complete sentences.
4. Find the average sentence length (L) by dividing the number of words in all of the complete sentences by the number of complete sentences (i.e. divide your answer to '3' by your answer to '2').
5. Count the number of words of three or more syllables (N) in the 100 word sample.
6. Add L and N, multiply by 0.4 and then add 5 i.e. $0.4(L+N)+5$.
7. This is the reading age.

You may wish to select three or four passages of a textbook to find the average reading age.

Example of Calculating the FOG Index

The following text is designed for use with students who have a reading age of 14. The FOG index has been applied to determine its suitability for such students.

Note that in the following passage there are 100 words between the two stars.

(*)Filament lamps are available with a single coil of tungsten wire or with a double coil, or coiled coil, which gives more light. All common filament lamps have an average life span of one thousand hours. This light is best for normal domestic usage since it gives a good balance between the amount of life obtained and the cost of the electricity.

Filament lamps should be bought to suit the voltage of the mains supply. If, for example, your residence is supplied at 240 volts, buy lamps of the same voltage. The common size of domestic filament lamps range from about (*) 8 watts (for the dimmest of night lights) to 200 watts. Almost all household lighting needs are met by 40, 60, and 100 watt lamps but the greater the wattage, the greater the heat generated and the greater the cost.

Number of complete sentences	=	5
Average sentence length (L)	=	$\dfrac{\text{No of words in all sentences}}{\text{No of complete sentences}}$
	=	$\dfrac{90}{5}$
	=	18
Number of polysyllabic words (N)	=	11
Reading Age	=	[(L + N) x 0.4] + 5
	=	[(18 + 11) x 0.4] + 5
	=	[29 x 0.4] + 5
	=	11.6 + 5
	=	16.6 Years

This means that the material would be unsuitable for students who have a reading age of 14 years. They would have too much difficulty with reading the text let alone with its content. You should recognise that the important aspect of Required Reading Age that makes the text difficult to read lines with the number of polysyllabic words and the length of the sentences. So to bring down the required reading age you must reduce the number of long words and the length of the sentences.

Consider the following text about the design of a teaching programme. It is intended to be used as a handout to students who have a reading age of 14 years. Will the students cope with the demands of the language?

(*) "*Basically* a teaching programme is a course prepared as a result of an *intensive analysis* of the learning task. It is *generally* presented to the students one stage at a time. Each stage presents *information* and demands a response from the students. They may be required to answer a question, make a *decision* or practise a *procedure*. The response that students make has two functions. First it ensures that they are *actively* involved in the learning process and practise the tasks that they are to master; *secondly* it provides a measure of their progress. This measure can be used by the (*) students as knowledge of results or by the course designer to identify and remedy weaknesses in the teaching."

Again use the FOG index to gauge the suitability of the text for these students. The two stars (*) represent the beginning and end of the 100 words. Within the extract there are:

(i) Six complete sentences within 94 words giving an average sentence length of 94/6 = 15.7 (L).

(ii) Nine words have 3 or more syllables (N) – these are shown in italics.

Thus, for this extract the Required Reading Age is:

$$
\begin{aligned}
\text{Age} \;&=\; [(L + N) \times 0.4] + 5 \\
&=\; [(15.7 + 9) \times 0.4] + 5 \\
&=\; [24.7 \times 0.4] + 5 \\
&=\; 10 + 5 \\
&=\; \underline{15}
\end{aligned}
$$

The extract is too difficult for the students and should be simplified. To do this you need to either reduce the length of the sentences or the number of long words or both *without* losing the sense of the original text.

We have rewritten the extract to reduce the number of long words to six, the semicolon has been omitted and an extra sentence has been created. Thus, the extract becomes:

(*) "In essence a teaching programme is a course prepared as a result of a thorough breakdown of the learning task. It is *generally* presented to the students one stage at a time. Each stage presents *information* and demands a response from the students. They may be required to answer a question, make a *decision* or practise a *procedure*. The response that students make has two functions. Firstly it ensures that they are *actively* involved in the learning process and practise the tasks that they are to master. *Secondly* it provides a measure of their progress. This measure can be used (*) by the students as knowledge of results or by the course designer to identify and remedy weaknesses in the teaching."

Thus:

$$
\begin{aligned}
L \;&=\; 95/7 \\
&=\; 13.6 \\
N \;&=\; 6 \\
\text{Age} \;&=\; [(L + N) \times 0.4] + 5 \\
&=\; [(13.6 + 6) \times 0.4] + 5 \\
&=\; [19.6 \times 0.4] + 5 \\
&=\; 8 + 5 \\
&=\; \underline{13}
\end{aligned}
$$

and the text will now be suitable for the students in terms of its Required Reading Age.

The SMOG index

SMOG is the Simple Measure Of Gobbledegook and may be calculated as follows:

1. Take a sample of 30 sentences.

2. Count the number of words with three or more syllables.

3. Find the square root of this number.

4.   Add 8.

This gives the reading age of the material. Again, three or four samples should be calculated to gain an average age of, say, a textbook. If your material contains fewer sentences you can try the following which should give very similar results.

1.   Take a sample of 10 sentences.
2.   Count the number of words with three or more syllables.
3.   Multiply this answer by 3.
4.   Find the square root.
5.   Add 8.

It has been said that calculations of Required Reading Age is an inexact science and, in fact, the SMOG index tends to indicate a required reading age about 2 years below that of the FOG calculation.

If the required reading age of the written materials appears to be too high then you can redesign the handout by reducing the number of words in each sentence and by reducing the number of words with three or more syllables. You cannot do this with books but you can consider recommending other books which your students may find easier to understand.

1.2.2 Reading age

APU vocabulary tests

The Applied Psychology Unit (APU) at the University of Edinburgh have produced standardised tests which measure the reading age of learners. These are relatively quick and easy to administer and are considered to be reliable.

The test that they have produced consists of 75 multiple-choice questions asking students to identify the meaning of words. The initial questions start off very easily. For example, which of the following words means the same as the one printed in capital letters?

BEGIN   1. ask   2. start   3. plain   4. over   5. away

However, later in the test the words become much more difficult. For example, the final question is:

PUSILLANIMOUS   1. loud   2. living   3. timid   4. averse

Thus, not only is the test assessing students' ability to understand words but it is also a time test. Once the test has been completed, it is marked and the raw score is placed on a graph to translate it into a reading age of the student.

CLOZE

Another technique that can be used to gauge whether students are able to cope with specific reading materials is the 'cloze' technique. This, unlike the APU test, does not give us a specific reading age, but allows us to assess whether a student can cope with a particular part of a book, a specific handout or worksheet.

So far we have considered the required reading age of materials and the reading age of students. The cloze technique can be used with your own materials to find the required Reading Age. It is based on 'closure'; a concept used in Gestalt psychology.

For example when we look at the figure we see a circle because we close the gaps.

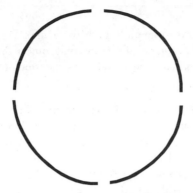

Similarly when we see gaps in prose we consider the meaning of the words before and after the gap and 'complete' the gap. The technique may be used on handouts, books, instructions etc. It matches an individual student with written materials and identifies if they have a concern.

The technique is relatively simple.

1. Take a passage and omit every 'n'th word (say every 5th word).
2. The learners have to supply the correct word.

Interpretation of the scores is not exact and tends to vary with n, i.e. 'n'th word which has been omitted. Figure 6.3 may act as a guide.

n = 5	n = 7	Comments
Score 50%+	Score 80% +	Learners should have no problems
Score 30%-50%	Score 65% - 80%	Some guidance needed
Score less than 30%	Score less than 65%	Materials too demanding

Figure 6.3 *Interpretation of Cloze Technique to Determine Readability*

Despite the problem of interpretation, the Cloze technique has several advantages.

1. It can be set for any student at any level because the learner relates to your material.
2. Your own relevant text can be used.
3. It is realistic to the student (own subject area).
4. It tests recognising words, semantics and skimming.

1.3 Listening skills

'Some students just don't listen'. The adage 'in one ear and out the other' describes fairly accurately what happens in some lessons with some students. Students, and teachers, sometimes hear what they want to hear and this invariably results in a breakdown in communication.

Listening, like reading and writing and, indeed, all communication skills, needs practising and can be improved. The skill for the teacher involves motivating students to listen. It involves more than telling them to listen hard and trying to pick out all of the important points. While motivation is necessary and should be encouraged, it is not enough. Students need to know when to 'tune in' and what to listen for.

To start with no one listens intently from one minute to the next. Students may look as if they are listening. But, while they may be hearing all of the time, only some of the time are they listening, that is, taking in information, storing, analysing or evaluating the content, and summing up what they hear.

The attentive periods when students listen vary depending upon their tiredness, anxiety, boredom or interest, the stimulation which you provide, and the extraneous noise that makes it difficult for them to concentrate. All people listen for periods ranging from twenty to forty seconds. This is followed by periods of processing of information. Listening involves this continual process of making sense of what is heard. If your talk has your student's attention, then the talk is making sense and students retain more information and are able to recall more details than if they are bored by what you are saying.

Both students and teachers listen: students listen to your explanations and you listen to your students' questions and explanations. Getting students to listen attentively involves using techniques of good talking. These are:

> Speak clearly and loudly so that all can easily hear.
>
> Do not read from notes; look at students when speaking and maintain eye contact.
>
> Be enthusiastic about the topic.
>
> Use gestures for emphasis and avoid distracting mannerisms.
>
> Use visual aids to assist the spoken word but be careful that they do not become the main form of communication.
>
> Encourage questions from the students.

Each of these assist with student listening and, combined, should ensure that most concentrate. Each of the techniques will be more or less attractive to individual personalities and, as such, will assist the concentration.

Teacher listening skills involve skills that students should be encouraged to use. These are:

> Organise.
>
> Summarise.
>
> Beware of distractions.

The first of these skills involves *organisation* and can be achieved through asking questions in your mind whilst the student is talking. Such questions are:

(a)   What are the main points that the student is making?

(b)   What supporting facts or reasons are given?

(c)   What advantages are being claimed?

(d)   What disadvantages are mentioned?

The answers to these questions can usually be summarised from the key words that the student uses. Most student answers contain relevant and irrelevant information and you need to sort this out.

Secondly, it is useful, when a student has finished speaking, to *summarise* the main points that have been said. This ensures that the main points have been understood and greatly assists with two-way communication.

Most classrooms are noisy places. So, finally, any *distractions* can be a barrier to effective listening. If the noise is too great, quieten the class, move closer to the students and delay the communication until it can be heard.

1.4 Questions and answers

1.4.1 Techniques of asking questions

Oral questioning is a very powerful way for you, the teacher, to interact with the students. It involves the student in the session through thinking and provides you with feedback on the level of learning.

Questioning is a skill which needs to be developed. 'Closed' questions usually only require the student to answer 'yes' or 'no' and as such are not particularly valuable. 'Open' questions cause the student to formulate a response. If you ask students to explain 'Why vaccines work', then they have to state in their own words their own understanding. This gives you feedback especially if you observe the students' body language – are they unsure?

Questions may be asked at various levels. For example in the cognitive domain you could ask: 'What are the main parts of a flower?' (Knowledge). 'What does this abrupt change in the graph mean?' (Comprehension). 'Knowing the properties of Sulphuric Acid and the composition of water, predict what would happen if the two were mixed' (Application).

Questions may be built up from knowledge to comprehension to application and above. You may pose questions at comprehension level and find no response from the students. In that case you ask questions at knowledge level to ensure that the students have the basis upon which they can answer the question.

Communication is a two-way process, where you want to communicate to your students and you want your students to communicate with you. Question and answer is a good way to develop this interactional style of communication.

As a teacher you need a certain amount of confidence in order to develop questioning skills in yourself and in your students. When you pose a question, you have no ideas as to what the student is going to say, despite your hopes! So, it means that you have to have the courage and confidence to deal with any answer no matter how bizarre. When you develop the questioning skills of your students, you are going to experience a wide range of searching questions which places significant demands upon you. You have to be confident in your subject matter and be well prepared even though the best of teachers are sometimes posed questions which they cannot answer. If you do not already use question and answer in your teaching, plan a short questioning session in the near future. You can then gain experience and extend the duration and frequency of the question and answer sessions.

Most teachers ask closed questions (that is questions that relate to specific facts and mainly to do with recall). What we should be trying to do is to get the students to think aloud. This gives a real insight into students' thought processes and assists both you and the peer group. You are also trying to get students to generate ideas and thoughts of their own and to explore the implications.

Open questions, on the other hand, allow the students more scope to state their views, postulate what could happen or put forward an argument. Developing the technique to pose open questions is a skill that teachers should practise. These questions need not just be at the start of a lesson or during the development phase. It may be useful to pose open questions at the end of one lesson which stimulates curiosity about the next lesson.

One of the first stages in questioning is getting the students to talk. This may seem strange when we are often trying to get them to be quiet. Students will engage in social talk very easily but your task is to get them talking about some aspect of your subject. It may be that the talking starts with an aspect not of immediate concern to the current topic.

For example you may be dealing with electrical circuit design and ask questions about the relative merits of using alternative sources of energy. Students talk to you but can also talk to their peers and it is at this stage that you ensure that you have control of the situation and do not allow a 'free for all'.

One thing about teachers is that we tend to talk far too much! What we need to do is to let others have a chance to speak. We need to plan our questioning. Before the lesson starts we need to think about the key questions which we should ask. The *order* in which we ask these questions is also important. Although we prepare these key questions before the lesson, we have to be prepared to change these questions, or use a series of unrehearsed questions, in order to respond to the answers that we receive. In other words we need to plan a questioning *strategy* but be prepared to develop *tactics* on the spot.

Another facet of good questioning technique is to distribute questions around the whole class so that answering is not left to a few students. One technique to achieve this is:

1.   Pose the question to the whole class.
2.   Pause – allowing all students to think   P.P.P.
     of the answer.   Pose, Pause, Pounce
3.   Nominate/name a student to answer.
4.   Listen to the answer.
5.   Reward correct answer with 'yes, correct, that's right' etc.
6.   Incorrect answer should not be.
7.   Spread the questions around the class so that all can participate.
8.   Encourage all to join in – in a regulated matter – for example by saying – 'Jean, can you give an example of what David means?'

However, non-verbal cues can be given by establishing eye contact, raising eyebrows, and so on. If you work around the class in an obvious systematic order, those who have answered tend to relax a little. Use a technique which is not obvious. There is also a tendency for us to act like a torch beam as shown in Figure 6.4.

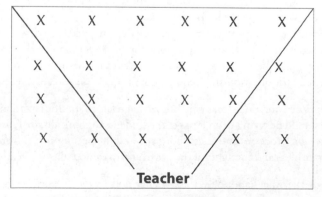

Figure 6.4 *'Torch Beam' Arc of Questioning*

If we are aware that most of us tend to concentrate our attention for questions on those students who sit in the beam, then we can deliberately pay attention to those we normally omit. There is also a tendency for students to sit in a classroom in such a way that it reflects their interest. Figure 6.5 shows the three zones into which students tend to sit according to their interest and you should try to relate it to one of your classes to see if it is true.

```
C    C      C       C      C      C

C    B      A       A      B      C

C    B      A       A      B      C

C    B      A       A      B      C
              Teacher
```

Figure 6.5 *Areas of Maximum and Least Interest in a Class*

The figure shows that 'A' is the area where students sit who have the most interest and 'C' is where they sit when they have the least interest. The least interested try to hide in the back corner of the room where they may not be seen and they may not have to answer questions.

Having posed our questions, dealing with the answers is another dimension. Student answers are sometimes difficult to hear. You can assist communication by repeating the correct answer so that all of the students are able to hear. Problems occur when students give incorrect answers. Derision from other students must be stopped otherwise some students will fail to answer for fear of ridicule. If you understand why a student has given an incorrect answer, you could reply, 'I can understand why you said that Sangeeta, but ...'. If you are puzzled by the student's answer try "Could you explain that a little more, Peter?" This then should identify the cause of the misconception.

Sometimes incorrect answers or no answers at all are due to the fact that students do not understand the question because of the vocabulary that has been used. You must take care to explain jargon or words that are familiar to you but may be outside the range of vocabulary used by the students. Remember, you are probably a generation removed from your students and language does change!

One of the problems that we encounter when we first start to use question and answer may be nervousness. We pose the question, no immediate response, so we answer our own question. If we are asking an open question, the students need time to recall facts, think about the relationships and formulate a response. Give the students time and look at their faces for clues about puzzlement, deep thinking or even pain. Encourage the answer with nods and other non-verbal encouragement. Praise good answers without becoming sycophantic. It may be useful to 'warm-up' the students with questions of the lower order like recall, before going onto the higher order questions.

Teachers differ in whether it is a good idea to ask nominated questions, that is, questions to named individuals or not. One of the aims of using question and answer is to increase student participation in the learning situation. However, a typical pattern is the teacher asking a question and then a student volunteering an answer. Those students who wish to be involved in the lesson participate and those not wanting to participate are unresponsive. This means that only a portion of the class are paying attention. (Some silent students may, of course, be paying full attention and learning.)

Research shows that teachers rarely direct questions at individual students (perhaps many teachers feel this is impolite). When teachers do ask nominated questions, these questions tend to be directed at the 'good' students.

Redirection

Redirection is a useful technique to use in question and answer sessions. This technique involves framing a single question for which there are many possible responses and allows responses from several students. The following example illustrates the technique:

T: 'We have all read about British Prime Ministers. Who do you think was the greatest Prime Minister? Mai Yip?'

S: 'Margaret Thatcher.'

T: 'David?'

S: 'Harold Wilson.'

T: 'Rashid?'

S: 'Churchill.'

You may note that at this stage the teacher did not discuss the students' replies. The original question was redirected thereby increasing student participation.

In the next sequence, a similar technique is used.

T: 'Why do you think these were great Prime Ministers? Yes, Jo.'

S: 'I think Thatcher was great because she was always right'

T: 'Tariq?'

S: 'I think Wilson was good because he understood ordinary people and could communicate with them.'

T: 'Ruth, do you want to add anything?'

S: 'They were all clever people and could speak well to large groups of people.'

You can see the three students who answered may not have been thinking about the same person but responded to the single question.

It is important to see that the teacher's questions were divergent, that is a number of answers were possible. The questions were high level questions. For example, they required descriptions or comparisons.

Prompting

We have discussed what happens when students fail to reply and have stated that teachers often end up answering their own questions. Allowing a silence to develop can and does work. Another approach is to prompt the students. It may be that the students fail to answer because they do not understand part of the question.

Consider the following:

T: 'Describe what is meant by equality of opportunity, John.'

John appears to be puzzled. It may be that the concept of 'equality' or the concept of 'opportunity' may be the problem. If it is 'equality' then you could say 'If I have 2kg of apples and 2kg of pears they are said to be ....?'

S: 'Equal.'

T: 'Correct. Equal in what way?'

S: 'Weight.'

T: 'Yes. If we put the apples on one pan of a scale pan and the pears on the other, what happens?'

S: 'They balance.'

T: 'Right – so this is a form of equality' and so on.

It is not easy to prompt students. Many aspects of your teaching may be planned in advance but prompting forces you to 'think on your feet'. You have to listen to student answers, identify the problem and then formulate your prompt. It requires practice. However, once you acquire the skill, the rewards are great.

So far we have concentrated on our role as teachers and posing questions to students. But how about getting students to ask us questions? We could set up a situation where the students have to formulate questions to us for which we can reply either 'Yes' or 'No' and *only* 'Yes' or 'No'. We will not give any other responses at all. This places real pressure on the questioner. An example could be: 'My car will not start. Why?'

The above technique helps the students to develop their communication skills and grow in confidence. However, there is a bonus. Such techniques give you interesting insights into how the students are thinking and, perhaps, show the concepts that they have attained and those that they have not.

Student Question	**Answer**
Is there any petrol in the tank?	Yes
Is the petrol getting through to the carburettor?	Yes
Has the battery given trouble recently?	No
and so on.	

Teachers at some stage in their careers, must be concerned about questions they cannot answer. The usual advice is to say that you do not know the answer but will find out for the next time. Perhaps someone else in the class may know. However, beware of the class who look for the most obscure question they can find for you each week! If you suspect this, give that question, or another, to the whole group as homework!

Classroom Relationships

2.1 Transactional analysis

Transactional Analysis (TA) was originally developed by Eric Berne (1968) as a model of human personality. As with all models and theories, there are imperfections but many teachers find TA useful.

Berne postulated that there are three ego states – Parent(P), Adult(A) and Child(C) shown diagrammatically in Figure 6.6.

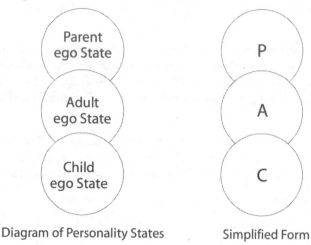

Diagram of Personality States   Simplified Form

Figure 6.6 *The Three Ego States*

Although people behave in many different ways, Berne argued that it is possible to classify their behaviour into the three ego states. All three states are usually present, but at any given time, one ego state tends to dominate. It is possible to move from one ego state to another very quickly although we are usually unaware which state we are in.

TA is based on two main assumptions: the first of these is memory. Memories from childhood are of particular importance as they contain many new feelings. Most of us have detailed memories of our parents or some guiding figures. The second main assumption is that we feel as a child feels. Perhaps this happens most when we are relaxing or when playing a sport.

As we move on to considering the three states it is important to say that TA does not imply that one of the ego states is superior to another. The TA suggests that the states are different from each other and that each person comprises three basic selves: parent; adult; child.

2.1.1 Parent

The Parent in us is often concerned with:

> Prescribing the limits of behaviour.
> Issuing moral edicts.
> Teaching 'how to'.

Protecting and nurturing.

Examples

Verbal Cues	Non-Verbal Cues
'If I were you ....'	Pursed lips.
'There's no question....'	Wagging fingers.
'That's ridiculous.'	Horrified look.
'Well done.'	Pat on back or head.
'This is the way to do it.'	

2.1.2 Adult

The adult in us is often concerned with:

> The acquiring and sorting of data.
>
> The choosing of alternatives.
>
> The planning of decision-making processes.

Examples

Verbal Cues	Non-Verbal Cues
'My view is ....'	Open alertness.
'In what way?'	Giving attention.
'Can you say more?'	
'I think ....'	
'Why,, what,, where,' etc.	

2.1.3 Child

The child in us relates to frustration, anger, fear or conformity and is connected to curiosity, creative delight, desire to explore and trust. It may also include competitiveness and dependency.

Examples

Verbal Cues	Non-Verbal Cues
'I'd like ....'	Delight.
'I don't care ....'	Rolling eyes.
'I can't stand ....'	Shrugging shoulders.
'Now!'	Laughter.
'Oh no!'	Raising hand to speak.

Before we consider how TA can help us with the teaching process, we need to develop the theory a little further. Two of the three ego states have subdivisions as shown in Figure 6.7.

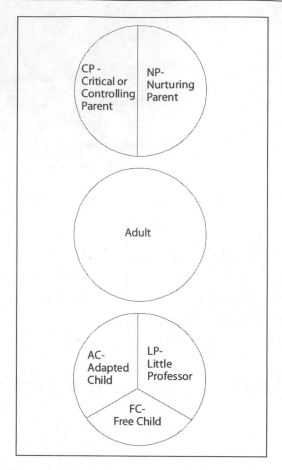

Figure 6.7 *Further Analysis of the Three Ego States*

The parent

Critical or Controlling Parent:

- Makes rules of behaviour.

- Strong, opinionated, prejudiced, critical.

- Authoritarian and judgmental.

Nurturing Parent:

- Supports.

- Helps by reassuring.

- Protective, sympathetic, understanding.

The adult

The Adult ego state is evaluating information from the other two states and this is 'normal'. However, if the adult cannot operate on its own, it is 'contaminated' by the Parent or Child.

If contaminated by the <u>parent</u> this results in <u>prejudices.</u>

If contaminated by the <u>child</u> then this results in <u>phobias</u> and <u>delusions.</u>

The child

Free Child:

- Impulsive, natural, untrained, expressive.

- Self-centred, pleasure loving.

- Angry when needs are unmet.

Adapted Child:

- Modifies behaviour with experience, particularly parental influences.

- Co-operative, obedient, sorry.

Little Professor:

- Intuitive, hunches, creative, inventive.

Most of us have a favourite ego state but we can, with practise, change to another ego state at will.

2.1.4 Transactions

Transactions are:

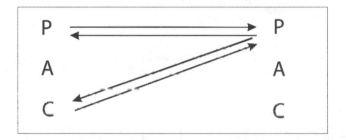

Complementary when the ego state corresponds to that to which it is directed.

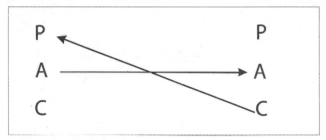

Crossed when the correspondence is not achieved.

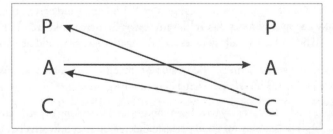

Ulterior where one correspondence is intended but another conveyed.

2.1.5 Transactional analysis and teaching

Much teaching may be classified to be in the parent ego state. The danger of this is that transactions will be directed at the child ego state which produces a corresponding childlike response in our students which perpetuates the parent ego state. If the child ego state produces a passive, teacher-centred approach, we need to change.

Consider the following comment from a student to a teacher:

'I'm really fed up. You gave us a reading list and not one of the books is in the library'.

This could be classified as C ⟶ C or C ⟶ P.

You could respond:

'You should have gone to the library straight after the lesson'.

This may be P ⟶ C

or you may respond:

'That's not my fault'.

The transaction is C ⟶ C

However, if you say:

'It is due to the usual under-funding of education. You could borrow my copy of Berne over the weekend and perhaps one of the group will help you with one of the other books'.

This is then A ⟶ C

and should result in the student moving from the child ego state to adult and hence to a better communication situation.

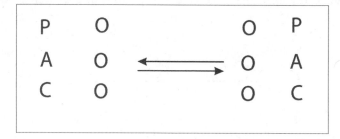

2.1.6 Stroking

Strokes are acts of recognition one person gives another. With babies and very young children these strokes may actually be physical touching. In the adult world, these strokes tend to be symbolic. A positive stroke would be, "That's a really good essay". A negative stroke would be "You're hopeless".

We all need strokes (unless we are hermits!). Berne suggests that if we cannot receive positive strokes we will look for negative strokes. This is better than being totally ignored.

If you have disruptive students, they may have been conditioned to seeking negative strokes. However, if positive strokes are given but only for good performance, no matter how small or trivial, then the student will tend to look for strokes based on acceptable behaviour.

2.2   Body language

A knowledge of body language is vital to every teacher. You need to be able to 'read' the students' body language and you need to be aware of your own. You cannot disguise your body language – but you may be aware of what sends negative feelings. You may not want to teach this particular group – and this may be communicated to the learners. You can minimise the negative signals and project more positive ones – which often means appearing to be more enthusiastic than you feel.

2.2.1   Posture

How you stand, sit and move indicate or communicate messages to others. Someone who stands and is constantly moving about is unsettled. Leaning forwards indicates interest, folded arms tends to indicate a defensive stance. A person who moves with confidence is very different from one who feels insecure.

2.3   Appearance and personal demeanour

How you dress has an impact on those you meet. We dress more formally for an interview than we would for a social event with close friends. A dinner party with friends would indicate less formal dress than that worn for an official dinner. We all tend to wear uniforms. Teenage students tend to wear jeans and tee-shirt type clothes. Look at your fellow teachers – you can often see an indication of their subject specialism from their choice of clothes.

2.3.1   Dress

Style of dress can enhance or inhibit your relationship and hence your communication with the students. Some students expect their lecturer to maintain a certain standard of dress, for example business studies students may expect their teacher to wear 'business wear'. This may mean that if the teacher appears in old jeans and a tee shirt then that teacher may not be perceived as being credible and hence is not taken seriously. Conversely Arts or Sociology students may expect their teacher to wear jeans and tee shirt and if they appear in a 'suit' then the teacher may not appear to be credible in the eyes of these students. Clearly, you need to develop a rapport or empathy with your students and the way in which you dress can be important.

2.3.2   Facial

The face is sometimes called the window on our feelings. When we are happy, we smile. It is difficult to stop doing so! Frowning can indicate difficulty with understanding or disagreement. There is a host of facial expressions and you need to look for the ones that signal the students are in trouble or following well. Asking if they understand almost always gets a 'Yes' – not always a reliable indication. Eyes are a key to feelings. Strong eye contact is usually a good sign.

2.3.3   Proximity

We all have our own 'personal space'. If we are talking to a stranger and they come too close, we move to increase the space. However too much space can indicate a barrier. Walk around the classroom, move from the front and show the students that you are not frightened of them.

2.3.4 Touch

The usual advice is never to touch students in any circumstances! There are exceptions and the main one is when teaching students with severe special needs. When observing these classes, it is obvious that touching is an important form of communication and perhaps the most effective. Care needs to be taken that you follow the guidelines of the organisation.

There are other exceptions including teaching some psychomotor skills. You may need to stand very near to the students and guide their hands. If you feel you need to do this, you should ask their permission.

Finally, do take care because your norms of touching with friends and family could be very different from those of your students, especially those from different cultures.

2.4   Class control

Careful planning should ensure that students are challenged appropriately with relevant learning activities. This should ensure that motivation is high. However, some post-16 student groups are not mature enough to fully respond to this situation. When this happens you need to have a protocol; a code of practice.

The following guidelines have been found to be useful:

Set acceptable standards for work.

Set high standards of behaviour and apply rules firmly and fairly.

Give respect and accept respect.

Treat everyone as an individual.

Relationships are important so take the initiative and for everyone:

- Greet and be greeted.

- Speak and be spoken to.

- Smile and relate.

- Communicate.

Students often try to see "how far they can go". Be prepared for this and be consistent and clear.

All classes present problems; success is achieved by the way we deal with problems.

Remember it is helpful to:

- Avoid confrontation.

- Listen.

- Establish facts.

- Judge only when all facts are known.

- Be careful with the use of punishments.

Within the college/organisation:

- Start the dialogue.

- Greet the students in corridors etc.

- Do not ignore misbehaviour.

- Set high standards of speech, manner and dress.

- Enjoy relating to students.

In the classroom:

- Arrive before the class and begin on time.

- Be prepared for the lesson.

- Keep everyone occupied and interested.

- Extend and motivate all students.

- Mark all work promptly and constructively.

- Encourage student contributions.

- Keep the room clean and tidy.

- Maintain interesting wall displays.

Avoid at all costs:

- Humiliation	–	it is hurtful and students resent it.
- Shouting	–	it diminishes you.
- Overreacting	–	the problem will grow.
- Blanket punishment	–	he innocent will resent it.
- Over punishment	–	always have something in reserve.
- Sarcasm	–	it is unnecessary and counter productive.

Try to:

| - Use humour | – | it builds bridges. |
| - Listen | – | it earns respect. |

- Be positive and build relationships.

- Know your students as individuals.

- Be consistent.

Finally, if you have a problem, do not brood. Talk over the issues with a colleague. If you are a part-time teacher, talk to a full-time member of staff; they may have the same problem with those students!

3.   Equal Opportunities

3.1   Language

Most of us become teachers because we enjoy helping others to learn. We agree that all students must have a fair and equal chance to learn. This essentially is embodied in equality of opportunity. We may be creating barriers to some students merely by the words we use. The following gives some examples.

3.1.1   Male – dominated language

Much of our language has expressions which contain 'man' e.g. mankind. We can, unconsciously, be creating barriers to some of our students. Further examples are listed below.

man in the street	average person
master copy	original copy
to man (the reception etc.)	to staff (the reception etc.)
to master	to learn
manpower	staff, workforce
manmade	synthetic, artificial
spokesman	official representative

Some examples of pronoun problems and how to overcome them are:

The student can complete his own enrolment form	Students can complete their own enrolment forms
A student with a physical disability should be able to gain entrance himself	A student with a physical disability should be able to enter without help
A student could get lost finding the college if he did not have a map.	One could get lost without a map.

There are many, many other examples and you can see that you really do need to take care.

3.2   Barriers to equality

There are barriers to equality and you need to look carefully at your own practice and that of the organisation for which you work. Mistreatment of one group by another, more powerful, group is possible in three main ways:

1. Individual   –   e.g. verbal or physical abuse.

2. Structural   –   e.g. employment, legal systems.

3. Institutional-practice   –   e.g. unequal provision of service.

Values, attitudes and assumptions may be transmitted in three main ways:

1. Expressed beliefs   –   e.g. they are all the same.

2. Cultural forms   –   e.g. books, jokes, literature.

3. Systems   –   e.g. the curriculum, learning resources.

You must not allow any form of discrimination in your classroom or learning situation. Not only is it morally wrong, it is likely to be illegal.

3.3   Assertiveness

3.3.1   Definition

Assertiveness can help you to exercise your rights when you need to. The danger is that you meet some people with assertion training who appear to be demanding all of their rights all of the time. You need to appreciate the rights of others and use assertiveness in a mature and sensitive manner.

This section deals with some of the techniques which may help you to become more assertive. However, it is necessary that you practise these techniques. The likely situations in which you sometimes need to be assertive are in dealings with colleagues and some students. When we get into situations where there is a difference of opinion we can become aggressive; we can get angry and fight to win our 'rights'. We may get our own way on one occasion but it is likely to be a hollow victory because of the ill feeling it causes. On the other hand, we could act in a submissive way, agreeing with everyone and thinking it is not worth making a fuss or making enemies. We could lose the respect of others, certainly the students, and even lose self-respect. Between these two cases lies being passive and manipulative. We actually do as we are asked but let it be known, perhaps through non-verbal signs, that we are resentful. None of these three positions is really satisfactory.

Being assertive can help us to improve or retain our self-respect and self-esteem. This, in turn, should increase respect with the communities of colleagues and students. Assertion is all about being able to express our thoughts, opinions and feelings whilst at the same time allowing others to do the same. Expressing our own values without listening to others is not being assertive, it is being rude! We should not expect to get all our own way all of the time but should be prepared to negotiate to find a common workable understanding and agreement.

The situations in which assertiveness might be necessary include 'refusing', 'poor treatment', 'anger', 'criticism', and 'activity'. Each of these have possible techniques, for dealing with them and are discussed separately below.

Refusing

Most of us when asked to do something we do not want to do either say 'Yes' and resent or regret doing so, or say 'No' and feel guilty. What we should do is think about the request and, if we do not want to do it, say 'No'. A technique to avoid feeling guilty is to rationalise it by refusing the request whilst showing that you are not refusing the person. Other helpful tactics are to ask for time to think about it. You might ask for more facts or information before making up your mind. If you decide to say 'No', say 'No' without thinking up excuses which could be attacked by the requester. Finally, you have said 'No', so do not linger to reassure that person – move on.

Poor assignments or poor treatment?

Sometimes students present work to us which we feel is well below their best. When we try to redress the situation, we are presented with responses which are intended to side-track us. Consider the following situation:

Teacher:	"Sam, I want you to resubmit this assignment. There are several spelling errors and your printer obviously needs a new cartridge. I can barely read the type."
Sam:	"I was in a rush and have a lot to do today – other assignments. I am happy with it."
Teacher:	"I appreciate your workload but I want the errors removed and a new printout."
Sam:	"Could I pencil in the corrections? The content is O.K."
Teacher:	"No, Sam. A new printout please. It is important that you present your work well at all times."
Sam:	"But the printer was rubbish!"
Teacher:	"Some of the equipment should be serviced more effectively and I appreciate your frustration but please resubmit."
Sam:	"O.K. I'll try my best."

This exchange showed the teacher using the 'broken record' technique, repeating the need to correct errors and for a new printout. The teacher was clear that the high quality of presentation was important and no amount of side-tracking had any effect. The teacher remained calm and did not criticise the student for sloppiness.

Anger

We are very fortunate if we never have to face a person who is angry with us. We tend to feel guilty and wonder why we have caused the situation. But, have we caused the anger? Perhaps it is up to that person to deal with situations without getting angry. Your task is to try to engage the person on a calm and rational basis.

1. Gain the person's attention by repeating a suitable phrase such as, "Could I say something please?"
2. Establish and maintain eye contact.
3. As eye contact is established, try to make progress with something like, "I can see you are upset, could you explain to me why?"
4. Try to get a 'sitting down' situation as people tend to be less aggressive in this position.
5. Listen to the person and determine why the anger is there. Move closer if you are at some distance to the person to avoid the need for shouting.
6. Finally, if you reach this stage, you should now be able to move to try to solve the problem.

Criticism

We all like to be appreciated by others and be held in high esteem. However, we are all subject to criticism from time to time. We have to be honest with ourselves about whether the criticism is justified. A way of coping with criticism is to use a technique called 'Fogging'.

This involves the following options:

1. You can agree with those issues that are true and say things like "Yes, you are right about that. I will get in on time in the future".

2. You can agree with issues which might be true and say something like "Yes, you could be right about that. I'll check it".

3. You can see why certain perceptions are held and say "I can see why you think that".

Negative enquiry can be used with fogging or in place of it and involves asking for more information and/or asking for more criticism. For example, the following might be said:

"Why do my comments upset you so much?"

"I don't understand. What do you expect me to do?"

"Could you explain why I should give you special treatment at the expense of your peers?"

3.4   Removal of barriers

Finally, it is crucial to point out that not only is equality of opportunity a matter of legal rights and responsibilities, it is a question of removing all possible barriers to access aspiration and achievement for everyone regardless of sex, gender, sexual orientation, age, race, religion, culture, differently abled, marital status, relationship, or health.

4.   Learning to Study

Teachers teach and students learn! But we can help students to learn more efficiently by cultivating study skills. What are study skills? This is a difficult area but if we can help students take more responsibility for their own active learning processes then these can be included in study skills.

4.1   Problem solving

Problem solving skills are important in everyday life such as, for instance, how to travel from A to B, or finding the best way to combine the demands of home life, working life and studying – and enjoy and benefit from each. With active learning we often ask the students to investigate a situation, explore a case study, and so on. We often leave the students to develop their own strategies for this and concentrate on our subject matter. Yet if we were to help with these problem solving strategies then the learning might be so much better. Three problem solving models are presented below and these are linked to Business, Science and Technology. You should use only one model depending upon the subject you teach. The models are only models and if experience shows that they could and should be improved to suit your students and their learning, then modify the models.

4.1.1   Business problem solving

Problems in the Business Studies area often involve people and their behaviour. For example, why is absenteeism higher in one section than another? A structured approach which involves separating fact from opinion is achieved as shown in Figure 6.8.

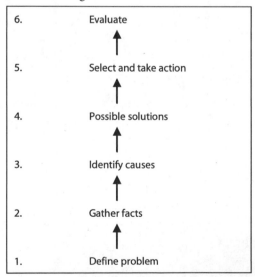

Figure 6.8   *Model for Solving Business Problems*

The first step is to state the problem. This seems to be rather obvious but if four people are working as a team to solve this problem then they may hold four very different perceptions, so it is useful to agree the problem (and any limitations). Secondly, facts need to be gathered and these need to be kept separate from opinions or conjecture. The third step involves exploring the cause or causes of the problem. There may be several interlinked causes. Some causes may be within your control but some may not. The fourth step is perhaps the most difficult. You need to get the students to generate at least three possible solutions. The danger, and it is a common trait in most of us, is that we identify a solution – the first idea – and use that. The difficulty is to structure the learning activity so that a number of solutions are generated. When using the problem solving model for the first few times, you may wish to set time limits for each stage and not allow progress until there are a number of possible solutions. The next step is to select the best solution and apply the solution to the cause(s) of the problem. Finally, students need to check that the problem has been solved by evaluating the solution.

4.1.2 The technology model

Technological Problem solving model is similar but often involves making something. The model is shown in Figure 6.9

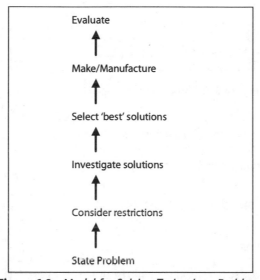

Figure 6.9 *Model for Solving Technology Problems*

In this case the restrictions could include limitations on space available, costs, material etc. An example could be to make a building without internal supports, for example an aircraft hanger, so that supporting the roof becomes the major design problem.

4.1.3 The science model

Science Model is yet another variation as shown in Figure 6.10

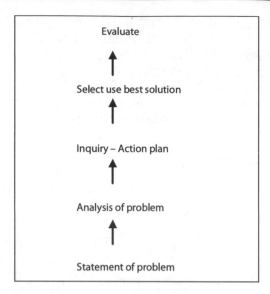

Figure 6.10   *Model for Solving Science Problems*

In this case the means of inquiry may be the most important stage. For example, how does temperature and humidity affect the strength of, say, nylon ropes? A structured approach to problem solving should give the students a framework for their learning activities. You may need to control the first uses of the models by setting time limits, checking progress, etc.

4.2   Strategies and techniques

4.2.1   Making notes

Learning is an active process so note making should be an active process. If you attend classes and try to write down every word the lecturer utters, then you feel as if you have complete set of notes – and you have worked hard. But think about what you were doing. You were passive. And did the lecturer intend you to write every word? You should turn your note making into an active, learning process which will help you to remember and understand. This section intends to help you to develop your own, individual style.

Note making is a vital study skill so let us examine some aspects. Firstly, you cannot write every word, listen *and* make sense of what is being said. So, you need to listen, be selective and then write notes. Remember, notes are simply an overview of the fuller picture. You should ask yourself why you are making notes, what is the purpose? How are you going to use them? Do try different methods of making notes such as key words, diagrams, pictures and so on.

You can make note making interesting – and more effective – by being proactive. As the lecture starts, listen to the introduction (and a good lecture should have one) and look for signposts. These should tell you what you are going to hear. You may wish to jot down key words and phrases. As the session develops, look for important sequences, structures or patterns, logic, relationships, key words, theories, people/names and so on. The lecture should have a conclusion. Do not relax and pack your notes away at this stage. Listen. Use the conclusion to check your notes. As you try to make patterns and relationships, you may have difficulties. Be ready with your question. 'Can you explain … please?'

You may have formed the impression that you only need to think about note marking during the session. Like the lecture, note making is a three stage process. Before the lecture pre-read about the topic looking at the materials and finding out what are the difficult-to-understand aspects. You can then concentrate on these aspects during the lecture. During the class you should listen and judge the material. Ask yourself, 'How does this fit/compare …?' Listen for signposts such as, 'This is crucial', 'A fundamental …', 'The three key aspects …', 'So, to summarise …' or 'By the way …'. With this last signpost, you can say this is just an aside and is unimportant. The lecture is over and you can relax, but then for the final stage: you must revisit your notes. Re-read your notes and change, add, omit, re-write and re-draw as you wish.

Throughout this section, we have talked about listening and listening is a skill. You should look at the speaker and show interest. This (apparent) interest will motivate the lecturer to respond to your body language, e.g. puzzlement, and adjust the pitch of the lecture to your level.

4.2.2 Reading strategies

We have already seen the importance of reading but know we need to help the students to develop good reading strategies. This may seem to be strange. If the students are good readers, what is the problem? The problem is that the students read everything in the book from start to finish when they need, and you want them, to be selective, that is read only three or four important pages. You may also want your learners to be able to skim read a chapter in order to identify and learn one or two key issues.

There are three approaches to reading a book, journal or part of them. These are:

(i)   *Skimming* – is where the purpose is to get a general idea of what the writer is saying. The reader looks at the headings, general points, and so on, in order to get a quick overview of the text.

(ii) *Scanning* – is when we are trying to find specific information – for example finding out what brainstorming is and how to use it.

(iii) *Intensive reading* – is where the text is read very carefully and thoroughly. You should only use this technique when you find the specific information you are looking for or when an item of interest is found when skimming.

Can you help your students develop these skills? The answer is for you to design activities which are an integral part of your teaching, which allow the students to develop these skills. If you want to try a more structured approach you could use the SQ3R method. SQ3R stands for

Survey

Question

Read

Recall

Revise

You could set a research exercise, based on this technique, which could involve the use of the library.

Survey – is where you ask students to 'skim' the source of information in order to find specific information.

Questioning – includes asking, for example, is this the most appropriate source of information? Is it providing the answers I need? Is it too basic? Is it too advanced and detailed?

Read – is reading with a purpose e.g. scanning, and then intensive reading. Note making may be part of the process.

Recall – after reading provides a good check on understanding and helps memory.

Revise – does not mean intensive reading for examination but the periodic revision of the key points.

You may wish to structure an exercise in your own subject area based on this technique. We are being asked to 'teach' more material in a shorter time. This is one approach which may be helpful.

4.2.3 Examination technique

There are still a great many courses which have formal written examinations. We often assume that our students know all about examinations and how to pass them. It may be worthwhile asking the students to form small groups and consider their worries about examinations, this may generate an agenda for discussion. The following five points may be in this agenda.

(i)   Research the examination

It is always valuable to see what the previous examinations were like. Again, the students should be guided to do this themselves. You could give them a framework as follows:

>   Look at the syllabus.
>   Look at past papers – What questions are likely to be asked?
>   Are the questions based on facts and/or application?
>   Practise on previous questions.

(ii)   Practice questions

It is usually valuable to set the students some questions from previous papers – even under simulated examination conditions – and give the students feedback which could include the following. Have they:

>   Read the question carefully?
>   Answered the question that has been asked and not what they hoped it would be?
>   Answered all parts of the question and included all relevant facts?
>   Given superfluous information? – this is wasteful.

Essay type questions should have answers which have:

>   Paragraphs.
>   An introduction.
>   A middle which contains key facts and argues the case, gives examples and generally demonstrates understanding.
>   A conclusion.

(iii)   Before the examination

The students need to be well prepared with all of the necessary equipment. You could get the students to draw up a 'be prepared' checklist which may look like this.

Pens + spare	Instruments e.g. ruler, protractor
Pencils (sharpened) plus sharpener	Eraser
Coloured Pencils	Reference books if allowed
Calculator	e.g. textbooks, dictionary
Watch/Clock	Sweets

(iv)   In the examination

Techniques which are common sense to you and I, often need to be explained to students.

(a)   *Read through the paper:*

Read instructions – any changes to previous papers.

Identify the questions you can – and want to answer.

(b)   *Plan the time:*

Equal marks for each question then spend an equal amount of time on each.

Plan your answer (see mind maps).

Leave space at the end of each answer in case you want to add anything.

Allow pre-reading time.

Allow time at the end for checking through all answers.

Allow time for planning answers.

(c)   *Answering the questions:*

Answer your best question first – but still to the time limit!

Do not do less than the specified number of questions.

Write legibly.

Check spelling and grammar (when checking answers).

(v)   *Multichoice questions*

Multichoice questions are common because they give good coverage of the syllabus and are easy to mark. Marking can even be automated. Students need practise with this type of examination because the instructions need to be understood. Guidelines could include the following points:

Read the instruction carefully.

Do you have to answer all questions?

Is there only one answer?

How much time is allowed?

Work straight through the paper and return to difficult questions later.

Do not spend too long on any one question.

4.2.4 Essays and Assignments

Essays and assignments are commonly used tools of assessment. We often assume that our students have the necessary skills to write good essays and assignments. However, this is not always the case. We have written the following section in a style so that you can use it with your own students.

Assessment on many courses requires you to write an essay or assignment. You can improve your grades by thinking about the best way to structure your work.

Most essays are in three parts: introduction, development and conclusion. The introduction is usually about 5% to 10% of the overall length. The introduction is your opportunity to create a good impression with the reader. You can discuss the title, your understanding of it and how you are going to deal with it. You need to say why the issue is important. You may rephrase the question as long as you not change its meaning.

The developmental section is the largest part of the essay. Here, you can develop arguments, state facts, make comments, introduce several main points with examples and data, and present a balanced case with points for and against. Signposts will help your reader and you should attempt to make your writing as clear and accessible as you can. Examples of helpful signposting include:

'There are two main aspects. Firstly …'

'Another factor is …'

'There are various definitions of …'

'What are the implications of …?'

'Finally …'

The concluding section, about 10% of the work, should be a summary of the main points and ideas. Do not introduce new materials. This is the final section so if you make it good, it will have a lasting impression.

What are you being asked to do?

It may appear to be obvious but the question or title of the essay is very important. Look at the key words in the question and analyse the question. Consider the following example:

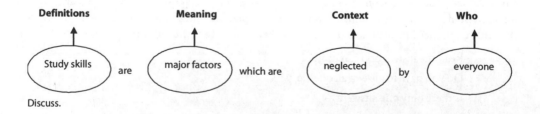

The key words are circled and now you can see the structure of your essay from the question itself.

The words used in the question are important and give a strong indication of the type of answer the questioner is seeking. Figure 6.11 gives some indication of what is required by some to the most commonly used words in questions:

Word	Expectation
Compare/contrast.	Explore two or more situations, ideas or concepts and show what they have in common and what is different.
Critique/evaluate/justify.	Discuss the merits and drawbacks of ideas, situations, statements, policy.
Describe/illustrate/outline/review/summarise.	Make something clear, recount events, give examples, give analogies, give an overview.
Explain/discuss/interpret.	Consider of examine an issue, make something clearer, relate to another situation.

Figure 6.11 *Words used in Essay Questions on Assignments*

(i)   The structure

A good essay has a clear structure and everyone plans their structure in different ways. Figure 6.12 shows the structure of an essay with three mind maps, one each for the introduction, development and conclusion. Planning in this way allow you to jot down key concepts and their relationships which leads you to write in a structured and logical manner. Not everyone finds mind mapping useful so Figure 6.13 shows an alternative approach which may suit you. As you can see, the introduction indicates what is coming in the development section. There are six very clear elements in the development and these are then summarized in the concluding section.

We all have our own way of 'creating' an essay. Figure 6.14 shows a typical sequence in the form of a flowchart. Do plan your time, allowing for recreation, eating, sleeping and things going wrong. Write a draft and *expect* to re-write. At the end of the creative stage edit to reduce (or increase) the word limit. Do proof-read paying particular attention to spelling, punctuation and grammar. Think about the style and effective use of paragraphs. Look at feedback from your tutors on previous assignments. Have you taken their advice? Do you have a copy of the assessment criteria? If so, ensure you have met these criteria.

(ii)   Paragraphs

Paragraphs are the building blocks of the essay. They should be complete in themselves and be linked to the previous and subsequent paragraphs. Very short paragraphs are a failing which make your work appear disjointed. A good paragraph deals with an idea or topic with the first sentence being the 'topic sentence'. This tells you about the paragraph. The format of a paragraph may be to introduce the concept or idea, discuss various definitions, consider evidence and conclude. Sequence is important. The first part of the paragraph should contain the most interesting point. Be brief so that you value your words and keep to what you really want your reader to know. Give examples and then make generalisations. Paragraphs are almost mini-essays.

Style

There are some general guidelines which may help you to improve your essay. Please remember these are guidelines and they are not rules which you must follow. You choose what suits you and your style.

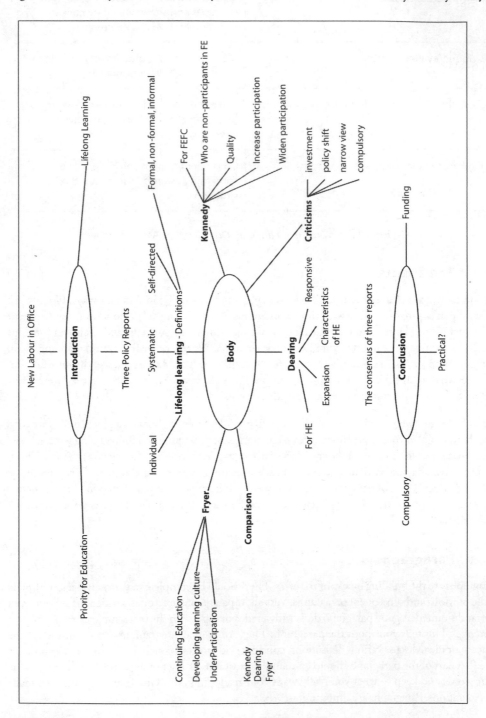

Figure 6.12 *Question: Compare and contrast three important reports on Education and Lifelong Learning*

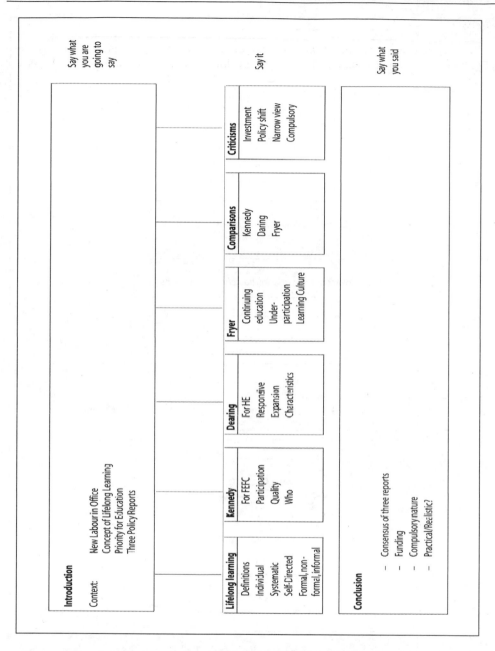

Figure 6.13   *Question: Compare and contrast three important reports on Education and Lifelong Learning*

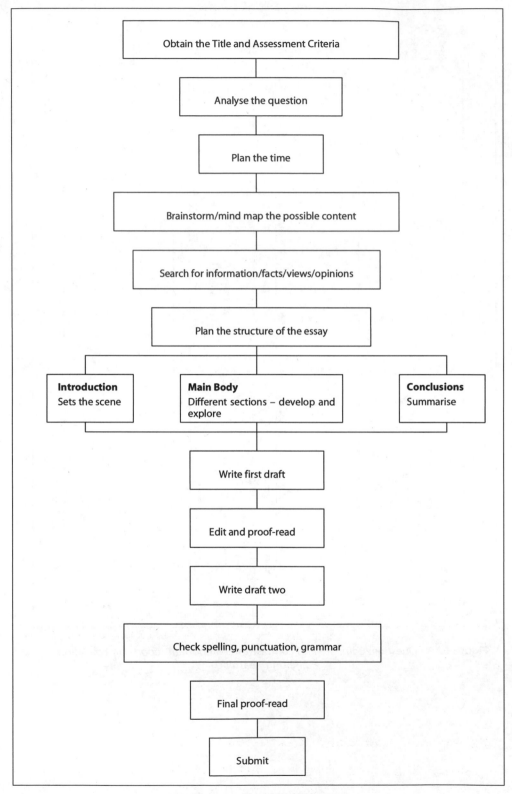

Figure 6.14 *How to Write an Essay*

Citation – be accurate, consistent and follow the College guidelines.

Quotations – use sparingly.

Avoid – vague generalisations.

Controversial views – always need evidence.

Arguments – be balanced with views for and against.

Keep to the topic.

Clarity – express yourself clearly and avoid unnecessary jargon.

Explain – new or unusual words.

Clichés – avoid these like the plague.

Active voice – is easier to read than the passive.

(iii)   Presentation

First impressions count so make your work look attractive. If you have not been provided with guidelines by your tutor, the following may help you.

(iv)   Typical guidelines for presentation of assignments

Your work must be word processed/typed.

Presented on one side of A4 paper only.

Lines should be double-spaced (except for quotations).

Blank line between paragraphs.

Main text should be 12 point (normally 14 point for heading) in a clear font style, e.g. Times New Roman, Arial.

Pages should be numbered in a single sequence covering the whole work.

Appendices may be included which do not count as part of the wordage.

Tables, illustrations and photographs may be used, but must be clearly identified, referenced and explained.

Margins of at least 2 cm at top, bottom and sides of each page.

Attention must be paid to spelling, punctuation and grammar.

Particular care should be taken to cite the works of others with due care and conforming to your colleges' edition of the Harvard System.

Acceptable binding should ensure each page is secure. DO NOT use plastic wallets.

The cover sheet should include the course title, the name of the college, the validating body, the title of your work, your name or enrolment number and the date of submission.

Two copies of your work, accompanied by a separate declaration that it is your own work, should be submitted to the course secretary.

The words limits are 3,000 ± 10%.

4.2.5 Spelling, punctuation and grammar

Many students, and especially mature students, take exception to comments being made about their spelling, punctuation or grammar. But it is important. You can lose marks for poor spelling etc. but, more importantly, you can lose credibility.

(i)   Spelling

There is a spell-check on your computer and do use it but remember it is not fool proof. It cannot distinguish between principal and principle. If you are unsure, use a dictionary. Learn from your mistakes by reviewing your previous assignment to see if you are misspelling or are using incorrect words.

(ii)   Punctuation

Good advice is to read your work aloud. This helps you to hear sentences which are too long and places where commas would help to make the meaning clearer.

Commas are usually used in lists as to give a breathing space in a long sentence. For example: 'The most frequently used teaching strategies are lecture, question and answer, and demonstration'.

Colons are mainly used to introduce a list. For example, *the benefits of using a lesson plan are:*

Apostrophes come in two flavours; possession, and missing letters. The apostrophe in 'the students work' shows that the work belongs to the student. To check if you need an apostrophe, change the order of the words to see if it makes sense, e.g. 'the work of the student'. If there is a plural, then the apostrophe goes after the 's', e.g. 'students' work can be…'.

Missing letters can be indicated by apostrophes, e.g. 'It's' for 'It is', 'don't' for 'do not'. In academic writing, it is better not to truncate words like this except when you quote direct speech.

(iii)   Presentation

When we go for, say, an interview, most of us take care over our personal appearance simply because we want to make a good impression by looking our best. Taking care over the presentation of our written work similarly produces a good impression. Obviously, we realise the importance of spelling, punctuation and grammar, and we need to conform to whatever criteria the course handbook stipulates. Have a cover sheet and use good quality paper. You must conform to the guidelines in your course handbook.

4.2.6   Time management

If you were to ask your students when they plan to go shopping for a new dress/shirt, to a disco, to buy the latest pop CD, and so on, they can probably give you a specific time because these are important events. If you were to ask which times in the week are set aside for study then you will probably find out that studying is fitted into 'spare' or unplanned time. It is important that time planning includes a positive approach to including studying.

(i)   *Planning the year*

This indicates examinations and could include deadlines for various assignments and projects. Indication of review and revision times is important.

(ii)   *Planning the week*

Some times cannot be changed e.g. coming to classes. It is important to stress that the students need to include time for sport, recreation, resting, meeting friends, and so on, but should also include study time. Does the planned study time reflect the importance of the learning programme?

(iii) *Planning the studying*

Research shows that an hour or so is the optimum time for studying a topic. For each hour the students should:

Set aside a few minutes to collect books and other requirements.

Set goals for the learning time.

Work for about 20 minutes.

Spend 3/4 minutes reviewing what has been learned.

5 minutes rest.

20 minutes working.

3/4 minutes reviewing.

Rest for 5 minutes or so.

Next topic or end there.

The above needs a disciplined approach but it is surprising how many students find it useful.

4.2.7 Feedback to students

We often tend to concentrate on the teaching of subject matter to the exclusion of core skills. But employers often tell us that they want their employees, our students, to be good communicators. The skills of communication pervade all subjects and all forms of education so each of us should help students to develop skills in oral and written communication. The use of question and answer will help students to receive oral information, process it and respond. Developing the students' own questioning skills is also a valuable asset. So, the frequent use of question and answer sessions in our teaching not only helps subject matter development, it aids the development of the students' oral skills. It is important that we encourage and support each student by giving feedback and encouragement. Written communication can be practised through assignments and homework tasks. You should mark this and return it to the students promptly. You should comment on the work rather than just give a mark of 6 out of 10. Comment about:

How the work can be improved.

What elements were missing.

Were some sections too verbose or unclear?

You should also correct any spelling and grammar errors. If you do not do it, no one else will and it is the only way that students will improve their written skills. With report writing, many students have problems writing in the third person, past tense. Re-write some sections for them correctly and get the students to practise this skill.

4.3 Using literature and referencing

Written assignment often cause students to panic. Inexperienced students are usually confused by terms such as references, citation, bibliography, reading lists and so on. We need to help them to use the literature (and the Internet) in order to inform their learning. But we also need to help them to avoid infringing copyright.

Many Colleges and Universities standardise on a referencing system and you may need to adhere to that system. Given a choice, most students appear to find the Harvard system the most practical.

The advantages of the Harvard system include: easy to use; in widespread use; commonly used by the academic press; allows presentation to be made of all publications cited and other reading in one, alphabetical list.

Citation and **reference** are usually taken to mean specific reference to the work of other authors in the text of the students' own assignment. On the other hand, bibliography is generally understood to mean a complete list of all sources consulted whether or not they were specifically cited in the final work. The bibliography is usually presented at the end of the written work, before the appendices.

4.3.1　Be systematic

Get into the habit of carrying around with you a number of index cards. Then when you see something of interest, note down all of the details of the publication – including any notes of your own. An example is given in Figure 6.15.

Reece, I. & Walker, S. (2006)

A Practical Guide to Teaching Training and Learning. 6th Edition
Sunderland: Business Education Publishers Ltd.

Own Notes:

A good overview of teaching
In College library at 374 but **must** buy my own copy

Figure 6.15　*Example of an Index Card*

4.3.2　Referencing in the text

Single authors

There are two main ways to refer to a publication using the authors name, the date of publication and page number.

Example:

   (i)   Smith (1996, 23) reports that less than half of the students used an accurate referencing system.

  (ii)   Less than half of the students used an accurate referencing system. (Smith 1996, 23).

Up to three authors

The same system can be used with up to three authors except all of the names are given.

Example:

   Smith, Jones, and Thomas, (1996, 310) established a novel way to analyse student evaluations.

Multiple authors

More then three authors can present problems but the Harvard system recommends the use of the first author followed by 'et al', (meaning 'and others').

Example:

> Students did not appear to understand how to cite publications which emanated from multiple authors (Able et al,. 1996, 12).

Prolific authors

Some authors are prolific, even to the extent of publishing more than once a year. Where do they get the time? In this case, you simply add a lower case letter after the year of publication.

Example:

> Cookson (1996, a, 108) discovered an interesting phenomenon …

In this case the bibliography would look something like this:

> Cookson, K. (1996, a) Concepts in Evaluation. Durham: Hangman Publications.

4.3.3 The bibliography

Entries in the bibliography, at the end of the written work, are arranged alphabetically according to authors surnames. The bibliography entries usually include, authors' surname(s) and initials in capital letters, the year of publication (not of reprint!) the title (which is underlined or bold or in italics), the edition, if it is not the first, the place of publication and the publishers name.

Example:

> Cookson, K. (1996, a) **Concepts in Evaluation.** Durham: Hangman Publications
>
> Reece, I. and Walker, S. (2006) **A Practical Guide to Teaching Training and Learning** 6th Edition. Sunderland: Business Education Publishers.
>
> Smith, M. et al. (1996) **Serious Education.** London: Meldon Ltd.

We have given a brief guide to the Harvard system. If you need further, detailed help, ask your college librarian for publications or guides. They are only too willing to help you.

4.3.4 Referencing Electronic Publications (Harvard)

When referencing individual works from internet sources the order of the reference is:

Author or Editor, year. Title [on-line]. Place of publication: Publisher. Available at: <URL> [Accessed Date].

> e.g. Johnson, A. (2003) *Reform of Teacher Training in Further Education: Johnson* [on-line]. London: dfes. Available at < http://www.dfes.gov.uk/pns/ DisplayPN.cgi?pn_id=2003_0223> [Accessed 28 July 2006].

5.   e-Communications

Much of the discussion in this chapter has evolved around the teacher and the student in a classroom situation; aspects such as listening, questioning, body language etc play an important role in teaching and learning. e-Communications have a role to play by allowing communications through Email, chat, forums and mobile phones, blogs as well as allowing the lessons to be recorded via webcasts, podcast and RSS feeds. So taking the lesson to students and allowing for a further preferred learning style to be used.

For example directing a question in a classroom to a younger student may not work. Peer pressure, embarrassment, lack of understanding may stop the student from answering. Pose the question in a Forum. Here the student can take their time in answering and hide behind the anonymity of the package. Most young students are brought up with a diet of text messaging, chat and forums and it becomes their preferred way of communicating.

5.1   Email, chat and forums

Email, perhaps the most widely known form of electronic communication can have advantages for both the teacher and the student. It allows for administration as well as teaching and learning. For example, it allows you to:

> Keep in touch with staff and students.
>
> Send and receive assignments.
>
> Share resources between staff and students.

However, by creating 'user groups' (that is a collection of like users, who all get the same information) then it allows you to:

> Send one email to all members of the group so improving communications.
>
> Share resources.
>
> Exchange ideas between individuals in the group.
>
> Efficiently exchange administration aspects such as timetable and room change, exam information, etc.

This last idea can be taken further by the creation of a *Mailing List*. A mailing list is an electronic discussion forum that anyone can subscribe to. Information is then shared to all members of the group. A search of the web identifies thousands of such lists on every conceivable topic. For example such lists exist for the sharing of ideas in teaching. Here problems, ideas, thoughts are shared amongst the group. Such lists are useful for the generation of ideas and problem solving.

Most email software contains an electronic diary and areas for writing down tasks and notes. The electronic diaries can be useful to share common themes such as assignment dates, exam times etc. The tasks and notes aspect allows the user to identify what they need to accomplish and by when. This is a useful aspect in many assignments when the student is asked to keep a log of their activities undertaken.

Email comes into is own for students undertaking distance learning or e-portfolio building, when the email is the main means of exchanging information quickly. Here distance does not matter.

The main advantage of the email over the telephone is that you can contact the person directly unlike the telephone where the person may not be available. In many cases the email can be accessed from anywhere doing away with the need to be in the office. Because of this it is more likely that you will answer the email. For distance learning rules need to be set up for answering emails. For example answering an email within 24 hours would be acceptable during weekdays but not at weekends.

Chat rooms

Chat rooms are places on the internet where people with similar interest can meet and communicate. They tend to be open to any individual to join or leave at will. Unlike email they are 'live' people communicating with each other just as they would over the telephone in 'real time' and messages go to everybody at the same time.

Chat rooms are very popular and most young students use them. It is in this aspect that a lot of bad and worrying publicity surrounds the use of chat rooms. Media coverage identifies bullying, stalking of members or paedophilia. To some extent this can be overcome by using a college Virtual Learning Environments (VLE) which have facilities such as chat and forums. Such facilities can be made into a 'closed user group' so that only certain users can have access. It is also useful to create a set of rules for students to follow such as language, what can be discussed etc. before allowing students use.

Many of the advantages of chat rooms are similar to those of email. However the aspect of 'in real time communications':

> Allows for discussion and points of view to be raised and argued.
>
> Queries can be answered immediately.
>
> Self help groups can be set up with or without teacher support.
>
> Setting a certain time when teacher is available allows for queries to be identified and answered outside the classroom.

Forums

Forums are similar to chat rooms but tend to have a themed or structured view allowing sharing of knowledge, expertise and opinions.

For example a teacher may post a question and students are encouraged to add their opinions. The teacher may then add a further response to these answers and so set continue the discussion. The idea of a theme or thread running through the responses is more apparent than in a chat room. As well a log of the discussion can be viewed identifying the users and responses. In this aspect it becomes useful for recoding group work and individual contributions.

Like chat rooms use of the college VLE allows the teacher to create a closed forum restricting access to certain students or classes.

There are a number of uses of forums:

> As an ice breaker to get to know your students.
>
> Group work to record individual contributions.
>
> Brain storming to identify new ideas.
>
> Discussion tool – to identify opinions.
>
> Expert knowledge to pool and allow sharing of knowledge. Many bodies such as City and Guilds are encouraging the creation of forums where teachers are invited to raise issues about courses, exchange resources or ideas for teaching, identify and solve issues.

Perhaps one of the most powerful uses of forums is in the brainstorming and generating new ideas. By bringing together a group of people and allowing them to freely discuss, argue and generate ideas outside the classroom environment, without time factors often generates original thinking.

5.2　Mobile phones and Personal Digital Assistants (PDAs)

Up till now we have looked at using personal computers linked through wireless or networks to communicate to each other. A major step is making use of the mobile technology that encompasses mobile phones and PDAs (handheld computers devices). Modern technology has enhanced these devices to allow for sending and receiving of text, images and many can now accept email and have internet capabilities. Although such devices, as yet, have not the capabilities of the personal computer they can communicate from almost anywhere. This coupled with the fact that nearly every student has access to a mobile phone allows for learning possibilities.

Such possibilities are:

> Keeping in touch with students or teachers.
>
> Contacting students who might not look at traditional means of communications e.g. letter or telephone (land line).
>
> Immediate.
>
> Deliver bite sized learning resources.
>
> Capture of data at a location e.g. field trip.

Perhaps the most important advantages in communications are:

> Spontaneity – learning activities can take place at any time including on the bus or train, when the student wants to learn.
>
> Immediacy – Learning takes place when or where it is needed e.g. in or outside the classroom.
>
> Widening participation – location is not a barrier to learning.
>
> PDAs – take this a step further by allowing immediate access to email, messages, timetables, tasks for the day etc.

Key areas that stand out using such technology are:

> *Keeping in touch with students and parents.* For many the mobile phone technology is a way of life and the first port of call. A simple message 'Why are you not in college today' has much more immediacy and urgency then contacting them using the land line phone. A letter identifying an open day is easily binned and forgotten compared with a mobile phone message reminding them to come.
>
> *Creation of online communities.* Creating support groups to help each other in the first instance.
>
> *Supporting basic skills and ESOL.* By using technology that students are comfortable with helps reduce the barriers to learning. The use of text messages and support groups are seen as a way of promoting basic skills. Often the students who have literacy and communications problems are the ones who disliked traditional learning methods. Mobile phones help to overcome such aspects.

The ideas identified above are not intended to displace traditional teaching methods, and should be used in conjunction with 'blended learning approach', but are seen as a way of giving a wider range of methods and for some students it is their preferred learning method. Also thought should be give to students with learning difficulties. Small screens and keypads may disadvantage students with visual impairment or motor coordination problems and alternative methods should be available. For more information about using mobile technology see JISC, Innovative Practice with e-Learning, 2005.

5.3   Video conferencing and web cameras

The original concept was to connect video camera to dedicated telephone lines (ISDN) to allow sound and video images to be sent between user/s. The use in education was:

> Allowed the participants to not only talk but to see each other.
>
> Allow lectures to broadcast to students wherever they were.
>
> Allow participation with students.
>
> To broadcast guest lecture/specialists to a wider audience.

Many of the initial ideas boarder around widening participation and allowed college/universities to deliver courses to regional centres where students would access the same resources as students sitting at the main site. Lectures were broadcast using video conferencing facilities and students and teachers could discuss concepts live. Although the ideas were sound it was not greatly successful partly due to cost of telephone lines, assembling the hardware and often the students themselves who preferred the face to face contact with teachers and peer groups.

With the advent of broadband which allows fast transmission of voice and video and the constant improvement in hardware technology such as very small and inexpensive web cameras and the ease of use (simply plug in and go technology) the idea of video conferencing is increasing in popularity. Web companies such as 'Skype allow free telephone and video conferencing between subscribers on the web.

It offers the facilities that video conferencing offered before but costs are much cheaper, hardware is simpler and more reliable and it allows widening participation in the true sense. By that it means students can access lecture, discussion from their own homes so giving them the same facilities without the need to travel to the centre. But far more is the access to student and teacher it that they can have a face to face discussion as simply as a telephone conversation.

The technology offers many of the facilities that video conferencing supported but simple and unobtrusive format allows for easy use within the classroom.

For example:

> For teachers and students studying languages or involved in European projects it allows easy access to their colleagues. As part of a lesson it allows for spontaneity and discussion.
>
> Similarly creating links with business allows for regular discussion with managers, teachers and students without the need for visits.
>
> Students on placement – progress can be discussed and problems identified without the need for visits.
>
> One-to-one or small group discussion with students.

It terms of using such technology planning is important to get out the best out of it. Rules such as:

> Identify times when conferencing will be available (in that teacher/students will be available to talk too).
>
> Prior to such a call identify the purpose of the session.
>
> Identify questions to be asked.

If working in group plan how this will be undertaken.

Allow for a backup plan if it all fails.

Bring in reflection and plan the next session.

5.4   Blogs

Blogs are the latest idea coming from the web. The term blog comes from the idea of a web log that is creating or maintaining an article on the web such as a diary/reflection or news story. They can be a source of information for other readers or a means of posting individual ideas. Early forms of blogs date back to 1995 when enthusiasts developed on line diaries but gained popularity in around the year 2000 where they developed into blogs as a medium of news dissemination, especially over the Iraq war. Rather like a newspaper article they tend to reflect the views of the writer unlike forums or newsgroups which reflect the wider views of the users.

Software is available to take the hard work out of creating blogs (see Blogger.com, Livejournal.com etc.) the user provide merely the content. Blogs tend to have a structured format along the lines of *Title* – main title of document, *Body* – main content; *Links* to other articles or web pages, hence are easy to create the software doing the hard work of linking to the user home page.

As stated earlier there are a wide range of uses of blogs from sharing of images, music and in our own areas, the creating of a diary or educational use.

> Online Diary – A means of recording or reflecting on activities and publishing them online, for other readers to read or comment about. Such example could be a reflection of teaching, or professional development activities.
>
> Educational – posting blogs for teachers to record what they have taught or for students to discuss what they have learnt. For a teacher they can post work for student to carry out including links to web, articles, research aspects, as a planning device, or recording field trips or scrap books of student life. These can be so posted as blogs and made readable to all.

It is argued that blogs encourage students to improve the standard of their reading and writing as their articles are being read by greater number of readers than just the teacher.

5.5   Webcasts, Podcast and RSS feeds and the VLE

With the exception of blogs the methods described previously have all allowed two way communications between the teacher and the student. The methods described in this section relate to the ways the teacher can communicate their lessons or information to students.

For example Webcasts or Podcasts (the Apple iPod version) are a way of delivering live or recorded lessons over the web. Students access the web to recall the lesson. Such methods allow for:

> Greater widening participation by allowing the students to view from any web connection be it their work or home.
>
> Students to view when they want to.
>
> Students to revisit aspects they want to clarify.
>
> Where the broadcast is live they can have the opportunity to be involved through questions or discussion.
>
> Efficient use of getting lesson to very wide audiences.
>
> Good platform for the use of guest speakers.

RSS feeds

RSS – Really Simple Syndication, is a format for syndicating news and the content of news-like sites direct to your own PC. Breaking news stories, updated websites, images video are linked directly to your PC without the need for accessing that particular site. Such services are becoming a key feature of the BBC website (www.bbc.co.uk) where they have a number of RSS web feeds to choose from.

Such services are increasingly becoming popular. For example the Learning and Skills Council website (http://www.learningandskillsweb.org.uk/home.do) provides access to educational information. It provides a series of RSS feeds to educational news services such as the BBC Education, JISC, FE News and others with the aim of providing a one stop education news service.

For teachers and students such services allow you to keep up to date without having to check each individual website.

The Virtual Learning Environment (VLE)

Bringing it all together, the VLE allows you a quick and easy way to make use of many, if not all of the services identified above. Most VLEs offer email, chat, forums services as well as RSS feeds identified above. All allow you to put on lesson materials and many allow access to Webcasts.

Not intended to be a substitute for the teacher, the VLE offers a further communications channel for your students. (See 4.2 page 187)

Achieving the LLUK Professional Standards

Standards
Domain A: Professional values and practice
AK3.1   Issues of equality, diversity and inclusion.
AK5.1   Ways to communicate and collaborate with colleagues and/or others to enhance learners' experience.
Domain B: Learning and teaching
BK2.2   Ways to engage, motivate and encourage active participation of learners and learner independence.
BK3.1   Effective and appropriate use of different forms of communication informed by relevant theories and principles.
BK3.3   Ways to structure and present information and ideas clearly and effectively to learners.
BK3.4   Barriers and aids to effective communication.
Domain C: Specialist learning and teaching
CK3.3   The different ways in which language, literacy and numeracy skills are integral to learners' achievement in own specialist area.
CK3.4   The language, literacy and numeracy skills required to support own specialist teaching.
CK3.5   Ways to support learners in the use of new and emerging technologies in own specialist area.
Domain D: Planning for learning
DK2.1   The importance of including learners in the planning process.
DK3.1   Ways to evaluate own role and performance in planning learning.

Achieving the LLUK Professional Standards

Standards	Ways in which you can show that you have achieved the Standards	See Section
AK3.1 BK3.1	1. Select two of your handouts, a text that you recommend and another resource (such as a video, website, etc.) and examine them with particular reference to equality of opportunity, diversity and inclusion. Record your findings noting examples of good practice and aspects for concern.	3
AK5.1	2. Describe how you collaborate with colleagues to share good practice and improve your own performance. You may wish to include aspects of methods of communication, planning and assessments.	1
BK2.2 BK3.1	3. Consider the textbooks on one of your reading lists for your students. Justify their inclusion with reference to readability.	1
BK3.3	4. With a group of your students set a question where they have to use a problem solving model. Comment on their use of the model and document the outcomes.	4
BK3.4	5. Select a class where student behaviour can, at times, cause concern. Consider the guidelines in section 2.4 of this chapter and plan a lesson using the most appropriate of these ideas. Review the impact on student behaviour and the effectiveness of the guidelines in the form of a short report.	2
CK3.3 CK3.4 DK3.1	6. Video-record one of your lessons. Consider: (a) the language; and (b) the body language used by yourself and your students. What can you say about each and how does this affect the learning of individual students?	3
CK3.5 DK3.1	7. Use an e-communication method with your students (e.g. email, chat, forum, mobile phone, VLE) and evaluate its effectiveness. Consider the effectiveness in terms of relating it to more conventional forms of communication with the advantages and limitations.	5
DK3.1	8. Identify one of the e-communication methods described in section 5 of the chapter that you have not previously used. Plan where its use might be appropriate, use it and evaluate its effectiveness.	5
DK2.1	9. Discuss how you negotiate with your students. You could include the benefits and concerns of negotiation making reference to a particular lesson.	2

For a model approach to show how you have achieved the LLUK Professional Standards See Appendix I.

Chapter 7

Assessment of Learning and Achievement

1. Principles of Assessment

- Introduction
- Formative Assessment
- Norm and Criterion Referenced Assessment
- Test Instruments

2. Assessing Practical Evidence

- Assessment of Competences
- Generation of Evidence
- Assessment of Student Practical Work

3. Assessing Academic Evidence

- Methods of Assessing Assignments
- Student Profile Formats
- Assessing the Minimum Core and Key Skills

4. Assessment in Lessons

- Assessing Individual Needs
- Motivating Students Through Feedback
- Assessment at the Design Stage
- Revising Assessment Procedures

5. The Role of ILT in Assessment

- Why Use ILT in Assessment?
- Using ILT in Assessment
- Concerns in Using ILT in Assessment
- ILT Assessment Resources

This chapter explores how you can assess your students' learning and achievement. It covers both formative and summative assessment, how you can design and use evaluation systems, and ways you may integrate core and key skills.

LLUK Professional Standards

The Knowledge and Understanding within the LLUK Professional Standards incorporated in this chapter are:

Domain A: Professional values and practice

AK1.1   What motivates learners to learn and the importance of learners' experience and aspirations.

AK2.2   Ways in which learning promotes the emotional, intellectual, social and economic well-being of individuals and the population as a whole.

AK4.2   The impact of own practice on individuals and their learning.

AK5.2   The need for confidentiality, respect and trust in communicating with others about learners.

AK7.1   Organisational systems and processes for recording learner information.

Domain B: Learning and teaching

BK1.3   Ways of creating a motivating learning environment.

Domain C: Specialist learning and teaching

CK2.1   Ways to convey enthusiasm for own specialist area to learners.

CK3.2   Ways to identify individual learning needs and particular barriers to learning in own specialist area.

CK3.5   Ways to support learners in the use of new and emerging technologies in own specialist area.

Domain D: Planning for learning

DK2.1   The importance of including learners in the planning process.

DK2.2   Ways to negotiate appropriate individual goals with learners.

DK3.1   Ways to evaluate own role and performance in planning learning.

Domain E: Assessment for learning

EK1.1   Theories and principles of assessment and the application of different forms of assessment including initial, formative and summative assessment in teaching and learning.

EK1.2   Ways to devise, select, use and appraise assessment tools including, where appropriate, those which exploit new and emerging technologies.

EK1.3   Ways to develop, establish and promote peer and self-assessment.

EK2.1   Issues of equality and diversity in assessment.

EK2.2   Concepts of validity, reliability and sufficiency in assessment.

EK2.3   The principles of assessment design in relation to own specialist area.

EK3.1   Ways to establish learner involvement in and personal responsibility for assessment of their learning.

EK3.2   Ways to ensure access to assessment within a learning programme.

EK4.1   The role of feedback and questioning in assessment for learning.

EK4.2   The role of feedback in effective evaluation and improvement of own assessment skills.

EK5.2   The assessment requirements of individual learning programmes and procedures for conducting internal and/or external assessments.

1. Principles of Assessment

1.1 Introduction

The first thing we should do is ask ourselves why do we assess? Some of the main reasons are categorised below:

Diagnosis:

> Establish entry behaviour.
>
> Diagnose learning needs/difficulties.

Feedback:

> Feedback to students on their progress.
>
> Diagnose strengths and areas for development.
>
> Reinforce learning.
>
> Feedback to teachers.
>
> Motivate students.

Standards:

> Maintain standards.
>
> Certificate achievement.
>
> Facilitate progression.
>
> Predict future performance/selection.
>
> Qualify as 'safe-to-practice' e.g. driving, nursing.
>
> Provide Data for Quality Assurance System.

It is important at the start of any study of assessment of student learning that you recognise the distinction between two types of assessment: formative and summative. The distinction between assessment to satisfy the needs of society ('summative' assessment) and assessment to help in both teaching and learning ('formative' assessment).

Summative assessment takes place at the end of a course or topic and is used mainly for certification purposes. It is used to see if a student has learned the material and is capable of going on to further study. Formative assessment, on the other hand, takes place during the course and is useful in telling the student how the learning is proceeding as well as telling the teacher about the success of the teaching. Figure 7.1 shows the different techniques that can be used for the two types of assessment.

Formative Techniques	Summative Techniques
Question and answer	End examinations
Supply type questions	Supply type questions
Selection type questions	Selection type questions
Projects	Projects
Assignments	Assignments
Essays	Essays
Practical tests	Practical tests

Figure 7.1   *Formative and Summative Assessment Techniques*

Many of the techniques are the same but the purpose to which they are put is what distinguishes them. Figure 7.2 indicates the different uses to which the techniques can be put.

Uses of Formative Techniques	Uses of Summative Techniques
Teachers for ensuring that learning has taken place.	Employers for job selection.
Teachers for improving methods of instruction.	Curriculum developers for curriculum reviews.
Students to gain an idea of their success.	Examining/Validating bodies for award of grades and diplomas.
	Students for selecting courses of higher study.

Figure 7.2   *Uses of Formative and Summative Assessment Techniques*

1.2   Formative assessment

The nature of formative assessment is essentially diagnostic. Black (1989) quotes research carried out by The Scottish Council for Research in Education, where teachers saw diagnostic assessment in terms of three basic modes as shown in Figure 7.3.

Mode	Focus of Assessment	Areas of Concern
I	The Class	Whether the success of the class in learning what was intended.
II	The Individual Student	Which students have not attained the intended learning?
III	The Individual Student	What is/are the reason(s) for the learner not attaining the intended learning?

Figure 7.3   *Assessment as a Contribution to Learning*

The answers to the question in Mode III pose other questions such as:

(a)   Are the objectives suitable?

(b)   Is the teaching strategy suitable?

In this way, both you and your students see assessment as a positive contribution to learning.

So, how do you use formative techniques; what must you do in the classroom to ensure that these ideals are achieved? The following three principles can be employed.

(i) **Use short-term informal assessment:** This first principle often means the use of question and answer but can also mean the use of test or homework questions which are given informally. The feedback concentrates upon the ways in which improvements might be made as opposed to giving a mark for the work.

(ii) **Provide rapid feedback:** If feedback is to be of most effect then it should be given immediately or as soon as possible. This is most effective through question and answer or through a tutorial situation. An effective technique is to get students to describe what they have done. In this way their understanding can be gauged and rapid feedback provided.

(iii) **Ensure feedback gives motivation to the student:** The third principle relates to the manner in which the feedback is provided. It is often said that students are not really motivated to learn until they revise for an examination. Yet, here we are making a case for you to use assessment methods which are part of the learning process; where feedback can be given without the formality of an examination or test situation and where the stress factors are removed as much as possible. The motivation must come from the *manner* in which the feedback is given. The emphasis must, at least initially, be upon what has been done well. The aspects that are done less well must be highlighted, as opposed to being condemned, and suggestions must be given as to how they might be corrected.

These three principles for formative assessment are outlined in Figure 7.4 with suggestions of how they may be achieved.

To apply these principles means that you should plan to use these techniques as part of your overall lesson plan. It is probably sufficient to plan the assessment times in the overall plan and to ensure you give feedback.

Principle	Methods of Achievement in the Classroom
Use short-term informal assessment.	Concentrate upon ways in which improvements can be made. Say why things are incorrect. Give comments as opposed to marks.
Provide rapid feedback.	Use question and answer as an assessment technique. Use tutorials to supplement assessment. Get students to describe their work.
Ensure that feedback gives motivation to the student.	Comment upon the good aspects first. Ensure that praise is given where due. Do not condemn the incorrect responses.

Figure 7.4 *Achievement of Principles of Formative Assessment*

1.2.1 Formative assessment techniques

The types of technique that you can use for formative assessment have been outlined in Figure 7.1. You can, however, use each of the different types of question in a variety of situations. One of your roles as a teacher is to decide which type of test to use in a particular situation. The main types of questions that are used are the various kinds of objective questions and essay type questions.

Multiple-choice questions can be an effective test. They are suitable for:

> Measuring a variety of complex learning outcomes such as vocabulary, explanations, calculations, facts and applications.
>
> Providing diagnostic information to help with the identification of student learning problems.
>
> Ensuring high test reliability.

Alternate-Choice (True/False) questions are *not* always particularly helpful as they are open to guessing and students have a 50% chance of getting them correct.

Matching Block questions are suitable for matching dates with events, causes with effects, principles with applications and symbols with meanings they represent. They are most suitable when:

> Lower level (knowledge) outcomes are to be tested.
>
> Associations between things that are to be identified.
>
> All the responses are plausible alternatives to a premise.

Short-answer questions can be useful for testing students' recall of names, dates, terms and generalisations. They are most suitable when:

> The learning outcome is recalling rather than recognising information.
>
> Simple computational problems are used.
>
> A selection-type would be too obvious.

Essay questions usually allow students a greater freedom of response. They test the students' ability to structure a response. Both structured and extended essay type questions are most suitable when:

> The objectives specify writing or recall rather than recognition of information.
>
> The number of students is small.

Figure 7.5 gives a comparison of factors which are to be considered when selecting test questions. In general, multiple-choice questions give greater coverage of the syllabus and are easy to mark, but, on the other hand they are difficult to write. Essay questions are just the opposite to this, easy to write but difficult to mark and they do not give good coverage of the syllabus.

Factors to Consider		Selection Type		Supply Type	
		Multiple Choice and Matching	**True/False**	**Short Answer**	**Essay**
Learning Outcomes	1. Number of specific learning outcomes which can be tested at a given time.	Many	Many	Many	Few
	2. Coverage of the syllabus.	Wide	Wide	Wide	Limited
	3. Abilities which can be tested.	All	Knowledge Comprehension	Knowledge Comprehension	High Levels
Influences on Student Behaviour	1. Suitability for testing writing ability.	Least	Least	Least	Most
	2. Suitability for testing reading ability.	Most	Most	Medium	Least
Teacher Requirements	1. Ease of preparation.	Hard	Hard	Medium	Easy
	2. Degree of skill required in preparation.	High	High	Medium	Least
	3. Speed of marking.	Quick	Quick	Medium	Slow
	4. Degree of skill required in marking.	Low	Low	Medium	High
	5. Objectivity in scoring.	High	High	Medium	Low

Figure 7.5   *Comparison of Different Types of Test Items*

1.3   Norm and criterion referenced assessment

End examinations are traditionally marked so that the normal curve of distribution (that is, a small percentage achieve distinctions and a small percentage fail, but the majority of the students obtain 'average' marks of between 40 and 60%) is achieved. This is termed norm-referenced assessment due to its relationship with the curve of normal distribution. This system is often employed in external examinations to ensure that standards are maintained. The argument is used that the level of the examination is difficult to maintain from year to year, whereas the level of students is more likely to be the same; the population remains more static than the level of the examination.

The forms of assessment related to norm-referenced assessment are the more traditional forms of end examinations and practical tests. These, of course, only assess a representative sample of the syllabus topics as time limits the amount that can be tested.

In terms of the marking of norm-referenced tests, to ensure the normal curve of distribution, scripts are awarded a 'raw' score depending upon the correctness of the student response and they are then 'adjusted' to ensure that the range of scores fits the curve of normal distribution. This is usually only done by the larger examination/validating bodies.

More recently, it has been realised that the concept of *mastery* learning is important where all students need to master a subject prior to moving onto another subject. This has been facilitated by the introduction of specific criteria given in terms of objectives and competences which state in detailed terms what the student must achieve. This *criterion-referenced* assessment is becoming more widely accepted.

Criterion-referenced assessment methods relate to assessment of assignments, projects; with profiles to record achievements as well as the more traditional forms of essays. Also, criterion-referenced assessment is associated with continuous assessment so that many more of the objectives and competences are assessed.

Criterion-referenced assessment relates to the objectives/competences. In this case all of the students can achieve full marks if they attain the required standard suggested, or, alternatively, they can all fail, if they do not reach the standard.

As a teacher you need to decide whether ALL of your students need to master the objectives of a topic before moving onto the next topic, or whether only a certain percentage will achieve all of them. This latter approach leads to the identification of minimum essential objectives (or competences) and developmental objectives. All students will need to learn the minimum essentials with the better students achieving the developmental ones.

1.4   Test instruments

A test is a *measuring instrument*; it measures the achievements of the students. The desirable characteristics of a test are similar to those that would be looked for in any instrument. A set of scales is an instrument that is designed for weighing articles. The scales will have a tolerance of, say, plus or minus two grams, to which it will be accurate. Similarly, a test needs to be accurate within limits. As a test consists of a series of items, questions or tasks, the quality of these is determined by their characteristics. Some of the desirable characteristics of the items, questions or tasks that effect their quality are:

> Power of discrimination.
> Objectivity of scoring.
> Validity.
> Reliability.

1.4.1 Power of discrimination

A test that consists of easy items only cannot bring out the differences in achievement of students. All students will score well and so it will not be effective in discriminating between good and poor achievers. A good test should have this power of discrimination.

You should, however, bear two points in mind about this:

(i)   It is not necessary on every occasion to discriminate between the students.

(ii)   How easy or difficult the question is depends upon the group of students. A question, for example, may be difficult for first year students but easy for final year students.

1.4.2 Objectivity of scoring

Depending upon the type of questions included, a test will be either objective or subjective. If different people are asked to independently score an essay question they will probably award different marks. This is because they will place different emphases on various parts of the essay. In other words *subjective* judgment or personal preference of the marker will influence the score. Essay questions, therefore, cannot be scored with complete objectivity.

In an objective test the same scores will be awarded by different people. The multiple-choice type of question has only one correct answer and can be marked by computer. A test made up of multiple-choice questions is *objective* in its marking.

1.4.3 Validity

Validity, in terms of assessment, is how well the test measures what it is supposed to measure. A paper and pencil test has low validity when assessing a student's ability to carry out a psychomotor skill but can have a high validity in assessing if a learner *knows* how to complete it. A valid test is one which assesses a representative sample of the content.

A valid assessment must also assess a sample of the abilities that are required in the curriculum. The questions must not only test the knowledge levels but also the comprehension, application and psychomotor skills; a cross section of all of the abilities that are required.

So, a test, having high *content validity* should:

(i)   Be based on a sample of the objectives in a curriculum.

(ii) Have all of the questions relevant to the objectives which have been chosen from the sample.

What has been described above is 'content' validity. However, validity is also affected by the appropriateness of the method of testing. This latter type of validity is termed 'construct' validity. The *construct validity* of an assessment is the extent to which it is appropriate to the course, subject or vocational area concerned. Assessment of work done in the student's own time, group work, assignment work, oral work or assessment of skills at work might all be relevant to the course. If methods of assessment are chosen purely because they are easy to administer or because they are easy to mark, the construct validity of the assessment may be questioned.

Ensuring that a particular type of test is used for a particular application ensures construct validity. Figure 7.6 shows possible assessment methods to improve construct validity.

Objectives	Possible Assessment Methods
Lower level cognitive	Multiple Choice questions Matching Block questions Short answer/completion questions
High level cognitive	Structured/Extended essay Assignment or Project
Psychomotor	Skill test observation Assessment of skills at work Self assessment related to a checklist Assignment or Project
Affective	Tutorial or discussion Peer assessment Observation
Personal effectiveness	Self assessment Discussion or tutorial Peer assessment

Figure 7.6 *Possible Assessment Methods to Improve Construct Validity*

There are no right or wrong answers for where you should use a particular test. There are too many variables to give more specific guidelines. What is right for one course might be different for other subjects or for different vocational areas.

Increasing validity by designing an assessment specification

One of the factors which relates to the success of your test instrument lies with your ability to design a high level of content validity. You can increase content validity by using an *assessment specification*. This is a technique which attempts to ensure that you sample:

(a)   The content of the course/topic.

(b)   The different abilities to be tested.

It is probably impossible that you will be able to cover all of the objectives or competences and all of the content in the time available for testing. You should ensure that this sample of questions is representative of both the content and the abilities. The *table of specifications* is used to show the relative importance of the various topics and abilities that are to be tested.

The following example specification (Figure 7.7) shows the percentage marks allocated to each topic distributed over the different abilities in the cognitive domain.

Topics	Knowledge	Comprehension	Application	Higher than Application	Total
A	6	6	2	3	17
B	8	6	2	2	18
C	4	6	2	4	16
D	6	4	4	3	17
E	6	8	10	8	32
Total	30	30	20	20	100%

Figure 7.7   *Specification to Increase Content Validity*

You can see from this table that, for instance, topic 'C' has been allocated 16% of the total marks and topic 'E', the major topic, has been allocated 32%. The first four topics have been allocated almost equal marks with the final topic allocated almost twice as much. On the other hand, the abilities of knowledge and comprehension are allocated the largest percentage of the marks (30% each). So, more marks are allocated within the assessment for the recall of information and its understanding.

You can design your own table by reflecting the objectives related to each of the topics and the abilities. This can be achieved either:

(a)   By completing the totals columns first and then the cells.

(b)   By completing each of the cells from the objectives and then the totals to see if this reflects the time allocated to the learning of the topics.

Once the specification has been completed you need to design questions which match both the abilities and topics with marks being awarded on the basis of the numbers within the cells. If you are using multiple-choice questions with one mark per question, you will need 17 questions at the different ability levels for topics 'A', 18 for topic 'B' and so on (or a percentage of these). If, on the other hand, you are using supply-type questions (say, structured essay-type) the number of marks need to be awarded as stated in the cells.

1.4.4 Reliability

The reliability of a test refers to the extent to which it consistently measures what it is supposed to measure. If a test is reliable then the following should happen:

> Different examiners assessing the same work should award the same scores.
>
> Examiners award the same score to the same script if they score it again on a subsequent occasion.
>
> Students get the same score on the test when it is administered at different times.

The reliability of a test is influenced by the objectivity of the scoring. If examiners are looking for the same aspects there is more likelihood of them awarding the same marks. Hence an effective marking scheme influences the reliability of a test.

Figure 7.8 gives an indication of the possible merits of different forms of assessment.

Assessment Form	Power of Discrimination	Objectivity of Scoring	Validity	Reliability
Essay	Medium	Low	Low	Low
Supply-type	Low	Medium	Medium	Medium
Selection-type	Medium	Medium	High	High
Project	High	Low	High	Medium
Assignment	High	Low	High	Medium
Practical test	High	Medium	High	Medium

Figure 7.8 *Possible Merits of Different Forms of Assessment*

You will see from the chart that the essay type of assessment scores quite low in all of the aspects. The selection type, on the other hand, scores quite high on all aspects. So, why do you use essays at all and why do we not all only use selection type questions. The rationale is that some forms are more applicable to some types of learning than other forms. The multiple-choice type of assessment is more applicable to knowledge and understanding whereas essays are applicable to the sorting and presentation of an argument. If the presentation of an argument requires assessment, you have to accept lower validity and reliability. However, there are techniques that can be used to increase reliability.

If you are still uncertain about the two concepts of reliability and validity, you may find the next two statements helpful:

(i)   Reliability is concerned with getting the *assessment right*.

(ii) Validity is concerned with getting the *right assessment*.

Increasing reliability by the design of a marking scheme

The value of *reliability* can be increased through using a *marking scheme*. A marking scheme is particularly important for those assessment forms which have low reliability like essays. An essay marking scheme, where the overall mark might be 40 marks, can be sub-divided as shown in Figure 7.9.

Aspect	Marks	Aspects
Style	15	Effectiveness of presentation in terms of sentence structure, and vocabulary range.
Accuracy	10	Spelling, grammar, sentence construction and use of tenses.
Content	15	How original and how relevant to the title.

Figure 7.9   *Essay Marking Scheme to Increase Reliability*

Using a marking scheme such as this, whilst it does not ensure that all of the essays will be marked in exactly the same way, does go some way towards ensuring that the basis of marking will be the same. You know that you are looking for the same things in each of the essays and, so you have increased the reliability of the marking.

A similar type of marking scheme can be used for a practical task where the abilities to be tested in each of the stages of the process are identified and marks awarded accordingly. An example for 'Flower Arranging' is shown in Figure 7.10 where the task is:

> *You are asked to decorate a table for a formal dinner party in June. All flowers and foliage must be available from the garden. Fruit and accessories may be included if desired.*
>
> *Table size 2 metres x 1 metre. Suitable covering to be used.*
>
> *Prepare a list of all plant materials used giving common and botanical names where possible.*
>
> *Describe briefly the china, glass, and cutlery that will be used.*

The framework of this marking scheme could be applied to almost any task in flower arranging. Any differences could be catered for in the individual cells. A further advantage of keeping to the same marking scheme throughout the course, is that students get used to it and know the aspects upon which they have to concentrate.

Assessment Stages	A Technical Skills	B Method of Work	C Use of Resources	D Application of Knowledge	E Creative Ability	Marks Available
1. Choice of design (style)			Related to materials (5)	Suitable for occasion (5)	Concept (theme) (5)	15
2. Selection of plant material	Knowledge of plants (plant identify) (4)	Sorting and packing (3)	Est. of amount req'd (5)	Appropriate design qualities (4)	Unusual colour, texture, etc. (4)	20
3. Selection of other components		Faultless appearance (2)	Ingenuity (3)	Harmony and Compatible (3)	Harmony and Compatible (2)	10
4. Mechanics	Neat, firm and well hidden (3)			Suitable for type of plant material & style of design (2)		5
5. Execution of design	Manual dexterity (5)	Tidy and methodical work (4)	Materials used well (6)	Application of design principles (10)		25
6. Presentation	Condition of plant material (3)	Staging and display (6)	Value for money (6)	Degree of craft skill (overall standard attained) (6)	Originality & Distinction (4)	25
Marks % available awarded	15	15	25	30	15	100

Figure 7.10 *Marking Scheme for a Practical Task*

Weighting, marking and grading

Reliability can also be influenced through awarding more marks for the more difficult questions and fewer for the easier questions. The problem with the weighting of questions is how do you decide what is a difficult question and what is an easy one? There are two ways in which you can do this:

(i) Those questions that take longer to complete can be considered to be more difficult and be awarded more marks.

(ii) Those questions that require higher level abilities to be used (application as opposed to knowledge) can be given higher marks. This is relatively easy with multiple-choice questions as knowledge questions can be awarded 1 mark, comprehension level questions 2 marks and application level questions 3, and so on. With other types of question it is not so easy, as say, an essay question requiring a number of different abilities together.

Whatever weighting factors are used it is always advisable to tell students what marks you intend to award for which questions or which parts of questions. When you do this, students know where to place their time and energies to obtain maximum marks.

Scores are notoriously unreliable when related to the assessment of student work. Even with a marking scheme it is very difficult to say with any conviction that a particular piece of work is worth, say, 56%. Depending upon the success of the marking scheme and the skill of the marker, there is probably a tolerance of plus or minus, at least, 5% on this mark. One way of overcoming this is to award grades instead of marks. On a graded mark scale the predetermined points are the pass and distinction or pass and merit points. For example a graded mark scale might have a pass mark of 40% and a distinction mark of 70%, or a pass mark of 50% and a merit mark of 65%. For example you might use:

Grade A - 75% and above
Grade B - 61% to 74%
Grade C - 45% to 60%
Grade D - 31% to 44%
Grade E - 30% and below

with D and E as fail, C as pass, B as merit and A as distinction. Also, for true criterion-referenced assessment, this scale can be related to only Pass and Fail to indicate whether the objectives have been achieved or not.

1.4.5 Assessing group work

It has been previously suggested that group work has many advantages; indeed, certain objectives can only be achieved through group tasks.

The size of the group depends upon the task. However, you should remember that small groups are probably better than large ones due to the ability of the weaker members being able to 'hide' in larger groups. Some teachers do not like groups larger than three students and, even then, consider this quite large as one student will often do less than the other two.

This type of work can give rise to problems in assessment both between groups and within them. First, group work tends to be marked higher than individual work: groups can achieve more than individuals and individual weaknesses tend to be covered up by others' strengths. Secondly, group marks tend to vary less than individual marks. If groups are randomly formed, the average ability will be similar and individual differences will be less. Problems within groups arise due to the differences in individual contributions.

To overcome some of these problems, you can use mechanisms which will allocate different members of a group different marks which reflect their relative contributions to the work. Gibbs *et al.* (1986) suggest that this can be achieved through (a) shared group grade, or (b) peer assessment.

The shared group mark means that students are invited to distribute a teacher's group mark amongst themselves. For instance if a group of four students were awarded 60% for a piece of work, they would be given 4 x 60 = 240 marks to distribute amongst themselves. Gibbs suggests that this distribution could be achieved by three different methods:

(i) Groups agree at the start of the work that all marks will be equally shared. This tends to motivate members into sharing the work equally.

(ii) Groups can agree the basis upon which marks can be divided. This might include creativity, some value of workload, leadership, communication, and so on.

(iii) Groups can decide at the outset of the work who will do which part of the work. This gives all members a specific task and, if this relates to the criteria for assessment can also lead to equitable distribution of the marks.

Another method is to allow, with the use of a rating sheet, each group member to rate every other member of the group in terms of several key aspects of their contribution to the group's work. An example is shown in Figure 7.11. These are only suggestions and might be very different depending upon the task. The average rating for each individual is then deducted from the group mark and allocated to that individual as their mark. So, a student who made a major contribution in every respect would have an average rating of zero and receive the group grade. Another student who contributed little in all aspects would receive the group grade minus 20 marks.

Abilities	Major	Some	Little
Leadership and direction	0	-1	-2
Organisation and management	0	-1	-2
Ideas and suggestions	0	-1	-2
Data collection	0	-2	-4
Data analysis	0	-2	-4
Report writing	0	-3	-6

Figure 7.11   *Peer Assessment Sheet for Group Work Abilities*

1.4.6 Selection type question design

Selection type tests are so called because students select the correct answer to a question from a given list. Examples of selection type tests are multiple-choice, multiple-response, matching-block and true/false.

The advantages of selection type questions may include:

> Good coverage of syllabus.
> Ability to balance topics.
> Possibility of compulsory questions.
> No need for students to write for long periods.
> Precise questions.
> Reliable marking.
> Consistent standard.
> Can be used each year (bank of questions).
> Student marking possible.
> Discourages 'question spotting'.
> Able to provide rapid feedback.

Disadvantages include:

> The time and skill needed to produce really good questions.
> Students are able to guess answers.
> No demand is placed on the students to express themselves in writing.

Multiple-choice questions

At first encounter, multiple-choice questions appear to be easy to write and easy to answer. However, experience shows that multiple-choice questions can be difficult to formulate – *and* can test student learning at a high level. The main advantages are:

> Good coverage of the syllabus.
> Tests at a variety of levels, e.g. knowledge, understanding and higher.
> Questions can be used many times over the years.
> Easy to mark (can be marked by a computer with an optical reader).

Cheap to mark (little or no use of expensive examiners' time).

High reliability.

Short time to answer and mark - hence feedback can be given at the end of a lesson.

There are disadvantages:

Time-consuming to write.

May lead to trivial questions or questions based simply on recall.

Students may guess.

The following is an example of a multiple-choice question:

Q.   If 6 is raised to the power of 2 then the answer is,   **(stem)**

    (a) 3   distractor

    (b) 12   distractor   **(options)**

    (c) 36   key

    (d) 64   distractor

The following are guidelines for constructing multiple-choice questions:

A well written question puts as much information as possible into the stem, the *options* are then brief and clear.

There should be one correct answer (known as the *key*). The other answers, the *distractors*, should be plausible, i.e. common or likely errors, e.g.

(a) $6/2 = 3$

(b) $6 \times 2 = 12$

(d) $2 \times 2 \times 2 \times 2 \times 2 \times 2 = 64$

Numeric answers should be in ascending or descending order.

Take care with the *key*. There is a tendency to make answer (a) or answer (c) correct. Look to see that you have a spread of correct answers e.g. some (a)s', some (b)s', some (c)s' and some (d)s'.

The *stem* and *options* should be grammatically correct.

The question must be based upon topics in the syllabus.

The *stem* should be positive, e.g. Which one of the following substances occurs naturally?

(a) Nylon

(b) Plastic

(c) Formica

(d) Coal

Avoid, where possible, double negative and 'which of the following is not' type questions. For example:

Which of the following is not a measuring instrument?

(a) Thermometer

(b) Bandage

(c) Sphygmomanometer

(d) Ruler

If you must use a negative, emphasise it by either **bold** type or an underline.

There should be only one correct answer.

Diagrams may be used to reduce wording if appropriate.

Try to avoid 'none of these', or 'any of these' as *distractors*.

If you are involved with the widespread use of multiple-choice questions then it is worthwhile considering:

The difficulty of each item (Facility Value).

The discriminating power of each item (Discrimination Index).

Modifying the scores with a factor to account for guessing.

Ensuring each of the distractors are attractive to the uninformed.

You may find the following examples of multiple-choice questions useful as they have followed the above guidelines:

Q1. Which is the main ingredient in Stroganoff?

(a) Chicken

(b) Lamb

(c) Beef

(d) Pork

Q2. A normal adult body temperature is:

1. 36.2°C

2. 37.1°C

3. 37.4°C

4. 39.0°C

Multiple-response questions

Multiple-response questions reduce the ability of the students to guess the answer correctly because there is a permutation of options. It is usual to award the mark only if the correct responses are made i.e. no half marks! It takes a little longer to mark the questions than with multiple-choice. However, they do share many of the same advantages. Examples of multiple-response questions are:

Q1. What ingredients would you require to cook cheese scones?

✓

(a) Sugar ☐

(b) Milk ☐

(c) Lard ☐

(d)   Margarine   ☐

(e)   Cheese   ☐

(f)   Suet   ☐

Q2. Which of the following are parts of the heart?

                                    ✓

(a)   Atrium   ☐

(b)   Cortex   ☐

(c)   Ventricle   ☐

(d)   Medulla   ☐

(e)   Bundle of his   ☐

(f)   Septum   ☐

Matching block questions

Matching questions require the students to match the correct answer to a series of questions. It is usual to have more answers than questions in order to reduce the guessing aspect. Some guidelines for matching questions are:

> Make the matches plausible.
>
> Offer more responses than questions.
>
> Use a logical order e.g. alphabetical or numerical.

Providing a response box eases the marking as the following examples show:

Q1. Match the Country to its Capital City

a. Brazil	1. Asunción
b. Paraguay	2. La Paz
c. Uruguay	3. Brasilia
d. Peru	4. Lima
e. Bolivia	5. Santiago
	6. Montevideo

a	b	c	d	e

Q2. Match the human organ to the appropriate instrument.

Instrument	Organ
a. Sigmoidoscope	1. Lungs
b. Auroscope	2. Ears
c. Gastroscope	3. Rectal
d. Bronchoscope	4. Eyes
e. Opthalmascope	

a	b	c	d	e

True/false questions

True/false questions are easy to design but the disadvantage is the very high guessing factor.

Well designed questions should:

> Be plausible.
> Avoid 'all', 'none', 'always', 'several'.
> Avoid negatives.
> Test one idea at a time.

Examples include:

Q1. The Language of the Inuit is Inuktituk.

True ☐

False ☐

Q2. The normal temperature of a healthy adult is 39^0C.

True ☐

False ☐

1.4.7 Supply type questions

Supply type questions require the students to 'supply' the correct answers to questions and the usual types include essays, short-answer questions, and structured questions.

Essay or free response questions

Essay or free response questions are often referred to or regarded as 'traditional' questions. Advantages include the student has to demonstrate:

The ability to organise materials, develop a theory or argument, write fluently and to structure an answer.

Original thinking and approaches to problem solving may be measured.

Inevitably there are disadvantages, including:

Student may not know if they have really answered the question.

Poor coverage of the syllabus.

Variable examinations! If students have to answer six out of ten questions then there are 210 possible combinations of questions.

Marking may be subjective and is difficult.

Students may be penalised for poor grammar, spelling and style.

An example of an essay question is:

1. The introduction of National Vocational Qualifications was a major milestone. Discuss.

It is often better to use structured questions which will overcome some of the disadvantages (see below) such as – 'how much do I write?'

Short-answer questions

Short-answer questions are an efficient way of testing a wide coverage of the syllabus. They are particularly useful for recall type assessment. They are relatively easy to set and to mark. You could have questions where the student has to supply a missing word or where the student is required to answer with a single sentence.

Advantages of short-answer questions include:

The students know what is required.

Marking is reliable, and quick.

No undue emphasis on writing ability.

However, the danger is that we assess rather trivial learning.

Examples of short-answer questions are as follows:

1. Name ONE acid and ONE alkali.
2. Name SIX essential foods in a balanced diet.
3. State TWO advantages of the National Curriculum and TWO disadvantages.

Structured questions

Structured questions help the students to know what is required of them. They are more specifically defined than an essay question.

Other advantages include:

Marking can be more reliable.

Questions can be related to more of the syllabus.

Easier to test higher abilities.

The disadvantages include:

> Difficult to set.
>
> Time consuming to set and mark.
>
> Subjectivity in marking.
>
> Students may be penalised for poor writing, expression etc.

The essay question outlined above (e.g. The introduction of NVQs was a major milestone. Discuss) can be structured as follows:

Q1.		Marks
(i)	Explain why NVQs were introduced and the system they replaced	5
(ii)	Discuss who were the main architects of NVQs	5
(iii)	What were the initial reactions of	
	(a) employers	2
	(b) trades unions	2
	(c) educationalists and trainers?	2
(iv)	In practice, what have been the	
	(a) benefits	2
	(b) problems?	2
		Total 20

As can be seen from the second version of the question, the student knows what the examiner is seeking rather than just guessing what the question is about. The marks allocated to each section helps the student gauge how much time to spend on each part of the question and the marking is more reliable.

The following examples may help you to make your questions more structured.

Q1. Describe the classes of bacteria likely to be found in cooked meats.

This may be improved as follows:

Q1. State THREE classes of bacteria likely to be found in cooked meats (with one mark for each class).

Q2. Discuss the materials used in the following situations

(a) Underground gas pipes.

(b) Cavity wall insulation.

(c) Ironing board covers.

An improvement would be.

Q2. For each of the following state ONE suitable material and ONE reason for your choice.

(a) Underground gas pipe.

(b) Cavity wall insulation.

(c) Ironing board cover.

Q3. Describe the construction of an electric bell.

Adding the following structure to this question and giving an indication of the marks to be awarded provides students with an indication of the required depth for each of the aspects.

Q3.   Marks

    (a) Sketch the circuit for an electric bell   6

    (b) Label four components   4

    (c) Describe how the system works   4

    (d) State one likely fault   2

As can be seen from each of the above three examples, the second version tells the student what the examiner is seeking rather than just guessing what the question is about.

1.4.8 Summary of methods

Figure 7.12 brings together various features of assessment instruments. As you may see if this is compared with Figure 7.8, there is no single ideal way to assess. If the test is easy to design, then it is likely to be difficult to mark accurately and reliably, and vice-versa.

Method	Validity	Reliability	Ease of Design	Ease of Marking
Multiple Choice	High	High	Low	High
Multiple selection	High	High	Low	Medium
Matching	High	High	Low	Medium
True/false	High	High	Low	High
Essay	Low	Low	High	Low
Short answer	Medium	Medium	Medium	Medium
Structured	Medium	Medium	Medium	Medium

Figure 7.12 *More Characteristics of Assessment Instruments*

2.   Assessing Practical Evidence

2.1   Assessment of competences

With the introduction and proliferation of National Vocational Qualifications (NVQs) major changes are occurring in the assessment systems of education and training of adults. Fundamental to these changes is the competence-based approach and the ways in which we assess and accredit the levels of attainment achieved.

The basis of Accreditation of Prior Achievement (APA) relates to the generation of evidence by students to show that they can achieve the competences. This evidence can be collected by:

> Students themselves.
>
> Other course members or colleagues.
>
> The student's line manager at work.
>
> Tutors.
>
> Mentors at the place of work.

Successful completion of a unit of competence will be on the basis of assessment. The requirements are illustrated in Figure 7.13.

Figure 7.13 *Pyramid of Competences*

The figure illustrates that at the base of the pyramid and the basis of achievement, lies the generation of evidence. Students can generate evidence either on a course, or at work or through exercises which are linked to criteria of assessment associated with units of competence. Once the evidence has been generated it needs to be collected into an acceptable form so that it can be assessed. The collected evidence is then judged as 'reaching the necessary criteria' and then verified by an external assessor.

In order to be awarded an NVQ, students need to achieve a number of units of competence which make up the overall competence related to a vocational job. The following principles should be followed for the award:

(a)   All of the competences must be achieved.

(b)   The evidence should relate clearly to the competences.

(c)   The evidence should cover the range of contexts for the competences.

(d)   The evidence should allow distinction between those who meet the criteria and those who do not.

(e)   The assessment must be open to verification by external examiners.

2.2   Generation of evidence

There are four major sources of evidence that can be collected to show that students have achieved a competence. Sometimes a mixture of sources will be used. The four sources are:

(i)   **Historical evidence:**

This is evidence resulting from activities that have been undertaken in the past either at work or elsewhere. The evidence may already exist (e.g. curriculum materials) or it may need to be generated (e.g. written reports of projects).

(ii)   **Performance at work:**

This is evidence generated by the student at work. Again, the evidence may already exist or alternatively it may be generated as part of the assessment requirements.

(iii)   **Performance on assignments:**

This relates to the assignments and projects completed as part of course work. This type of evidence gives greater freedom and students can demonstrate more fully their capabilities. However, there is more chance that the evidence will not relate directly to the competence.

(iv)   **Questioning:**

This relates to questioning during tutorial sessions. It may be combined with other sources of evidence.

The evidence collected can usually be built up into a portfolio of work. The type of evidence can be included in a portfolio to be considered for APL (Accreditation of Prior Learning) and APEL (Accreditation of Prior Experiential Learning) includes:

(i)   Direct evidence (students own work) such as:

        Projects/assignments from previous courses.

        Tutor assessments of projects/assignments.

        Artefacts – models, videos, photos, etc.

        Documents used in professional practice.

        Evidence from written tests.

(ii)   Indirect evidence (information from others) such as:

        Reports of professional practice.

        Endorsed statements from an employer.

        Curriculum vitae.

        Certificates and awards.

        References.

Accrediting both prior learning and prior experience has the advantage of using what has been completed previously to show competence in relation to a specific area of an NVQ. The problem when using either direct or indirect evidence is to ensure that the past skills relate exactly to the performance criteria. This can often be a time-consuming process.

2.3 Assessment of student practical work

The usual technique for the assessment of practical work involves direct observation, where you watch the completion of the task and assess the process, (how the work is done), and the product, (what has been done).

2.3.1 Direct observation assessment

Direct observation of practical work may be used to identify learning needs of students in relation to personality, attitudes, behaviours and skills. You can use direct observation in either a formative or a summative manner. Observation as a formal means of assessment over a long period, however, is subject to two problems. First, your students may feel threatened and second, your prejudices as the observer can affect the validity and reliability of the assessment. When identifying learning needs, it is best that you use short, focused periods of observation of a sample of tasks.

There are four common methods of direct observation:

(i) **Global Impression:** This, essentially, is a technique where you 'look and describe what you see'. The method has no structure and, as such, lacks reliability. However, it is a useful first step in the development of the more sophisticated approaches.

(ii) **Semi-structured:** This consists of a number of open questions which you determine in advance and are relevant to the task. You write answers to the questions for each student either during, or after, observation.

(iii) **Rating Schedules:** This is where you rate a performance on a, say, five point scale as to your impression of each component of the task as carried out by the student.

(iv) **Checklists:** This is where you mark whether the student did or did not carry out specific features of the task.

These four methods range from the global and impressionistic to the relatively specific and analytical. Each has its own strengths and weaknesses. Global methods allow you to take account of individual differences and spot unsuspected learning needs but they are also susceptible to personal idiosyncrasies. By contrast, semi-structured observations do provide you with a framework which goes some way to checking your idiosyncrasies. Rating schedules concentrate your attention on the major aspects to be assessed but you may differ in your ability to interpret the 5-point scale compared with your colleagues. One assessor's 'very good' may be another assessor's 'mediocre'. Detailed checklists provide a very reliable method of diagnosing strengths and weaknesses but they may exclude some important unforeseen and rarely occurring characteristics. Of the four techniques, the checklist is probably the best for identifying student needs and provides you with some useful feedback for the improvement of your performance as a teacher. Once you have devised a checklist you can use it to develop rating schedules and to provide you with a framework for semi-structured observation.

Examples of the four approaches are shown so that you can see the relative merits of each:

1. **Global observation:** This approach is ambiguous as the instructions do not specify the items that are to be commented upon. Also, the notion of 'ability' is included so you are asked to predict as well as to comment upon present achievement. No criteria are given so it is difficult to compare a group of students. Finally, the meaning of A B C D E is not specified.

   Example:

   Please write comments on the student's ability to decorate a table for a dinner party.
   Ring the grade you feel is appropriate: A B C D E

2. **Semi-Structured Observation:** This structured approach provides you with some guidelines in the form of questions. It can be used for observing the student but there is a temptation to answer the questions with a YES/NO. Additional instructions and questions would be required if you intend to estimate the student's achievement.

    Example:

    > Did the student choose an appropriate style?
    >
    > Were appropriate plant materials selected?
    >
    > Were other components appropriately selected?
    >
    > Were the mechanics of the design well applied?
    >
    > Was the execution of the design completed well?
    >
    > Was the presentation appropriate?

3. **Rating Schedule Observation:** This approach concentrates on the five broad dimensions of table decoration which are important. The rating scales are labelled but observers would have to be trained to ensure that they use the scales in the same way. It is, implicitly, a norm-referenced scale.

    Example:

    Please rate the student on the following:

Choice of Style.	6 5 4 3 2 1
Selection of appropriate plant materials.	6 5 4 3 2 1
Selection of other components.	6 5 4 3 2 1
Application of the mechanics of design	6 5 4 3 2 1
Execution of design.	6 5 4 3 2 1

    6 = very good, 5 = good, 4 = quite good, 3 = just satisfactory, 2 = unsatisfactory, 1 = very poor

4. **Checklist Observation:** This approach sets out the criteria clearly. Even if you do not agree with the criteria, you do at least know what they are. The checklist, when given to learners, gives them a useful guide on how to cope with the decorating of a table for a dinner party. The terms 'appropriate' and 'correctly' clearly still require some personal judgment by you as assessor, but different assessors are more likely to agree when using such a checklist than they are when using a rating schedule. The checklist is, therefore, likely to yield reliable assessments and they may also be valid. It is essentially a criterion-referenced instrument.

    Example:

Criteria	Yes	No	Not Observed
The student related to available materials.			
The design was appropriate for the occasion			
Choice of theme was appropriate.			
Plants were identified correctly			
Plants were sorted and packed correctly			
Correct estimate of quantities made.			
Appropriate design qualities used.			
Unusual combinations of colour and texture			

Thus, from the four types, the checklist is the most complex but is more likely to provide accurate results in terms of validity and reliability. It does, however, take more time and expertise to design and you need to observe a student closely in order to complete all of the aspects. In the class situation this latter point might cause difficulties. It is evident that the checklist is at one end of a spectrum with a high degree of structure with its closed, specific and systematic approach but there is less inference involved in interpretation of the instrument. The global approach is at the other end of the spectrum with low structure through its open, general and unsystematic approach, with the resultant high inference level required in order for you, as assessor, to interpret it, which results in different interpretations. The rating schedule and semi-structured approaches lie between these two ends of the spectrum as shown in Figure 7.14.

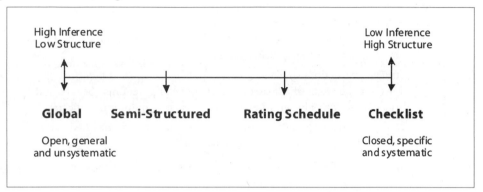

Figure 7.14 *Relationship Between Different Observation Techniques*

2.3.2 Preparation of practical tests

You should follow logical steps in the preparation of a series of practical tests for your students. Typical logical steps are:

Step One: prepare, from the syllabus, the objectives that require assessment by means of practical work. This will, in effect, be the minimum essential objectives from the syllabus.

Step Two: decide upon the number of tests that will assess the objectives and the type of test exercise that will be required for each of them. For this you will use:

(a) The number of objectives noted in the list prepared from the syllabus.

(b) The importance of each of these objectives.

(c) The ways in which the objectives can be grouped together as relating to similar exercises.

(d) The time which each of the tests can be expected to take, and the maximum time reasonably available from the course.

Step Three: prepare each test exercise. This is sub-divided into four parts:

(i) Design a test exercise to ensure that students demonstrate attainment of the objectives which have been grouped together.

(ii) Decide how the test will be marked, by designing an assessment scheme which will comprise a list of criteria to show whether the student's performance is satisfactory. This might be a rating schedule, a checklist or a semi-structured format. Probably the most appropriate of these is a checklist which requires either a tick or a cross to show the student achievement or non-achievement of the criteria. The criteria should refer to both the final product and the method of work. It might also refer to the speed of work if this is important.

(iii) Decide how the result will be determined. Assessment criteria can be classified as either essential or desirable. Essential criteria are those which, when they are not met, can lead to the complete failure of the exercise, or, alternatively, lead to unsafe practices. The remaining criteria can be classified as desirable.

The requirement for a pass should include all essential criteria plus however many of the desirable criteria as is judged reasonable for a student to achieve.

(iv) Draft the test in three sections using clear, simple and unambiguous language. The three sections are:

> Preparation which includes:
> Where the test will be held; details of any necessary preparation and a list of materials, tools and equipment required.

> Student instructions which include:
> What is to be done; what materials, tools and equipment may be used and a brief description of how the test will be assessed, including any time limits.

> Design the marking scheme which comprises marking criteria listed in the order that will be most convenient to be checked.

The example shown in Figure 7.15, is an example of a test sheet for a task of wiring a three pin plug.

Preparation

The test should be held in normal working conditions. Students should be able to use tools and plugs normally available. They should be instructed to provide their 'usual' tools.

Student Instructions

This test is to assess whether you have reached a basic standard in wiring a 3-pin electrical plug. Using your own tools, a standard 3-pin plug and 13 amp wire, within ten minutes, wire the plug so that it is mechanically and electrically sound.

You should:

(a)   Collect the appropriate equipment.
(b)   Strip the outer sheath and core insulation to the appropriate lengths.
(c)   Secure the outer sheath correctly.
(d)   Connect the cables to the correct terminals.
(e)   Reassemble the plug correctly.
(f)   Use the appropriate tools correctly.
(g)   Check your work.

Marking

Each point to be marked with a tick if satisfactory and a cross if it is not satisfactory. To obtain a pass, all the square boxes and 50% of the circles must be ticked.

Cable stripper used appropriately.	○
Cable cores bared to terminals but not away from them.	○
Connected cable to correct terminals.	□
Cables connected securely to terminals.	□
Outer sheath clamped securely	□
Fuse fitted correctly.	□
Body of plug reassembled securely.	□
Used correct screwdrivers for different screws.	○
Worked tidily and neatly.	○

Figure 7.15 *Example Marketing Scheme for a Practical Test*

3. Assessing Academic Evidence

3.1 Methods of assessing assignments

You may encounter some confusion in the difference between projects and assignments. When used in the context of teaching methods the two are often ill defined despite being widely used and are sometimes inter-changed. The two are very similar and it is the time that is taken to complete them that often differentiates the two: an assignment generally taking a shorter time to complete than a project.

However, the major difference between the two lies in design. In a project the student decides the parameters of the work within overall guidelines whereas in an assignment the teacher decides on the parameters. Thus, a project is more open and is liable to more differences in the way in which it is tackled whereas the assignment has more structure which is likely to lead to similarities in the approaches taken by the students. In many ways a project may be considered as the extreme to which you may go in arranging student-centred learning approaches, whereas an assignment is more teacher-centred.

Both assignments and projects have the advantage that they provide the opportunity for the assessment of a great range of skills within all of the domains and at all levels within the domains. Also, Edexcel have pioneered the use of what they term 'integrative' assignments where they also give the opportunity for assessment across the subject matter boundaries. They argue that this is the way that learning takes place at work; not within subjects but across them. The problem is the basis. This has given rise to 'work-based' assignments which also give the opportunity for the assessment of common (transferable) skills, which are problem based.

In this section we are going to concentrate upon the methodology of assessing assignments. The reason for this is that (a) assignments are more commonly used than projects, but (b) the principles and techniques described are applicable to both strategies.

An example of a work-based Assignment given by Edexcel relating to National Awards in Leisure Studies is given below. The general guideline to the student is:

> *You are to investigate security arrangements in a chosen leisure organisation.*

This, however, is only a general guideline that is given to the student. Remembering that an assignment has been defined as being:

    (i)   structured by the teacher; and

    (ii)   giving opportunity for assessment across subject matter boundaries,

both student activities and the objectives from the different subjects need to be identified. These are shown diagrammatically in Figure 7.16. The student activities are shown as a step-by-step guide for the students to follow and it is from these that the objectives are identified from the different subject areas. The objectives become the basis for the assessment.

The assessment of the assignment is based on amalgamation of the student activities and the objectives from the different styles. This means that you will need to identify assessment criteria for each of the student activities. There are also the common skills which must be included in the criteria. These can be achieved as shown in Figure 7.17.

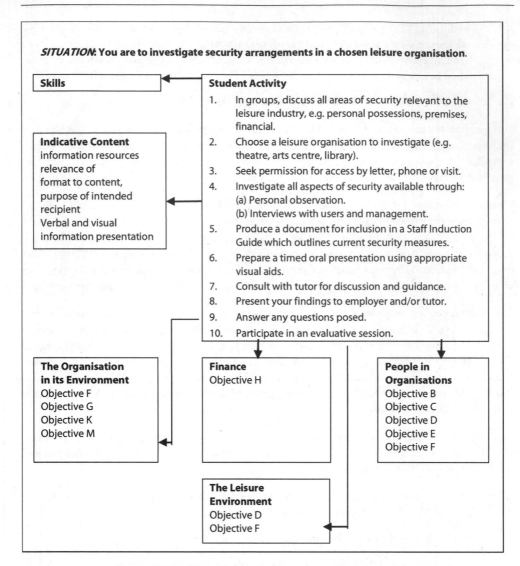

Figure 7.16 *Example Layout for an Integrated Assignment*

Student Activity	Assessment Criteria
1. In groups discuss all areas of security relevant to the leisure industry.	Uses a variety of sources of information. At least three different areas of security should be discussed. Helps the group reach decisions. Participate in verbal and non-verbal communication effectively.
2. Etc.	

Figure 7.17 *Assessment Criteria Related to Student Activities*

So, you need to design assessment criteria for each of the student activities and these can be given to the students along with the other information prior to the start of the assignment.

Instead of showing you all of the assessment criteria for each of the student activities in the previous example, it is of more use to you to indicate a checklist as shown in Figure 7.18. This is subdivided into aspects to achieve validity (ensuring that it assesses what it is supposed to assess), reliability (ensuring that the assessment is the same for all the students who are observed) and utility (ensuring that it can be used effectively). In order to use the checklist for an acceptable assignment assessment all of the aspects should be checked as either 'YES' or 'NOT NEEDED'. Any aspects that are checked as 'NO' should be reconsidered in order to improve the assessment schedule.

	Aspect	Yes	No	Not Needed
1.	**Validity of Assignment Assessment**			
1:1	Are the objectives of the assignment stated?	1	2	3
1:2	Do the objectives cover:			
	(i) all the necessary domains?	1	2	3
	(ii) all the necessary subjects?	1	2	3
	(iii) all the necessary core skills?	1	2	3
1:3	Are the necessary student activities produced?	1	2	3
2.	**Reliability**			
2:1	Do students receive:			
	(i) written information of the assessment scheme?	1	2	3
	(ii) details of how gradings are arrived at?	1	2	3
	(iii) a timetable of key assessment events?	1	2	3
3.	**Utility**			
3:1	Is there any duplication of sampling of student performance?	1	2	3
3:2	Is there an effective balance between process and product assessment?	1	2	3
3:3	Is informal observation of student performance possible to achieve?	1	2	3

Figure 7.18 *Checklists for Assignment Assessment*

You might use a wide range of assessment methods for assessing performance in assignments. The following examples illustrate some of the range that you might use:

(i)   *Teacher observation* of group activity, team tasks and, sometimes, individual activity.

(ii) *Student diaries* of work experience which include reflections on learning and students' strengths and weaknesses.

(iii) *Portfolios/work files* which may include students' working papers as well as completed assignment work and tutor comments.

(iv) *Self-Assessment statements* on skills development at regular stages during the assignment.

(v)   *Peer assessment* which may take the forms, for example:

Agreeing with a team member a statement of their contribution to the task.

Commenting in a group review on the work of different aspects.

Making a written comment, against set criteria, of the work of different teams.

(vi)   *Assignment products* which may be reports, designs, or artefacts.

(vii)   *Process reviews* in which the students and tutor review the ways in which the assignment was approached.

3.2   Student profile formats

You will realise from Chapter 1 that a profile is a way of reporting student achievements; it is not an assessment technique in itself. Profiles can be used for both formative and summative processes. Traditional methods of reporting student progress are through an examination and a brief comment about these results, the work completed in class and, perhaps, the attitude of the student. It can be argued that traditional methods:

Are very crude, global and mask individual differences.

Are subject-based reports which tend to hide the overall student abilities.

Offer little incentive to many students.

Offer little worthwhile information to students.

Give no real assistance to students with self-assessment.

Give teachers very little to go on when they are asked to give an account of their work.

Are very impersonal, giving students very little opportunity to discuss them.

Consider the aims of a typical vocational course given in Figure 7.19.

Aims	Objectives
• To identify personal opportunities and prepare for progression. • Further explore selected occupational and non-occupational roles. • To become an effective member of a team. • Assist an ability for organisation and leadership. • Develop confidence in working independently. • Equip students to communicate effectively with a range of people in a variety of situations.	• Apply enterprise skills. • Recognise the need for a career plan. • Work co-operatively in a team. • Assist colleagues to plan tasks. • Assess results of own work without assistance. • Present a logical and effective argument and analyse others' arguments.

Figure 7.19   *Typical Aims/Objectives of a Vocational Course*

These mainly fall within the affective domain and, it is suggested, are not assessed and reported upon by traditional methods of assessment and reporting. Indeed, generally traditional methods of assessment neglect the affective domain to a large extent. Profiles attempt to pass information on to students, employers and other teachers on all aspects of learning.

Four different types of profile are described. When looking at each of them you should consider:

The method that appears to be particularly helpful to you in your teaching situation.

Methods that might hinder you in your teaching situation.

Methods that might assist you to overcome problems that you might have presently in reporting on student learning.

3.2.1 Grid-style hierarchical profile

This type of profile (Figure 7.20) shows the specific abilities that the students must exhibit and, alongside each, a three-point scale of individual progress in the abilities. A space is also provided for examples of how individual students have exhibited the abilities (what task they were involved in when they were observed, what they did, and so on). Additionally there is a space between each statement where either the teacher or the student can sign and indicate a date to confirm that, at that time, the student had achieved that level.

Abilities		Examples of Abilities	Progress in Abilities		
C O M M U N I C A T I O N	*Talking/ Listening*		Can make sensible replies.	Can follow and give explanations.	Can present a logical argument.
	Reading		Can read words and phrases.	Can follow written instructions.	Can judge materials to support an argument.
	Writing		Can write words and phrases.	Can write instructions.	Can write a critical analysis.
	Use of diagrams		Recognises everyday sign/symbols.	Uses basic graphs/codes/ charts.	Can make graphs to support conclusions.

Figure 7.20 *Grid-style Hierarchical Profile*

Only abilities in communication are shown in the example. However, practical, numerical, social and decision making skills can be added to cover all of the skills in a course of study.

It will be seen that the statements alongside each ability are graded starting from the simple and going to the complex. In the example given, a three-point scale is used. This results in quite large jumps between each level. If a five-point scale were used the jumps between each would be smaller.

A completed example for a 'Practical' skill is given in Figure 7.21 to indicate how the spaces might be used. The ability has been assessed on two occasions with different tasks and shows the progression between the two dates.

Abilities	Examples of Abilities	Progress in Abilities		
Safety	1. Changed wheels and oil filter on a car.	Can explain the need for rules.	Can spot safety hazards.	Can suggest safety improvement.
		Sig. Date(1)	Sig. Date(2)	
	2. Changed points on a distributor.			

Figure 7.21 *Completed Grid-Style Hierarchical Profile*

The *advantages* of the grid-style profile are:

> Specific examples for the abilities can be identified.
>
> Reliability is improved through the nominating of the three points on the scale.
>
> Progress can easily be shown.
>
> Can be completed by the teacher, the student, or through a mixture of both.
>
> Can be used as either a formative or summative document.
>
> Contains a lot of information for employers.
>
> Has both tick box and statement information.

However, there are also the following *limitations*:

> Can be restricting as there is no space for abilities other than those listed.
>
> Can take employers a long time to read if they have a lot of them and if they are used as summative documents.
>
> Teachers might think that all of the abilities need completing.
>
> Can be time consuming to complete.
>
> There is no specific space for students to write their own comments.

3.2.2 Bank of statements profile

This profile consists of a set of objectives which are available for both the teacher and the student. The intention is that they are used as the basis for negotiation between teacher and student to decide how and when individual students will achieve the statements. The teacher will also use them as a basis for assessment and reporting.

Banks of Statements can be written for any area of the curriculum. However, they are mainly associated with affective domain areas covering the core skills such as 'personal development', 'career development', 'manual dexterity', 'evaluation of performance', and so on. Figure 7.22 shows an example bank of statements from the core area of 'personal and career development'. These are just a representative sample of the type of statement from this core area. Additionally, there would be objectives under other core areas of:

industrial, social and environmental studies;

communication;

social skills;

numeracy;

science and technology;

information technology;

creative development;

problem solving;

or whatever are the demands of the particular curriculum.

It will be seen that these are, as the name implies, just a bank of statements. The use of these in profiling is open to interpretation but, often, they are used as a checklist for teachers and individual students to check individual abilities.

Factor	Ref. No.	Core Competence Statement
Personal Development	01.1	Can identify own strengths and weaknesses.
	01.2	Can recognise opportunities to develop interests and abilities.
	01.3	Can make the most of opportunities to develop interests and abilities.
	01.4	Can show initiative in developing own interests and abilities.
Career Development	02.1	Can recognise the need for a personal career plan.
	02.2	Can identify factors influencing local job opportunities.
	02.3	Can make a realistic assessment of own career potential.
	02.4	Can produce a realistic career plan.

Figure 7.22   *Bank of Statements Related To Personal/Career Development*

Again, this system has its advantages and limitations:

Advantages:

Gives a clear picture of what is intended in the curriculum.

Gives an excellent basis for negotiation with students.

Validity is assisted with the pre-specification of the statements.

All students know what is required from the curriculum.

Can be used either formatively or summatively.

Contains a lot of information.

Limitations:

There are a lot of statements.

It can be difficult to keep track of all of the statements with what students do.

Students might not understand what is meant by the statements when tasks are negotiated.

Some form of overview sheet is needed for individual student records.

It is likely to be time consuming to assess.

Can be constraining as only the nominated objectives are likely to be reported.

There is no indication of need for open comments.

3.2.3   Free response profile

This type of profile is in the form of a booklet with headings under which both the teacher and the student make comments (see Figure 7.23). It can be completed at any time during the learning process and will form the basis of a summative report.

The *advantages* of this type of profile include:

The compilation can be specifically geared to the needs of the individual students and the activities that they have completed.

Having a space for student completion ensures their involvement in the process.

There are few restrictions for the teacher and the student.

Is used as a formative document but is a basis for a summative report.

On the other hand it also has *limitations*. These include:

The openness might lead to bland comments being made about individual students.

Validity might be low due to the open nature of the profile.

Can be time-consuming to complete.

Relies on the writing ability of the tutor and the student.

Reliability might be low.

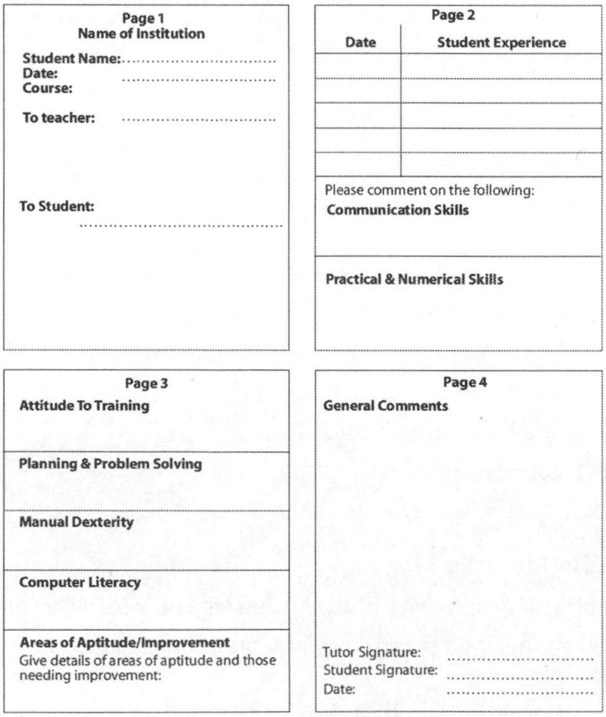

Figure 7.23   *Example of Free Response Profile*

3.2.4 Joint review profile

This profile is a formative document between the teacher and the student (see Figure 7.24) It reviews what a student has completed over a period of time (say over a month) and sets targets for the following period.

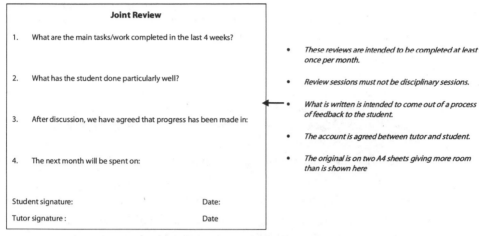

Figure 7.24 *Example Joint Review Profile*

The main difference between a joint review profile and the previous profiles is the emphasis on the consultation between the teacher and the student. The principle here is that, if students see the need for change, then they are more likely to accommodate that change. Also, it places the emphasis upon self-evaluation by the student. This is a skill that must be learned and the format can be a useful teaching tool for that purpose.

The joint review profile, then, has the following *advantages*:

> The completion can be specifically geared to the needs of individual students and to the activities that they have completed.
>
> The involvement of the students assists the self-evaluation process and is more likely to be meaningful to them.
>
> Setting targets can be useful for improvements.
>
> It is used as a formative document but also provides useful evidence for a summative report.

The format also has the following *limitations*:

> The openness might lead to bland comments being made about individual students.
>
> Validity might be low due to its open nature.
>
> Can be time consuming to complete, especially as it involves discussions with individual students.
>
> Discussions must take place in private; a quiet room must be provided for this to take place.
>
> Relies upon the writing ability of the tutor.
>
> May be used for disciplinary purposes.
>
> Can be difficult to get the involvement of the more recalcitrant students.

3.2.5 Profile reviews

We have already described profiling as a *process*; it takes place in a formative framework. In order for you to achieve this, the following principles should be followed:

(i)   Profiling requires one-to-one tutor-student reviews on a regular basis.

The joint review format suggests completion at least once a month. This is time consuming but, it is suggested, is well worth the time that is devoted to it. A further problem is that this tutorial time must be completed in private and the remainder of the class might be unsupervised at this time.

(ii)   Profiling involves negotiation with individual students.

The negotiation with individual students, no matter which of the formats is used, is to ensure that students are involved in the process; involved in their own assessments, involved in making judgments about themselves and involved in their own target setting.

(iii)   Profiling is a teaching strategy which allows student to:

Reflect on success and failure.

Take responsibility for their own learning and development.

When considered as a teaching strategy, profiling is looked at in a different light. You should not consider it as an assessment strategy and your students should not look at it as a session for discipline. It is an opportunity to discuss both strengths and weaknesses.

(iv)   Profiles should record positive statements of achievement with respect to:

Abilities or skills/competences demonstrated.

Personal qualities exhibited.

Tasks or activities experienced.

You should note that the intention of a profile is that it reports what students can do as opposed to what they cannot do. You can see that, in all of the examples, the statements are written positively. In addition it should report the abilities, competences, personal qualities, tasks and activities in which the student has been successful.

Four different formats of profile have been identified and the advantages and limitations of each have been stated. The main points relating to these are contrasted in Figure 7.25.

Profile Format	Characteristics	Advantages	Limitations
Grid-style Hierarchical Statements	Space for list of activities and nominated scale for indication of progress in abilities.	• Has tick box and statement information. • Progress can be easily shown.	• Might be restricting for some students. • No specific space for student comment.
Bank of Statements	List of objectives as basis of the curriculum.	• Clear basis for negotiation. • Valid and reliable.	• Lots of statements. • Can be confusing and limiting.
Free Response	A list of headings with spaces for mainly the tutor.	• Easy to link what student has achieved.	• Relies on the tutor's writing ability.
Joint Review	Similar to Free Response but more open in terms of headings.	• Easy to link to what the student has achieved. • Space for setting of targets.	• Is very open. • Might be hard to get the student involved.

Figure 7.25   *Contrasting Different Formats of Profile*

When you have designed your assessment it may be worthwhile using the following checklist (see Figure 7.26) based upon a CNAA/BTEC project report.

Is your assessment:

Reliable? *It is helpful to:*	Reliable assessment will produce the same score from different assessors. • *Agree about what is being assessed.* • *Agree standards.* • *Have evidence and verdict open to scrutiny.*
Valid? *It is helpful to:*	Does your assessment measure what it is supposed to measure, i.e. the stated learning outcomes? • *Match assessment to the standard/objectives/competences.* • *Have clear performance criteria.*
Credible? *It is helpful to:*	Assessment is likely to be seen as credible if the assessors agree that it is effective. • *Design simple methods of assessment as opposed to complex.* • *Use tried and tested methods of assessment.* • *Use a range of assessment instruments.*

Authoritative? *It is helpful to:*	If the assessors are experienced, knowledgeable, fair, and work to professional standards, then the assessment will be seen as authoritative. • *Maintain standards.* • *Have a sense of justice.*
Feasible? *It is helpful to:*	Assessment has to be manageable, i.e. it can only measure what it is cost effective to measure. Some skills and abilities are elusive and difficult to measure. • *Have outcomes which are realistic and measurable.* • *Have all resources available.*
Enabling? *It is helpful if:*	Assessment should influence and improve student performance. • *It encourages better practice.* • *It is motivating.* • *It encourages learning so that the student becomes competent.*
Transparent? *To encourage openness and agreement it is helpful to agree:*	Does everyone have a shared understanding? • *What is to be assessed.* • *When assessment is to take place.* • *What the consequences and outcomes will be.*

Figure 7.26 *Checklist for Assignment Assessment*

3.3   Assessing the minimum core and key skills

In the previous chapter (see section 4.3) we discussed Key Skills. The **minimum core** of these skills refers to a set of standards in literacy and numeracy that form an integral part of all teacher training programmes. This minimum core is included so that when you, as a teacher, have these skills you will be able to support your own students' development of them. The six Key Skills are:

> communication;
>
> information technology;
>
> application of number;
>
> working with others;
>
> improving own learning and performance; and
>
> problem solving.

Although the Key Skills Qualification is not as yet mandatory, many students will be following these courses as part of their studies.

3.3.1   Diagnostic assessment of key skills

Many students introduction to Key Skills is when they undertake a diagnostic test in literacy and numeracy, often within the first few days of their study. These diagnostic tests identify to what level the student is presently working. Students taking an Intermediate or GCSE programme will be expected to be working at level 2 NVQ standard or above, whilst those studying 'A' level or BTEC National will be expected to be working at level 3 standard. The intention of the diagnostic test is to identify students who are working below the prescribed level so that you can provide the necessary support for them. The tests are usually administered using ILT.

Examples of Diagnostic testing software including Diagnosys™ and Basic and Keyskill Builder (BSKB™). These individualise tests by generating random questions and can also increase or decrease the level of difficulty depending on the users response, quickly identifying the level at which the student is working. At the end of the test the student obtains a printout identifying their level of working and areas that need additional work. Such software frees the teacher from marking and allows them more time to work with the student on improving. An example of diagnostic testing can be seen at www.bbc.co.uk/keyskills/website.

3.3.2 Supporting the student in key skills

Some teachers do not think that it is their responsibility to teach literacy or numeracy or any of the other key skills. These teachers argue that they were appointed to teach their own subject and that there are specialist teachers in literacy and numeracy who are much better equipped to teach these key skills than they. However, it is generally accepted today that this is not true. We would argue that we are all responsible for teaching key skills and, indeed, these skills are much easier understood and learned by our students when they are learned within our own subject matter.

All teachers need to take on responsibility for both the teaching and the assessment of Key Skills. We have already identified in Chapter 4 the importance of using correct spelling when preparing handouts or when using the whiteboard and this is one way in which we support our students in this important area. However, you can also support your students by including the assessment of key skills in your student assignments.

Traditionally, ILT has been included as part of an assignment by requiring students to present their work through the use of a word processor or by asking them to word process their research. However, although this is useful in terms of the legibility of the work, it is really a bolt-on part of the work for the sake of coverage of the ILT key skill. Compare this to asking your students to post their research ideas to a 'closed-user Forum' rather than as a Word document. A user forum is an area on the web where people can exchanges ideas. A closed user forum is restricted to certain users set up by the teacher. The teacher may start such a forum by posting a number of key questions which the students respond to by using an email type response. Unlike email, all users can see and respond to the questions at the same time. Your students will still have researched the subject and made use of ILT to post their ideas but you can take this further. During the next lesson you can review, with individual students or with groups, the research that has been completed and recorded in the Forum.

To successfully implement and assess Key Skills they should be mapped across the unit and between units. In this way you can think of exciting ways to bring Key Skills into your subject. We use the word 'exciting' as the three Key Skill subjects of particularly numeracy and literacy, and perhaps information technology, often bring back bad memories from previous education for your students.

Numeracy can be daunting to many students. In fact it is often much easier in practice when it is in the context of the topic. For example, for hairdressing students, fractions, ratios and percentages can be introduced when looking at measurement of hair colouring. The importance of getting it right becomes critical when students mix hair dye in the ratio of 3:1. For Certificate of Education students, numeracy can be related to retention and achievement figures and their comparison to the appropriate bench marks.

Literacy can similarly be introduced by 'Using appropriate language for your audience'. For example, when designing a leaflet or worksheet for a client, both spelling and grammar should be checked by you and your students. Producing the document in Microsoft Word or Publisher will allow your students to try different styles, colours and formats of text all relating to the understanding of the leaflet by a specific audience. Getting your students to send the finished leaflet for comment can bring in additional skills such as using email and attaching documents.

Another example can be for students to create a new information technology suite and asking them to plan and cost a solution. Students can propose measurements for the unit and create scale models or computer-aided drafting layouts of their proposals. The students then present their chosen solution. This activity can incorporate all of the six Key Skill aspects and the interest of the students is maintained as it is a real-life scenario and there is no one right answer.

Here the Key Skills had been thought through and integrated across a number of units rather than simply being 'bolted on'. The idea can be adapted to hairdressers, tour operators, and so on.

4.   Assessment in Lessons

4 .1   Assessing individual needs

The identification of training needs is an interesting concept and one which only relatively recently has attracted the importance that it deserves. Traditionally, in post-16 education and training, students have 'signed-on' for a programme of study so long as they had the necessary entry requirements. There was little attention paid to the requirements of the individual, to the appropriateness of the programme or to making any changes to the programme to meet individual requirements. However, greater attention is now being paid to retention rates, Ecclestone (1996) identifies the different times when identification of needs can take place. These are:

> **Initial diagnostic assessment** which includes pre-course screening and diagnostic assessment to help students onto the correct programme and to accredit their prior learning.

> **Pre-programme guidance** to gain information about an individual's aims and to identify help that might be required, including an action plan.

> **In programme assessment** and guidance to ensure an individual's aims are being met and if any further assistance is required.

Additionally, there is a fourth which can be identified as:

> **End of programme guidance** to identify the next stage in the student's learning programme.

These have been shown diagrammatically in Figure 7.27 with each of the four stages in the learning programme identified together with some of the mechanisms that could be used.

For 16-year old students the **first** important stage (Initial diagnostic assessment) is often completed by careers guidance personnel in school. Most pupils are involved in 'work experience' activities and interviews with careers guidance staff to identify their interests and aptitudes together with their aspirations. Additionally, when 16-year olds are interviewed for a job, they may be required to complete standardised diagnostic aptitude and skill tests. The information gained from these activities can help individuals choose which programme or qualification will be of benefit to them.

The **second** stage (Pre-programme Guidance) aims to find what help and support is needed by individuals who are enrolled onto a programme. There are two main types of test that can be used to gather data for this stage: (i) induction and diagnostic tests to find what type of help and support (if any) are needed (for instance APU literacy and numeracy tests); and (ii) questionnaires to find out an individuals aspirations and expectations of the programme. An example is shown in Figure 7.28 which is given to students during their induction and can form the basis for the first tutorial. This first tutorial can be used for initial action planning processes. One of the advantages of this type of questionnaire is that it requires students to be self-evaluative. This can lead to other assessments where students can assess both themselves and each other.

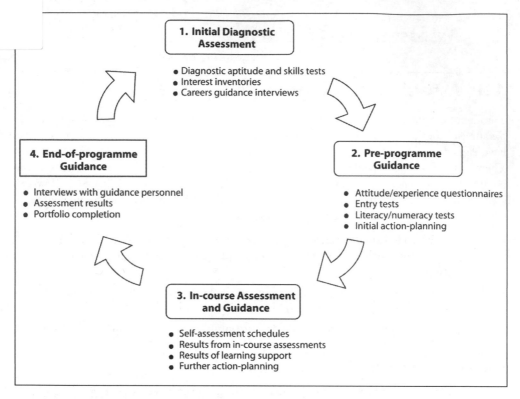

Figure 7.27 *Needs Assessment Opportunities and Mechanisms*

The self-evaluation element of needs assessment can become an accepted practice on the programme. One way of achieving this is to ask students to complete a Development Journal or Profile (or Practice Portfolio). This is a profile in which records can be kept of (i) initial and subsequent tutorials with their action plans, (ii) topic planning and reflections, and (iii) critical incident records. This Journal (see Figure 7.29 for the typical contents) has the benefit of informing the students about the programme and assisting them in becoming self-evaluative: it gets students thinking about, and planning for, the work that they are to complete. It helps to identify strengths and areas for development. The contents of the Journal is shown in Figure 7.29, with separate sections for:

(i) Programme details – where the aims, learning outcomes and assessment criteria can be recorded.

(ii) Self-analysis – for initial, interim and final stages.

(iii) Topic planning and reflection – where a student can make plans for learning on a unit-by-unit basis and then reflect upon their learning.

(iv) Critical incident recording – perhaps three or four incidents are recorded.

Programme Title	
Name:	Place of Employment:
Qualifications:	
Role and Tasks carried out at work:	
What are your main strengths?	What are your main weaknesses?
What do you expect to gain from the programme?	
What work do you expect to have to do on the programme?	
What do you expect of your tutors?	
What informal learning opportunities exist at work?	
Any other comments?	

Figure 7.28 *Example Student Questionnaire to Gather Data about Expectations*

Contents

Personal Details

Unit Details

Self Analysis:

      - Initial analysis

      - Interim analysis

      - Final analysis

Topic/Unit Planning and Reflection

      - Unit 1 Title

      - Unit 2 Title

      - Unit 3 Title

      - Etc.

Critical Incident – Description and Reflection

      - Incident 1

      - Incident 2

      - Incident 3

      - Etc

Figure 7.29   *Typical Contents of a Development Profile*

Initial Analysis		
What is your experience of the topics to be covered during the session?		
A Good Deal of Experience	Some Experience	No Experience
	Strengths:	Areas for development:
Action Plan for session:		
Key Skills to be developed:		

Figure 7.30   *Typical Contents of an Analysis Page of a Development Journal*

Planning for Unit 'X'	Reflection On Unit 'X'
1. Plan how you will meet the learning (outcomes) for the unit.	This page is for you to reflect on Unit 'X', you could include: (a) the main points of the unit; (b) how this relates to what you do at work;
2. Comments (to be completed during tutorial) Student / Tutor	(c) what you might do in the future.
3. Notes on the type of evidence to be provided (work to be produced).	
4. Key Skills to be used during the Unit.	

Figure 7.31   *Typical Contents of a Planning and Reflection Pages of a Development Journal*

The typical Initial Analysis format shown in Figure 7.30. It is intended for students to analyse their strengths and areas for development in relationship to the aims and objectives, they can then design an initial action plan. Students do not find this easy and tutor assistance may be required. The inclusion of 'topics to be covered' tries to ensure that students think about the content of their programme from the start. It can be seen that Key Skill development has been included. Subsequent analysis (e.g. interim and final) can follow-up the points that have been made in this initial analysis.

The initial analysis is quite general. Asking students to plan for a unit (or topic) can be made much more specific to the content. Figure 7.31 indicates a typical format for the planning and the reflection. That the completion of both of these pages has implications for tutorial supervision. The planning page has a space for both student and tutor comment which can be completed at the start of the unit. The reflection is completed at the end of the unit and should be reviewed by the tutor.

A further possible inclusion in a Development Journal is a description and reflection of 'critical incidents'. Critical incidents are described in Chapter 8 where we discuss your own professional journal (see section 4.1 page 422).

Examples of critical incidents could include:

> Understanding a difficult concept or procedure.
> Receiving a particularly good mark or a particularly poor mark.
> Working with a set of guidelines with less tutor direction than normal.
> Using different tools/techniques/methods.
> Simulation of a typical work situation.
> An incident when you felt 'under pressure'.

Figure 7.32 shows a typical format which may be used in a Development Journal to record critical incidents.

Critical Incident 1	
1. Description of the incident	4. How did you overcome concerns?
2. What were the important aspects?	5. What have you learned?
3. What are your concerns?	6. What will you do next?

Figure 7.32   *Typical content of the Critical Incident pages of a Professional Development Journal*

Although the suggestions for the pre-programme guidance include aspects of the Professional Development Journal, some of these (like unit planning and reflection and critical incidents) cross over into in-course assessment and guidance, the **third** stage (in-programme assessment) which was identified in Figure 7.27. Additionally for this stage of needs assessment, it might have been that the diagnostic phase identified the need for learning support. Educational organisations for post-16 education and training are increasingly being funded for good retention and achievement figures. It is, then, important that once enrolled on a course, students stay and complete the programme and are successful at the end of it. To this end much more interest is shown in 'student support' procedures with committed staff employed specifically for the purpose. After initial screening (possibly using ALBSU tests), support is provided to assist students on an individual basis with any shortfalls in literacy, numeracy, problem solving, and so on. The results from such learning support can form part of the in-course assessment and guidance.

The **fourth** and final phase of needs assessment lies with the end of programme guidance. This might consist of an interview with guidance personnel in order to provide information on the possible sources for further professional programmes and qualifications. Also, it might review the completion of a portfolio as evidence of the work to show either a prospective employer or to an admissions tutor of a College or University.

4.2   Motivating students through feedback

The quality and type of feedback given to students is crucial if it is going to lead to improvement. Feedback can be given as a mark or grade, or comments, or a mixture of the two. You will also know that if a mark is given then this is perhaps the first, and only thing, that is looked at. Comments take time to write, but should benefit the student in terms of future improvements. Immediate feedback is beneficial as the work is still fresh in the mind of the student.

There are many ways of attempting to ensure that students use your feedback. The main way is to relate your comments to the assessment criteria. Alternatively you can ask students themselves what kind of feedback they want.

The following (adapted from Gibbs, *et al.*, 1986) is a checklist for giving feedback to students:

1. Keep the time short between submission and feedback. Where possible make feedback instantaneous.
2. Substantiate a grade/mark with comments both in the text for specific aspects and with a summary at the end.
3. Balance negative comments with positive ones and ensure that negative ones are constructive.
4. Follow-up written comments with oral feedback and aim for a dialogue.
5. Make the criteria clear to students when setting the work, preferably in writing.
6. Make further suggestions (e.g. for further reading or for further developing ideas).
7. Give periodic oral feedback on rough drafts.

4.3   Assessment at the design stage

Assessment should be an on-going activity throughout both the lessons and the course. You can assess through written work and through question and answer. Different types of cognitive lessons are shown in Figure. 7.33 with different types of assessment taking place during the lesson. The important thing is that assessment is an integral part of each lesson, the course and of the learning.

	Introduction		**Development**				**Conclusion**	
A	State lesson aim	Entry level test	Concept No 1	Concept No 2	Review of Concepts	Test	Homework & next lesson topic	
B	Review test last lesson	State lesson aim	Introduce concepts by Q & A		Concepts 1 and 2	Application of concepts through Q and A	Test of concepts and next lesson topic	
C	Q & A last lesson	State lesson aim	Entry level test	Concepts 1 and 2	Review of concepts through Q and A		Test	Next lesson topic

Figure 7.33   *Assessment in a Cognitive Lesson*

4.4   Revising assessment procedures

Earlier in this chapter we discussed methods of increasing validity and reliability.

It is suggested that you periodically evaluate all aspects of your assessment. An evaluation might consider the following points which have been adapted from Ward, C. (1980):

1. Does the assessment appear to be valid? Is it assessing all of the required topics and abilities in the right proportions?
2. Does it appear to be meeting the needs of employers or prospective employers?

3. Do the students see the assessment as valid and reliable? If not, why not?

4. Is the standard of assessment appropriate to the aims of the course? i.e. does the table of specification relate to the course aims?

5. Are most of the students succeeding in the assessment? If not does the fault lie in the selection of the students, in the teaching, in the students' motivation, or in some other factor?

6. Are the results of most of the students consistent with your expectations? If not, why not?

7. Were most students able to complete the work in the time available?

8. Was the assessment of appropriate difficulty judged by the average mark obtained?

9. Does the assessment differentiate between students of different levels of ability? This may be indicated by the numbers of students with high, low and middle range marks.

10. Are all of the questions in the assessment appropriate, clear and technically correct?

The answers to all, or some, of these points can assist in giving you an overall view of how your assessment is working. The main point, however, is that you should periodically try to identify any problems that might occur in your assessment procedures.

5.   The Role of ILT in Assessment

5.1   Why use ILT in assessment?

We explored in Chapter 4, section 4, how ILT is transforming the way in which students learn. It is also transforming the assessment processes. No longer is assessment confined to the classroom: it can take place wherever students can access the web. We now need to consider the role of ILT in the assessment process in terms of:

> **how** it can be used;
>
> **where**; and
>
> **when** to use it.

Consider the following two scenarios:

Classroom 1

It is the end of a two hour, teacher-centred Food Hygiene lesson to a group of Catering National Diploma students. The students are getting tired but the teacher attempts to recap the main points of storage conditions for raw meats and asks the students to provide examples from their own experiences. The response from the students is slow with none of them really wanting to provide any answers. It is hard work.

Classroom 2

A similar group of National Diploma Catering students are coming to the end of their session. However, the session has been student-centred where they have decided, from their own experiences both in College and in the local shops, what storage conditions have been used for raw meats. The students have used the interactive whiteboard to record their findings. The conclusion to the session requires the students to give a PowerPoint presentation of the main points learned about raw meat storage and to give four different examples. Most of the students are joining in and the lesson seems to have been fun.

Has assessment been used in both of the classrooms? The answer is yes – in the first classroom the formal question and answer is slow with students not showing much interest. Compare this to the second classroom in which the whole group is presenting the information with ILT providing the means of presenting that information. In both situations the teacher is getting individual and group feedback about what has been learned in the lesson. The assessment of the students of the second session the assessment was part of the learning process. The use of ILT in the second classroom has added to the student-involvement and made it enjoyable for both the students and the teacher.

Using ILT in assessment can enhance:

> motivation;
>
> diagnostic testing;
>
> tracking of students;
>
> portfolio building;
>
> discussion;
>
> differentiation; and
>
> summative assessment.

Each of these is considered in turn below:

5.1.1 Motivation

ILT assessment can increase student's motivation by bringing a 'fun-element' into the session. You can assess individual students or groups as described in 5.1 above. However, like all teaching and learning methods, the use of ILT can be 'overdone'. Using nothing else but electronic quizzes, PowerPoint or Word will soon have a demotivating effect for students but when used to provide variety, can be effective.

5.1.2 Diagnostic testing

Diagnostic testing is often used to identify students' entry behaviour i.e. the level of their existing knowledge and skills. When using ILT it can provide immediate feedback to both the students and the teacher about the student's current learning. Again, assessing students using an electronic diagnostic assessment tool can be motivating in what might be a boring and repetitive task. From the teacher's point of view, it saves repetition in marking as well as providing a summary of areas of concern which need strengthening for both individual and groups of students. For students who miss the original test-time, ILT provides a convenient way to 'catch-up'.

Mature students are often reluctant to take such tests often wanting to hide their problems especially in numeracy and literacy, but also feeling threatened by the technology. In instances like this, much reassurance is needed to help the student to overcome their fears.

5.1.3 Tracking of students

When assessing students using a Virtual Learning Environment (VLE), or through an electronic portfolio, it makes it possible and easy to track students. Examples of VLEs could include:

> electronic photographs;
>
> use of intranet for assessment or portfolio documents; and
>
> video demonstration of a working practice.

Teachers using VLE can easily identify what each individual student has achieved and, perhaps more importantly, what they have yet to achieve. In this case early warning to the teacher and feedback to the student can quickly get them back on track or identify learning problems. Where students are involved in distance or on-line learning, the tracking can be audited by both internal and external verifiers. It is then possible for example, to record and hence track;

> time and date of teacher/student discussion;
>
> agreed action;
>
> competences achieved; and
>
> feedback provided.

5.1.4 Portfolio building

Portfolio building is an essential part of many programmes, including NVQs. ILT provides an effective way of gathering and sharing information between student, teacher and assessors in one central location. Portfolio building documents have been discussed in Chapter 5 (see page 237-241) and in Chapter 8 (see pages 394-396) and these documents can usefully be designed and placed on the college intranet or VLE using either a CD or the intranet. If the information is available via the web it means that it is available anywhere, at any time, and hence reduces the number of visits the assessors and verifiers need to make.

A major advantage of this system is that the quality of feedback often improves. It is available more quickly and, because the students are tracked more readily, it becomes easy for the students and teacher to identify what has, or needs to be, achieved. Many teachers have also identified that their students are more likely to stay on the course so reducing high drop-out rates which are often the norm on distance learning or NVQ programmes.

With regard to practical work (such as hairdressing or bricklaying), using electronic photographs of a finished artefact, video demonstrating of a working practice or voice recording of student's comments are much more motivational and convenient to the student, teacher and manager than the written word.

5.1.5 Discussion

Discussion plays an important role in both learning and assessment. Electronic discussion through the use of:

> email;
>
> chat lines; and
>
> forums

can be made available to students. The advantage of electronic discussion is that it allows students to discuss, with their own peer group, problems on homework or assignments in or outside the classroom and it avoids the problem of the teacher only being available during the session. Similarly, it allows the teacher to keep in contact with the students: especially important in these days of good retention and achievement. Additionally, if a student is away due to illness or is posted to another part of the country/overseas, or is part of a distance learning group, electronic discussion allows them to feel part of the group.

5.1.6 Differentiation

Students are individuals, having different experiences and different requirements for their learning. Yet an entire class of students are required to reach a minimum essential level to achieve a pass grade for the programme which they are studying. In order to achieve this minimum standard, the teacher needs to provide learning activities and assessment tasks which allow for differentiation between the students. The quicker and more able students probably need different perhaps, additional learning experiences so that they are constantly engaged in learning. Differentiation is an important teaching and assessment element which enhances the teachers opportunity to treat students as individuals. In terms of assessment, by putting together a series of different assessment tasks (e.g. multiple-choice questions, short answer questions and long answer questions) it not only maintains the interest of the students but allows students to work at their own pace and, consequently, differentiates between the different level of student. Alternatively, by making the questions progressively harder, allows differentiation between the individual students.

So, we can see the use of ILT greatly enhances the ability of teachers to provide tasks and activities which allow for differentiation between students. For example:

Making use of a computer's ability to create tests and tasks with different levels of ability for different students. For example a computer can choose a number of questions from a bank of questions to give individual students a different set of questions at different levels. The overall level of the test can be designed to be more challenging for the faster students.

5.1.7   Summative assessment

Summative, or end of programme, assessment is often carried out by examination boards such as EdExcel and OCR. These examination boards are beginning to evaluate ways of transforming traditional assessment methods into electronic formats. The Health and Safety Executive published a research report in 2004 (HSE, 2004) of a summative assessment supported by the Internet for a Professional Diver Competency Theory Assessment System (DCTAS). DCTAS is a computer software system used to generate paper-based examinations using 5-option multiple-choice, short-answer or mixed format questions depending upon the subject being assessed. The report concluded that, while the online database continues to evolve, the online format appears to have been successful and assessment organisations are supporting the continued development.

Additionally, much research work (e.g. Cooper and Love, 2001; Barrett, 2000) is being carried-out in the development of electronic portfolios for summative assessment purposes and the automated marking of them. Cooper and Love conclude that online portfolios are useful as assessment tools and offer benefits in the 'process of student assessment' and the 'management of the process of student assessment'. Used in conjunction with appropriate software solutions, online portfolio-based assessment may relieve teachers of some of the more tedious aspects of assessment and allow some of the aspects to be automated. There still, however, remains a problem with the assessment of the more subjective elements of the portfolio that need the judgement of an examiner.

5.2   Using ILT in assessment

We all use assessment in our lessons. This assessment could be in the form of verbal question and answer, a test, an exercise (either theoretical or practical and either individual or group), or a discussion. Each of these types of assessment can be adapted to use ILT. ILT, when used sparingly and creatively, can enhance learning and motivate your students. On the other hand, as with any teaching approach, 'overkill' – we have all heard of 'Death by PowerPoint', where every lesson starts and ends with PowerPoint slides – is a sure way to bore students.

This section gives you some ideas of the potential of ILT in assessment. The references identified will help you to embed ILT into your existing assessment.

5.2.1   'Off the shelf' software

There is an increasing number of specific software packages that will help you to design multiple-choice, crossword, quiz and 'hangman' types of assessment. Two of these are 'Hot Potatoes' (http://hotpot.uvic.ca) and 'Quia' (http://www.quia.com).

The **Hot Potatoes** site enables you to create:

    (i)   interactive multiple-choice questions;

    (ii)   short-answer questions;

    (iii) jumbled-sentence questions;

    (iv)   crossword assessment;

    (v)   matching/ordering questions; and

    (vi)   fill-in-the-gap exercises.

Each type provides you with a framework into which you can place your own questions and activities. The site is freely available so long as it is used for educational and non-profit making activities.

The **Quia** site is more comprehensive than Hot Potatoes in that it allows the creation of 16 types of games and learning activity including quizzes with eight types of question being included. It also has a built-in management tool which allows you to create and track your own students. There is a 30-day trial offer before you have to purchase the package. However, it is affordable and offers discounts depending upon the number of users.

Both **Hot Potatoes** and **Quia** work in a similar way in that you decide upon the type of assessment and the number of questions that you want to ask. You then use given frameworks to type in the questions, followed by any clues that you want to provide. The software then creates the format of the assessment and publishes it to your chosen website. The package allows you to test and change the questions quite easily. Students access the assessment via the website that you have nominated. At the end of the assessment the students are informed of their score, and also those answers which have been correctly and incorrectly answered. Both of the packages allow you to input images as well as text.

An advance on these two packages is an interactive voting system (Active Studio) from **Promethan** (http://www.promethan.co.uk). It is a version of the television game-show that asks you to vote on a subject. Using this software and an interactive whiteboard you can create a bank of questions. The students are then given a hand-held voting device which allows them to choose and vote on a particular answer. Using the quiz, the students see the question on the whiteboard, they then vote from a choice of answers and then have the option of either continuing to the next questions or looking at the scoring and voting pattern for that question. Immediate feedback and analysis coupled with anonymity of the answers lead to accurate and interesting feedback.

Where and when to use

These assessment methods coupled, with an interactive whiteboard, help you to control assessment anytime during a session: at the start of a session to identify entry behaviour or to recap and assess the current topic at the end of the session for feedback and evaluation. It can also be placed on a shared area of the network or VLE with students working either individually or in groups, during or after the session, at college or at home.

As we have stated previously in this chapter, by careful creation of the questions and, paying particular attention to the choice of the optional answers, bespoke software can be used effectively at all levels within the cognitive domain. Combined with a discussion after the event, they can be used effectively to challenge and progress to the higher levels within the cognitive domain (i.e. higher than application)

5.2.2 Commercial (general purpose) software

Every teacher and student has access to Microsoft's range of software including Word, PowerPoint, Excel, and to a lesser extent an Access database. This range has been used for a long time to create traditional assignments which allow students to incorporate clipart, photos, sound and video. In this way an assignment is enhanced by making the tasks more interesting than traditional pen and paper.

However, we could be missing a lot of the features that these packages have to offer! Word, for instance, has features to create an input form, cut and paste, drag and drop, along with review features that allow hiding and revealing comments. PowerPoint allows you to create multiple-choice questions incorporating music and images. This enables you to animate so that you can, for instance, demonstrate particular mathematical principles. You can also create links to pages, other software and to the web.

The creation of a photo portfolio can easily be achieved by both teachers and students. All of these can be used in the creation of assignments.

Where and when to use

As with the previous section, this software can be used as an aid to the design of assessments at any time on an individual or group basis. Creating assessment methods that make use of the more sophisticated aspects of the packages bring in an element of problem solving and can be used on an individual or group basis.

As you may have realised you need to good knowledge of the packages to create the desired effects which have been described and you may need to be able to programme the software. However, in some situations, you may have knowledgeable and skilled technicians in your organisation to help you. A simple search of the web under 'Quizzes in PowerPoint' may be enough to find a readymade quiz or simulation.

5.2.3 e-Communication

It might be argued that email, chat forums and mobile phones have little place in assessment strategies. Email has for some time been the vehicle for students getting in touch with their teacher or for sending an electronic copy of an assignment. On the other hand, 'Chat Lines' and 'Forum' have, in many cases, suffered a 'bad press'. However, most VLEs have both Chat and Forum facilities on a 'closed-basis' (i.e. this can be constrained so that access is only between teacher and students or between students within the specific class). This software can be fascinating and addictive by (particularly adolescent) students and it offers a vehicle to engage them in learning.

Most methods of e-communication can be used within assessment, including the archiving of chat rooms, forums, blogs etc. to illustrate communication, discussion and debating skills. Mobile phones also fall into this category and how many times do we see students glued to their phones, texting their friends. We can make use of this technology in assessment in a number of ways; students can take photographs, voice recordings and in some cases videos which can be sent via SMS and MMS through mobile technology into school or college or vice versa, from college to student

When and where to use

Using VLEs or e-portfolio allows us to keep in touch with our students. These discussion tools can become essential when sending and receiving assignments. In the case of widening participation it becomes available to all students no matter where they live or where they attend our classes. The growth of the personal PC and broadband has enhanced access to all.

A major problem of assessment using group work, lies in the identification of who takes responsibility for the overall decisions and who undertakes which task and sub-task. Setting up students with email allows them to record minutes of meetings, emailing each other with specific tasks, ideas and so on. As well as the email facility, students can keep a diary as a method of recording tasks and who does what. Using these facilities allows the teacher to keep track of progress, and milestone schedules and deadlines effectively.

Posing a question in class often results in a silence. Pose a question on a 'chat line' or 'forum', and it is a different story. Here all students can dip in and sample what has been said or voice their own opinion without fear of embarrassment or constraint. Posing a controversial question as the starting point for a 'forum' allows the students the chance of reply and the facility to voice their own opinions at any time. It also provides evidence and can easily be followed up next lesson as the basis for further discussion.

Mobile phone and text messaging allows you to keep in contact with your students at all times. At its simplest, it is a way of checking why a student was absent from class, or to remind them of next week's test. A list of email addresses and mobile phone numbers at the start of the session allows you to quickly get in touch with your students. However, there is nothing to stop you asking for comments, posing a question, even getting students to assess the standard of a lesson using the mobile phone or text message. Text messaging students is effective as it gets directly to them quickly and allows them to reply in a medium with which they are comfortable.

5.2.4 Virtual Learning and e-portfolio

We have discussed in sections 5.1.3 and 5.1.4 the role of the VLE in assessment. A further development alongside the VLE is in the e-Portfolio.

An e-Portfolio is defined as (see www.FuturEd.com) 'an electronic portfolio of acquired learning, knowledge, skills and abilities acquired through formal, accidental and incidental learning. Placing the portfolio on the web allows for the exchange of information easily and quickly as well as adding and editing the documents.

It takes the personal 'record of achievement to new levels by putting together not only a comprehensive record of education, employment, volunteer work, life experiences, skills and recognition, but rather as a artist presents a portfolio of their work, so allows for the input of essays, images, video clips and sound to provide a more in depth and fuller picture. The portfolio is stored 'securely online and allows easy access. It is suggested that this could be a way of students keeping a record of the accomplishments through school and then into work. An example is (see http://channelcontent.dal.ca/portfolio/over_01.html), which gives a wider picture of the e-Portfolio.

A more specific development of the e-Portfolio is in the work based programme of NVQs where students traditionally gather evidence of competences achieved by putting together a portfolio of evidence. The need to cross reference the evidence makes a paper based system time consuming leading to high drop out rates and low motivation on both the student, who has to present the information and the teacher who has to mark it. The role of the e-Portfolio is to take out the drudgery of portfolio building process and allow the students to present their evidence in a simple manner. Once assessed by the teacher, it becomes relatively easy to cross reference the work to the competences achieved.

Figure 7.34 shows how a VLE can be used to record the progress made by a student. The figure identifies the units studied on the left and the progress made on the right hand side of the document.

Name			Available Until	Progress
Higher Education at			Description	21%
	HE Courses			21%
		HNC Business		100%
		HNC/D BIT		21%
		HNC in Hospitality		0%
	HE Study Skills			11%
	Frequently Asked Questions			100%
	Open Day Event			0%
	Aim Higher Video			0%
	Graduation Photographs			0%

Figure 7.34 *Example VLE Showing the Student's Progress*

Figure 7.35 shows the teachers view of the students progress in much more detail. Frequent observation of the progress warns the teacher of possible problems which can, by the use of email, be quickly checked out with the student.

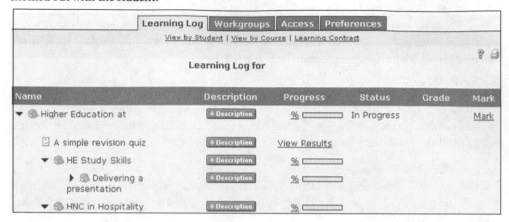

Figure 7.35   *Teacher's View of the Students Progress*

More powerful and purpose built e-Portfolio software maps out the competences required. As this is web-based the student can send, from home or work, the evidence that they are using to support this competence. The evidence need not be written but could be voice, image and video format (electronic format). So for example a hairdresser demonstrating a cutting style may produce a short video clip. This becomes incorporated in to their personal e-Portfolio as evidence. The teacher can then check their portfolio, again at anytime and from any web accessed computer, and can agree the work submitted and sign off the competence or disagree and request additional work to be submitted electronically. Once agreed the competences are electronically ticked off and the evidence becomes cross referenced to it.

As all of this is achieved electronically, it is up to date and can be inspected by the student, teacher, internal and external verifier at any time.

The advantages are:

> Information is transferred electronically and therefore quickly.
>
> It prompts a faster response by teacher and student.
>
> Use of email to advise, chase up, give instructions reduces time.
>
> Easier to map and cross reference.
>
> Provides an audit trail for administration and finance purposes.
>
> Monitoring of adherence is vastly enhanced.
>
> Promotes equality by allowing the most appropriate evidence to be submitted.

Software manufacturers have commented (See Inspection comments from ALI inspectors http://swwetn.virtualcollege.ac.uk/DYSG_conference_html/Speaker_Details/Other/ENVQ.htm) that the initial and running costs are recouped by a higher rate of retention and achievement (increase of 60% has been noted) and reduction in administration costs.

When and where to use

There are various ways to assess and record a student's learning, e.g. test results, performance appraisal at work, personal diaries. The e-portfolio is a new form of recording learning, and can make portfolio assessment more effective and efficient.

Any electronic resource can be used for an e-portfolio. The student can select evidence from word-processed documents and also make use of images, sound clips and video. This evidence becomes a very powerful medium as evidence from the workplace can be videoed and placed in the portfolio.

FutureEd (op cit) research has demonstrated that the e-portfolio is closely linked with:

> human resources development as the means of identifying and managing what a person knows and can do;
>
> lifelong learning as the method of tracking and recognising on-going learning;
>
> prior learning assessment;
>
> education and training at all levels as a teaching tool (reflection as a basis for learning) and as an alternative form of learning assessment.

This shows that the e-portfolio can be used effectively for a wide variety of purposes and a wide variety of study. Additionally, it can be used at various times throughout the operation of a programme from entry to final assessment.

5.2.5 Administration

We have concentrated on using electronic assessment from the students' point of view. As a teacher, having assessed the students, you will need to provide feedback to the students and record the results.

You will also need to identify and assess the students' views of the programme on which they have been through. The Learning Skills Council (LSC) randomly targets students undertaking college courses to establish their views. ILT can be used to gather this data for evaluation. For example, an electronic questionnaire asking for views about courses can be analysed easily. Feedback about a lesson can be quickly obtained using an interactive voting system and be filed and used as part of a course review.

Setting up an electronic spreadsheet containing student marks and placing it on a shared area of a network allows colleagues to view its content. As a vehicle for internal verification, it provides accurate information very quickly.

5.3 Concerns in using ILT in assessment

It would be unfair to only discuss the advantages of the use of ILT in assessment without mentioning some of the disadvantages. A number of concerns are explored below:

> Unable to access ILT in the classroom.
>
> Time involved in creating assessment resources.
>
> Tests basic knowledge only.
>
> Student tracking.
>
> Cheating and plagiarism.

5.3.1 Unable to access ILT in the classroom

It might be argued that if the computer or projector is not available in the classroom then there is no point in creating e-assessment methods. However, most new educational establishments are now equipped with most forms of ILT such as interactive whiteboards or portable projectors. Even if this is not the case, you could consider placing your assessment onto a Virtual Learning Environment (VLE). If you put a test on the web or use mobile phones to assess the learning you can overcome the problem of lack of equipment in the classroom.

Even when ILT is available, it is sometimes argued that computers are prone to failure at the crucial time. However, a similar argument existed for using the overhead projector in that the bulb would fail at the crucial moment. A wise teacher ensures that a spare bulb is available. The difficulties arising from the use of ILT go far beyond the carrying of a spare bulb. Failure of the computer, bulb, fuse, the network going down, the software not being on the computer, and no sound available, are all likely problems. In these cases, you should have a back-up procedure. Sometimes it is simply testing the equipment before the event to ensure that it works. For other aspects like power failure you will need to have a back-up plan in place. For example the electronic crossword reverts to the paper-based resource once again.

5.3.2   Time involved in creating assessment resources

It takes time to create ILT assessment resources. However, once created they can be used again or quickly changed or adapted for different learners. Much of the software used for creating quizzes, multiple-choice questions, or crosswords, is very easy to use and, once the questions and answers are thought through, they are often much easier to make than the traditional handout version.

However, creating video, animation, cartoon or even games in PowerPoint can be very time consuming and often you need to have expert knowledge of the packages or programming language to create to a high standard. But you have the Web and a simple search of the Web for an interactive quiz in PowerPoint can often bring you the results that you require and you may simply have to drag and drop your questions and answers onto the given template.

5.3.3   Tests basic knowledge only

A major criticism voiced with using ILT is that it only tests the students' most basic knowledge and, indeed, this can be said of using multiple-choice questions, crosswords, and so on. However, as with all areas of assessment, well planned multiple-choice questions can be set to assess the high levels of analysis, synthesis and evaluation by choosing answers carefully and using subtle wording so that students have to think very carefully before answering. This, coupled with a strict time element ensures you have a very powerful method of assessment.

5.3.4   Student tracking

A really valuable aspect of VLE is that it can track students progress and achievement. However, the problem is that a programme often only comments that '50% of the Unit has been completed'. This is easy to overcome depending upon how the software was created. More advanced software brings in frequent testing so that the student reads part of the unit and then completes an assessment before going further. LearnDirect uses this method making student tracking more accurate and informative.

VLEs by default monitor student hits and can be used to identify who has accessed materials, chat rooms, forums and resources etc. Other features of VLEs track downloads and uploads of assignments, marks and grades awarded. Tests held within a VLE also hold student marks and dates of assessments individually in by groups/classes etc.

5.3.5   Cheating and plagiarism

By far the major criticism of using ILT is cheating and plagiarism. Since the creation of 'Copy' and 'Paste' it has been possible to copy text from one source and paste it into your own word-processed document. With the advent of the web, some users are keen to publish their own assignment answers as a resource. There are websites which contain essays that cover a whole course. So, what was once a simple copy and paste of key paragraphs, has become the complete copying of documents, in some cases without making any changes and in the hope that teachers will not be aware of the blatant plagiarism involved.

Advice on plagiarism can be found at the national Plagiarism Advisory Service (PAS), which is based at Northumbria University. The service offers advice and guidance on all aspects of plagiarism prevention and detection. The service also provides advice for students on how to avoid unintentionally plagiarising or colluding with other students, on referencing and citation practices as well as providing information on legal issues relating to plagiarism. All of the Plagiarism Advisory Service information is freely available on the website, and can be provided in other formats if required.

Some limited Plagiarisms services are free but most do have a subscription fee attached. All of them require registration. Advice can be found at: JISC Plagiarism Advisory Service at: http://www.jiscpas.ac.uk/

Another website (www.flinders.edu.au/aims/staff/references.html1) suggests the clues to plagiarism which include:

> URLs left at the top of students' pages;
>
> strange changes of font and layout;
>
> American spelling either throughout a document or in scattered sections;
>
> lack of citations or quotations in a long piece of prose;
>
> unusual or highly specific professional jargon in a student starting out in the discipline;
>
> introductions and conclusions written in grammatically incorrect English and not addressing the body of the paper that is written in flawless, complex English;
>
> bibliographies that only cite material not available locally;
>
> bibliographies that do not reflect the content of the coursework;
>
> mixed bibliographies where two or more citation systems are used;
>
> bibliographic references from 1996 and before (for example) in a paper on a topical issue;
>
> essay being off topic; many of this type have oddly placed 'on-topic' paragraphs that the student inserts themselves to bring it more in line with the required subject;
>
> essay is much better than previous writing samples (from the same student) clear presence of unacknowledged material from other sources .

Apart from using sophisticated software to validate student's work or by using the clues suggested above, you could also:

> get to know your students well, building-up a picture of their words, writing and styles;
>
> ask a student to explain the key points of their work;
>
> look for words and phrases you know the students would not say or write;
>
> look for choice of assessment method other than the essay.

5.4   ILT assessment resources

The following websites (current at time of going to print) support the discussion topics raised in section 5.2: Using ILT in assessment.

Quality Improvement Agency, Excellence Gateway: http://excellence.qia.org.uk

The online service for post-16 learning and skills providers and the new home for Learning and Skills Web and Excalibur. Here you will find examples of good practice, self-improvement, suppliers of improvement services plus materials to support teaching and learning. It has a simple search facility, typing in 'hot potatoes' or 'Quia' will give you information on how to download the software, give real examples of its use and even licensing information.

The BBC: http://bbc.co.uk

The BBC website has a wide range of resources and assessment materials which can be found at http://www.bbc.co.uk/schools.

They support key skills numeracy and communications, as well as information technology at http://www.bbc.co.uk/keyskills/.

Hot Potatoes: http://hotpot.uvic.ca

The Hot Potatoes suite includes six applications which enable you to create interactive multiple-choice, short-answer, jumbled-sentence, crossword, matching/ordering and gap-fill exercises for the World Wide Web.

Quia: http://www.quia.com

The Quia software allows you to create a wide range of games and learning activities including: quizzes, multiple-choice, true-false, Pop-up, multiple-correct, fill-in, initial answer, and short-answer and essay type activities. A trial version is available.

Plagiarism: http://www.submit.ac.uk/static_jisc/ac_uk_index.html

The Jisc recommends TurnitinUK, an online service hosted at www.submit.ac.uk that enables institutions and staff to carry out electronic comparison of students' work against electronic sources including other students' work.

Achieving the LLUK Professional Standards

Standards
Domain A: Professional values and practice
AK1.1   What motivates learners to learn and the importance of learners' experience and aspirations.
AK2.2   Ways in which learning promotes the emotional, intellectual, social and economic well-being of individuals and the population as a whole.
AK4.2   The impact of own practice on individuals and their learning.
AK5.2   The need for confidentiality, respect and trust in communicating with others about learners.
AK7.1   Organisational systems and processes for recording learner information.
Domain B: Learning and teaching
BK1.3   Ways of creating a motivating learning environment.
Domain C: Specialist learning and teaching
CK2.1   Ways to convey enthusiasm for own specialist area to learners.
CK3.2   Ways to identify individual learning needs and particular barriers to learning in own specialist area.
CK3.5   Ways to support learners in the use of new and emerging technologies in own specialist area.
Domain D: Planning for learning
DK2.1   The importance of Including learners in the planning process.
DK2.2   Ways to negotiate appropriate individual goals with learners.
DK3.1   Ways to evaluate own role and performance in planning learning.
Domain E: Assessment for learning
EK1.1   Theories and principles of assessment and the application of different forms of assessment including initial, formative and summative assessment in teaching and learning.
EK1.2   Ways to devise, select, use and appraise assessment tools including, where appropriate, those which exploit new and emerging technologies.
EK1.3   Ways to develop, establish and promote peer and self-assessment.
EK2.1   Issues of equality and diversity in assessment.
EK2.2   Concepts of validity, reliability and sufficiency in assessment.
EK2.3   The principles of assessment design in relation to own specialist area.
EK3.1   Ways to establish learner involvement in and personal responsibility for assessment of their learning.
EK3.2   Ways to ensure access to assessment within a learning programme.
EK4.1   The role of feedback and questioning in assessment for learning.
EK4.2   The role of feedback in effective evaluation and improvement of own assessment skills.
EK5.2   The assessment requirements of individual learning programmes and procedures for conducting internal and/or external assessments.

Achieving the LLUK Professional Standards

Standards	Ways in which you can show that you have achieved the Standards	See Section
AK1.1 AK2.2 AK4.2 AK5.2 BK1.3 DK2.1 DK2.2	1. Use one of your lesson plans to indicate when, where and how you assess your students (either formally or informally). Describe how you give feedback to the students and the effect of this feedback.	1 and 4
AK1.1 AK2.2 AK4.2 AK5.2 BK1.3 DK2.1 DK2.2	2. Discuss the provision of feedback from assessment with your students and comment upon: (a) the form required by the group; (b) its motivational effectiveness; (c) if it promotes well-being of individuals; and (d) their perceived need for confidentiality.	1
AK7.1	3. Choose the assessment of one of your classes and comment upon your recording the assessments in terms of its effectiveness in: (i) the retrieval of information; and (ii) meeting the needs of your organisation.	1
CK2.1 CK3.2 CK3.5	4. Design or use a questionnaire to give to your students at the start of their course to identify the expectations they have about the course. Explain how you will make direct use of the student responses to each of the questions.	4
CK2.1 CK3.2 CK3.5	5. Use one of the methods of assessing individual needs discussed in section 4 of the chapter and evaluate its effectiveness in terms of: (a) its ability to gather information about individuals; and (b) your ability to provide the necessary guidance.	4
CK3.5	6. Use software such as Hot Potatoes or Quia to create an assessment such as multiple-choice, short answer, jumbled questions, crosswords, etc. Identify how you could use such assessment in your lessons and comment upon the advantages and limitations.	5
DK3.1	7. Review the assessments that you use for a particular course. Justify their design and any changes that you need to make.	1,2,3 and 4
EK1.1 EK1.2 EK1.3 EK2.1 EK2.2	8. Compare and contrast the use of (a) selection-type items, (b) short-answer questions, (c) structured questions, and (d) essay-type questions with regard to their validity, reliability, ease of design and marking in relation to your own subject.	1
EK2.3 EK3.1 EK3.2 EK4.1 EK4.2 EK5.2	9. Design an assessment for your students and discuss how you have made it valid and reliable. Describe how the design of your questions, and the feedback that you provide for your students, leads them to self-assessment.	1, 3 and 4
CK3.5	10. Show how you use, or intend to use, ILT in your assessment techniques. You may wish to indicate the merits of using ILT in both the assessment processes and in record keeping.	5

For a model approach to show how you have achieved the LLUK Professional Standards see Appendix I.

Chapter 8

Evaluating and Improving Professional Practice

1. Teaching and Learning Standards

- Introduction to Teaching and Learning Standards
- The Standards
- Achieving the Standards

2. Evaluating Teaching and Other Professional Tasks

- Autonomy and Accountability
- Evaluating Teaching and the Wider Role of the Professional
- Getting Feedback on Teaching
- Teaching Observations

4. Developing Professionally

- Evaluating One's Own Practice
- Self-Assessment Documents (SAD)
- Engaging in Continuing Professional Development (CPD)

3. Course Evaluations

- Aims of Course Evaluations
- Models of Course Evaluation
- Instruments for Course Evaluation
- Data Collection and Presentation
- Writing a Course Report

This chapter deals with the practical aspects of different types of evaluation including evaluating our own practice and our courses. Of increasing importance is the production of a self-assessment report (SAR) and how this links with continuing professional development (CPD) as the basis of our continuing annual registration with the Institute for Learning. The methodology for producing both the SAR and CPD portfolio are discussed.

LLUK Professional Standards

The Knowledge and Understanding within the LLUK Professional Standards incorporated in this chapter are:

Domain A: Professional values and practice

AK4.2   The impact of own practice on individuals and their learning.

AK4.3   Ways to reflect, evaluate and use research to develop own practice, and to share good practice with others.

AK7.2   Own role in the quality cycle.

AK7.3   Ways to implement improvements based on feedback received.

Domain B: Learning and teaching

BK2.6   Ways to evaluate own practice in terms of efficiency and effectiveness.

Domain D: Planning for learning

DK2.1   The importance of including learners in the planning process.

DK3.1   Ways to evaluate own role and performance in planning learning.

Domain E: Assessment for learning

EK4.2   The role of feedback in effective evaluation and improvement of own assessment skills.

EK5.1   The role of assessment and associated organisational procedures in relation to the quality cycle.

EK5.2   The assessment requirements of individual learning programmes and procedures for recording internal and/or external assessments.

---

1.   Teaching and Learning Standards

1.1   Introduction to the teaching and learning standards

The LLUK Professional Standards in Teaching, Tutoring and Training for the Learning and Skills Sector have been devised in England by Lifelong Learning UK (LLUK). These standards form the basis of an Initial Award to be attained by all new teachers, trainers and tutors, leading through a structured framework, to the Qualified Teaching Learning and Skills (QTLS) status conferring a 'Licence to Practice' award.

A new award, Initial Teacher Trainers Tutors in Education (ITTTE), is a response to weaknesses highlighted by OFSTED in November 2003. (See (http://www.ofsted.gov.uk/whatsnew/index.cfm?fuseaction=newsStory&id=317) 'which pointed out that Further Education teacher training courses are failing to provide trainee teachers with a satisfactory foundation in the professional skills needed at the start of their careers'.

Johnson (2003) states that the standards aim to improve the quality of teacher training by:

- The introduction of formalised subject-specific mentoring as part of the workplace development of trainee teachers.
- A full initial assessment, leading to an individual learning plan with agreed objectives. Trainees will receive additional support to make sure they all reach satisfactory levels of literacy and numeracy before they gain a teacher training qualification.

Initial teacher award

The starting point for new teachers is the Initial Teachers Award. For this the student teacher has to:

- Identify an individual learning plan.
- Work with a subject mentor.
- Identity and address literacy, numeracy and eSkills.
- Undertake 30 hours of guided learning.

This qualification would be at level 3.

Qualified Teaching Learning and Skills (QTLS) status

The student teacher, by following a credit based framework of core and optional elements will, if successful, obtain QTLS status and have 'licence to practice' conferred by the Institute for Learning (ILT). To achieve this the teacher needs to:

- Complete the qualification within 5 years.
- Be working at a level 5 status (minimum).
- Undertake and pass a minimum of 8 teaching observations.
- And undertake continuous personal development.

This qualification would be at a Level 5 or higher status.

1.2   The standards

The key purpose of the LLUK Professional Standards for teachers in the learning and skills sector is to create effective and stimulating opportunities for learning through high quality teaching. The standards are based around six Domains, replacing the Further Education National Training Organisation (FENTO) standards. They are:

1.	Domain A:	Professional Values and Practice
2.	Domain B:	Learning and Teaching
3.	Domain C:	Specialist Learning and teaching
4.	Domain D:	Planning for Learning
5.	Domain E:	Assessment for Learning
6.	Domain F:	Access and Progression

1.3   Achieving the standards

All teachers should become increasingly competent throughout their teaching careers. The teacher in training, however, need to prove this competence and show how they have achieved it. The following process is one such practical way:

(i)   Diagnose your learning needs.

(ii)   Plan a learning programme.

(iii)   Negotiate the further learning needed to provide evidence to show competence.

(iv)   Build a portfolio of evidence of competence.

(v)   Record evidence in a logbook or diary.

(vi)   Reflect on the learning activities.

There are many variations to this sequence but it seems to us that this is logical and covers the important aspects of the process. Such a process revolves around the *generation of evidence* to show competence in each aspect of the teaching role.

To assist with the learning process and to show that you have achieved evidence to prove that you are competent, it is suggested that you might use a Profile and a Logbook to record the above activities, as discussed in Chapters 5 and 7. The *profile* provides an accredited record of your learning activities. It can consist of:

(i)   A record of the evidence that you negotiate with your accreditor.

(ii)   Your record of learning activities.

(iii)   Reflections on those learning activities.

The *logbook* is a document for recording progress as you attempt the different aspects of competence. It is similar to a diary and runs parallel with the development of the profile of evidence. It assists you in reflecting on the learning process underlying that development.

It is becoming increasingly important when attending courses and going for job interviews that, you also keep a *portfolio* of work that you have completed as part of the learning process. This, like an artist's portfolio, gives examples of the different parts of work that you have completed whilst you are learning.

So, there are three important documents, profile, logbook and portfolio, and each of them are interlinked. All of them are your responsibility to keep up to date. You can, if you wish, ask your line manager, tutor, or a colleague to assess what you have done, comment upon it and sign that they have seen it.

The starting point, then, for the achievement of competence lies with the generation of evidence to show that you are competent and this evidence must be related to the assessment criteria.

The generation of evidence is important and it is vital that you plan and organise your learning programme. Each of the stages in the process is described below with ideas of ways in which you can present your evidence.

1.3.1   Diagnosis of learning needs

You need to start with a diagnosis of your learning needs. For each competence ask yourself:

- What competence, if any, do I start with?
- What evidence do I have of existing practice?
- What competence do I need or want to achieve?
- What action do I need to take?
- How will I know when competence has been achieved?

Suppose that you want to achieve competence in 'employ appropriate assessment of student practical work'. In order to diagnose your learning needs it will be necessary for you to think about your requirements for assessment of practical work. If you are attending a course you will be given assistance through the assessment criteria for that area of work. Thus, it might be as shown in Figure 8.1.

Competence	Assessment Criteria
Employ appropriate assessment of student practical work.	(a) Use a range of test instruments for the assessment of practical tasks. (b) Use appropriate formats for the assessment of projects/assignments. (c) Employ effective student profiling formats. (d) Present feedback to students in a positive manner.

Figure 8. 1 *Assistance with Diagnosis of Learning Needs*

You can now link the five questions above with the content areas contained within the assessment criteria. So you ask yourself:

What competence have I with:

- A range of test instruments?
- Using appropriate formats?
- Employing profiling techniques?
- Presenting feed back in a positive manner?

What evidence do I have with:

- A range of test instruments?

- Using appropriate formats?

- Employing profiling techniques?

- Presenting feed back in a positive manner?

What competence do I need to achieve with:

- Etc.

Figure 8.2 gives an example of what your diagnosis of needs might look like in response to the questions above.

Diagnosis of Need

I already use what I consider to be valid and reliable test instruments for workshop practical tasks. The evidence that I have for this includes test schedules and associated marking schemes for 1st year work.

I need to consider which type of marking scheme is best for the subject, for me and my students. I need to increase my competence in the assessment of project work for the end of year project for 1st year students I need at least one and possibly three project briefs with associated marking schemes covering both content and common skills.

I have no experience with profiles but can see that they could be useful when associated with the practical work and projects.

Figure 8.2 *Example of a Completed Diagnosis of Needs*

Such a diagnosis needs to be carried out for each of the competences that you want to achieve. In this manner you start to identify competences that you already have together with the evidence that you can assemble to prove that you have the competence, along with those competences that you need to achieve to make you better at your job.

1.3.2 Planning a learning programme

One of the requirements of the Initial Teacher Award is the development of an Individual Learning Plan. The main purpose of this plan is to map out your strengths and areas for development to form the basis for your professional development leading to Qualified Teaching Learning and Skills (QTLS) status. It is envisaged that this plan would be created through discussions with your staff development tutor, mentor and, possibly, line manager.

Figure 8.3 gives an indication of what a completed plan might look like for the diagnosis completed in Figure 8.2.

Plan of Learning Programme

1. Investigate different formats for the assessment of practical work and identify one that will be most appropriate for 1st year students. This to include:

    - Whether to give marks, grades or pass/fail.

    - Whether the marking will be on-going or terminal.

    - What will be given to the students (brief, assessment scheme, task sheets, and so on).

2. By looking through the syllabus and scheme of work, identify optional (possibly 5) practical tests.

3. Use one of these practical areas, to identify the skills (both subject and common) that students will need to complete the test. These skills to be limited to those that can be assessed.

4. Prepare a possible scheme of work that students can follow in the completion of a project area.

5. For each of the tasks identify the assessment criteria that will form the basis of the assessment scheme for marking the project.

6. Investigate profile formats to include:

    - Where these are best used.

    - Teacher and student tasks associated with their completion.

    - Aspects to be included in their design.

    - What is available and what I need to design.

Figure 8.3   *Completed Example – Plan of Learning Programme*

The completed plan indicates not only what is required to be learned, but gives an indication of the order in which this might be completed. The criteria for making these decisions is likely to revolve around what you are doing at work and the type of possibilities that you see in the achievement of the competence with your students.

The argument here is that, when you plan your own programme, it is more likely to be relevant to your needs and be able to be applied, and be related to, your teaching. This, then, is more likely to give you motivation for your learning.

You may find it beneficial to select one of your groups of students and base all or most of the work on them. This could save you duplication of work and it will certainly be easier for your mentors, guides and the assessor.

1.3.3   Negotiating the criteria and evidence

After planning the learning programme, you need to concentrate upon how the assessment criteria will be met when you negotiate, collect and present evidence of your competence.

In meeting these criteria, it means that your work:

1. *Establishes and maintains quality.*

    In all your work you need to ensure that its quality is the best. This is of prime importance in meeting the criteria.

2. *Diagnoses students' learning needs and problems.*

    Your work needs to be based on the needs of your students.

3. *Is based on an understanding of the learning process.*

    Not only do you need to gain the various competences based on doing your job better in the classroom, but the competences need to take account of a clear understanding of the learning processes. This might well mean wide reading of educational psychology which can often underpin classroom practices.

4. *Demonstrates an awareness of the alternatives that can be used in achieving the criteria.*

    Often, in solving a problem, we use the first solution that comes to us.
    It is important that you consider the alternatives that are available to you and choose the most appropriate of these. The appropriateness might be in terms of what is available, what will best suit your students, what will best suit your situation, and so on.

5. *Explores the use of IT.*

    The use of IT is a common skill upon which you must concentrate.

6. *Contains its own evaluation.*

    In meeting criteria you must ensure that you can evaluate what you are proposing and doing. This self-evaluation must become a way of life.

7. *Demonstrates your research skills.*

    The achievement of all of the above indicates that you must be able to research what you are doing. This research might involve reading, asking tutors and colleagues, asking students, trying things out and evaluating them, and so on.

All of these will not be achieved with every piece of work, every piece of evidence that you produce and for every competence. However, you should aim to achieve all of them by the end of a period of study. They are all equally important to the practising teacher. How you are to meet the criteria should be recorded in a Logbook or Diary.

The negotiation of appropriate evidence is a key stage in the overall process. Having decided on the competences to be achieved and having undertaken an initial diagnosis, the questions are: What further learning and development is needed? What form will it take? What evidence will emerge that learning has occurred and that competence has been gained?

You may decide that no further work is needed to meet a given assessment criteria – you may feel competent enough and you can assemble evidence to prove it from work that you have already completed. If you do feel competent, gather your existing evidence in a document such as a portfolio of your work. You do, however, need to be fully prepared to justify your decision and to show that you have checked out all of the possibilities.

Sharing ideas and practices with colleagues and other teachers on a teacher training course can sometimes enable you to discover applications and practices that you have never thought about yourself. It is sometimes hard to identify the gaps in your knowledge until you know what is available. It is therefore important that you are 'open' about what you have done and be willing to show it to others and discuss its advantages and limitations. This sharing is an important learning tool.

One way that you might use to negotiate your evidence to prove that you are competent is shown in Figure 8.4. This, when associated with a teacher training course, would need to be completed either in association with the course tutor, or, when not on such a course, with your line manager. Whichever situation, it provides the basis for a discussion of what you are attempting to achieve.

Competence Area:	Negotiation of Evidence of Competence		
Competence:	Establishment: _____		
Aspects of Competence	*Proposed Evidence*	*Location of Evidence*	*Date*
1.			
2.			
3.			
4.			

Figure 8.4   *Model for the Negotiation of Evidence of Competence*

The completion of the above becomes a simple matter when you have competently and accurately completed a diagnosis of need as suggested in Figure 8.2. The diagnosis should indicate the type of evidence that is proposed (for example the project briefs and assessment criteria). However, you might have indicated that you can already meet some of the criteria and the type of evidence that you have to show this can be indicated on the form.

We have provided a completed pro-forma in Figure 8.5 for the assessment of practical work.

Competence Area: Assessment	Negotiation of Evidence of Competence		
Competence:	*Establishment:* XYZ Adult Training Centre		
Aspects of Competence	*Proposed Evidence*	*Location of Evidence*	*Date*
1. Employ appropriate assessment of student practical work.	5 practical tests.	Year 1.	October
	Marking Schemes.		
2. Use a range of test instruments for practical assessment.	Year 1 projects.		
	Marking Schemes.		
3. Employ student profiling formats.	Essay on formats.	ABC college.	December
	Report on discussion.		
4. Present feedback to students in a positive manner.	Results of questionnaire to student's practical assessment.	Year 1 work.	July

Figure 8.5 *Example Completed Pro-Forma for the Negotiation of Evidence*

The negotiation process can suggest alternative types of evidence that you might collect as well as assisting you with the things that are available. It is important that you have the evidence agreed before you start work. The evidence builds into a Portfolio which you should maintain and develop as you are achieving competences.

1.3.4   Building a portfolio of evidence of competence

Probably the most important aspect of this type of learning involves the building of a portfolio of evidence. The portfolio consists of all types of work that you have been involved with and shows the depth of skill that you have applied to the competence. It does not only show your assessor the work with which you have been involved, but is also available for future reference to be used as accreditation of prior learning. It will ensure that you do not have to repeat work.

So, what do you include as evidence in your portfolio? There is both direct evidence, that is the results of work that you yourself have completed; and indirect evidence completed by others as a result of your work, such as testimonials and certificates.

You can include many kinds of *direct* evidence in your portfolio like:

- Teaching plans: schemes of work, lesson plans.
- Visual aids: handouts, transparencies, slides, charts.
- Evaluation materials: tests, projects, assignments, questionnaires, interview schedules, and the data from these.

- Course work: papers from working parties, proposals for new courses, reports of meetings, conferences and visits.
- Summaries: of books, articles, radio and TV programmes.
- Analysis of classroom, workshop and other activities.
- Artefacts: photographs, models, video recordings, audio tapes.

The types of *indirect* evidence that you might include are:

- Reports on your practice (such as practical teaching reports).
- Certificates and awards.
- References and evidence of work done on short courses.

The portfolio can also be a useful place to file *your thoughts* (or reflections) on:

- Learning activities that you have undertaken.
- Your development of competence.
- Practical teaching visits.
- Projects and assignments that you have completed.

Whichever of the above types of evidence that you keep in your portfolio, when it is part of a course, it should be in line with the evidence agreed in advance and must meet the criteria for that particular competence. The portfolio will also help you to decide whether, in your opinion, you are competent or not and, again if it is part of a course, whether you are ready to claim competence.

1.3.5 Record evidence in a logbook or diary

A 'Logbook' or 'Diary' can be used to record progress as you tackle the different competences. You can keep a Logbook in parallel with the development of your Portfolio. The process might follow the sequence of:

(i) Start with your diagnosis of learning needs and continue with what has been agreed (Figure 8.2) and then record what is agreed in your learning plan (Figure 8.3); that is, the proposed evidence and the criteria by which it is to be judged that has been negotiated with a tutor (Figure 8.4).

(ii) Make a note in your logbook when you are actually engaged in the learning process. For example, record when you try a new method of teaching, use a particular visual aid, plan a lesson in a different way, try out a particular method of assessment, go to a meeting and try a new skill. (A completed example is shown in Figure 8.5.)

Date	Competence: Assessment of Student Practical Work
Oct 6th	*Practical Test 1* *Designed a marking scheme by completing a breakdown of the complete job and for each sub-task, allocated marks (as appropriate)* *to (i) technical skills, (ii) method of work, (iii) use of tools, (iv) application of knowledge, and (v) creativity.*
Oct 10th	*Used marking scheme with Year 1. It was perhaps too thorough in that it took a long time to complete. I only completed three students.*
Oct 21st	*Practical Test 2* *Designed a marking scheme using a rating schedule.* *The scale designed using sub-tasks like Test 1.* *Designed questionnaire to give to students to see which type of marking scheme they (a) find most helpful and (b) prefer.*
Oct 31st	*Used Marking scheme and distributed questionnaire. The analysis of the results showed ...etc.*

Figure 8.6   *Completed Logbook Entry to Show Record of Evidence*

This shows the date on which aspects were completed for student practical work and it follows on from the entry in the Negotiated Evidence by expanding on the entry 'Design Five Practical Tests with Associated Marking Schemes'. The intention being to try different types of marking scheme and to try to find out which is preferable.

1.3.6   Reflection of learning activity

The next stage is to record how things went – to *reflect*. This can indicate what success you had, how you as the teacher felt about it (was it worth the amount of time and effort that was invested in it?), what results or feedback you obtained, what you need to do next, and so on. It is a record of your thoughts and actions. It does not, of course, have only to be your thoughts, for the reflection can often be most useful when you talk to someone else (a colleague, your students, and so on) about it and share and talk through the problems and difficulties. A completed example of such a reflection is shown in Figure 8.7.

Reflection of Learning Activity

Assessment of Practical Work

Test 1:   *The marking scheme took a long time to prepare (about 4 hours). It was decided to give a copy of the marking scheme to the students (which I had not done before) and they did not really know what to do with it. Perhaps I should get them to mark their own tasks which might make them concentrate more on each of the aspects.*
It was difficult to use the marking scheme for method of work as it was difficult to watch the 15 students at the same time and I felt that I missed some aspects. This was similar for Use of Tools. Students only tended to look at their overall mark when I gave them their results and not the marks for the individual sub-tasks. The reliability of the results was judged to be higher than my previous assessments as it is more closely related to the course aims.
The next scheme (rating scale) I will not add the marks for individual students.

Figure 8.7   *Completed Example – Reflection of Learning Activity*

A discussion on Reflection and the use of a Professional Development Journal follows in Section 4.1.

2.   Evaluating Teaching and Other Professional Tasks

2.1   Autonomy and accountability

Evaluation, especially course evaluation, has emerged because of the increasing acceptance of two related concepts: professional autonomy and accountability.

The idea of autonomy is that professionals should be free to determine how they practice but, in return for this privilege, they should be rigorous in maintaining and developing their standards of practice. Accordingly, examining and validating bodies increasingly allow you, the teacher in post-16 education and training, to determine what you teach, to whom, and how you teach it. Your external syllabuses and externally set examinations are being replaced by college devised and assessed courses which are approved by central bodies and by lead bodies setting competences and associated performance criteria. However, in return, these central bodies are increasingly requiring you to monitor, review and evaluate your programmes and to report on them periodically. Such reports contain a critical analysis of the operation of the programmes together with proposals for improvements.

The public served by professionals, increasingly expect those professionals to be accountable to them or their representatives. In education, the move to accountability has been promoted by public concern over the relevance and standards of education in schools and colleges.

This means that you have to have the knowledge and skills to evaluate your own performance and your courses.

2.2   Evaluating teaching and the wider role of the professional

We need to consider the main tasks for which we are responsible. Once these have been identified, they can be the focus for a self-audit.

There has been a move recently to base many of the teaching tasks on a competence model. In terms of competences that are required by the teacher, we need to consider, firstly, those aspects required to teach our subjects and secondly, aspects of management of both the classroom and the curriculum. Thus, these tasks can be sub-divided into (i) teaching and (ii) other professional duties.

2.2.1   Evaluating teaching tasks

Teaching may be seen as having **six** main elements, as follows:

(i)   *Preparation*:
- Identification of student needs.
- Analysis of a subject/topic into a logical sequence.
- Indication of expected student learning.
- Selection of appropriate teaching/learning methods.
- Writing systematic lesson plans.
- Selecting and preparing learning resources.

The **second** element, that of presenting the lesson to students, relates to the application of the preparation. Aspects relating to this element include:

(ii)   *Presentation*:

- The implementation of selected teaching/learning methods.
- Provision of appropriate:
  - Introduction.
  - Development.
  - Conclusion to a session.
- Flexible response to classroom situations.
- Using learning resources effectively.

The **third** element relates to the manner in which you as the teacher are able to relate to your students. This operates on the premise that the better the relationship between you and your students, the more likelihood there is of optimising learning. Aspects relating to this element include:

(iii)   *Trainee/student relationships*:

- Securing student participation in lessons.
- Promotion of a classroom climate that facilitates learning.

An element that could be considered as going across all of the other elements is the **fourth** element, communication. However, it is considered so important that it is thought worthwhile to separate it and make it an element on its own. Aspects relating to communication include:

(iv)   *Communication*:

- Using appropriate language registers.
- Employment of effective skills in verbal and non-verbal communication.

The **fifth** element is the final one in the basic teaching model, assessment of student learning. It is from here that you are able to identify any problems that might have occurred with the operation of the previous elements. Thus the aspect to be considered is:

(v)   *Assessment of learning:*

- Making an assessment of the extent to which the students achieved the stated intentions.

The **sixth** and final element relates to your knowledge of the subject that you are teaching. Within this element you also need to consider the integration of key skills into the lesson.

(vi)   *Subject matter:*

- Demonstration of mastery of the subject matter.
- Integration of key skills.

There are a number of key aspects that relate to the whole teaching and learning experience. These are:

- Widening participation: Widening access and improving participation of our learners.
- Differentiation: Tailoring teaching environments and practices to create appropriately different learning experiences for different students.
- Inclusiveness: The integration of learners with special or particular learning needs or disabilities (physical, intellectual, emotional).
- e-Learning: Using ILT to enhance teaching and learning.

Each of these impact on the some or all of the elements identified above. For example, widening participation identifies the following:

- Preparation: Identify student needs. What are the most appropriate learning methods? Do I need different resources?

- Presentation: How can I best present the information across?

- Communications: e-Learning? Distance learning? Identify most appropriate communication methods.

- Assessment: What are the most effective methods to use?

- Subject Matter: Do I need to make any changes with the different learning methods?

These aspects, provide you with the basis on which you can evaluate your own teaching or, on the other hand, the basis on which someone else might evaluate your teaching. They can be used in total to give an overall impression or they might be used one at a time to provide feedback on specific elements.

If you are inviting someone else to evaluate your teaching performance you might use a form such as the one indicated in Figure 8.8.

PRACTICAL TEACHING OBSERVATION

Date: Class:

Time: Subject/Topic:

Place:

Competences to be displayed and assessed with associated comments:

Competences (completed by you)	Comments (completed by observer)

Additional comments by the observer:

(i) Preparation:

(ii) Presentation:

(iii) Trainee/Student Relationships:

(iv) Communication:

(v) Assessment of Learning:

(vi) Subject Matter:

Figure 8.8 *Practical Teaching Feedback Form*

From the lesson plan it will be possible for you to identify the range of competences on which you want feedback. If you identify these prior to the observation and write them onto the observation form, you will obtain the specific feedback. These might be, for instance:

(a)   Use teaching strategies that are appropriate to the group.

(b)   Organisation of the environment in a way that assists learning.

(c)   Use appropriate language.

(d)   Analyse strengths and weaknesses of the students.

It may be that you want to practise and gain feedback on a specific skill, such as your ability to use the question and answer technique effectively. In this case you might design and use a schedule related only to this specific aspect (see Figure 8.9).

An advantage of such a schedule is that you think about the main aspects of the competence related to question and answer both in the planning and the presentation stages. That is, you plan your question and answer technique to try to ensure that you cover the aspects that you have highlighted.

Question and Answer Technique		
	Circle as appropriate	
1. Questions were clearly understood by students.	YES	NO
2. Pauses were used after asking most of the questions.	YES	NO
3. Some of the questions were asked of specific students.	YES	NO
4. The questions were distributed amongst the whole group.	YES	NO
5. Prompting techniques were effectively used to assist students in answering.	YES	NO
6. Some of the questions were at the higher levels of thinking.	YES	NO
Comments:		

Figure 8.9   *Example Schedule About a Specific Aspect of Teaching*

This can, then, be used either by yourself or by an observer. If it is to be used by yourself, it can be useful to (a) write your impressions of what happened immediately after the teaching episode and (b) to arrange to either audio or video tape and, at your leisure, watch/listen to the tape and remark your schedule in the light of what you hear/see.

This type of self-evaluation allows you to compare your initial reactions with those that are evoked.

2.2.2 Evaluation of other professional tasks

Teaching is not only related to what you do in the classroom or in preparation for it, it also involves many other aspects that go to make up the 'extended professional'. Tansley (1989) suggests the following list of tasks when discussing the role of the course team:

- Managerial and Administrative Tasks: Timetabling/accommodation, resource allocation.

- Liaison with outside bodies: Arranging work experience, liaison with schools and employers.

- Liaison within the organisation: Reporting to line management, liaison with support staff including external support (such as social workers), liaison with other departments e.g. key skills areas

- Student responsibilities: Student guidance and tutoring/assessment/ discipline.

- Course responsibilities: Curriculum development, course evaluation and profiling.

- Examination administration: Clerical administration, examination administration, liaison with qualification bodies and internal and external verifiers.

This list gives some idea of the complexity of other tasks that the teacher is expected to complete. Although they are directly related to a course leader, many people tend to delegate these duties to different members of the course team. Indeed, there are distinct advantages in this delegation taking place so that it gives all of the course team members an overview of the whole of the course, its changes and developments. The line management and the course team are the best places for you to gain feedback about how you are doing with such tasks. Alternatively, you can make your own checklist of tasks and rate yourself on each of them.

2.3 Getting feedback on teaching

There are several sources for obtaining feedback on your teaching performance which can give assistance with your evaluation. These include your students, peers, and your line manager or tutor. However, all of these people should give you feedback in such a manner as to assist with your own self-evaluation. They can provide information (data and impressions) which it is difficult for you to gather when you are involved in the teaching yourself. The only true evaluation, however, is self-evaluation. You can find a multitude of excuses why someone else's evaluation is incorrect but, when you find a fault for yourself, there is less scope for such excuses. In consequence, the principles of providing feedback should be:

(a) To apply and have assessed competences identified by you.

(b) For the observer to provide constructive feedback about the identified competences and about aspects of practice.

(c) For the observer to collect data about practice for detailed subsequent analysis.

(d) For you to try out new methods and approaches to the development of student learning and obtain feedback on them as opposed to obtaining feedback on aspects in which you know that you are proficient.

(e) To assist you to evaluate your own teaching.

If these are the principles, it is important to look at the pros and cons of the different sources of feedback so that you can try to accentuate the positive aspects and minimise the negative ones.

Students are the people who have to suffer our teaching quirks and styles. They are omnipresent and, in consequence, you are not able to 'put on a show' for them. If you do something that is not usually done, they will be aware of it and are able to comment upon it from the standpoint of comparison with what they are used to. Thus, they have distinct advantages over the casual observer.

On the other hand students, especially adolescent ones, might not have the skill to be able to express themselves and tell you their feelings. Also, as you have the upper hand, especially as you assess their work and say whether they are to pass or fail their course, they are likely to give you answers that they think you expect. They might well be fearful of being honest, especially if this involves critical comment, thinking that it might have a bearing on their chances of success. Even if they complete a questionnaire anonymously you are going to know their handwriting so you are likely to be able to trace who has said what.

When you ask *colleagues* and *peers* to give you feedback, they are likely to be busy people and will have to find the time to complete the observation. Thus, any instrument that is given to them will have to be easy to complete and will have to be completed during the period of observation. Also they may make unfair comparisons between your practice and their own.

The main advantage of *tutors* is that they will have gained skill in observation and can provide effective feedback to you. However, they only see you on a limited number of occasions and might have some difficulty in 'tuning-in' to both your needs and requirements.

There are occasions for more formal feedback. Two which you will come across in your teaching career is the self-assessment report (SAR) and OFSTED/ALI inspection.

Self-assessment is an internal inspection method where line managers and senior staff judge how successful the college is. Support for Success Quality Improvement Programme website http://www.qualityacl.org.uk/quality/selfassessment.aspx, comment that 'Self-assessment should be integral to organisational development; not only should the self-assessment report (SAR) reflect your organisation's goals and the needs of your learners, but it should also take account of external requirements, for example those of the Learning and Skills Council (LSC) and the inspectorates'.

OFSTED has the responsibly for inspecting sixth form, tertiary, general further education and specialist colleges. The Adult Learning Inspectorate (ALI) undertakes joint inspections with Ofsted of colleges where there are significant numbers of learners aged 19 and over. OFSTED is responsible for the publication of all college reports. Further information can be found form the OFSTED website http://www.ofsted.gov.uk/colleges relating to college inspection.

In both situations your teaching will be observed. The duration of these observations needs to be between 30 and 50 minutes, and you may be observed more than once. They will give no warning of who they will inspect. Feedback will be given at the end of the session or at another suitable point. The inspectors will grade your teaching but they will not reveal your grade to you or other senior mangers. In their report back they will simply identify that they saw 3 exceptional lessons, 10 satisfactory lessons. Although inspections are stressful, the feedback given does form a valuable pointer to the quality of your teaching and your students learning.

2.4   Teaching observations

It is useful to note that a PowerPoint presentation by HMI inspectors Vincent Ashworth (HMI) and David Martin (ALI), [Standards in Business Education 2004-05, http://www.nabse.ac.uk/docs/conf 2005 presentations/vashworth.ppt] identified the following weaknesses in teaching:

- Insufficient variety of teaching and learning strategies.
- Uninspiring teaching in many lessons.
- Unsatisfactory IT resources for effective teaching.
- Insufficient assessment and review of students' progress.

- Insufficient enrichment experiences for full-time students.
- Insufficient development of Key Skills.

Evans, D. (2001) is a useful publication which deals with teaching observations.

As a final check on the aspects that you might consider in your teaching the following checklist can be useful. You need to consider each of the points and decide if specific points are applicable to your teaching and, if they are, whether you have taken them into consideration with a specific group of students. The completed checklist should be used with a specific group of students.

	Yes	No	Not needed
Preparation			
Have you:			
A clear statement of aims/objectives/competences?			
Explicitly identified the needs of the students?			
Clear **plan** for the lesson with:			
• Times indicated?			
• A choice of appropriate resources?			
• A choice of teaching strategies and learning styles?			
• An identified introduction, development and conclusion?			
• Planned assessment of student learning?			
Is the amount of material about right for the time available?			
Have you anticipated problems and made the necessary contingency plans?			
Presentation			
Have you:			
Identified the learning needs of the specific group?			
Determined the entry behaviour of the students?			
Considered the background, age, gender, racial and cultural issues?			
Identified possible barriers to learning?			
Managed the time effectively?			
In the **introduction** have you:			
• Given an overview of the session?			
• Shared with the group the required outcomes (aims/ objectives competences)?			
• Made links with other sessions?			
• Created interest?			
• Negotiated with the students within the constraints that are set?			
In the **development** have you:			
• Used a logical sequence for the sub-topics?			
• Modified the plan to suit responses?			
Have you used a range of teaching/learning aids including:			
• OHP?			
• Chalkboard?			
• Handouts?			
• White board?			
• Flip chart?			
• Audio?			
• Computers?			
• Video?			
• Programmed learning?			
• Resource-based learning?			

	Yes	No	Not needed

Have you:
  - Used a range of teaching strategies effectively?
  - Paced the presentation to suit the students and the demands of the syllabus?
In the **conclusion** have you:
  - Given a summary of the lesson?
  - Reviewed the key issues?
  - Made links to the next lesson?			

Communications and Relationships
 	
Have you:
  - Communicated effectively with the students?
  - Spoken clearly?
  - Introduced and explained jargon?
  - Managed question and answer sessions effectively?
  - Answered student questions clearly?
  - Used clear diagrams via OHP, chalkboard, flip chart?
  - Written clearly on the OHP, chalkboard, flip chart?
  - Obtained student feedback?
  - Provided positive reinforcement?
  - Managed group work effectively?
  - Used tutorial time effectively?
  - Developed student communication skills (e.g. writing, talking, questioning)?
  - Communicated enthusiasm for the subject?
  - Motivated the students?
  - Encouraged student contributions?
  - Observed the non-verbal reactions of the students?
  - Kept discipline and order?
  - Managed disruptive student(s)?
  - Been approachable?			

Assessment
 	
Have you:
  - Identified prior knowledge and skills (entry behaviour)?
  - Identified and used assessment criteria?
  - Selected and used a range of assessment instruments?
  - Designed a range of assessment instruments e.g.
    • Essays?
    • Practical tests?
    • Observation?
    • Objective tests?
  - Ensured validity and reliability?
  - Used assessment to facilitate learning?
  - Selected and collected evidence of learning for profiles?
  - Encouraged self-assessment?
  - Encouraged peer group assessment?
  - Kept accurate, up-to-date records in an appropriate, confidential system?			

	Yes	No	Not needed

Evaluation
 	
Have you:
 	
-Used a range of evaluation techniques for:
    • Lessons?
    • Modules?
    • Courses?
    • Programmes?
-Reviewed teaching strategies?
-Taken appropriate action in response to evaluation?			

Subject Matter and Others *Have you:* -Given due regard to the safety of the students? -Given regard to equality of opportunity for all? -Allowed for a range of different Learning Styles? -Allowed for differentiation? -Set tasks that challenged students? -Integrated key skills numeracy and literacy? -Developed student study skills? -Set homework? -Given appropriate guidance?			
ILT and e-Learning *Have you:* -Have you made use of ILT in your presentation? - Have you made use of ILT as a resource? -Have you made use of ILT in assessment? -Are materials available on the VLE or Web for student to use outside the lesson? -Are any materials available for delivery using e-learning?			
Personal Development *Have you:* -Updated your own subject knowledge? -Updated your own teaching expertise? -Considered your own staff development needs?			

You can gain feedback from many sources but this information is valueless unless you use it. The following section asks you to take all sources of information and evaluate your own practice.

3.   Course Evaluations

3.1   Aims of course evaluations

In order to take part in course evaluation in any realistic and motivated manner, you have to recognise the benefits that will come to you personally and to your teaching, your course and your students. This leads to your consideration of your aims of course evaluation; what is likely to accrue from them. Once the aims have been formulated, and only then, are you able to formulate an effective scheme to evaluate your course.

One of the problems of formulating a course evaluation scheme is the number of aims that might be achieved. Some of the aims are:

- To find the appropriateness and achievement of the aims and objectives of your course/subject.
- To consider the structure of your course, its progression, balance and coherence.
- To identify the relevance and currency of the course syllabus.
- To understand the quality and effectiveness of your teaching approach used on the course.
- To find the abilities and skills of the graduates.
- To assist with the student input profile and its match to the initial stages of the course/subject.
- To improve and develop skill in your assessment methods and techniques in relation to the objectives and their effectiveness in revealing student achievement.
- To give an appreciation of the staff who teach on the course, their development and cohesion.
- To promote a positive attitude in the provision and deployment of resources.

As you can see, the aims are very comprehensive and to achieve them all would involve a very stringent evaluation. You need to be selective in deciding what you want to achieve in order to make a manageable task for your evaluation. You might achieve only one or two of the above aims in any one evaluation; you might make a three year development plan in order to achieve them all but only tackle some of them each academic year. You might decide, initially, on more general headings like:

- Finding information to improve educational processes and programmes.
- Identifying problem areas.
- Evolving new approaches.
- Improving your ability to plan and effect the necessary changes.

Thus, you as an individual teacher, or with colleagues, might want to find the relevance of your course or subject to industry and students, find out if your teaching approaches are acceptable or if others would be better for your students, and so on. Once you have identified your aims, you might want to plan and effect the necessary changes. However, all of these should be reflected in your aims of the evaluation.

Figure 8.10 gives a typical list of aims for the evaluation of a subject.

Aims of the Evaluation of a subject	
1.	To consider whether the objectives are consistent with the needs of industry and other subjects in the course.
2.	To examine the entry behaviour of the students and to link this with subject objectives.
3.	To investigate the appropriateness of the teaching and learning approaches to (a) the curriculum documents and (b) the students' needs.
4.	To find the trends in percentage of passes and 'drop-outs' over the past five years.

Figure 8.10 *Typical Aims of Evaluation*

Aims 1 and 2 are linked to the appropriateness of the objectives of the subject which will be found in the curriculum documents. However, their appropriateness to: (i) the industry that the course serves; and (ii) to the students, indicate that either questionnaires will have to be designed or interviews carried out. Similar methods may be used with respect to aim 3 where it is necessary to find out how appropriate the teaching approaches are to the students. The trends in pass rates and drop-outs will be obtained from course records.

A checklist for writing the aims of course evaluation is given in Figure 8.11.

Are the aims that you have written for the evaluation of your course or subject:		Yes	No
1.	Of practical use?		
2.	Able to be used in the design of evaluative instruments?		
3.	Able to be achieved through the process of evaluation?		
4.	Within your scope to achieve?		
5.	Sufficiently comprehensive to cover all of the aspects that you want to achieve?		

Figure 8.11 *Checklist for Writing Aims of Course Evaluation*

One of the problems that you will find in deciding the aims of evaluation lies in their scope. The aims have to be wide enough to cover all of the aspects that you want to achieve, but, on the other hand, they need to be manageable. In other words, you need not too many aims and not too few. They need to be written to be helpful in terms of the things that need to be identified and also to assist in the choice of evaluative instruments that you might design.

3.2   Models of course evaluation

In order to achieve comprehensiveness in terms of the design of the aims, you need to consider the types of question that you might ask. Several models of evaluation have been suggested but probably the most useful in terms of post-16 education and training is the one suggested by Stufflebeam (1971). He suggests that we should think of evaluation in terms of four main headings:

Stufflebeam calls this the **CIPP** (the first letter of each of the elements) **Model** and suggests that a comprehensive evaluation should answer questions relating to each of the elements. However, this might comprise quite an onerous task, especially for an individual teacher, and even for a course team. You might want to consider a long-term evaluation and write aims only for one of the elements for one set of students. So, the complete evaluation might take two or more years to complete.

Context: This is the setting of the course or subject and relates to the aims of the curriculum.

Input: The input elements relate to the students, the staff and the resources that are used.

Process: This relates to the appropriateness of what happens on the course – how the input elements are used to achieve the aims and objectives.

Product: This relates to the outcomes – the students who have gone through the course and what they have learned.

The type of questions that you might want to find answers to under each of Stufflebeam's elements could be:

Context

1.   Are the aims of the curriculum consistent with the needs of industry/society/the individual student?
2.   Does the curriculum foster purposeful co-operation and interaction with the world of work?
3.   Are the aims broad enough to ensure further education and mobility of the students?
4.   Are the aims up-dated regularly?

Input

1.   Do the students possess the entry behaviour assumed when designing the curriculum?
2.   Do the teachers have the competences required for implementation of the curriculum?
3.   Are the resources for teaching and learning, explicit or implicit in the curriculum documents, available to the teacher and to the students?

Process

1.   Do the teachers make use of the curriculum documents and, if so, for what purposes?
2.   Do the teachers understand the curriculum documents?
3.   Is there a system of feedback from students and teachers on the problems faced in the achievement of the aims and objectives?
4.   Are the teaching strategies (classroom, laboratory and workshop) in line with those proposed in the curriculum?
5.   What is the extent of the use of instructional resource material?
6.   Is the student assessment system valid, reliable and practicable?

Product

1.   What are the trends in percentage of passes and drop-outs?
2.   Do the students get absorbed into industry? Is there a time lag? Do they get appropriate employment?

3. What are the opinions of students and ex-students regarding the relevance of the course/subject/topics?

4. What are the staff development needs that have arisen and to what extent have they been met?

5. What are the views of employers on the curriculum?

This is not an exhaustive list of questions, but it gives an indication of the areas that a curriculum evaluation might want to address.

Each of the aims of evaluation, then, can have questions associated with them. Figure 8.12 shows how questions might be associated with the aims of the evaluation suggested in Figure 8.10.

Aim	Possible Questions
1. To consider if the objectives are consistent with the needs of employers.	Do the objectives cover cognitive, psychomotor and affective domains? Are any additions or deletions necessary? Do the objectives reflect industrial needs? How many employers take graduate students? What questions can be asked of employers to determine if the objectives are relevant?
2. To examine the entry behaviour of students.	Is an entry behaviour test available – if not, can one be designed? What is the best time to give an entry behaviour test? Does the entry behaviour for one subject need to reflect other subjects?
3. To investigate the teaching and learning methods.	What teaching strategies are suggested or implied In the curriculum documents? What teaching strategies are used and what strategies *could* be used? What questions should be asked of students and should these be through interview and/or questionnaire?
4. To find the trends in passes and drop-outs.	Who keeps records over the past five years? How can reasons for drop-outs be found - how can student addresses be found?

Figure 8.12 *Questions Related to Aims of Evaluation*

These, of course, are only a sample of the questions that might be asked. Each of the aims has a whole host of questions that might usefully be associated with them to find specific aspects of the operation of a course or subject. The skill in evaluation is to ensure that the questions are relevant to the information required and useful to the improvement of a course or subject.

We mentioned previously, 'What are the trends in percentage of passes and drop-out?' and this issue is worth taking further. A major focus of course evaluation is based around Retention and Achievement figures and a comparison to benchmark figures for similar courses. This comes about due to funding issues, in that further education colleges are paid for retaining students on a courses and a further percentage is paid on students passing the course. Hence the need for accurate data to compare success rates and drop-out figures. The purpose of the benchmark is to make a direct comparison to a national standard. This information allows the course team to judge the success of their course or determine weaknesses against these national standards.

Part 2 (CPRD2) - Course Data Sheet			
Course:			**Academic Year: 200 / 200**
	Criteria	**Current year**	**Notes**
A	**Enrolment** Target number		
	Actual enrolment (X)		
	% performance		
	Number of places offered (Y)		
	% offered place actually enrolled (X/Y x 100)	18	
	number of males		
	number of females		
	number of 16-19		
	number of 19+		
	number of white		
	number of other ethnic groups		
B	**Retention** Target (%)		
	number completing (N)	16	
	% performance (N/P x 100)	88%	
	National Benchmark		
	number at Nov Yr 1 (P)		
	Feb Yr 1		
	May Yr 1		
	Nov Yr 2		
	Feb Yr 2		
C	**Highest Qualification On Entry** number with no qualifications		
	number with Level 1		
	number with Level 2		
	number with Level 3		
	number with Level 4		
D	**Achievement**	15	
	Target (%)	94%	
	number passing (S)		
	% performance (S/N x 100)		
	National Benchmark		
	Breakdown of achievement (please annotate with grades or equivalent)		
E	**Progression** number going relevant job/training		
	number going to non-relevant job/training		
	number not progressing		

Figure 8.13   *Example of Statistical Information for a Particular Course of Study*

Information asked for in the example Figure 8.13 includes students interviewed and progression at the end of the course.

Much of the data produced is assembled onto computer software such as ProAchieve (http://www.compasscc.com/proachieve/) which allows detailed analysis of student retention and achievement and comparisons to the benchmark figures. This information feeds directly to the Learning and Skills Council (LSC) and is key information used by OFSTED during college inspections.

3.3   Instruments for course evaluation

If the evaluation is to serve the aims that you have listed, it must be a continuous process rather than an intermittent or once only event. It must consist of constant observation, measurement and reporting of how the course/subject is being implemented so that appropriate corrective measures at the most convenient stage of curriculum development might be taken.

The methods of obtaining information can be:

- Questionnaires.
- Checklists.
- Student performance.
- Structured interview schedule.

These might be used on the following:

- Teachers.
- Students: present, drop-outs, graduates employed.
- Industry.
- Support staff.
- Organisational set-up.
- Text and reference books.
- Teaching/learning resources: availability, use.

3.3.1 Questionnaires

An example questionnaire to be given to students about text and reference books is given in Figure 8.14. The aim of this evaluation is 'to examine how students use the suggested reading list of books for the course'.

The questions associated with this are:

1. How easy is it for students to locate the required reading?
2. How useful to students is the list of references given for the course?
3. What use has been made of additional reading?
4. Why have students found additional reading useful?

Student Questionnaire – Use of Reading List

1. How useful have you found the reading list given at the start of the course? Circle the number that best represents your feelings.

   Of little use 1 2 3 4 5 6 *Very Useful*

2. Have you used the readings for? Tick the appropriate boxes.

Doing homework.	
Completing assignments.	
As a backup to lectures.	
Preparation for examinations.	
For topics missed when absent.	
Others (please state).	

3. Which of the texts have you found **MOST** useful:

   (a)

   (b)

4. Why have you found them useful?

5. Which of the texts have you found **LEAST** useful?

   (a)

   (b)

6. Why have you found them least useful?

7. Where have you obtained the required books? Tick as appropriate.

	YES
Institution Library.	
Home Library.	
Bought.	
Borrowed from friend.	
Other (please state e.g. Internet).	

Figure 8.14 *Example: Questionnaire for Students*

You will see from the example that there is a mixture of open questions (those that require a written response) and closed questions (those that only require a tick). The closed questions are both easier to answer and easier to analyse. As you can see a mixture of both qualitative and quantitative data will be collected.

Whatever the design, the questionnaire should be easy to answer and quick. A lengthy questionnaire will not get the necessary attention paid to it and will be difficult to analyse. As a general guide, the questionnaire should not take longer than 5 minutes to answer. The questions need to be directly related to the aims of what you want to find out and its design should be easy to follow and appealing to the eye. Plenty of white space is useful and each question should be clearly separated from the others. It could be helpful, for example, for questions 3 and 5 to indicate the titles of the specific texts that have been given as, say, required reading so that you are not relying upon the student memory to answer the questions. If this was the case you could combine these two questions with tick boxes for the most and least useful.

3.3.2 Checklists

A checklist can be a useful *aide memoire* to ensure that you have covered all of the necessary aspects in an evaluation. It can also be used as a basis for the design of a questionnaire.

The example shown below (Figure 8.15) is a checklist of tasks that a course leader might wish to complete in order to consider the staff development of the course team.

Checklist for Course Team Staff Development	Yes	No
1. All of the staff teaching on the course understand their roles and responsibilities.		
2. Course team members have received specific training in working as a team.		
3. Structured curriculum-led staff development has been offered to all of the course team.		
4. The expertise of staff in helping other course team members to develop has been used.		
5. The following course tasks have been delegated as far as possible: • Administration. • Assessment design. • Use of new teaching strategies.		
6. Part-time and support staff have been included in all staff development programmes for course teams.		

Figure 8.15   *Example: Checklist for Course Team Staff Development*

Checklists must contain terms which the respondent understands and which more briefly and succinctly express views than would be the case with answers from open-ended questions. They are inevitably crude devices, but careful pilot work and design can make them less so. They are at their best when they are designed and used to be related to specific aims.

3.3.3　Student assessment

Information about how well the course is going, can be obtained from the results of student assessments. If, for instance, a large proportion of the students fail the end examination, then this is important information and questions will need to be asked as to why this has happened. This does not only have to be at the end of the course. If students do badly (or well) on your formative tests, then this is also useful information about the success of that part of the course which is being assessed.

3.3.4　Structured interview schedules

An Interview Schedule is structured and prepared as a basis of a one-to-one interview.

In a structured interview schedule you are unlikely to be able to cover as many aspects as you can in a questionnaire but it has the advantage that you can cover the items in greater depth: subsequent questions being dependent upon the response to the previous one. Also, you have much greater control over the responses in that you can ask the questions to ensure that they are understood and ensure that *all* of your questions are answered.

Although you are going to have a face-to-face discussion it is still important that you prepare a schedule upon which to base your questions. In such a schedule you should structure your questions from the general to the specific. You can ask questions about:

(a)　Knowledge and skills.

(b)　Common and study skills.

(c)　Work related skills.

Usually, you will want to find out opinions of individuals about various aspects of the course. The schedule shown in Figure 8.16 is for employers, to find out their opinion of a course of study upon which they send students.

It will be realised from the example schedule that the actual aims and objectives of the course, the knowledge and skills that are applicable, can be inserted into the design itself.

In completion of the schedule, spaces are left for you to insert notes on the responses that the employer makes. You make these notes as the discussion proceeds.

Your design should ensure the following:

- The questions must be directly related to the aims of what you want to find.
- There are a limited number of questions.
- Adequately prepare both the schedule and any other information that is required.
- Structure the schedule from the general to the specific.

Name: Position:

Company:

No of Employees: Course Title:

Q1.   Outline of course aims and objectives. Is this how you perceive the course?

Q2.   If this is not what you thought, what differences would you wish to see?

Q3.   Do you agree with the course content?

Q4.   The course provides training in the following skills and knowledge.
      Does this reflect your requirements?

Q5.   Stress will be laid on the following skills. Do you agree with this?

Q6.   Where should the greater emphasis be laid?

Q7.   How satisfied have you been with the student(s) who have attended the course?

Q8.   How do you see your future needs?

Q9.   What should be added or subtracted from the course?

Figure 8.16   *Example: Structured Interview Schedule for Employers*

3.4   Data collection and presentation

Data collection can either be qualitative, that is when it is related to opinion, or quantitative when it is related to a numerical scale. For comparative purposes it is easier to deal with and draw conclusions from quantitative data than qualitative. It is necessary, therefore, for us to look at transferring qualitative into quantitative data.

Figure 8.17 shows a small part of a questionnaire given to students to evaluate their opinion of the effectiveness of a short, in-service course for teachers. The part shown refers to the overall organisation of the course.

In your opinion was the overall organisation of the course:					
	QUALITY				
	Poor	Fair	Good	Very Good	Excellent
1. Well prepared?					
2. Properly sequenced?					
3. Intelligently time-tabled (e.g. to give variety)?					
4. Etc.					

Figure 8.17 *Part of Student Questionnaire*

It may be assumed that the questionnaire is given to a class of 25 students. In order to collate the data, each of the responses from the individual students can be transferred to a blank questionnaire. When this is done the completed blank questionnaire might look as shown in Figure 8.18. In each of the appropriate spaces a slash (/) mark indicates where a particular student has responded. The slash marks are then summated within each of the cells.

In your opinion was the overall organisation of the course:					
	QUALITY				
	Poor	Fair	Good	Very Good	Excellent
1. Well prepared?			///// //// (9)	///// ///// (10)	///// / (6)
2. Properly sequenced?		/// (3)	///// (5)	///// ///// //(12)	///// (5)
3. Intelligently time-tabled (e.g. to give variety)?	//// (4)	///// / (6)	///// ///// (10)	///// (5)	
4. Etc.					

Figure 8.18 *Data Collection on a Blank Questionnaire*

The next task involves changing the qualitative scale into a quantitative one (that is assigning numbers to each of the points on the scale). This can be done as follows:

Poor   = 1
Fair   = 2
Good   = 3
Very Good   = 4
Excellent   = 5

A further section of the questionnaire asked questions about the 'group tasks' involved in the course and students were requested to indicate their opinion of the tasks by either agreeing or disagreeing with a number of statements. A five-point scale of SD = Strongly Disagree, D = Disagree,; N = Neutral; A = Agree, and SA = Strongly Agree was used. This type of scale, known as a Likert Scale, is shown in Figure 8.19.

Similarly, the qualitative responses can be given a numerical value by assigning numbers to each of the five values of opinion.

	Opinion				
	SD	D	N	A	SA
1. The group work was useful in gaining insights into problems.					
2. The variety of group work helped to maintain interest.					
3. The group work needed more resource materials.					
4. Etc.					

Figure 8.19 *Example: Questionnaire using a Likert Scale*

Once the scale has been decided for each of the questions, the responses to them can be converted to the numerical scale and then correlated. So, for question 1 in Figure 8.10, the number of responses in each cell has to be multiplied with the number assigned to that point on the scale. As nine (9) students considered the preparation to be 'good' and 'good' = 3, a total for this cell would be 3 x 9 = 27. This can be completed for all of the cells as shown in Figure 8.20.

In your opinion was the overall organisation of the course:					
	QUALITY				
	Poor 1	Fair 2	Good 3	Very Good 4	Excellent 5	Mean
1. Well prepared?			9 x 3 = 27	10 x 4 = 40	6 x 5 = 30	97/25 = 3.9
2. Properly sequenced?		3 x 2 =6	5 x 3 = 15	12 x 4 = 48	5 x 5 = 25	94/25 = 3.7
3. Intelligently time-tabled (e.g. to give variety)?	4 x 1 = 4	6 x 2 = 12	10 x 3 = 30	5 x 4 = 20		66/25 = 2.6
4. Etc.						

Figure 8.20   *Calculation of a Mean (Average) Response*

For comparative purposes the mean (average) response can be calculated for each of the questions. This can be achieved by adding the totals for each of the cells and dividing this by the number of students responding (25 in this case). So, for Question 1 the mean response is (27 + 40 + 30) = 97 / 25 = 3.9.

In consequence, the mean response for each of the questions will allow specific comparisons between the questions to be made. It can be seen that there is 1.1 difference between questions 2 and 3, but only 0.2 difference between questions 1 and 2, and that question 1 receives the 'best' result and question 3 the worst.

3.5   Writing a course report

A necessary part of any evaluation that you have completed is the preparation of a report to convey the results and conclusions to interested parties. There are many different ways in which your report may be written but generally there are commonalities in the different formats. Reports usually contain four main divisions: an introduction, the methodology used, presentation and analysis of data, and conclusions and recommendations. This format reflects the stages of the evaluation process. The headings shown in Figure 8.21 expand upon each of the main divisions and may help you to write your report. This list of items is fairly comprehensive but is not meant to be a rigid guideline of every step you must take.

---

1. Introduction

    (a)   Reasons for the evaluation.

    (b)   Aims to be achieved.

    (c)   Key questions to be answered.

    (d)   Any limitations.

2. Methodology

    (a)   Sources of data.

    (b)   Data gathering instruments.

    (c)   Procedures employed.

3. Presentation and Analysis of Data

    (a)   Presentation of findings.

    (b)   Tables and Figures (usually incorporated into the findings).

4. Conclusions and Recommendations

    (a)   Conclusions.

    (b)   Recommendations.

Figure 8.21 *Format of a Report*

Before deciding upon the final format it is necessary to ask yourself what is essential in order to provide an easily understood report, and how do you provide evidence that the recommendations are solidly based? An outline is effective if it helps to identify and order the sub-divisions of the report's major sections. Obviously the outline must precede the actual writing of the report since it is expected to serve as a guide for the writing that lies ahead. An effective outline is a check for coverage and an assurance for sequence and logical presentation of ideas and items.

Conclusions and recommendations of a course report

These two aspects of the report are very important: they are why all of the work has been completed. Often, the two are confused but, in fact they are very different. The conclusion represents your judgment based on the evaluation data. There are two types of conclusion: (i) pre-determined decision situations and (ii) exploratory conclusions. In pre-determined decision situations a conclusion would be based on a synthesis of information about the particular decision. You have to draw your conclusion in the light of, say, political and social forces both inside and outside the education or training establishment. It is no good drawing conclusions that you know could not work due to cost. The second type of conclusion is more exploratory in nature. Exploratory evaluation is initiated to explore general concerns or feelings about the adequacy of a course. That is, if a course leader believes that a course has its shortcomings, but has not collected data on which to base the opinion, an evaluation study may be carried out to identify areas or components of the course which need changes.

Recommendations must be based on the conclusions. It can be useful to organise the recommendations around areas upon which you have placed special importance. For example the recommendations may be organised under content area, teaching, personnel, course management, or support services. Good organisation will assist the reader to have a clearer appreciation of the importance of your recommendations. Conciseness in the recommendations section is a desirable characteristic. A lengthy section may produce boredom and lead to the rejection of even the good recommendations that are presented.

You should remember that the recommendations are a basis for action, and will be translated into policy by the decision makers. Therefore, you need to consider that decision makers have their own barriers to overcome. The recommendations, to assist this, may be presented in rank order. Recommendations that are socially, economically or politically unacceptable need to be adapted accordingly.

4.   Developing Professionally

4.1   Evaluating one's own practice

It is difficult to read anything about teacher education without coming across the terms 'reflection' or 'reflective practitioner'. These are indeed very important concepts and in this section we explore reflective practice, see its relationship to Kolb's model, and then the value of the simplification of Kolb's model by Gibbs. Throughout this book we have endeavoured to relate theoretical aspects to your own teaching situation, so we show how Gibbs is the basis for a structured PDJ (Professional Development Journal). Reflection is not an easy process and, initially, this structured approach is beneficial. Finally, just to prove that it can be done! we show an example of an entry in a PDJ.

Have you ever had a disagreement with someone and afterwards thought to yourself, 'I wish I had said so and so?' We often replay a scenario in our minds and think about what was actually said and what we could (or should) have said. This is quite natural and is a good basis for learning. Indeed it is, in very basic terms, the essence of the reflective process.

The key figure in the Reflective Education movement is Donald Schon. He was interested in how people in different professions solve their work problems and how their learning develops with experience in their chosen profession. He examined five professions: Engineering, Architecture, Management, Psychotherapy and Town Planning, and reported his views (Schon, 1983). His work was well received and his second book on the subject, Educating the Reflective Practitioner (Schon, 1987), rapidly became a classic text. There are many definitions of reflective practice, and perhaps an appropriate one is given by Reid (1993) who states, 'Reflective Practice is a process of reviewing an experience from practice in order to describe, analyse and evaluate and so informs learning from practice.' This relates rather well to the work of Kolb (1984) who expanded the Experience, Reflection, Learning model into his own four stage model of learning. (See Figure 8.22).

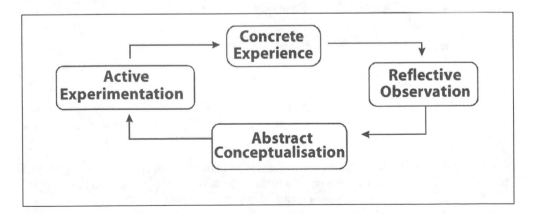

Figure 8.22 *Kolb's Four Stage Model of Learning*

As we found in Chapter Two, Kolb's use of unusual concepts, e.g. concrete experience, and other jargon can make his work rather difficult to understand. Gibbs (1988) comes to our rescue with his much more accessible model, the Reflective Cycle, which is shown in Figure 8.23.

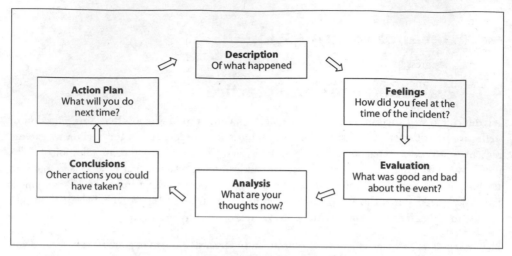

Figure 8.23 *The Reflective Cycle*

If we return to the above scenario, rather than just thinking about the disagreement in general as we do normally, the Reflective Cycle ensures a more rigorous approach. We start with the description: this is merely recall and is the lowest level of learning in the cognitive domain. However, the remaining five steps cause us to think more deeply about the issues and can lead to very valuable insights.

A sign of a true professional is to undergo an experience, reflect upon it, and learn so that there is an improvement in their professional practice. It sounds easy and to some extent it is. However, becoming reflective is, generally speaking, not a quick process. Most colleagues find that they need some form of framework in order to make a start. They also find that the views of an experienced colleague often provide valuable insights. Our experience shows that the process of moving from intuitive teaching to a structured, reflective process takes a year or more.

The following is an example of the structure of a professional journal, which we have used successfully with our own students. You can see the links to Gibbs Reflective Cycle.

4.1.1 Your PDJ

Your PDJ (Professional Development Journal) is a very important part of the process of becoming a better teacher. Its prime purpose is to provide a framework which helps you to reflect on your own development. The nature of your PDJ should, therefore, be *reflective* rather than *descriptive*. It is easy to describe what you do, but becoming and remaining reflective is much more demanding. The ideas we describe in this section will give you a good start.

Your thoughts should focus around the aims of the teacher-training course you are following as well as the Standards. Your PDJ may well become part of the evidence you present to show your progress and achievements. If you are working with a mentor or tutor (even both), you should ask for them to review what your write and too add their own comments to your PDJ, when appropriate. A well-proven structure for your PDJ is as follows:

- Initial analysis.
- Critical incidents.
- Periodic reviews.
- Final review.

You are encouraged to reflect upon your:

- Ability to carry out an initial analysis of your strengths and weaknesses.
- Progress in teaching, training and assessment.
- Writing assignments required on your course of study.
- Personal learning during the course.
- Performance as a teacher.
- Strengths and potentials for further development.

The *Initial Analysis* should be, as its name suggest, your first entry. You should focus on your strengths, potential, your perceived concerns and perhaps your ambitions. As with all entries in your PDJ, you should be as honest as you can. This initial analysis now forms the benchmark for your reflections.

We shall come to critical incidents soon. *Periodic Reviews* provide a regular opportunity for you to examine your progress. You may find it helpful to consider:

- Progress in preparing to teach.
- Experiences of teaching to date.
- Reactions your teacher-training course.
- Achievement of the Standards so far.
- Reading, visits and other activities.
- Evaluations of teaching sessions.
- Reaction to tutor or mentor guidance.
- Any other issues which are important to you.

The Final Review and Evaluation should be as comprehensive as possible in order to demonstrate your progress and achievements. Go back to the Initial Analysis and read the Periodic Reviews and Critical Incidences. You will be amazed at the progress you have made and so can start to develop an action plan for your further development. You could include your views on:

- Personal achievements in your own learning.
- Progress as a teacher.
- The value of your teacher-training course.
- The value of the Standards.
- Progress in your use of ILT.
- Future developments and progression in the college/profession.

The use of *Critical Incidents* was pioneered by an American psychologist called Henagan. The critical incident technique is a valuable way of encouraging reflection. The word 'critical' tends to make you think of a negative situation such as critical care in a medical emergency but Benner (1984) suggested a range of incidents such as a lesson which:

- The style of your teaching really made a difference to student learning.
- Went unusually well.
- Was not as successful as planned.
- Was very ordinary/typical.
- Was particularly demanding.

You should try to analyse the incident as fully and as clearly as possible. You could include:

- A description of the context (class, topic, venue, time etc.).
- A detailed account of what happened.
- Why the incident was 'critical' to you.
- What were your concerns at the time.
- What were your feelings during and after the incident.
- What was the most demanding aspect.
- What was particularly satisfying about the incident.
- What will you do next time.
- What have you learned.

Notice how the above list takes you from being merely descriptive to being more thoughtful i.e. becoming reflective. Becoming a reflective teacher is not easy and it does take some time and effort to achieve, but once you are using reflective practices, you will find teaching a much rewarding role.

The following is a worked example of a critical incident: *I work as a lecturer in a small FE college teaching catering students. I am in the early stages of my teacher-training so I am going to use the Reece and Walker framework so that I have some structure for my account of a critical incident.*

Description of context: *My students are 16-18 year-olds who work in the college kitchen learning how to prepare and cook food for use in the college training restaurant which serves customers from the locality. I want my students to know what is meant by good customer service, their part in the process and how they need to work together with the servers (waiters/waitresses). My students, instead of cooking, are exchanging places with the trainee servers who are taught by one of my colleagues.*

What happened?: *I worked with my colleague (Sam) and we briefed our respective students, my students dressing as and (briefly) training for, the servers role. Then disaster! Some of the customers telephoned to say that they could not attend. Help! I had too many servers for too few customers. I rushed to Sam who said 'why not use some of your students as customers rather than servers'. I was not sure about this but Sam is a very good teacher so this is what I did. The mail went quite smoothly and the students appeared to enjoy their new roles, especially the 'customers'. We had a debriefing session as usual (perhaps I should call it reflection). The students were even more vocal than usual but their views and comments were really good. I got the 'content' that I expected to get about the need for the servers and kitchen staff to work as a team, to be professional, and so on. But what really surprised me was comments from the students in the role of customers. They felt intimidated by some of the servers (yes, their own classmates). As we explored this we found that few young people go to 'posh restaurants' and the servers appeared to be aloof or snobbish. So then we discussed getting the balance right between respectful serving and being too matey. I did not expect this but the students were really interested.*

Why it was critical: *This was the first time I had planned to do a simulation to teach students rather than just telling them in the classroom. It was also a lesson which looked as if it would have to be abandoned when some of the customers did not turn up.*

My concerns: *It would be 'safe' to tell the students about service but I thought the experience in the training restaurant would be better. However, lots of things could go wrong and the students night not learn what I wanted them to learn.*

Feelings during and after: *When some of the customers did not turn up, I really felt in a panic. San reassured me and I followed Sam's advice. The session went well but the best bit was the discussion at the end. It was good to see the students so animated and excited. I was surprised about some students (the eaters) feeling intimidated. I would never have thought of that.*

Most demanding: *Two aspects were demanding. Firstly, trying to keep cool when things appeared to be going wrong i.e. customers not attending. Thank goodness for Sam! Secondly, having the courage to allow the students to take a different role to that I planned.*

Most satisfying: *The lesson went really well and the students really enjoyed it. I think they like being treated as adults! We had unplanned learning – and it was good. We have just covered concept attainment models in our teacher-training course (I like de Cecco best). I suddenly realised that I was already teaching concepts and when I compared the way I was teaching 'service', it was just like the model. I did not think of using negative example as mentioned in the model but the students themselves managed to bring that out.*

Next time: *I will have more confidence to be flexible and accept there will be times when I have to depart from my lesson plan.*

What I have learned: *I must try to keep cool under pressure and make the best of the situation. The theory of concept attainment works and I can use it in future.*

You can see from the account of a critical incident that the teacher started with a *description* of the event. As the framework was followed, simple recall was replaced by a more *reflective* view of the experience. The framework provides a good starting point for your PDJ and as you gain more experience, you will find that you will reduce your reliance on the model.

You will find that using a PDJ is a good way to structure your reflection. We suggest that you make an entry every two weeks or so and obtain feedback from your tutor or mentor. You will probably find that your initial entries tend to be descriptive but, with experience and thoughtful feedback, your entries will become more and more reflective. It is one thing to read about something but it is another to actually do it, so we have provided a 'worked example' in order that you can see a typical journal entry.

4.2   Self-Assessment Documents (SAD)

Many colleges use the Course Team Report to feed directly into self-assessment and operational planning document. Figure 8.24 shows part of a typical document. The document forms the basis of an operational plan which is a working document for the following year. The Self-assessment grid maps also maps to the OFSTED, Common Inspection Framework (CIF) covering the 5 Key Questions set out in the New CIF, as well as the Quality Criteria which are featured in the Framework. Note the Common Inspection Framework sets out the principles requirements for inspections in post 16 non higher education. For further information see OFSTED/ALI, (2001), The Common Inspection Framework.

Once combined with all other college courses, the self-assessment document identifies strengths and weaknesses of the college as a whole and forms the basis for the OFSTED inspection.

COURSE TEAM SELF ASSESSMENT AND OPERATIONAL PLAN JULY 2005 – C&Guilds 7407

FACULTY:		COURSE TEAM:		
1. HOW WELL DO LEARNERS ACHIEVE?				
EVALUATION ISSUES	*QUALITY CRITERIA*	**Key Strengths/*Areas for improvement***	EVIDENCE	LOCATION
1.1 success in achieving challenging targets, including qualifications and learning goals, with trends over time, and any significant variations between groups of learners e.g. 16-18 year olds and adult learners (3)	*Results and retention rates compare well with local and national averages*	• **Stage I achievement rates above B/M** • **Stage II Retention and Achievement rates above benchmark** • *Stage I retention figures below B/M*	• Ach %, BM • Ret 94%, Ach 97% Benchmark 89%, and 79% • Ret %, BM	• CTH
	Trends in performance over time show continuous improvement or the maintenance of very high standards	• **Continued improving of Retention and Achievement figures**	• 03-04 90% 97% • 02-03 87%, 80%	• CTH
	Analysis of added value indicates that learners make at least the progress expected of them		•	•
	Learners reach appropriate levels in key skills consistent with their main programme of study or training		•	•
1.2 the standards of learners' work in relation to their learning goals	*Standards are consistently high across the provider's work*	• **External verifiers endorse high standard of learners portfolios**	• EV reports • 2005, 2004	• CTH
	Challenging learning goals and targets are achieved	•	•	•

Figure 8.24   *Part of a Course Self-Assessment Document and Linked to OFSTED common inspection framework (CIF)*

4.2.1   Internal and external verifiers

Although not strictly a course review, the internal and external verifiers give feedback on quality issues relating to the course.

Most courses where work is assessed and compared to a standard is subject to internal and external verification. The internal verifier is internal to the college and often is responsible for quality procedures. These not only reflect the standard of work submitted and assessed but also procedures such as plagiarism, re-submissions of work, standards of teaching and teacher qualifications etc.

The external verifier (EV), appointed by Qualification Body, has the responsibility of ensuring the college is working to a nationally set standard. Many courses have a visit from the EV at least once, often twice a year. Current trends of reducing costs have often limited the number of visits or visits have been replaced by materials being sent through the post. Like the internal verifier, they will look at work to ensure standard are met but they will often ask to meet and talk to students on the course asking questions about teaching, problems they have had, any resources issues and so on. Figure 8.25 shows a section of an External Verifier form.

Management Systems	Yes/always						No/never						
There is an effective communication system between all levels of staff and in all directions (including satellites, placements and peripatetic staff).	o	o	o	o	o	o	o	o	o	o	o	o	
An appeals procedure that candidates understand is issued.	o	o	o	o	o	o	o	o	o	o	o	o	
Equal opportunities/access policy is documented.	o	o	o	o	o	o	o	o	o	o	o	o	
Implementation of equal opportunities/access policy is reviewed.	o	o	o	o	o	o	o	o	o	o	o	o	
Induction materials for new assessors/IVs/QA staff are adequate.	o	o	o	o	o	o	o	o	o	o	o	o	
Centre model. *Please shade all responses that are appropriate.*	o	o	o	o	o	o	o	o	o	o	o	o	

Assessment is mostly: at the main site	o	in satellites	o	in the workplace	o
Assessors are mostly: based at the main site or satellite	o	peripatetic	o	Work based	o
IVs/QA staff are mostly: based at the main site or satellite	o	peripatetic	o	Work based	o
Evidence from the workplace is mostly based on witness testimony			o		
The EV has confirmed the expiry date of awards with the centre staff	Yes		o	No	o

Resources	Yes/always						No/never						
Equipment, procedures and accommodation are suitable, appear safe and are fit for use.	o	o	o	o	o	o	o	o	o	o	o	o	

Figure 8.25 *Example of the Typical Feedback Form from an External Verifier*

4.2.2 Producing the Self-Assessment Report (SAR)

In section 2.3 we discussed the SAR and in section 4.2, the SAD (Self-assessment Document). Now we are going to concentrate upon the *process* of self-assessment.

The Learning of Skills Act (HMSO, 2000) requires all FE providers to undertake an annual self-assessment. The focus is on the quality of provision, with the need to produce a development plan. The Act defines self-assessment as a 'structural way of involving teaching staff in evaluating their provision', which implies input from all levels in the organisation: individuals, course teams, departments and the organisation as an entity. The key feature of the process is the need to *improve* quality, not merely to report the state of play. Evidence is crucial. You need to:

- Review your performance against agreed goals.
- Compare your performance against previous years and that of others.
- Compare your performance against other providers.
- Identify your strengths and weaknesses.
- Identify and respond to the needs of your students and other interested groups.
- Prepare for reviews and inspections.

The (NIACE) National Organisation for Adult Learning, and the Learning and Skills Development Agency (formerly known as FEDA), (Kenway, and Reisenberger, 2001) jointly produced a guide for producing the SAR. They proposed a four-stage process which has been adapted in Figure 8.26 below. It identifies a logical flow from (i) preparation to (ii) carrying out, to (iii) development and, finally, to (iv) review. The sequence is designed to match the tasks and decisions that you should follow for the successful completion of the SAR and the development plan. You should note that effective self-assessment (i) encourages all levels of staff to evaluate their performance, and (ii) involves students, employers and others in the process. We will now consider each of the four stages shown in Figure 8.26.

1. Preparing for self-assessment	☐ What is to be self-assessed? ☐ Who will do what? ☐ When will it be carried out? ☐ How will it be carried out?
2. Carrying out self-assessment	☐ Identify and gather evidence. ☐ Analyse data and decide strengths and weaknesses. ☐ Draft self-assessment report (SAR). ☐ Decide grades.
3. Development Planning	☐ Produce plan to improve performance. ☐ Get approval for plan. ☐ Monitor actions systematically. ☐ Report regularly on progress.
4. Review	☐ What worked? ☐ What didn't work? ☐ Changes to processes.

Figure 8.26 *The Process of Self-Assessment*

The preparation for writing the SAR involves you making decisions about *what* to assess, *when* it will be done and *how* it will be completed. Remember that the judgements made in the SAR must be based on evidence. The 'how' is crucial and should include:

- A regular system of classroom observation with grades.
- Records of guidance given to students.
- Up-to-date feedback and evaluations from students and others.
- Up-to-date and analysed enrolment, retention and achievement data.
- Explicit internal and external moderation systems.

The first task involved in the second step, *carrying out self-assessment,* is the gathering of evidence. Typical evidence required includes:

- Feedback from student questionnaires.
- Results of evaluations.
- Achievement rates.
- Results of classroom observations together with grades.
- Internal and external verifier/examiner reports.

The SAR is a summary of the evidence that has been collected. It will help inspectors greatly if you indicate where the evidence can be found. Individual members of staff need to complete their own assessments and evaluations. These feed into course, curriculum area, and college annual self-assessment reports and eventually into the Development Plan.

The data needed to support judgements about student achievements and performance include: enrolment, retention, achievement and progression rates in the manner shown previously in Figure 8.13.

Data to support the quality of teaching and learning could involve:

- Grades and reports on lesson observations.
- Student satisfaction surveys e.g. (see Figure 8.14).
- Course evaluations.
- Staff development activities (e.g. see Figure 8.15).
- Course handbooks, minutes of team meetings and reviews.

Data to support learning could include:

- Needs analyses and individual student learning plans (see Figure 7.28).
- Tutors' assessment records.

Records of trends in performance are expected by the (LSC) Learning and Skills Council and the (ALI) Adult Learning Inspectorate at their inspections. Typical trend data for a three year period are shown in Figure 8.27 using the data from the forms in Figure 8.13.

Enrolment Rates

	2006/2007	2005/2006	2004/2005
	18	21	20

Retention Rates

	2006/2007			2005/2006			2004/2005		
	Start	Finish	%	Start	Finish	%	Start	Finish	%
National Benchmark	18	16	88	21	17	81 75	20	15	75

Proposed Retention Targets

	Start 2006/2007 18	Finish 2006/2007 16 (88%)	Target for 2007/2008 91%

Achievement Rates

	2006/2007		2005/2006		2004/2005	
	Pass	%	Pass	%	Pass	%
National Benchmark	17	95	18	86 75	15	75

Observation of Teaching and Learning Grades and National Average

	Grade 1	Grade 2	Grade 3	Grade 4	Grade 5
Course Team	0	2 (33%)	4 (66%)	0	0
National Average	(17%)	(45%)	(31%)	6%	0%

Figure 8.27 *Examples of Trend Data for a Course Self-Assessment Report*

Your data needs to be compared in terms of how you are doing within your course team, within your department, within your college and compared to the national average benchmarks. For instance from the data shown in Figure 8.27, the following might be indicated:

- Enrolments have varied little over the last three years.

- Retention rates have increased from 75% in 2004/05 to 88% in 2006/07 and it is planned that these should continue to rise in 2007/08 to 91%.

- Achievement rates have also climbed over the three year period and are well above the national average. This would indicate a strength to be noted in the SAR.

- 33% of the lessons observed were considered outstanding (grades 1 or 2) which is below the national average. This would indicate a weakness to be noted in the SAR.

The drafting of the SAR involves encouraging staff to be 'reflective practitioners'. It is easier if there have been regular lesson observations and reviews. Each course team should have a leader to plan and manage the team self-assessment process and take responsibility for producing the report. Figure 8.24 has already shown part of a Course SAR that has been completed for a course. This concentrates on the key strengths and weaknesses of the course, what evidence is available and where this evidence is located. On inspection, both LSC and ALI will look at your evidence and decide whether it is adequate justification for what has been claimed. As a general guide, evidence should be:

- Valid – it directly supports your claims.

- Quantifiable – using internal and external performance indicators.

- Sufficient – adequate to support your claims.

- Current – recent to provide an accurate picture.

- Accurate – verifiable from evidence.

Writing evaluative statements is a skill. NIACE (op cit) provide us with some examples of evaluative statements which could lead to problems and how they might be improved. These include:

Original Statement	Concerns	Improved Statement
There is a file of fully minuted teaching team meetings.	This is a statement of fact. It is a norm (if it did not exist it would be a weakness).	Well minuted monthly meetings of the teaching team address emerging issues promptly. Outcomes that are reviewed at future meetings and shared with other teams.
Student achievement on the course is high.	This is vague. It lacks impact.	Achievement on the course has consistently improved, exceeding national level benchmarks by 10% over the last 3 years.
All students on the course receive relevant and informative course handbooks.	This is a statement of fact and not an evaluative judgement. It could be a norm. It lacks impact. What is the consequence?	All students receive timely (in some cases pre-course), relevant and informative course handbooks with full assessment schedules, which students report usefully assist them in planning their work.

An important aspect of both self-assessment and inspection lies in the grading of work. The Inspectorate's five point-scale for learning and leadership and seven point scales for lesson observation are shown in Figure 8.28.

Five-point scale for areas of learning and leadership	Five point scale for lesson observation
1. Outstanding	1. Excellent/very good
2. Good	2. Good
3. Satisfactory	3. Satisfactory
4. Unsatisfactory	4. Unsatisfactory
5. Very Weak	5. Poor/very poor

Figure 8.28   *Scales for Grading Learning and Leadership and Lesson Observation*

The problem, of course, with grades is that most of us tend to concentrate upon the grade at the expense of the justification that is provided. We are like our students: they only look at their mark and tend to ignore the written comments. You should avoid the temptation to state that you are better than you really are. When you are honest about weaknesses and show how you plan to tackle them in a development plan, you have a better chance of getting supportive feedback from an inspection.

The third step in the process *development planning* identifies how you expect to improve by building upon strengths and addressing the weaknesses. These strengths and weaknesses provide the main information for the development plan.

Objectives and targets for improvement will need to be precise rather than vague. The objectives should be SMART (Specific, Measurable, Achievable, Results-oriented, and Time-bound). A simple improvement may only need a straightforward action with an end date. Some will be more complex and need staff development and may involve others outside of the team.

An example of how a weakness of 'low retention rates' might be addressed is given in Figure 8.29.

Weakness identified in SAR: Low Retention Rates			
Concern	**Action**	**By whom**	**Timescale**
1. The reason for previous years drop-out rate will be thoroughly investigated.	Develop a questionnaire.	Course Team	September 2006
	Send questionnaires to last years drop-outs.	Course Leader	October 2006
	Analyse results.	Course Leader	November 2006
2. Lesson plans will be investigated to see if variety for students is built into lessons.	Collect lesson plans from all full and part-time staff.	Course Leader	October 2006
	Interrogate plans to see if appropriate learning methods are used.	Course leader	November 2006
3. Course timetable will be investigated.	Is induction period adequate?	Course Team	September 2006
	Are needs analyses of students adequate?	Course Team	November 2006
	Should more tutorial time be given?	Course Team	January 2007
4. Present cohort to be monitored.	Develop questionnaire and distribute to measure student satisfaction.	Course Leader	Sept-Dec 2006
5. Review changes.		Course Team	June 2007

Figure 8.29   *Example of how a Weakness Might be Addressed*

Figure 8.29 has three different stages which are relevant to many areas:

- *Preparing* – developing of materials (and staff) to make the investigation.
- *Implementing* strategy involving a series of actions.
- *Review* – monitoring of how it is going.

The fourth and final stage of the self-assessment process involves *review* of the process. As suggested in Figure 8.26, this involves the identification of (i) what worked, (ii) what didn't, and (iii) changes that are needed. There is no doubt that self-assessment, although initially a part of an external requirement, should become a regular and integrated part of all quality assurance procedures.

4.3 Engaging in Continuing Professional Development (CPD)

An outcome of the self-assessment process is professional development. Not only do you need to produce a plan to improve professional performance for a specific issue, you need to ensure that professional development becomes a continuous process.

In 2005 the government announced plans for the reform of initial teacher training (DfES, 2005). Future teachers entering the profession will be required to have a 'licence to practice'. Trainee teachers into FE will be required to complete an initial 'passport to teaching', assessed at level 3 or above involving about 30 guided learning hours. They will subsequently need to complete full teacher training within 5 years of completing their initial passport. This will result in the award of Qualified Teaching Learning and Skills (QTLS) status. Teaching licences will be renewed annually by completing an annual tariff of continuing professional development (CPD).

The Foster Report (DfES, 2005) noted the need for a major enhancement of workforce development. Support for teachers and trainers to develop and improve their practice was considered crucial. (ITT) Initial Teacher Training needs to be reinforced by CPD. It was proposed that, by September 2007, the government would introduce a regulatory CPD requirement for FE colleges. The requirement involves:

- All teachers to fulfil, at the very least, 30 hours of CPD a year, with a reduced amount for part-time teachers, (there are similar expectations for managers and leaders).
- Colleges and providers to draw-up development plans for CPD.
- Teaching staff to maintain a portfolio of CPD that shows evidence of industrial/subject updating including:
  - membership of appropriate professional bodies;
  - development of skills in subject teaching;
  - effective application of e-learning techniques;
  - application of diversity and equal opportunities principles;
    use of student feedback to improve performance.

The Institute for Learning (IfL) was launched in 2002 and has been given an increasingly important role by the government dealing with initial teacher training in Post Continuing Education and Training (PCET). IfL will be the body who are to be responsible for the awarding of the licence to practice in the PCET sector of education. In the proposed new system, due to start in 2007, the IfL will be responsible for:

- Designing a professional development record that staff can use while undergoing ITT and CPD.
- Registering trainees with a 'passport to learning' once they have undertaken initial assessment.
- Awarding staff a threshold licence to practice.
- Registering staff who then enrol for a full qualification.
- Awarding QTLS to those completing the full qualification.
- Continuing to register staff who complete appropriate CPD.

(Deasy, M, 2006)

From this it is clear that IfL is the organisation that will help individuals through the range of CPD on offer. To this end, the Institute has researched the recording of CPD activities for an online pilot scheme. Using a portal on the IfL website (www.ifl.ac.uk/cpd_portal/cpd_index.html), staff can highlight:

    (i)   Their CPD needs.

    (ii)   Record activities.

    (ii)   Plan further staff development.

    (iv) Provide evidence to show that they remain in good professional standing.

It is going to be important to have a strict process to both design and implement an annual CPD plan to initially gain an ITT award and to have your licence renewed annually. Currently many of the ITT providers have developed their own Professional Development Records (PDRs) which consist of self-assessment tasks and the setting of targets for their own professional development both during and after their ITT programme. The IfL has developed a five-step planning cycle process to assist you. These steps are:

    Step 1. Initial reflection to support CPD.

    Step 2. Estimating areas for development.

    Step 3. Designing a personal development plan.

    Step 4. Making a personal development record.

    Step 5. Keeping track of professional activities.

Each of these important areas are now considered in detail.

Step 1   Initial reflection

IfL suggest that you need to reflect upon your previous activities and current needs in order to plan your self-development. They suggest that you use standards (e.g. FENTO standards), to help with your reflection. The standards will get you thinking about the key areas involved in teaching and learning like planning and preparing teaching, assessing the outcomes of learning, evaluating one's own performance, and so on. IfL also suggest that you might access other standards through the LLUK website (http://www.lifelonglearninguk.org/standards/standards_index. html).

Apart from the teaching skills discussed above, you might also reflect upon your own:

Personal Skills – such as time management, problem solving skills, reflective skills and handling conflict.

Studying Skills – such as analytical skills, speed reading, research methods, note-taking.

Student Support – such as dealing with Dyslexia, IT skills.

Subject Skills – such as subject specialist knowledge, current initiatives in your own subject.

You could also use the self-assessment that you have made in preparation for your SAR. You might reflect upon the information that you have gathered from feedback and evaluations from your students, enrolment, retention and achievement statistics for your classes, feedback from classroom observations, feedback from internal and external moderators, and so on.

The importance of this first step lies in the identification of aspects that you think might be helpful for your continuous professional development.

Step 2   Where am I?

The second step involves the identification of key issues and current strengths and weaknesses to help with the preparation of the-personal development plan. This builds on the outcomes of your initial reflection and key issues and areas that you think need developing. IfL suggest a format shown in Figure 8.30 as the basis for recording the decisions that you make.

Current Activities	Strengths
This is a list of your current activities and responsibilities.	List the strengths that you have developed in the current activities that you perform.
Areas of Development	**Unused Competences**
Note here any aspects identified in the initial reflection that you consider need developing	Here list any aspects that you are good at but are not presently using.

Figure 8.30   *Format for Identification of 'Where am I'*

The importance of this second stage lies in the identification of your strengths and the areas to be developed. You will need to not only build upon your strengths but also to minimise any weaknesses.

Step 3   Designing PDP (Personal Development Plan)

You have now reflected and identified strengths and development needs which leads naturally to the design of a plan. The suggestion for this third step is that, using the outcomes from Areas for Development in Step 2, you write a list of

    (i)   what you want/need to learn,

    (ii) personal development objectives, and

    (iii) what will I do?

For instance, in response to (i) above you might need to learn how to make use of e-learning methods in your classrooms. The SMART objective associated with this could be:

> 'I will attend workshops to learn how to use interactive whiteboard, PowerPoint and chat rooms by June 2006 so that I can use them in next session's teaching'

Generic Training	
Accredited	**Accredited**
City and Guilds 7407 Training for Trainers (OCN)	Assessor Awards First Aid Courses
Non-Accredited	**Non-Accredited**
Induction programme Observation and review as probationer Use of independent learning materials	Observation from internal or external assessor Appraisal review discussions Local workshops (e.g. equal opportunities) Local conference Use of independent learning materials
Initial Training	**On-going Training**
Accredited	**Accredited**
CLAIT Course Developing Skills for IT Tutors (OCN) City and Guilds Certificate for Adult Learning Support	Higher qualifications in own subject Higher pedagogic qualifications
Non-Accredited	**Non-Accredited**
Basic Skills awareness training Pre-entry curriculum training ESOL curriculum training	Team meetings Support from local curriculum groups ALBSU and ESOL Conferences Dyslexia awareness groups Local conferences Techniques for dealing with conflict talk Time management course Speed reading course
Subject/Curriculum-specific Training	

Figure 8.31   *Types of Programme and Activities to Achieve a PDR or PDP*

The final part of this third step is to decide what you will do. Figure 8.31, which has been adapted from a NIACE publication (Ewens, D. 2003) shows the types of programme and activity that might be useful to achieve the objectives of your PDR. The figure helps you to identify 'What will I do?' to achieve your objectives.

Step 4 Personal Development Record

Those of you who have recently completed an ITT programme may well be familiar with the completion of a professional development record (PDR). Typically these require the following aspects to be recorded:

- Personal information including personal and programme details and a professional context showing teaching institution, subjects taught, mentor's name, etc.
- Log of tutorials with tutor and/or mentor detailing what was discussed and agreed.
- Log of key tasks/assignments completed with date when achieved.
- A self-assessment profile to identify current personal skills and needs which you intend to achieve.
- Setting targets for tutorials in relation to language, literacy, numeracy and IT.
- Assessment of practical teaching with assessors comments, and your own reflection on the lesson.
- A reflective overview of the programme.

The IfL suggest that you note (i) activities that you have completed, (ii) what you learned from each, (iii) how you will use them, and (iv) any further actions and goals for the coming year. This latter aspect ensures the continuity of the planning processes.

Step 5 Keeping track of professional activities

To achieve this step you need to keep a journal, diary or database of all activities, week by week, that have added to your professional development. This, IfL suggest, could include reflective practice with mentors or colleagues, INSET sessions, moderation meetings, updating knowledge and skills, attendance at conferences, and workshops, current reading on your subject, recent industrial or commercial experience, mentoring experience, visits to other institutions, and so on.

It should also be remembered that, as you are required to show at least 30 hours per year involvement on CPD activities, for each of the activities that you note in this step, you should also indicate the time that you spend on them.

Achieving the LLUK Professional Standards

Standards
Domain A: Professional values and practice
AK4.2   The impact of own practice on individuals and their learning.
AK4.3   Ways to reflect, evaluate and use research to develop own practice, and to share good practice with others.
AK7.2   Own role in the quality cycle.
AK7.3   Ways to implement improvements based on feedback received.
Domain B: Learning and Teaching
BK2.6   Ways to evaluate own practice in terms of efficiency and effectiveness.
Domain D: Planning for learning
DK2.1   The importance of including learners in the planning process.
DK3.1   Ways to evaluate own role and performance in planning learning.
Domain E: Assessment for learning
EK4.2   The role of feedback in effective evaluation and improvement of own assessment skills.
EK5.1   The role of assessment and associated organisational procedures in relation to the quality cycle.
EK5.2   The assessment requirements of individual learning programmes and procedures for recording internal and/or external assessments.

Achieving the LLUK Professional Standards

Standards	Ways in which you can show that you have achieved the Standards	See Section
AK4.2 AK4.3	1. Use the checklist in section 2.4 of this chapter to review your own teaching. For each of the questions that you have answered 'No', explain how you could change your response to a 'Yes'.	2
AK4.2 AK4.3	2. Obtain a copy of the Self-Assessment document for one of the courses that you teach and identify the 'Areas for Improvement'. Explain how you would address these areas and ensure that you are able to justify that they have been addressed.	4
AK7.2	3. Obtain a copy of your organisation's Quality Assurance document and identify your own role in the quality cycle. Evaluate your own contribution in terms of the course evaluations' timing and effectiveness.	3
AK7.3 BK2.6	4. Explain how you obtain feedback on your teaching from students, colleagues, internal verifiers/examiners, external verifiers/examiners, inspection reports and self assessments. Explore which of these you find most helpful and how you use the information to improve your practice.	2 and 3
AK7.3 BK2.6	5. Explain how you identify opportunities to keep your own specialist subject knowledge up-to-date.	4
AK7.3 BK2.6	6. Devise a scheme which allows you to identify, plan and engage in and record your own professional development.	4
AK7.3 BK2.6	7. Keep your Professional Development Journal up-to-date with regular and frequent entries. Ensure that you include all of the suggested aspects, especially feedback from colleagues. Examine the use that you have made of ILT within your lessons especially in areas such as resources, communications and assessment. Where there is little evidence of use, consider why this is the case and the steps that you need to take to correct these issues.	4
DK2.1 CK3.1	8. Review one of your lessons in terms of the planning processes. You might include: (a) The lesson planning process. (b) The methods and resources and assessments designed and used. (c) The use made of student opinion.	4
EK4.2 EK5.1 EK5.2	9. Explain how you obtain feedback on the effectiveness of your assessment planning, use of assessments and feedback you provide to your students.	2
EK4.2 EK5.1 EK5.2	10. Explain and justify the procedures that you use for the recording of internal and/or external assessments and judge the effectiveness of these procedures.	2

For a model approach to show how you have achieved the LLUK Professional Standards see Appendix I.

Appendix I

A Worked Example of how you may achieve the Professional Standards

The purpose of this 'worked example' or model is to indicate to you one approach that shows how you may demonstrate your achievement of the Professional Standards:

My initial thoughts

I have to demonstrate that I can achieve the Standards through developing and reflecting upon my own practice. On my teacher-training course, we have just finished the aspect which explored teaching strategies. This has given me confidence to move from my 'comfort zone' to try some new strategies with my students. I intend to achieve the standard AK 4.3.

What shall I do?

I find that a mind map or spider diagram helps me to explore what I can do and to decide what I will do.

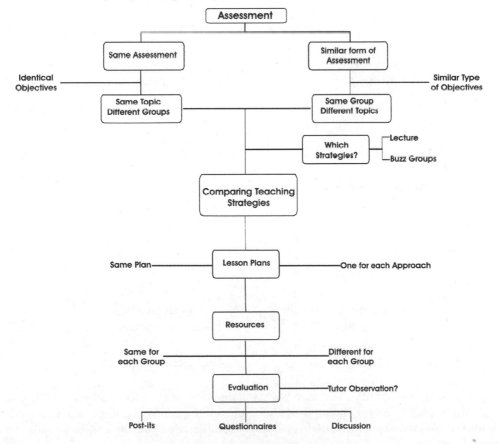

Mind map to help decision making

Decisions

I have decided:

> To teach the same topic to two similar groups.
>
> The topic selected is … … … … … …
>
> My usual teaching strategy is 'lecture' and I will use this with one group.
>
> My experiential strategy is 'buzz group' and I shall use this with the other group.
>
> To evaluate each lesson by leading a discussion with each group.
>
> To ask my tutor or mentor to observe the lessons (if they can) and give me additional feedback.

Evidence

You now need to design the two lesson plans and produce the resources.

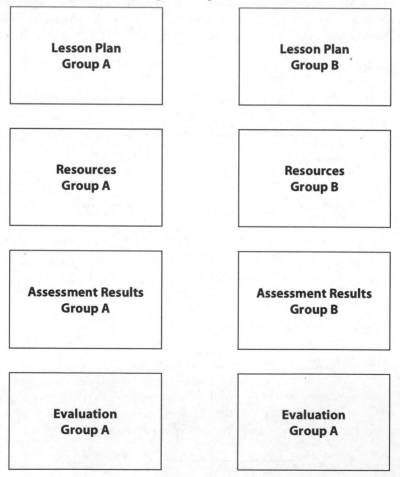

Lesson Plan Group A	Lesson Plan Group B
Resources Group A	Resources Group B
Assessment Results Group A	Assessment Results Group B
Evaluation Group A	Evaluation Group A

After teaching and evaluation has taken place, you should record your conclusions regarding the experiment and decide upon the implications for your future teaching. You should also identify the limitations of your experiment and what you would do differently if you had to repeat or undertake a similar experiment.

Glossary of Educational Terms

Adult Development and Adult Learners	Stages in adult cognitive, affective and psychomotor development and their impact on the education; social and physical environment issues typical of adults in learning settings.
Affective Domain	Involves feelings, emotions, attitudes and values.
Andragogy	The science of adult learning (usually related to a student-centred approach).
Assessment	Measurement of how effectively the students have learned; usually measured against stated learning outcomes.
Assessment – Learning	Criteria, values, methods, techniques and instruments for evaluation of learning.
Assessment – Teaching	Criteria, values, methodology, techniques and instruments for evaluation of teaching.
Assignment	Students are presented with a topic/subject or problem for an in-depth analysis.
Behaviourism	The prediction of human behaviour or learning through actions or tasks and based on responses to stimuli.
Blended Learning	Blending traditional and modern technologies to add enhance and support students learning.
Brainstorming	Teaching strategy where students generate a large number of ideas in a short time.
Byte sized Learning	Breaking the lesson down into manageable chunks of information using a wide a range of teaching strategies.
Case Studies	Use of real life incidents, critical or otherwise, or single phenomenon issues, to illustrate subject related or pedagogical issues with greater relevance..
Chalkboard	Either roller or fixed boards with a surface which will take chalk.
Checklist	A list of aspects (for example to assess) which can be 'checked-off' when they are completed.
Class Journals	Records of classroom events kept on a regular periodic basis by a class sometimes including the lecturer, to improve student-student and student-teacher communication.
Classroom Assignments	Exercises or other work intended to be performed within the class period.
Classroom Discussion	Teaching technique focused on enabling verbal feedback from students as a class to encourage participation and to evaluate the degree of learning that has taken place by both teachers and learners.
Classroom Dynamics	The process or agreed conventions of interaction among teachers and students during a class over time, and how it impacts on learning.
Classroom Research	Techniques and processes focused on formative evaluation by students of learning, teaching, and/or classroom dynamics, conducted in class.

Cognitive Domain	Involves mental processes.
Cognitivists	School of human learning with the focus on students and how they gain and organise their knowledge.
Collaborative Grading	A method of evaluation where students grade each other's work, usually in pairs.
Collaborative Learning	A generic term for learning in groups facilitated by a teacher, as opposed to learning as individuals from a teacher: includes seminars, discussion groups, etc.
Collaborative Testing	Instruments designed for testing by students of each other, teaching techniques which contemplate collaborative grading.
College Extranet	An external (private) network for sharing of resources and information across the web.
College Intranet	A network within the organisation which allows the sharing of computer hardware and software but also information such as policies, procedures, announcements, or information about new products.
Colloquium (or seminar)	Presentation of research to some group, usually at department level, and usually open to colleagues and students.
Common Skill	General or transferable skills (sometimes called core skills).
Competence	The ability to perform actions/procedures effectively in the workplace.
Computer-assisted Instruction	Instruction which includes various levels of interaction with data processing equipment; in the limit 'programmed instruction' where the student works directly with the equipment without a teacher.
Concept	Mental pictures of relationships and qualities of objects or ideas.
Concepts of Teaching	One's basic attitude or world view towards teaching and the respective roles of teacher, content, and student.
Constructivism	School of human learning which believes in the need to identify current learning prior to constructing new meaning.
Contiguity	The almost simultaneous occurrence of stimulus and response in psychomotor skill learning.
Convergent	Search for a single correct answer or solution.
Cooperative Learning	A highly structured form of collaborative learning which focuses in particular on small group approaches to problem-solving.
Copyright	The legal exclusive right that authors have to print, publish and sell their own work.
Counselling by Teachers	Teachers advising students on matters not directly connected with the course being taught, e.g. personal problems.
Course Content	The material to be covered within a course outline, which collectively for courses within the framework of a programme constitutes a curriculum.
Course Design	Sequencing modules or elements of course content in an order that facilitates learning.
Course Overlap	Material covered by more than one course in a programme of study.
Criterion	Set standard, usually to be attained during assessment.
Critical Thinking	The ability to assess and evaluate particular assertions or concepts in the light of either evidence or wider contexts.

Curriculum	Programmes for learning and those factors which influence the quality of learning.
Curriculum Development	Qualitative change in the course structure or courses making up a particular programme intended to bring a particular curriculum closer to the goals and objectives of the programme.
Curriculum Planning	The process of evaluating curriculum and implementing curriculum development.
Debate	Teaching strategy where students put points for and against an argument or motion.
Deductive	Moving from generalisations to the particular.
Demonstration	Teaching strategy usually associated with showing students a practical skill which they will then practise.
Discussion	Teaching strategy where it is planned that students will talk to each other about a topic and report back on their findings.
Differentiation	Tailoring teaching environments and practices to create appropriately different learning experiences for different students.
Distance Education	Formal learning settings where the students and the instructor are separated geographically and there is no classroom; in some applications, e.g. open learning there is no formal teaching, only prepackaged materials and a tutor.
Divergent	Process or search for a solution to a problem which has more than one answer.
Domain	A category of learning.
DST	Display screen technology – includes interactive whiteboards, televisions, plasma screens and data projectors.
e-Communications	Using a wide range of electronic communication devices such as e-mail, chat , forums to much newer technology such as blogs, webcasts and RSS feeds to keep in contact or deliver the curriculum.
e-Learning	Using a range of computing and communication devices to support learning.
e-Portfolio	Electronic version of the traditional paper based system made available via the web.
Educational Innovation	Applying creativity to teaching process, practices, or techniques.
Educational Technology	Artificial aids to teaching and learning; formal knowledge about educational processes.
Entry Behaviour	What the student knows about the topic at the start of instruction.
Essay	Student response to a question where they have structured their response themselves.
Evaluation	Applying assessment to particular situations, processes, settings, persons, or time periods, in order to derive conclusions about efficiency and/or effectiveness.
Examinations	Formal and summative evaluation of learning, usually written, but may be oral, administered periodically and as a conclusion to most credit courses.

Experimental Learning	An outcome of teaching practices generally known as 'learner-centred', where the learner's knowledge, particularly from experience is considered important, and where learners, 'act out' or simulate the content of the course in order to develop familiar as well as formal knowledge of it.
Extrinsic	Coming from outside oneself. For example, extrinsic motivation is that provided by the teacher.
Feedback	The passing of information to the student of their ability to perform a task.
Feltboard	Board covered in felt which can be used to stick pictures, shapes or words.
Field Trip Methods	Techniques and processes used for research, teaching and learning in settings outside the classroom.
Flipchart	Large pieces of paper fixed to a stand to be used in the same way as a chalkboard.
Formative	Type of assessment to help with teaching and learning. On-going assessment throughout the learning process.
Gender Differences in Instruction	Ways in which males and females differ behaviourally in instructional settings, including motor skills, participation and assertiveness, personal needs, and implications of those differences for teaching and learning.
Gestaltists	Study of human learning where understanding is based upon insight.
Grading and Testing	Assigning some rank order to students via the design and marking of assignments, including examinations e.g. criterion referenced, norm referenced etc.
Group Projects	Assignments some by two or more students, which typically take several weeks to complete, and are normally graded on an combination of individual and collective criteria.
Homework	An informal term for assignments to be done outside class, normally consisting of reading, problem sets, or writing short pieces, not usually numerically graded, in preparation for succeeding classes.
Humanist	Person who believes that learning should be based upon worth, self esteem and dignity of the individual.
Handout	Pieces of paper containing information to be given to students.
ICT	Information Communications Technology – The integrated use of computers and communications systems to process, transmit and store data and information.
ILT	Information Learning Technologies – The use of Information and communication technology to support teaching and learning, such as multimedia, e-mail, VLEs.
Inclusivity	Practices to ensure that all students in the class have an equitable opportunity to participate, achieve successful completion of the course, and develop multicultural and gender awareness.
Independent Thinking	The ability to appreciate, create, analyse, synthesise, assess and evaluate without outside assistance.
Inductive	Going from particular examples to a generalisation.
Interactive Whiteboards	Presentation device coupled to a computer. Allows the user to interact with the software, write, present as well as print directly from the board.

Institutional Environment	The culture of a particular institution, including collective and unwritten attitudes, predisposition, values etc.
Instructional Design	Principles or procedures or guidelines upon which instruction is modelled before it is put into operation.
Instructional Development	The process of assessing, improving, and updating instructional design, including measures to improve the skills of instructors.
Instructional Media	Means of communication used in teaching.
Instructional Objectives	Concise statements of what the learner is expected to accomplish during a lesson, consisting of a general instructional goal, and specific learning outcomes, normally denoting something observable or assessable.
Interdisciplinary Approach	An approach which focuses on structures or tasks of interests, regardless of disciplinary boundaries and which leads to a task-force or problem-based rather than programme orientation.
Intrinsic	Coming from within oneself.
IT	Information Technology the computer infrastructure hardware and software to retrieve, store and transmit information. Tends to have been replaced by the term ICT with the emphasis on communications.
Jobsheet	Handout containing instructions or a specification so that students can complete a piece of work.
Just-in-Time Teaching	Using e-learning devices such as chat and forums to identify students' prior knowledge of a subject to help shape the forthcoming lesson.
Keller Plan	A personalised system of instruction which is individually paced and based on mastery learning principles.
Key Skills	Are a range of essential skills that underpin success in education, employment, lifelong learning and personal development. The key skills are: communication, application of number, information technology, working with others, improving own learning and performance and problem solving.
Kinaesthetic	The perception of muscular effort.
Laboratories	Specialised classrooms, generally of two types; scientific, where experiments are carried out in support of theoretical curricula, and language, where students receive conversational practice.
Large Classes	Generally, classes with over 50 students.
Learner Productivity	The degree to which or rate at which learners advance their knowledge in terms of content and learning process, usually assessed on criteria of efficiency and effectiveness.
Learning Style	A coherent set of learner preferences for ways and means of teaching and learning.
Lecture	Teaching strategy where the passage of information is from the teacher to the student.
Lectures – Alternatives	Methods of teaching that do not involve a unilateral presentation or transmission of information by the instructor.
Lecturing	Method of teaching where the instructor transmits information to the students in a basically unilateral fashion, i.e. defines the topic, the approach, and the salient substantive information to be presented, with limited time for discussion.

Lesson Plan	A guide to what the teacher plans for the students to do in order to achieve the intended learning outcomes.
Liberal Arts Education	Curricula orientated towards the humanities and softer social sciences with an emphasis on basic knowledge of the arts and theories of social interactions and communication.
Library Research Methods	Ways and means of accessing and assembling bibliographic databases and conducting literature review, including familiarity with cataloguing and in-library citation indices and other databases.
LSC	Learning and Skills Council. Has responsibility for the funding, planning education and training for over 16-year-olds in England.
Magneticboard	Board with a steel backing upon which magnets or magnetic-backed pictures can be placed and moved around.
Mastery Learning	Where a student must learn one topic (objective) before proceeding to another.
Matching Block	Type of question where students have to match aspects in one column with those given in another.
Memory	The ability to recall information.
Mentoring	A relationship where a more experienced person provides advice, guidance, and resource to a less experienced one.
Minimum Core	A level 2 standard of literacy and numeracy that all teachers undertaking teacher training programmes must now obtain to achieve Qualified Teacher Learning and Skills (QTLS)status.
MLE	Managed Learning Environment incorporating the VLE (content and assessment) the MLE looks at the information systems such as quality assurance, student records and other data.
Model	Theoretical relationships between aspects.
Module	Discrete units of identified learning materials.
Motivation	An inclination to become involved in the learning process.
Motivating Learners	Providing incentives for or enabling learners to seek their particular learning aims, goals, or values.
Multiple-choice	Type of question where a student chooses from a number of options.
Multicultural Awareness	Sensitivity to the needs of those who come from different cultures than one's own, or that typical of the institution.
Needs Assessment	Criteria, values, methods, techniques and instruments for evaluation of conceptual and substantive requirements for learning, teaching course content and activities, and curricula.
Norm	Related to the normal distribution of the population.
Norm Referenced Assessment	Relating performance with that of a typical student population.
Objective	May be behavioural (product) or expressive (process) but is concerned with what students must be able to do.
Open Learning	Sometimes called distance learning where the teacher and the student meet infrequently. The learning material is usually written.
Overhead Projector	Machine used to project images (words and diagrams) to students.
Pedagogy	The science of teaching (usually related to a teacher dominated approach).

Peer	Of equal rank or status (e.g. a colleague or fellow student).
Peer Coaching	A type of peer consulting where pairs of teachers visit each other's classrooms, and assess performance based on pre-agreed criteria.
Peer Consulting	Collaboration with co-workers or co-paractitioners, in this context generally students and teachers, for the purposes of dealing with common problems or issues, arriving at consensus, or assessment of performance.
Peer Review	Assessment and critical review of performance by colleagues, usually applied to academic and professional activities in general.
Philosophical and Conceptual Approaches	World views, theories and schemata of teaching and learning in adult, higher and continuing education.
Preparation for Teaching:	Work done prior to classroom time assembling materials, activities and techniques, in general advance planning for classes.
Principle	A statement of the relationship between two or more concepts.
Problem Based Learning	An approach to learning inclined towards clinical practice, emphasising tacit or familiar as opposed to propositional knowledge.
Problem Solving	A high level cognitive activity using two or more principles.
Professional Education	Postgraduate programmes leading to professional designations, e.g. law, teaching, medicine, etc. as opposed to those oriented to academic research; also continuing upgrading of qualified practitioners.
Profile	A means of recording achievement.
Programme Development – Financial Aspects	Developing, planning, budgeting, and administering funding at the programme or course of study level.
Programme Review	Critical analysis or proposals for improvement of programmes from the viewpoints of theoretical, substantive, and instructional matters.
Project	A method of problem solving which involves the student in research, finding a solution and reporting either in writing or verbally.
Psychomotor	Involves physical movement and co-ordination.
QTLS	Qualified Teaching Learning and Skills (QTLS) status the new standards qualification for new and unqualified teachers and trainers within the further education sector to be introduced in 2007.
Question and Answer	Teaching strategy where the teacher asks a question and a student responds.
Questioning Techniques	Teaching techniques designed to evoke independent thought, to motivate learners, to inquire into present learner familiarity with content, or to test learner mastery of material by conversation with learners.
Rating Schedule	Rating students according to a fixed scale.
Reading Assignments	Written material to be read by the student in preparation for a subsequent lesson.
Reading Pairs	An informal collaborative learning technique where two students assist each other with reading assignments by checking each other's comprehension of the material assigned.
Real Time Simulation	A teaching method in which some hypothetical situation is acted out or modelled in some way, by students or sometimes by computers, and where there are dynamic time-constraints on solutions.

Reflective Practice	The process of reviewing an experience from practice in order to describe, analyse and evaluate and so informs learning from practice.
Reliability	The ability of a test to consistently measure what it is supposed to measure.
Research Design	An outline preliminary to research in which the topic is justified within some, usually disciplinary framework, where some general assertions are made, and comprehensive plan prepared to justify those assertions based on empirical or textual evidence.
Role Play	Teaching strategy where students act out a part or role.
Scheme of Work	The sequence in which topics are to be taught.
Science Education	Curricula oriented towards the more quantitatively based biophysical and social sciences, with an emphasis on basic knowledge of the theories and engineering of physico-chemical, biochemical, biological systems, and technological artifacts and infrastructures.
Self-assessment – Teachers	Criteria, values, methods, techniques and instruments for evaluation by teachers of their own teaching performance.
Self-directed Learning	Some course of study where the primary aims, goals and objectives are established by the learner.
Seminar	A type of course design where the instructor sets broad topics or guidelines for the course, but most of the actual instruction is done by the participants.
Simulation	An event or situation that is set up to be as similar to the real thing as possible.
Staff Development Programmes	Techniques, conceptions and processes intended to bring about qualitative change in the competence and/or confidence of faculty members, some criteria usually applied by an educational institution as part not the promotion or reader/professorial assessment process; often programmes are voluntary (but not always).
Student Evaluation	Rating of teaching performance, usually summative, by students on the course.
Student Interviews	One-on-one conversations with students, usually in the sense of tutoring with regard to substantive or theoretical issues in a course, but also at times a sort of informal counselling regarding time management, organisation, and issues of personal morale.
Student Journals	Day-to-day records of events in the classroom or the field kept by students.
Student Responsibilities	Those parts of a course in which students are expected to direct their own activity, e.g. attendance in class, topical readings, applying writing skills to assignments.
Student self-Evaluation	Students applying assessment criteria to their own work to determine efficiency, effectiveness etc.; also students grading their own assignments.
Students with Disabilities	Those who have difficulties with mobility, or for whom some primary sensory system or secondary perceptual system is partly or fully inoperative (contentious definition).
Summative	Type of assessment used at the end of a period of instruction and used for certification purposes.

Teaching Portfolio	A short document summarising one's teaching accomplishments, strengths, and areas of improvement, used either as part of a curriculum vitae, or as a basis for reflecting on teaching and making a development plan for acquiring or enhancing teaching skills.
Teaching Environment	The general biophysical and/or social conditions under which teaching is carried out, including general conventions of behaviour, student-faculty and collegial relations, reporting and recording requirements etc.
Teaching in the Classroom	That part of instruction spent in active one-on-many contact with students, excluding field trips and laboratories.
Teaching Methods	As opposed to teaching practices, more global views on appropriate ways and means of accomplishing instructional duties, i.e. not restricted to classroom practice, including philosophical and ethical issues.
Teaching Practices	Generalised ways and means of accomplishing general instructional objectives, e.g. creating discussion groups.
Teaching Process	The time progression of particular teaching techniques through various phases of a course, or lesson or section of a course.
Teaching Style	A coherent set of instructor preferences for ways and means of teaching and learning.
Teaching Techniques	As distinct from teaching practices, specific ways and means of accomplishing specific instructional objectives, typically of the more short-term or informal variety.
Teaching Tips	As distinct from teaching techniques, situational and/or anecdotal ways and means of accomplishing specific instructional objectives, or responding to issues and concerns while teaching in the classroom.
Test anxiety	Apprehension commonly experienced by students prior to, sometimes during, a formal examination, which inhibits the ability to think and/or express oneself clearly.
Total Quality Management	In general, quality control applied at each stage of the production process in faculty development contexts, ongoing evaluation by instructors of classroom productivity, in terms of both efficiency and effectiveness criteria, with coordination by a separate staff department, as opposed to by administrators after the fact.
Transparency	Acetate sheet upon which words or diagrams are drawn to project to students.
Tutorials	Specialised classes, typically led by a teaching assistant, where the focus is on solving assigned problem sets or practical applications of lecture content.
Understanding	Doing something with recalled information (e.g. interpreting, translating or summarising).
Whiteboard	Similar to chalkboard but using dry-marker pens on a white plastic surface.
Worksheet	Incomplete handout given to students for their completion.
Workshop	An intensive and short-term form of course design, typically delivered to small groups, and relying on active participation by learners.
Written Assignments	Work intended to be performed outside class and submitted for evaluation in writing, typically part of the term mark for a course.

Written Communication Skills:	The ability on the part of a person to transmit information to or exchange views with another by written means.
Validity	How well a test measures what it is supposed to measure.
VLE	Virtual Learning Environment – Software that allows interaction of students and teacher. Such software includes for the administration, communications, content and tracking of students undertaking a course of study.
Widening participation	Widening access and improving participation for all learners.

Bibliography

Armitage, A. *et al.* (1999). *Teaching and Training in Post-Compulsory Education.* Open University Press.

Ausubel, D. P. (1968). *Educational Psychology: a cognitive view.* Holt, Rinehast and Winston.

Barret, H.C. (2000). *Create Your Own Electronic Portfolio. [on-Line]* Available at <http://electronicportfolios.org/>. [Accessed 5 February 2006].

Barrett, H. C. Ed (2002). *Electronic Portfolios* [on-line] Available at <http://www.electronic portfolios.org/TelEd98Abstract.htm. [Accessed May 2006].

BBC, (2006). *Keyskills. London: BBC Education* [on-line]. Available at <http://www.bbc.co.uk/keyskills/> [Accessed 28 July 2006].

BBC, (2006). *Schools Learning resources for homes and schools* [on-line]. London: BBC Education. Available at <http://www.bbc.co.uk/schools> [Accessed 28 July 2006].

BBC, (2006). *BBC Open News Archive* {on-line]. London: BBC. Available at <http://www.bbc.co.uk/calc/news/content_intro_results.shtml> [Accessed 28 July 2006].

BECTA, (2003). *What the Research Says About Interactive Whiteboards* [on-line]. Coventry: BECTA IT Research. Available at: <http://www.becta.org.uk/page_documents/research/wtrs_whiteboards.pdf> [Accessed 28 July 2006].

Bell, D., (HMI), (2004-5). Annual Report of Her Majesties Chief Inspector of Schools [on-line]. London: OFSTED. Available at <http://www.ofsted.gov.uk/publications/annualreport0405> [Accessed 28 July 2006].

Berne, E. (1996) (Re-Issue Edition). *Games People Play: The Psychology of Human Relationships.* Ballantine Books, New York.

Black, H. *et al.* (1988). *Assessing Modules,* Scottish Council for Research in Education.

Black, H. *et al.* (1989). *The Quality of Assessment,* Scottish Council for Research in Education.

Bligh, D. (1971). *What's the Use of Lectures?,* Penguin.

Bloom, B. S. (1956). *Taxonomy of Educational Objectives, Handbook 1: Cognitive Domain,* David McKay.

Boud, D. *et al.* (Eds) (1985). *Reflection: Turning Experience into Learning,* Kogan Page.

Bransford, J., Brown, A. and, Cocking, R. (Eds) (2000). *How People Learn: Brain, Mind, Experience and School.* New York. NAS Press.

Brookfield, S. D. and Preskill, S. (1999). *Discussion as a Way of Teaching.* Open University Press.

Brown, G. and Atkins, M. (1988). *Effective Teaching in Higher Education.* Methuen.

British Pathe, (2003). *News British Pathe News* [on-line]. London: ITN Source. Available at <http://www.britishpathe.com> [Accessed 28 July 2006].

Brown, S. (2005). *Interactive Whiteboards in Education* [on-line]. York: TechLearn. Available at http://www.jisc.ac.uk/uploaded_documents/Interactivewhiteboards.pdf [Accessed on 28 July 2006].

BTEC, (1988). *Course and Unit Design*, Business and Technician Education Council.

Buzan, T. (1989). *Use Your Head*. 2nd Edition. BBC.

Castling, A. (1996). *Competence-based Teaching and Training*, MacMillan.

City and Guilds (1979). *Constructing Practical Tests*, City and Guilds of London Institute.

City and Guilds (1994). *Producing a Portfolio of Evidence for an NVQ:* Assessment Resource Book. City and Guilds of London Institute.

Cole, H. P. (1982). *Process Education*, Education Technical Publications.

Collins, J. (1998). *Perfect Presentations*. Marshall Publishing.

Cooper, T. and Love, T. (2001). *Online Portfolios: Issues of Assessment and Pedagogy. [on-line].* Available at <http://www.aare.edu.au/01pap/coo01346.htm> [Accessed 6 February 2006].

Curzon, L. B. (2000). *Teaching in Further Education*. 2nd Edition. Holt Education.

De Cecco, J. P. (1968). *The Psychology of Learning and Instruction: Education Psychology*. Prentice Hall.

De Cecco, J. P. and Crawford, W. R. (1974). *The Psychology of Learning and Instruction*, Prentice Hall.

Dave, R. H. (1975). In Armstrong, R. J. *et al. Developing and Writing Behavioural Objectives*, Educational Innovators Press.

Davies, I. K. (1971). *The Management of Learning*, McGraw Hill.

Deasey, M. (2006). *Somewhere to turn to for Advice and Support on CPD. [On-Line]*. IfL Research Articles. Available at <http://www.ifl.ac.uk/research/research_articles.html>. [Accessed 10 April 2006].

DfES, (2005). A Review of the Future Role of Further Education Colleges. (The Foster Report). DfES November 2005.

Driver, R. and Bell, B. (1986). Students' Thinking and the Learning of Science, *School Science Review*, March pp 443-456.

Ecclestone, K. (1996). *How to Assess the Vocational Curriculum*, Kogan Page.

Eggen, P. D. and Kauchak, D. P. (1998). *Strategies for Teachers*. 2nd Edition. Prentice Hall.

Elliott, J., Hutton, N., Hildreth, A. (1999) Factors Influencing Educational Motivation: A Study of Attitudes, Expectations and Behaviour of Children in Sunderland, Kentucky and St. Petersburg. *British Educational Research Journal* 25 (1) pp75-94.

Emler, N. (2001). *Self Esteem: The Costs and Causes of Low Self Worth*. York/Rowntree Publishing Services, York.

Entwistle, N. (1990). *Student Learning and Classroom Environment*. in 'Refocusing Educational Psychology, Eds Jones, N and Fredrickson, D. P. Falmer London.

Entwistle, N., Skinner, D., Entwistle, D., Orr, S. (2000). Conceptions and Beliefs about Good Teaching: an integration of contrasting research areas. *Higher Education Research and Development*. Vol 19, No. 1.

eNVQ, (2004). *Product review eNVQ* [on-line]. UK: eNVQ. Available at <http://swwetn.virtualcollege.ac.uk/DYSG_conference_html/Speaker_Details/Other/ENVQ.htm> [Accessed 28 July 2006].

Ewens, D. (2003). Managing Staff Development in Adult and Community Learning. NIACE and Learning and Skills Development Agency.

Farrington, I. (1996). How Adults Learn Best. *Journal of Further and Higher Education* 20. (1) Spring.

FEDA (1998). *Learning Styles Inventories.* A FEDA Publication. Coventry. FEDA.

Felder, R. (2003). *Learning Styles.* [on-line]. Avaliable at <http://www.ncsu.edu/felder-public/learning-styles.html.> [Accessed June 2003].

Felder-Silverman, A. (2001). *Teaching Learning and Learning Teaching: An Introduction to Learning Styles.* [on-line]. Available at <www.ubs.ac.in/cms/learning style pdf> [Accessed July 2006].

Ferl, (2002). *The JISC Plagiarism Advisory Service* [on-line]. Coventry: Ferl. Available at <http://ferl.becta.org.uk/display.cfm?resID=4468> [Accessed 28 July 2006].

Ferl, (2006). *News and Resources* [on-line]. Coventry: Ferl. Available at <http://ferl.becta.org.uk> [Accessed 28 July 2006].

Ferl, (2006). *Teaching and Learning: Welcome to the Pedagogy Focus Area* [on-line]. Coventry: Ferl. Available at < Welcome to the Pedagogy Focus Area> [Accessed 29 July 2006].

Fesmire, M., Lisner. M., Forest, P., Evans, W. (2003). Concepts Maps: A Practical Solution for Completing Functional Behaviour Assessment. *Education and Treatment of Children,* 26 (1) pp89-104.

FEU (1981). *Experience, Reflection, Learning.* Further Education Unit.

Fitts, P. M. and Posner, M. I. (1967). *Human Performance,* Brooks Cole.

Foster, A. (2006). *Review of the Future Role of FE Colleges* [on-line]. London: DfES. Available at <http://www.dfes.gov.uk/furthereducation index.cfm?fuseaction=content.view&CategoryID=20> [Accessed 28 July 2006].

Fry, H. Ketteridge. S, and Marshall, S. (1999). *Teaching and Learning in Higher Education.* Kogan Page.

Gage, N. L. and Berliner, D. C. (1983). *Educational Psychology.* Houghton Mifflin.

Gagné, R. M. (1973). *The Conditions of Learning.* Holt Rienhart and Winston (NY).

Gagné, R. M. (1975). *Essentials of Learning for Instruction.* The Dryden Press.

Galperin, D. (1957). in Simon, B., *Psychology in the Soviet Union,* Routledge and Kegan Paul.

Gardner, H. (1992). Multiple Intelligences as a Partner in School Improvement. *Educational Leadership.* Vol 55, No. 1 pp20-22.

Gardner, H. (2002). Good Work, Well Done: A Psychological Study. *Chronicle of Higher Education.* Vol 48, No. 24, pp7-10.

Gibbs, G. (1984). *Learning by Doing.* Further Education Unit.

Gibbs, G. (1988). *The Reflective Cycle.* [on-Line] Available at <http://www.nursesnetwork.co.uk/forum/lofiversion/index.php/t1355.html>. [Accessed 6 April 2006].

Gibbs, G. (1992). *Improving the Quality of Student Learning,* Technical and Educational Services.

Gibbs, G. Habeshaw, S. and Habeshaw, T. (1986). *53 Interesting Ways to Assess your Students*, Technical and Educational Services.

Gibbs, G. Habeshaw, S. and Habeshaw, T. (1988). *53 Interesting Things to do in your Lectures*, Technical and Educational Services.

Gibbs, G. and Habeshaw, T. (1988). *253 Ideas for Teaching*, Technical and Educational Services.

Gibbs, G. and Jenkins, A. (1992). *Teaching Large Classes in Higher Education*. Kogan Page.

Gilbert, T. F. (1973). Mathetics: The Technology of Education, *Journal of Mathetics*, 1st July.

Gordon, W. J. J. (1961). *Synetics*. Harper & Row.

Grasha, A. F. (2002). Encounters with Active Learning in Four Disciplines. *College Teaching*. Vol 50, No. 3, pp82-83.

Gronlund, N. E. (1970). *Stating Behavioural Objectives for Classroom Instruction*. Macmillan.

Guardian, (2006). *Guardian Newspaper* [on-line]. Manchester: Guardian Unlimited. Available at http://www.guardian.co.uk [Accessed 28 July 2006] Guardian, 2006. Guardian Education.Co.UK [on-line]. Manchester: Guardian Unlimited. Available at <http://education.guardian.co.uk/> [Accessed 28 July 2006].

Habeshaw, S. Habeshaw, T. and Gibbs, G. (1984). *53 Interesting Things to do in your Seminars and Tutorials*, Technical and Educational Services.

Habeshaw, S. Gibbs, G. and Habeshaw, T. (1992). *53 Problems with Large Classes*. Technical and Educational Services Ltd.

Harkin, J. (2005). Discussion Paper 16: 14-16 Year olds in Further Education [on-line]. Oxford: Oxford Brookes University. Available at <http://www.nuffield14-19review.org.uk/files/documents94-1.pdf> [Accessed 28 July 2006].

Harvey, J. and Mogey, N. (1996). *Implementing Learning Technology: Learning Technology Distribution Initiative (LDTI)* [on-line]. Herriott-Watt University. Available at <http://www.icbl.hw.ac.uk/ldti/implementing-it/cont.html> [Accessed 1 August 2006].

HMSO, (2000). Learning and Skills Act 2000. HMSO.

HMSO, (2001). *Special Education Needs and Disability Act 2001* [on-Line] London: HMSO. Available at <http://www.opsi.gov.uk/acts/acts2001/20010010.htm>. [Accessed 28 July 2006].

Hodkinson, P., Gleeson, D., James, D. and Postlethwaite, K. (2001). *Transforming Learning Cultures in Further Education [on-line]* Available at <http://www.tlrp.org.uk.> [Accessed 3rd Feb 2003].

Honey, P. and Mumford, A. (1982). *Manual of Learning Styles*. London: P. Honey.

Hot Potatoes, (2006). Hot Potatoes: From Half-Baked Software Inc. [on-line]. Victoria: university of Victoria. Available at < http://hotpot.uvic.ca/> [Accessed 28 July 2006].

Howard, R. W. (1987). *Concepts and Schemata*, Cassell.

HSE, (2004). *Research Report 243. Health and Safety Executive.* [on-line] Available at <http://www.hse.gov.uk/research/rrhtm/rr243.htm>. [Accessed 15 May 2006].

Huddleston, P. and Unwin, L. (1997). *Teaching and Learning in Further Education*. Routledge.

ITN Source, (2006). *ITN Source* [on-line]. London: ITN Source. Available at <http://itnarchive.com/britishpathe> [Accessed 28 July 2006].

Jenkins, A. (1992). *Break up your Lectures*. Kogan Page.

Jessup, G. (1991). *Outcomes: NVQs and the Emerging Model of Education and Training,* The Falmer Press.

JISC, (2005). *Moving Image Gateway (MIG)* [on-line]. London: JISC. Available at <http://www.jisc.ac.uk/index.cfm?name=coll_mig> [Accessed 28 July 2006].

JISC, (2006). *Plagiarism Advisory Service* [on-line]. Newcastle upon Tyne: Northumbria Learning. Available at <http://www.jiscpas.ac.uk> [Accessed 28 July 2006].

JMC, (2005). *The Common Inspection Framework (CIF): Proposed Changes September 2005* [on-line]. Birmingham: JMC. Available at <http://quality.jmc.ac.uk/OFSTED_ALI/New_Inspection_Agenda.pdf> [Accessed 28 July 2006].

Johnson, A. (2003). *Reform of Teacher Training in Further Education: Johnson* [on-line]. London: dfes. Available at <http://www.dfes.gov.uk/pns/DisplayPN.cgi?pn_id=2003_0223> [Accessed 28 July 2006].

Joyce, B. and Weil, M. (1986). *How to Learn a Teaching Repertoire*, in Models of Teaching, Prentice Hall.

Joyce, B. and Weil, M. (1992). *Models of Teaching*. 4th Edition. Prentice Hall.

Joyce, B., Calhoun, E., and Hopkins, D. (1997). *Models of Learning – Tools for Teaching*. Open University Press.

Kenway, M. and Reisenberger, A. (2001). *Self Assessment and Development Planning* [on-line]. London. NIACE/LSDA. Available at <http://www.qualityacl.org.uk/quality/docs/seAssess.pdf> [Accessed 28 July 2006].

Knowles, M. (1970). Andragogy: an emerging technology for Adult Learning, in Tight, M. *Adult Learning and Education*, Croom Helm, 1983.

Knowles, M. (1983). *The Adult Learner: A Neglected Species*, Gulf Publishing.

Kolb, D. A. (1984). *Experiential Learning – Experience as a Source of Learning and Development,* Prentice Hall.

Kolb, D. (2003). *Learning Styles.* [on-line] Available at <http://www.suppot4learning.org.uk> [Accessed June 2003].

Kramlinger, T. and Huberty, T. (1990). Behaviourism Versus Humanism *Training and Development Journal*, December.

Krathwohl, D. R. *et al.* (1964). *Taxonomy of Educational Objectives, Handbook 2: Affective Domain*, David McKay.

Lampert, M. (2002). Appreciating the Complexity of Teaching and Learning in School. *Journal of the Learning Sciences,* 2(3) pp365-369.

Learning and Skills Web, (2006). *Access to a wide range of educational information* [on-line]. Available at <http://www.learningandskillsweb.org.uk/home.do> [Accessed 28 July 2006].

LeTTOL, (2006). *Learning to Teach Online* [on-line]. Sheffield: The Sheffield College. Available at < http://www.sheffcol.ac.uk/lettol> [Accessed 28 July 2006].

Litow, A. (1991). Negotiating Teaching/Learning Interactions: A Study of Reciprocity in Tutorial Discourse. *Dissertation Abstracts International.* 52-04, #313A.

LLUK, (2005). *Working with young learners: Teaching and Learning* [on-line]. London: LLUK. Available at <http://www.lifelonglearninguk.org/wwyl_cd/tl_unit1/tl_unit1.html> [Accessed at 28 July 2006].

LLUK, (2006). *New Professional Standards: Teacher/Tutor/Trainer Education In The Lifelong Learning Sector* [on-line]. London and Leeds: LLUK. Available at <http://www.lifelonglearninguk.org/standards/new_prof_standards.html> [Accessed 28 July 2006].

Lockitt, W. (2004). *Unlocking the Potential of ILT.* [on-line] Avaliable at ,http://www.futurelab.org.uk/images/downloads/14-19pdf> [Accessed July 2006].

Love, T. and Cooper, T. (2004). Designing Online Information Systems for Portfolio-Based Assessment: Design Criteria and Heuristics. *Journal of Information Technology Education,* 3, 65-81 [on-line].Available at <http://www.love.com.au/PublicationsTLminisite/2003/Online portfolios IS.htm> [Accessed 28 July 2006].

Lovell, R. B. (1980). *Adult Learning.* Croom Helm.

LSRN Project, (2004). *14-16 Year Olds in Further Education.* [on-line]. London and South East Learning and Skills Research Network. Available at <http://www.nuffield14-19review.org.uk/files/documents94-1.pdf> [Accessed 28 July 2006].

MacDonald-Ross, M. (1973). *Behavioural Objectives - A Critical Review.* Instructional Science 2.

Mager, R. F. (1970). *Preparing Instructional Objectives,* Fearon Publishers.

McLay, M. and Brown, M. (2003). Using Concept Mapping to Evaluate the Training of Primary School Leaders. *Interactional Journal of Leadership in Education.* Vol 6, No. 1, pp73-92.

Meziorw, J. (1981). A Critical Theory of Adult Learning in Tight (op cit).

Microsoft, (2006). *Product Information* [on-line]. Washington: Microsoft Corporation. Available at <http://www.microsoft.com> [Accessed 28 July 2006].

Microsoft, (2006). *Microsoft in Education* [on-line]. Washington: Microsoft Corporation. Available at <http://microsoft.com/education> [Accessed 28 July 2006].

Minton, D. and Castling, A. (1997). *Teaching Skills in Further and Adult Education.* 3rd Edition. City and Guilds Co-Publishing Series.

Myers-Briggs, (2003). *The Myers-Briggs Foundation* [on-line] Available at <http://www.myers-briggs.org/> [Accessed 2 August 2006].

NLN, (2006). *National Learning Network* [on-line]. UK: NLN. Available at <http://www.nln.ac.uk> [Accessed 28 July 2006].

Newble, D. (1987). *A Handbook for Medical Teachers,* 2nd Edition, MTP Press.

OfSTED/ALI, (2001). *The Common Inspection Framework for Inspecting Post-16 Education and Training.* Office for Standards in Education and Adult Learning Inspectorate.

Pea, R. (2002). *The Digital Video Inquiry Collaboratory.* The Centre for Innovative Learning Technologies. Stanford, CA.

Quia Corporation, (2006). Quia: Where Learning Takes You. San Mateo Quia Corporation. Available at http://www.quia.com/ [Accessed 28 July 2006].

Ramsden, P. (1992). *Learning to Teach in Higher Education.* Routledge.

Rawlins, K. (1993). *Presentation and Communication Skills.* Macmillan Magazines.

Reece, I. (Ed) (1982). *Aspects for Curriculum in Technical Education*, Colombo Plan Staff College, Singapore.

Reece, I. and Walker, S. (1995). *A Practical Guide to the Overhead Projector and Other Visual Aids.* Business Education Publishers Limited.

Reid, B. (1993). *Reflection [on-Line}* "But we're doing it already" Exploring a response to the concept of reflective practice in order to improve its facilitation. Nurse Ed Today 13: 305-309. Available at <http://www.trainer.org.uk/members/theory/processes/reflection.html> [Accessed 6 April 2006].

Rosenthal, R. and Jacobson, L. (1968). *Pygmalion in the Classroom*, Holt, Rinehart & Winston.

Rowntree, D. (1977). *Assessing Students: How Shall We Know Them?,* Harper and Row.

Rowntree, D. (1981). *Developing Courses for Students.* Harper and Row.

Rowntree, D. (1982). *Educational Technology in Curriculum Development.* Harper and Row.

Schon, D. A. (1983). *The Reflective Practitioner: How Professionals Think in Action*, Basic Books.

Schon, D. A. (1987). *Educating the Reflective Practitioner: Toward a New Design for Teaching and Learning in the Professions.* Jossey-Bass.

SENDA, (2001). *Special Education Needs and Disability Act 2001* [on-line]. London: HMSO. Available at <http://www.opsi.gov.uk/acts/acts2001/20010010.htm> [Accessed 28 July 2006].

Simpson E. J. (1976). *The Classification of Educational Objectives: Psychomotor Domain*, University of Illinois.

Sternberg, R. J. (2003). Creative Thinking in the Classroom. *Scandinavian Journal of Educational Research.* Vol 47, No. 3, pp325-339.

Stenhouse, L. (1975) *An Introduction to Curriculum Research and Development.* Heinemann.

Stoner, G. (Ed), (1996). *LTDI, Implementing Learning Technology* [on-line]. Edinburgh: LTDI. Available at <http://www.icbl.hw.ac.uk/ltdi/implementing-it/implt.pdf> [Accessed 28 July 2006].

Stones, E. (1982). *Educational Psychology – A Pedagogical Approach*, Methuen: London.

Stufflebeam, D. (1971). *Educational Evaluation and Decision Making*, Peacock Publishers Inc.

Shulman, I. (2002). Making Differences. *Change*, Vol 34, No. 6, pp36-45.

Tansley, D. (1971). *Course Teams: The Way Forward in FE.* NFER Nelson.

TechDis, (2003). *Inclusive Learning and Teaching: ILT for Disabled Students* [on-line]. York: techDis. Available at <http://www.techdis.ac.uk/resources/files/Theme1.2.pdf> [Accessed 28 July 2006].

TechDis, (2006) *Welcome to TechDis.* [on-line]. York: TechDis. Available at <http://techdis.ac.uk> [Accessed 28 July 2006].

Tight, M. (1983). *Adult Learning & Education*, Open University Press.

Vargas, J. S. (1972). *Writing Worthwhile Behavioural Objectives*, Harper Row.

Walkin, L. (1990). *Teaching and Learning in Further Education*, Stanley Thornes Ltd.

Ward, C. (1980). *Designing a Scheme of Assessment,* Stanley Thornes.

Warren Little, J. (2003). Inside Teacher Community: Representations of Classroom Practice. *Teachers College Record.* Vol 105, No. 6 pp913-946.

W3C, (2006). The World Wide Web [on-line]. USA: W3C Consortium. Available at <http://w3.org> [Accessed 28 July 2006].

Yorke, J. (2004) *RR243 - Summative assessment supported by the Internet: the Professional Diver Competency Theory Assessment System (DCTAS)* [on-line]. London: HSE. Available at <http://www.hse.gov.uk/research/rrhtm/rr243.htm> [Accessed 28 July 2006].

Index